From China to Canada

GENERATIONS

A History of Canada's Peoples

From China to Canada

A History of the
Chinese Communities in Canada

Harry Con, Ronald J. Con, Graham Johnson,
Edgar Wickberg, William E. Willmott
Edited by Edgar Wickberg

Published by McClelland and Stewart Ltd. in association
with the Multiculturalism Directorate,
Department of the Secretary of State
and the Canadian Government Publishing Centre,
Supply and Services Canada.

Catalogue No. Ci44-10/1982E

McClelland and Stewart Limited
The Canadian Publishers
25 Hollinger Road
Toronto, Ontario
M4B 3G2

CANADIAN CATALOGUING IN PUBLICATION DATA
  Main entry under title:
  From China to Canada: a history of the Chinese
  communities in Canada

  (Generations: a history of Canada's peoples)
  Bibliography: p.
  Includes index.
  ISBN 0-7710-2241-7

  1. Chinese Canadians – History.*   I. Con, Harry.
  II. Wickberg, Edgar, 1927-   III. Series.

  FC106.C5F76   971'.004951   C82-094863-2
  F1035.C5F76

Printed and bound in Canada

Contents

Editors' Introduction

Canadians, like many other people, have recently been changing their attitude towards the ethnic dimension in society. Instead of thinking of the many distinctive heritages and identities to be found among them as constituting a problem, though one that time would solve, they have begun to recognize the ethnic diversity of their country as a rich resource. They have begun to take pride in the fact that people have come and are coming here from all parts of the world, bringing with them varied outlooks, knowledge, skills and traditions, to the great benefit of all.

It is for this reason that Book IV of the *Report of the Royal Commission on Bilingualism and Biculturalism* dealt with the cultural contributions of the ethnic groups other than the British, the French and the Native Peoples to Canada, and that the federal government in its response to Book IV announced that the Citizenship Branch of the Department of the Secretary of State would commission "histories specifically directed to the background, contributions and problems of various cultural groups in Canada." This series presents the histories that have resulted from that mandate. Although commissioned by the Government, they are not intended as definitive or official, but rather as the efforts of scholars to bring together much of what is known about the ethnic groups studied, to indicate what remains to be learned, and thus to stimulate further research concerning the ethnic dimension in Canadian society. The histories are to be objective, analytical, and readable, and directed towards the general reading public, as well as students at the senior high school and the college and university levels, and teachers in the elementary schools.

Most Canadians belong to an ethnic group, since to do so is simply to have "a sense of identity rooted in a common origin . . . whether this common origin is real or imaginary."[1] The Native Peoples, the British and French (referred to as charter groups because they were the first Europeans to take possession of the land), the groups such as the Germans and Dutch who have been established in Canada for over a hundred years and those who began to arrive only yesterday all have traditions and values that they cherish and that now are part of the cultural riches that Canadians share. The groups vary widely in numbers, geographical location and distribution and degree of social and economic power. The stories of their struggles, failures and triumphs will be told in this series.

As the Royal Commission on Bilingualism and Biculturalism pointed out, this sense of ethnic origin or identity "is much keener in certain individuals than in others."[2] In contemporary Canadian society, with the increasing number of intermarriages across ethnic lines, and hence the growing diversity of peoples ancestors, many are coming to identify themselves as simple Canadian, without reference to their ancestral origins. In focusing on the ethnic dimension of Canadian society, past and present, the series does not assume that everyone should be categorized into one particular group, or that ethnicity is always the most important dimension of people's lives. It is, however, one dimension that needs examination if we are to understand fully the contours and nature of Canadian society and identity.

Professional Canadian historians have in the past emphasized political and economic history, and since the country's economic and political institutions have been controlled largely by people of British and French origin, the role of those of other origins in the development of Canada has been neglected. Also, Canadian historians in the past have been almost exclusively of British and French origin, and have lacked the interest and the linguistic skills necessary to explore the history of other ethnic groups. Indeed, there has rarely ever been an examination of the part played by specifically British – or, better, specifically English, Irish, Scottish and Welsh – traditions and values in Canadian development, because of the lack of recognition of pluralism in the society. The part played by French traditions and values, and particular varieties of French traditions and values, has for a number of reasons been more carefully scrutinized.

This series is an indication of growing interest in Canadian social history, which includes immigration and ethnic history. This may particularly be a reflection of an increasing number of scholars whose origins and ethnic identities are other than British or French. Because such trends are recent, many of the authors of the histories in this series have not had a large body of published writing to work from. It is true that some histories have already been written of particular groups other than the British and French; but these have often been characterized by filio pietism, a narrow perspective and a dearth of scholarly analysis.

Despite the scarcity of secondary sources, the authors have been asked to be as comprehensive as possible, and to give balanced coverage to a number of themes: historical background, settlement patterns, ethnic identity and assimilation, ethnic associations, population trends, religion, values, occupations and social class, the family, the ethnic press, language patterns, political behaviour, education, inter-ethnic relations, the arts and recreation. They have also been asked to give a sense of the way the group differs in various parts of the country. Finally, they have been asked to give, as much as possible, an insider's view of what the immigrant and ethnic experiences were like at different periods of time, but yet at the same time to be as objective as possible, and not simply to present the group as it sees itself, or as it would like to be seen.

The authors have thus been faced with a herculean task. To the extent that they have succeeded, they provide us with new glimpses into many aspects of Canadian society of the past and the present. To the extent that they have fallen short of their goal, they challenge other historians, sociologists and social anthropologists to continue the work begun here.

Jean Burnet
Howard Palmer

[1] *Report of the Royal Commission on Bilingualism and Biculturalism.*
[2] Ibid. Paragraph 8.

Preface

In preparing this history we have assumed that it would have many audiences. In addition to the Canadian general public interested in the social history of this country, many groups in and out of the Chinese-Canadian communities will be interested in specific ways. Although we cannot hope to satisfy everyone, we have tried to offer something of interest and value to every group.

The history of an ethnic community is almost inevitably a celebration of achievements, institutions, and leaders. Thus, we have included short biographies of a few past leaders and lengthy discussions of some of the more important organizations. We hope that organizational activists and Chinese traditional-style historians will find these passages of interest and importance. Scholars interested in the comparative analysis of Overseas Chinese social institutions will also, we hope, find this information and our observations about it interesting and useful. Indeed, our extensive treatment of Chinese organizations reflects our belief that both Chinese Canadians involved in community affairs and sociologists looking from the outside will find this subject particularly important. It also grows from our belief that during most of the history of the Chinese communities in Canada, such organizations performed essential community services, and, indeed, made life bearable for most Chinese.

Although our broad approach tends to be inclusive, in some ways we have had to be exclusive. There is less information here than there should be about the histories of both the Chinese Benevolent Associations and the chapters of the Kuomintang across the country because we were unable to obtain from those bodies the co-operation needed for that purpose. We hope that they may see fit to publish their own versions in the near future, thereby making available the full story of their important contributions to Chinese-Canadian history. Politically sensitive Chinese Canadians will be aware that some of the authors of this history have been associated with the Chinese Freemasons and some others with the Canada-China Friendship Association. Our project team of five authors

1

came together accidentally and without any political motivation. We have our viewpoints, as readers will see; but we believe readers will find that we have been fair in our presentation. Since most of us were located in British Columbia during our period of research, we have had more western Canadian materials to work with, and our coverage of eastern Canada is often not what we would have wished. Perhaps subsequent studies by groups based largely in the East will be able to supplement what we have done.

An ethnic history may be a celebration but, given limitations of time and space, it cannot celebrate every important person or group. Nor, as a first effort, were we able to exploit all important sources. Lack of research time prevented our full use of church materials, printed and archival. We particularly regret that. There is, in fact, much more material in archives of all kinds – public and private – that future researchers may use. Although we have made extensive use of the files of one Chinese-language newspaper, the surviving scattered issues of others could be used with profit by other researchers. Western-language newspapers, too, have not been used nearly to the degree possible. Finally, although we have included a few extracts from oral histories we have made slight use of this approach, believing that there are now many people better equipped than we are who are engaged in this effort. Indeed, oral histories of Chinese-Canadian communities and individuals may well become a genre of their own.

Most previous studies of the Chinese in Canada have been done by white persons from white perspectives. We have, instead, attempted to present a view of Chinese-Canadian history from what is at least in part a Chinese perspective, talking about themes of interest to the Chinese communities and using viewpoints derived from Chinese sources. There are many possible Chinese perspectives on Chinese-Canadian history. Ours is only one possibility among those.

It is our hope that this history will assist Canadians of all backgrounds to understand Chinese-Canadian history, grievances, and contributions. We hope that the problems discussed and the sources referred to will stimulate further research and may partly set the agenda of research questions. We also hope that our book will provide reliable information that can be the basis for teaching materials about Chinese Canadians for secondary school use. In our opinion, secondary school coursework that includes ethnic histories is greatly in need of development.

In preparing this history we divided the labour as follows: Harry and Ronald Con were primarily responsible for collecting material and carrying out interviews; Johnson, Wickberg, and Willmott did library and archival work and supervised the work of research assistants. Chapters Two through Five were written by Willmott; Chapters Six through Fourteen by Wickberg; Chapters Fifteen through Eighteen by Johnson. The Preface, Chapter One, and Conclusion were prepared by Johnson and Wickberg, and Wickberg edited the manuscript as a whole.

Dr. Ronald J. Con passed away during the course of our work. We wish to express our deep sense of grief at his passing and our appreciation for his achievements while he was among us. May the completed history honour his memory.

It remains for us to make a few explanations and acknowledgements. In rendering Chinese names of persons or institutions we have used the form common in Canada, whenever known. If not known, we have rendered the name in standard Chinese using *pinyin* romanization. Use of *pinyin* is not intended as a political statement on our part. *Pinyin* is simply becoming the most widely used form of romanization for English readers outside of China as well as inside. The glossary and name list in the back of the book give equivalents in the older Wade-Giles system and in the standard Cantonese system of Meyer and Wempe. One exception to the general rule of using *pinyin* has been when names of Kuomintang members are being cited, or names of others to whom the use of *pinyin* would clearly be offensive. In such cases, we have used Wade-Giles.

Our debts are numerous and we can only name a few of those who have helped. For research assistance we are indebted to Jenny Yue, Bessie Yu, William F.W. Yee, Sheila Wong, Thais McKee, Kerry McPhedran, Harriet Simmons, Robert Zajack, Ji-ming Wang, Timothy Brook, Charles Sedgwick, Karin Straaton, Sen Ma, Brij Lal, Lydia Chung, Roxana Ng, Manuel Diaz, Fanny Davies, Amy Lau, and Ada Chiu. Research materials, advice, and assistance in other ways were furnished by Bernice Kwong, Keith Ralston, W. Peter Ward, Ronald Adams, David Chuen-yan Lai, Howard Palmer, Jean Burnet, F.Q. Quo, Gordon Taylor, Mrs. Foon Sien Wong, Mrs. E.C. Mark, Dr. Ivan Mark, Mrs. Hilda Cumyow, Paul Levine, H. Mark Lai, Stanley Horrall, Eve Armentrout-Ma, David T.H. Lee, J.E.A. Parnall, Stan Kita, and Erwin Epp. Staff members at the Public Archives of Canada, the Public Archives of British Columbia, and the Vancouver City Archives were generous with their time and assistance. There is also a much larger, though anonymous, group of people who deserve special thanks. These are persons who were interviewed or who contributed information or advice on a confidential basis. We are greatly in their debt. Finally, essential funding was generously provided by the Multiculturalism Directorate, Department of Secretary of State, Ottawa. A grant from the University of British Columbia assisted us in the final stages. We gratefully share credit with all of these people and organizations for whatever merit this study may have; but we reserve for ourselves the responsibility for its demerits.

Edgar Wickberg
Graham Johnson
Vancouver, 1982

ONE

The Background to Emigration

The history of Chinese immigration to Canada is part of a much larger story of Chinese migrations to various parts of the world in the modern era. The 200,000 or so people of Chinese background who today are part of the population of Canada make up only one per cent of the approximately 20 million persons of Chinese origin who live outside of China.

Emigration from China to Canada began in 1858. Long before that time there had been large-scale migration to other parts of the world, particularly Southeast Asia, where opportunities for business under European colonial rule proved attractive to the Chinese immigrants. Thus, there were already sizable and fairly stable Chinese settlements in Southeast Asia by the 1850's, when large numbers of Chinese started to migrate to the Western Hemisphere.

Most Chinese emigrants were single men, and migration in general assumed two forms: coolie broker and chain migration. Coolie broker immigration usually involved an indenture arrangement by which the immigrant worked off his indebtedness to the broker who had paid his passage from China before he was free to seek employment on his own. Coolie broker labour, normally used to provide gangs for specific construction jobs or resource extraction, was a major part of Chinese-Canadian history in the late nineteenth century but of much less significance thereafter. In chain migration, on the other hand, which was common in Canada after 1900, the immigrant came on his own and worked until he had saved enough for a trip back to China. During this first return to his village he might marry, or, if already married, he might arrange to bring back with him a teen-aged son or nephew. Through subsequent return trips accompanied by teen-aged relatives, fractional families without women were assembled abroad. Depending on his financial condition and the opportunities in his country of settlement, he might bring his wife and thereby establish family life in the new land. Many Chinese emigrants, however, never reached this stage, and remained what emigrant Chinese have often been called in modern times: Overseas Chinese.

Patterns of close ties to native villages through remittances and frequent trips back are indicative of what has been called a "sojourner mentality," as is the accompanying expectation of many migrants that they would retire to China. Although there were many emigrant Chinese who went abroad seeking adventure and new frontiers and fully expecting to settle permanently in their host country, if given decent opportunities and fair treatment, all Chinese were bound to be influenced by certain Chinese cultural norms. In China the sense of native place is extremely strong. Even those Chinese who migrated within China itself, looking for opportunity and income, did not readily abandon their native places and kin; they sent remittances and assumed they would return eventually, if possible. The same was true of Chinese who migrated farther afield. By the time Chinese began to come to Canada, the expectations and patterns of sojourning migration were well-established in South China communities that had sent generations of emigrants to Southeast Asia and were now to send generations to North America.

What produced the phenomenon of Chinese migration overseas, however, was not just the attractiveness of new opportunities. The "pull" from without was matched by a "push" from within. Chinese migration is very much a product of the major forces that have shaped modern Chinese history – population pressure, political weakness and disruption, foreign intervention, and a series of natural catastrophes. As the rapidly growing Chinese population after 1700 began to press upon a limited stock of farm land, one of the responses of the Chinese was to migrate. Sometimes migration was rural to rural in that peasants sought new lands away from their original villages. Just as often it was rural to urban as peasants sought work in trade and as artisans in the cities of China or in urban settlements overseas.

Political instability was another factor that had a bearing upon overseas migration. A weak and corrupt imperial government was succeeded by incompetent republican governments which could neither impose new political institutions nor control the rampant banditry and persistent chaos and warfare in the country. A major complicating factor was the intervention of foreign powers whose diverse influences included Christian missions, a corrupting opium traffic, and limitations on China's sovereignty.

In the mid-nineteenth century, when Chinese began to migrate to Canada, China was in the throes of the great Taiping Uprising, a radical millenarian movement that produced a vast civil war in which, by the most conservative estimates, 20 million persons perished. Yet the Taiping was only the largest of several mass uprisings that rocked China in the middle decades of the century. It was small wonder that the tempo of Chinese overseas emigration increased during those years. By the 1870's the authority of the central government had been formally re-established, but banditry remained endemic in the countryside and private armies of all kinds were becoming a way of life in rural China. Increasing population continued its relentless pressure on farm land. Since the stock of new farm land was by now exhausted, more people had to be fed from the existing stock. Yet there was no agricultural revolution that would have allowed the land to become more productive. And the bare beginnings of an industrial revolution that took place in the first half of the twentieth century did little to alleviate the pressure on the land. It is not surprising, therefore, that the parts of China that provided the emigrants should be among the least arable and the most crowded. Those areas also were most accessible to the sea and had the traditions and experience of several centuries of migration to Southeast Asia.

THE ORIGINS OF CHINESE EMIGRANTS TO CANADA

Chinese migrants came predominantly from the southern coastal province of Guangdong and the neighbouring coastal province of Fujian. Both areas were in the van of Western efforts to break down the cultural and commercial barriers surrounding China from the early nineteenth century. Canton, the Guangdong provincial capital, was the point of contact with European commerce before the disastrous First Opium War in 1839. As one consequence of that war, the island of Hong Kong was ceded to the British and treaty ports were established in Canton, Amoy, and Foochow and at Shanghai and Ningpo in the lower Yangtze valley. It was through the original treaty ports in Guangdong and Fujian and the British and Portuguese possessions of Hong Kong and Macau that Chinese went abroad.

South and southeast China is characterized by sub-cultural complexity, one index of which is language. Cantonese, as the language of the great commercial centres of Canton, Macau, Hong Kong, and Wuzhou in Guangxi, was dominant among Chinese abroad. It has several sub-dialects, the most distinctive of which is that spoken in the four adjacent counties (*xian*) to the southwest of Canton: Sun-wui, Hoi-ping, Toi-san, and Yin-ping. Cantonese in its standard form (known colloquially as "provincial speech") is spoken in the three counties surrounding Canton: Poon-yue, Nam-hoi, and Sun-dak. Chung-san county, immediately adjacent to Macau, has its own variant of Cantonese. The overwhelming majority of Chinese migrants to Canada have come from a small area of eight contiguous counties in the heart of the Canton delta, in particular the four adjacent counties of Sun-wui, Hoi-ping, Toi-san, and Yin-ping, known collectively as *Sze-yap* ("Four Districts").

The Canton delta, as the heartland of Cantonese Guangdong, is distinct. Language marks it off from other regions of China and its long association with foreign commerce has made it open to influences different from those that predominate in northern China. From a northern Chinese perspective Guangdong was at the margins of the Chinese cultural system. It was and still is considered "complicated." But the Cantonese are self-consciously distinct. They regarded themselves as "people of the Tang," in contrast to the more typical term for ethnic

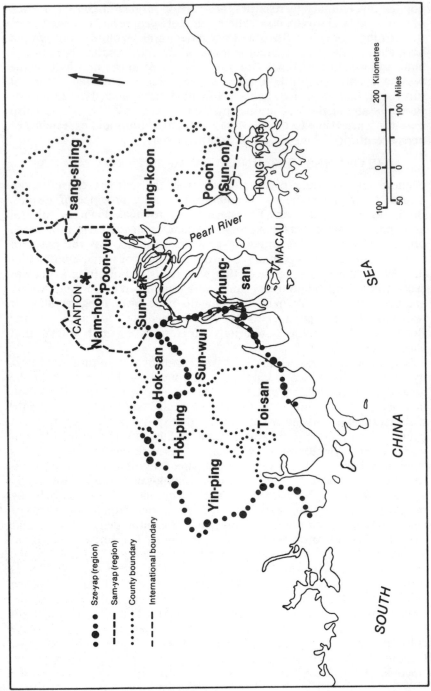

Canton Delta Region, Guangdong Province

Chinese, "people of the Han." Their sub-culture is noted for a fine regional cuisine and a distinctive tradition in the arts, poetry, and letters. Guangdong represents particular traditions in philosophical and political thought.

The vast majority of Chinese who migrated to Canada were of rural origin. The problems of mere survival for South Chinese peasants were so overwhelming that many decided to abandon the struggle and face the uncertainties of earning a living abroad. Population pressure was especially severe in the Canton delta. By the late nineteenth century overall densities were about 600 persons per square kilometre, although density variations within the region and per unit of crop land were enormous.[1] The typical peasant household cultivated less than one-third of a hectare of land; in the area that provided most of Canada's Chinese population they worked with a great deal less.[2] The paucity of land was not, however, the only issue. Land ownership in Guangdong as a whole, and in the delta in particular, was concentrated in the hands of the few. The vast majority of the Cantonese peasant population was composed of tenants renting their cropland, inadequate though it was, from landlords.[3] The consequences were disastrous. As one commentator in the early twentieth century, Chen Han-seng, notes:

> The land tax in Kwangtung [Guangdong] has been greatly increased by two new policies. The first is the recent extensive building of public roads, with the pretext of improving rural communications but primarily for facilitating military movements. The second is the reorganization of village administration under the beautiful name of rural self-government; however, it is chiefly for furthering the purpose of taxation. Within the past five years the total tax burden has trebled, and this burden is being largely shifted upon the shoulders of peasants who have to pay rent. The rent, which is usually paid in grain, amounts to 50-57% of the entire harvest. . . . Such a high rent, together with all its consequent burdens, crushes the peasant and sends him to the usurer. In any one district of the province, 60-90% of all the peasant families are in debt. Many peasants have to seek a loan in grain; others have to pawn their clothes, furniture, and even hoes, rakes, harrows, ploughs, etc. The usual interest charged on a loan in grain is 30% for six months. . . . The bankrupted peasants rapidly give up their land through the process of mortgage; as landless peasants not taken in or "absorbed" by industry are ever on the increase, wages in general are falling down, and rents in all forms are rising. Thus, bankruptcy repeats itself and accelerates the process till the speed of rural proletarization, or in China to be more exact, the speed of pauperization, far exceeds that of peasant exodus and possible industrialization. The present system of land monopoly in China can only bestow perpetual ownership to a selected few, and simultaneously force perpetual indebtedness upon an ever growing mass.[4]

One response to the apparent inability to change social arrangements was to leave the Chinese homeland and seek economic opportunities elsewhere.

SOCIAL VALUES AND EXPERIENCE OF THE EMIGRANTS

It is not possible to understand social organization among Chinese communities in Canada without an appreciation for the values and rules of social behaviour which prevailed in the Chinese homeland. The peasant migrants from Guangdong were born into a society firmly rooted in an agrarian mode of production. They were familiar with a form of social organization in which kinship had an important role to play and in which economic organization, political power, sources of prestige, and religion were oriented toward kinship groups. At one level a highly localized form of community was determined by a system of peasant marketing.

Kinship was one of the most important forces integrating the Chinese peasant into his local system. South and southeastern China are notable for the elaboration of the principle of kinship. A prominent position was occupied by localized kinship groupings known as lineages. A lineage is composed of a group of men, and their families, who trace their descent from a common male ancestor. In Guangdong and Fujian, where the population was somewhat more stable in traditional times than in parts of China more subject to natural calamities, villages were often composed of only a few surnames. An individual's status was determined in part with reference to his family and his kin group. Beyond his kin group he was involved in certain political relationships and in a socio-cultural system determined by his local market. His lot as a peasant was subject to a great deal of privation, but the local social system of which he was part was clear in its allocation of status.

With migration, this system influencing behaviour was destroyed. The peasant became a coolie, a railroad worker, a miner, or a cannery worker. His occupation propelled him into a new economic system. He lived in a milieu away from his kinsmen, no longer quite so aware of the social rules and without a familiar, unified community for support. Nonetheless, his attachment to traditional forms was intense. The breaks were never considered final. The migrant believed that it was in his best interests to remain involved, as far as possible, with his native cultural system.

China was traditionally an agrarian society in which rural peasants had been the most numerous social class. But there had always been urban areas in China and there had always been migrants to those urban areas. Such migrants within China had faced the problem of moving between two distinct social systems with different behavioural expectations and had created voluntary organizations as one possible mechanism for helping the migrant to cope with the demands of a new urban milieu. When there is change – and migrations involve change – voluntary associations often arise to deal with problems implicit in the change.

Voluntary associations had always been a feature of traditional Chinese society. Even in rural areas voluntary associations were formed, especially to raise short-term credit. In traditional urban China there were two broad kinds of voluntary associations of urban migrants: (1) those oriented to specific economic ventures, which can be called guilds; and (2) "provincial clubs," or *landsmannschaften*, whose aims were to provide various facilities, often of mutual aid, for fellow countrymen who were forced for whatever reasons – trade, scholarship, employment – to spend periods of time away from their native places.[5]

It is not necessary to discuss in detail here the nature of such organizations in the traditional Chinese city;[6] it is sufficient to say that when Chinese went overseas they carried with them certain organizing principles relevant to the problems of migration. But it is important to add that they also were free to behave according to a number of principles not open to them in China. Released from the constraints of Chinese bureaucratic dominance, new forms of economic organization could emerge.

The Chinese overseas have been typically an ethnic minority, in many instances in a colonial setting. In general, the non-Chinese majority has remained aloof from involvement in the affairs of the Chinese community. As long as order was preserved, and revenue collected, a laissez-faire attitude prevailed. This meant that, within limits, the Chinese were free to organize their own communities as they saw fit.

Chinese migrants to Canada, although disadvantaged in terms of education, language, and ethnicity, thus had an inventory of cultural strength which could be applied to the process of adaptation to Canadian society. Their cultural background encouraged a veritable genius for association formation. The history of the Chinese in Canada can be seen largely as a history of the communities they formed. Until the very recent period the core of those communities was a set of associations.

NOTES

1. We are grateful to Dr. David Fu-keung Ip for the detailed references in the following section. See his "The Design of Rural Development: Experiences from South China, 1949-1976" (Ph.D. thesis, University of British Columbia, 1979), pp. 22-97. On densities in Guangdong, see Amano Motonosuke, *Shina no gyo keizai ron*, I (Tokyo, 1942), pp. 175-6; and Liang Rencai, *Guangdong jingji dili* (Beijing, 1956).

2. *Guangdong jingji nianjian*, 1941 (Lienxian, 1941), pp. G. 47-8. See also Zhao Chengxin, "Guangdong Xinhui: Cixi tudi fenpei diaocha," *Shehui xuejie*, V (1929), excerpted in Feng Hefa, *Zhongguo nongcun jingji ziliao* (Shanghai, 1933), pp. 936-95; Zhuo Zhengfeng, "Zhongshan xian nongye diaocha baogao," in *Guangdong nongye gaikuang diaocha*

baogao shu, Book 2, Vol. 2 (Canton, 1930), pp. 141-8; and Zhuo Zhengfeng, "Kaiping xian nongye gaikuang diaocha baogao, in *ibid.*, pp. 48-55.

3. See D.H. Jefferson Lamb, *The Development of the Agrarian Movement and Agrarian Legislation in China* (Shanghai, 1934), p. 40.

4. Chen Han-seng, *Landlord and Peasant in China* (New York, 1936), pp. ix-x.

5. J.S. Burgess, *The Guilds of Peking* (New York, 1928); H.B. Morse, *The Guilds of China* (London, 1909); and Ho Ping-ti, *Zhongguo huiguan shilun* (Taibei, 1966).

6. See the recent work edited by G.W. Skinner, *The City in Late Imperial China* (Stanford, Calif., 1977); and M. Elvin and G.W. Skinner (eds.), *The Chinese City Between Two Worlds* (Stanford, Calif., 1974).

PART ONE

1858-1911

TWO

Foundations, 1858-1880: Early Immigration and Settlement

THE BRITISH COLUMBIA GOLD RUSH

The news of gold on the Fraser River brought thousands of prospectors from California in April, 1858. Those who came by sea disembarked at Fort Victoria, on the southern end of Vancouver Island, where they sought whatever transportation was available to ascend the Fraser. In a few short weeks, Victoria was transformed from a "quiet English village" into a "busy commercial centre" with several streets, two hundred shops, and several thousand residents.[1] At the same time, thousands were trekking north through Montana, Idaho, and Washington to enter the goldfields overland.

Among the first wave of prospectors came a Chinese merchant, Ah Hong, an agent from a Chinese company in San Francisco, who was prospecting for business rather than for gold.[2] His findings, reported in the San Francisco *Daily Globe* on May 16, 1858, painted a sufficiently optimistic picture (he claimed to have been offered a job as a cook at twenty dollars per day) that soon many Chinese were travelling northward from California to Victoria, most continuing thence into the interior.

According to Lee Tung-hai, the leading Chinese writer on the subject, the first group of Chinese arrived in Victoria on June 28, 1858.[3] Hop Kee and Co. of San Francisco arranged with the shipping company Allan Lowe & Co. for passage to Victoria on the *Caribbean* for 300 Chinese.[4] This contract indicates that Chinese migration to British Columbia began in an organized manner, and implies that subsequent charters were similarly arranged by companies in San Francisco and Hong Kong. The first arrival of Chinese from Hong Kong took place in the spring of 1859.[5] In 1860 several of the ships coming from Hong Kong carried an increasing number of passengers. The Victoria *Daily Colonist* estimated that a total of 4,000 Chinese arrived in Victoria during 1860 alone. The rate had increased somewhat by the following year, with an estimated 2,875 arrivals

13

in the first half of that year.[6] Many, perhaps two thousand, came overland from Portland, Oregon, to New Westminster, B.C., in the first two years of the gold rush, 1858-59. Some came northward from further east, up the Columbia River or from Portland to Kamloops through the Okanagan.[7]

There may have been as many as six or seven thousand Chinese in what is now British Columbia in the early 1860's. Those who came in the 1850's and 1860's were a continuation of the migrations to California in the previous decade. A large proportion of them had moved northward from California as the boom subsided and anti-Oriental feeling became more widespread there. They were almost all men, although by the end of the 1860's Victoria's business community included several establishments employing small numbers of women. Very few Chinese brought their wives to live with them. Even in 1871, when the census counted 1,548 Chinese, there were only fifty-three women in the province, a ratio of only 35 per 1,000. A Chinese couple at Port Douglas, at the head of Harrison Lake, produced the first Chinese baby born in Canada in March, 1861; he was Won Alexander Cumyow, who was to have a long and colourful career, dying in 1955 at the age of ninety-four.

Most of the original merchants who established themselves in Victoria were from the Sam-yap ("three counties") region of Guangdong Province,[8] but we know nothing of the provenance of those who ventured into the interior.

In July, 1858, only three months after the gold rush began in British Columbia, a Chinese by the name of Ah Sou purchased land in Esquimault with the idea, so the *Victoria Gazette* reporter surmised, of "making arrangements to facilitate a heavy immigration of his countrymen to the new El Dorado of the North."[9] As it turned out, the Chinese businesses were established, not in Esquimalt, but in downtown Victoria, along Fisgard, Cormorant, and Johnson Streets. According to Lee Tung-hai, a Chinese doctor by the name of Ah Chi opened a dispensary for non-Chinese on Johnson Street in 1859; it soon moved to Cormorant Street, which became the centre of Victoria's developing Chinatown. A Chinese laundry had been established as early as July, 1858, and the Sacramento House had opened its doors for meals and rooms in Waddington Alley by the beginning of 1860.[10]

From the start, the major Chinese company was Kwong Lee, established in San Francisco some years before. Its Victoria agency was opened on Cormorant Street in 1858 by Lee Chong, a merchant from San Francisco. In the *Colonist*, Kwong Lee advertised itself as "Importers and Dealers in all kinds of Chinese Goods, Rice, Sugar, Tea, Provisions."[11] Because the company name was so familiar in the area, Lee Chong was often known as Kwong Lee, which means "Expansive Profit." He was the first Chinese to bring his wife and children to Victoria. The other major Chinese company was Tai Soong (Tai Sun),

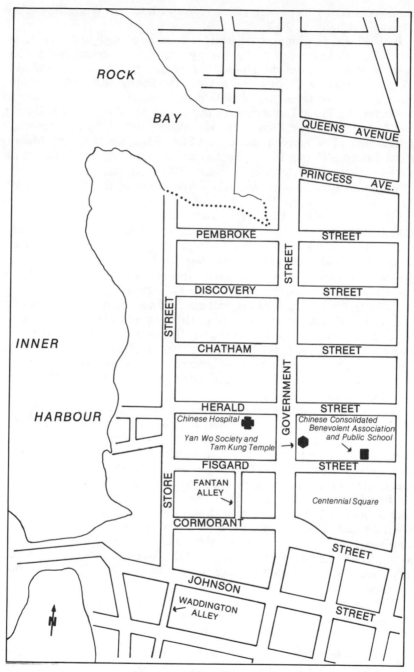

Victoria, B.C., Chinatown

managed first by Tong Kee (Dong Ji) and later by Wong Soy Chew (Huang Ruichao).[12]

By 1862, eleven Chinese companies were large enough to pay tax under a new Trade Licence ordinance. Kwong Lee was the second largest company in Victoria (after the Hudson's Bay Company), being assessed at £6,500. Two other Chinese companies, Tai Soong and Yan Wo Sang, were assessed in the £2,000-£6,000 class. The other Chinese listed as liable for the Trade Licences were the following: Ah Sing, Du Quong, and Si Long, traders; Fock Sing, washman; Hong Sing (Quong Sing), restaurateur; Lee Yon Sin, doctor; and Lee Song, apothecary.[13] Missing from this list is Chong Tsoo, who was mentioned in an early article in the *Victoria Gazette* (30 July 1858) as already having raised a business sign (presumably for a laundry) and who owned three of the twenty-four lots belonging to Chinese in Victoria in 1861.[14]

Of the thousands of Chinese who arrived in British Columbia, the vast majority travelled up the Fraser River into the gold fields. Many also joined them overland, avoiding Victoria altogether. The Chinese going to the gold fields were said to *yap kong* (*ru kuang*), "enter the mines." As early as August, 1858, there were thirty-seven Chinese among the 206 residents of Port Douglas, at the head of Harrison Lake.[15]

By 1860, the gold rush had spread up the Fraser River beyond Lillooet and up the Thompson to Kamloops. Three thousand of the four thousand miners were above Lillooet, and "the original diggings, both bar and bench, along the lower Fraser were now practically given over to the Chinese," who were earning "from one to four cents a pan." In January of that year, the *Daily Colonist* estimated that there were 1,195 Chinese in the gold fields.[16]

As the prospectors were moving even further into the Cariboo and up the various tributaries of the Fraser, the most advanced parties tried to keep the Chinese out of their areas, even by violent means – many of them having come from the California fields where anti-Oriental feeling was already running high. The major concentrations of Chinese settlement, therefore, remained in the lower reaches of the Fraser until Barkerville suddenly burgeoned in 1862. In 1861, however, as many as three hundred Chinese arrived in Kamloops, the western extent of the Cariboo gold rush.[17] By 1863 there were some 4,000 Chinese in the whole Cariboo region, most of them labourers. Although they earned an average of $10 a day, they had to pay $35 a week for board, which usually meant sleeping on the floor of a cabin wrapped in their own blankets.

The following account by Walter Moberly of an incident on a trip through the Fraser Canyon in 1859 gives some indication of the conditions of Chinese settlement at that time:

> On my way down from Boston Bar the first night I reached a camp where a few Chinese were mining. It was situated on a narrow shelf of rock about six feet in width and twenty feet in length. The

Chinamen received me kindly and made me some tea and mixed some flour and water and made thick cakes of dough which they cut into strips about an inch in width and boiled. They had no other provisions but were looking forward to the spring run of salmon which were then on their way up the river. I left my kind friends early the next morning.[18]

A British traveller remarked that "the Chinamen form the largest section of the dwellers" around Yale during his travels there in the 1860's:

This much-enduring and industrious race are generally to be found in little clusters, at work upon the diggings deserted by the whites; and sometime one meets a string of them migrating in search of a fresh field of enterprise, with all their worldly belongings in a pair of baskets suspended from either end of a pole carried across their shoulders.[19]

While most sought gold along the Fraser, some Chinese were collecting jade. Since the green stone was not recognized as precious by other prospectors, the Chinese were able to mine it without competition.

On January 28, 1860, the *Daily Colonist* reported the arrival at Victoria of one Chinese miner from the interior with five thousand dollars' worth of gold ore, indicating that some of the early Chinese prospectors were able to make large returns quite rapidly. While their compatriots were goldmining the lower Fraser, many Chinese in the Cariboo were in service occupations, particularly after 1860, by which time they came mainly from Hong Kong rather than from California and therefore had no prior mining experience. As a supply centre for the miners on the various creeks in the Cariboo, Quesnel Forks began to attract Chinese who could provide services required by a population of single males, such as laundries and restaurants. Some began vegetable gardens as well; one even established a fishing company at Rock Bay, near Victoria, where fish were caught on rod and line, salted and dried, and then shipped to the protein-hungry miners, both Chinese and white.[20]

In 1862, news of Billy Barker's spectacular strike brought thousands of new prospectors into the area. The population of the settlement of Barkerville rose rapidly into the thousands, and at its height at least 3,000 Chinese lived there.[21] In that year alone, sixteen Chinese business houses opened, including brothels and opium dens and eight Chinese restaurants.[22]

Quesnel Mouth, at the junction of the Quesnel with the Fraser River, was also growing and when the road was cut through to Barkerville in 1865 it became even more important as an entrepot centre, completely eclipsing Quesnel Forks. As the white prospectors and businessmen moved out of Quesnel Forks, it became an almost entirely Chinese settlement, with some 400 Chinese working gold diggings that were by then not sufficiently rich to attract other prospectors. In 1884, the only white resident was the government agent, W. Stephenson.[23] This Chinese community survived until 1922, when it was rapidly deserted because of a minor gold rush at Likely. Several elderly individuals remained, however, as happened in Barkerville and then Cumberland after major Chinese communities had dispersed. The last Chinese died at Quesnel Forks in 1956.[24]

Throughout the 1860's, the Chinese companies in Victoria developed a network of subsidiaries and agencies in all the towns of British Columbia. Kwong Lee and later Tai Soong, in particular, were involved in the transportation business, first with mules and subsequently with wagons, up the Fraser Valley and into the Cariboo. In Langley's *Pacific Coast Directory* of 1866, Kwong Lee was the only Chinese listed among the forty-three transport companies. Although it cannot be said with any certainty just what proportion of the upcountry supply trade was in Chinese hands, it is clear that they made a major contribution to the provisioning and development of British Columbia.

In 1863 Governor Douglas commissioned a wagon road into the Cariboo to provide easier access for the growing mining industry. It began at the head of Harrison Lake, struck north to Lillooet and thence over the Pavilion Mountain to Williams Lake, from which point steamer traffic on the Fraser was possible as far as Quesnel Mouth. An alternative route was commissioned through the Fraser canyon to provide access to the various mining towns and sites on the lower Fraser. The various sections of the Cariboo Wagon Road were let to tender, and several of the contractors found that Chinese were the most satisfactory labourers available for the work. Walter Moberly, in charge of the work on a section between Lytton and Spence's Bridge, discovered that when he paid his white labourers, most of them immediately absconded from their debts and went further north in search of gold. He commented:

> This contemptible proceeding on the part of these men, which was brought about by the reports of fabulously rich deposits of gold having been discovered on Antler and other creeks in Cariboo, reduced the force of men needed to insure the prosecution of the work in accordance with our contract with the government, and compelled me to employ, much against my wishes, a large force of Chinese labourers. It will thus be seen that the bad faith and unscrupulous conduct of the white labourers was the cause of the employment of Chinese labour in constructing the Cariboo wagon road. All the other contractors on this road experienced the same treatment from their white labourers that befell me.
>
> I found all the Chinese employed worked most industriously and faithfully and gave me no trouble.[25]

It has been estimated that about one thousand Chinese worked on the Cariboo Wagon Road and "another thousand were hired to build dikes and ditches in Victoria and New Westminster."[26] In July, 1864, the road from Quesnel Mouth to Cottonwood was being constructed by 200 Chinese and 100 white workers. In 1866, 500 Chinese were hired by Western Union to string the telegraph wires from New Westminster to Quesnel.

In 1865 a minor gold rush occurred in the Kootenay, bringing about 2,000 men into the district, including many Chinese. By 1866, the rush was already subsiding, and of the 700 men still in the district half were Chinese, some of whom had bought claims from departing whites. The Chinese "had paid high prices for claims – from $2,000 to $7,000 – and promptly met all engagements. There was considerable litigation, however, arising from the whiteman trying to take advantage of the Chinese."[27]

The first census of Canada, in 1871, gave the number of Chinese in British Columbia as 1,548. There is reason to doubt this figure, for the same source estimates the Chinese population in 1874 as 3,000. Even this figure is well below the estimate of 6,000 for 1861, however, and it is therefore to be supposed that many Chinese departed Canada after the gold rush had petered out and the provisioning and servicing of mining communities no longer provided the lucrative employment it had in the early 1860's.

During the next decade, the Chinese community in Victoria increased considerably. Perhaps more important than their absolute numbers is the fact that their distribution became increasingly urban during the decade of the 1870's, with over a third living in Victoria itself (see Table 1). This followed a similar shift in the distribution of the non-Indian population generally as the gold rush dwindled and men started moving out of the interior toward the towns.

As the individual miners moved out of the interior, mining companies replaced them, many of them owned by Chinese. By 1875, there were more than thirty Chinese-owned companies mining gold in the Cariboo, the largest ones being Quong Lee, Dang Sing Dang, Sing Dang, and Loo Gee Wing, which four companies together produced gold to the value of $300,000 per year. Furthermore, a major non-Chinese mine, the Dancing Bill, was bought by Chinese and produced $900,000 worth of gold in 1878.[28] Clearly, the Chinese who remained in the interior were able to continue lucrative mining long after the first "killings" had been made during the rush itself.

Chinese were attracted north from Victoria on Vancouver Island by the coal industry. Coal had been discovered at Nanaimo in 1850 and indeed was the colony's major source until the gold rush began in 1858. When a depression hit the regional economy in 1866, the two coal-mining companies at Nanaimo brought in Chinese workers above ground, since they could be hired at $1 per day compared to the white workers' minimum wages of $2.50 per day. However, a month after they were hired, the Chinese workers struck for $1.50 and won.[29] Few were involved in coal-mining; the 1871 census counted only thirty-six Chinese in

19

Nanaimo. The companies hired another sixty-two Chinese that year, but the main influx came to nearby Wellington, where the Dunsmuir mines were opened in 1869 and began to hire Chinese labour above ground in 1871.[30]

Another occupation into which Chinese moved at this time was domestic service. This began in 1864, when several American families from San Francisco hired Chinese servants. Given the gross imbalance in the sexes at the time, the wealthy families in Victoria were unable to keep white women as servants for any length of time before they left to get married, so Chinese soon replaced most others in domestic services. "Without the Chinese in British Columbia," one prominent citizen told the Royal Commission on Chinese Immigration some years later, "there would have been no domestic service at all." Even in 1884, he considered that they would serve that function "for some years to come."[31] By the end of the 1870's, it was estimated that there were 400 Chinese servants and cooks in Victoria; since there would have been a score of restaurants at the most, almost all of these would have been in domestic service.

BUILDING THE RAILROAD

On October 7, 1877, the Victoria *Colonist* announced that the Canadian government had at last called for tenders for construction of the railroad that had been promised six years before, when British Columbia entered the Confederation. The construction tendered was from the head of navigation on the Fraser to the western end of the Kamloops Lake, 127 miles up the Fraser and Thompson canyons. Attempts by Premier Walkem of British Columbia to have clauses inserted into the contracts prohibiting Chinese labour were rejected by Sir John A. Macdonald, who argued that the government could not dictate to its contractors how they should carry out their work as long as it was done well.

Although this section of construction was let in four contracts, a young American contractor, Andrew Onderdonk, managed to buy them all from the lowest bidders on the grounds that one contractor could do a more efficient job than four. Onderdonk already had experience in major public works around San Francisco and knew the capabilities of Chinese workers. Nevertheless, because of a growing anti-Chinese feeling in Victoria, he gave his assurances that he would give white labour preference and would "with reluctance engage Indians and Chinese" only if he could find no other workers in eastern Canada or elsewhere.[32] Many of the workers Onderdonk hired from San Francisco proved to be unreliable, totally unsuited to construction work in the difficult circumstances of the Fraser Canyon, "the most useless lot of broken down gamblers, barkeepers, etc. ever collected in one place."[33] Quite a few of these "roughnecks" deserted the work almost immediately. Within a month of starting operations at Yale, Onderdonk was hiring Chinese labourers recruited from San Francisco and Portland, Oregon. In all, some 1,500 experienced Chinese railroad workers came from the United States in 1880 and 1881. Henry Cambie, the surveyor and engineer for the CPR, later described them as "trained gangs of rockmen, as good as ever I saw."[34]

The recruitment of Chinese from San Francisco and Portland was undertaken by a Chinese company, the Lian Chang Company, established for the purpose by Li Tianpei, a Toisanese businessman from San Francisco. Li joined with several relatives and other people from Toi-san County to organize the Lian Chang Company, with offices in Victoria and Hong Kong. At first, the Victoria agents were the Tai Yuan Company, managed by Li Yide, and the Guang An Long Company, managed by Li Youchin, although by 1882 Lian Chang itself appears in the Wells Fargo list of Chinese companies in Victoria. The Lian Chang Company began to recruit workers even before they were contracted, so that it was paying expenses for travel and maintenance before positions were guaranteed. Tai Chong and Lee Chuck were also mentioned as involved in contracting labour from Hong Kong in 1882, as were two non-Chinese transport companies in Victoria, Stahlschmidt & Ward and Welch and Rithet. Stahlschmidt & Ward seem to have had the lion's share of the business, for they received over five thousand of the eight thousand Chinese landed in Victoria during 1882. Another leading contractor was Kwong On Wo, whose superintendent, Yip Sang (Yip Chun-tin), was later to become a leading Chinese merchant in Vancouver.[35]

In 1881, Onderdonk contracted with Lian Chang for two thousand workers from Hong Kong. To bring them across the Pacific, Onderdonk chartered two ships, the *Escambia* and the *Suez*, which arrived in May, 1882, along with several ships from the south bringing still more workers for the railway. Of the eight thousand who arrived in Victoria during 1882, 6,500 disembarked in the three months of April, May, and June. Many suffered from scurvy when they disembarked, and Cambie estimated that "nearly ten per cent died of it."

Most of the Chinese stayed only briefly in Victoria before they embarked on river steamers for the trip across the Straits and up the Fraser to Emory, the head of river transport just two miles below Yale. This part of the journey was not particularly comfortable, and one group of nine hundred suffered the indignity and discomfort of being "penned in the wharf overnight like so many cattle" at New Westminster. Once off the river steamers at Emory, the Chinese then moved up the line on flat cars to their construction camps, a tedious ride, especially in inclement weather.

Chinese workers were used extensively on the sections of construction contracted to Andrew Onderdonk. While white workers graded the section from Yale to North Bend (27 miles), the section from North Bend to Lytton (26 miles) involved both white and Chinese labour, and all the remaining sections from Port Moody to Yale (90 miles) and from Lytton to Savona's Ferry (70 miles) were graded entirely by Chinese labour. Except for the section from Port Moody to Yale, however, it appears that white labour usually outnumbered the Chinese.

The 1885 Royal Commission on Chinese Immigration reported that 15,701 Chinese entered Canada during the period January, 1881, through June, 1884, "more than half of whom came in the years 1882 and 1883, when the demand for labour for the construction of the Canadian Pacific Railway was at its height."[36] Another 1,306 Chinese had arrived in the port from July to October, making a total of over 17,000 Chinese immigrants in the four years of railway construction. Of these, over 10,000 came directly from China.

Little is known about life in the railway camps to which the Chinese were sent because almost no Chinese records or diaries have been found that survive from that time. Perhaps the misery of their conditions precluded the workers from speaking much about them after they returned to China or settled elsewhere in Canada. Pierre Berton mentions one descendant of a railway worker, Dr. George Pon of Toronto, whose grandfather, Pon Git Cheng, worked on the railways, returned to Toisan to collect his family, and then settled in British Columbia. Pon Git Cheng's son worked as a "houseboy" for Benjamin Rogers, son of the man who had agreed not to hire any Chinese labour in his sugar works in Vancouver. Dr. Pon told Berton that he had learned something of his family background in China but nothing at all about his grandfather's time on the railway.[37]

A little about the organization of the Chinese railway camps can be inferred from indirect evidence. Most of the labour was contracted and therefore arrived in the camps in organized groups. Probably, an agent of the contracting company was resident in each camp. On the job thirty labourers worked as a gang with its own cooks and bookman. Each gang had a non-Chinese foreman, or "herder," who was responsible to the construction company. As many as 1,000 or more Chinese might be living in the same locality and such a camp would contain its own Chinese services, such as restaurants, barbershops, and stores. There were such large camps at Yale, Port Moody, and Savona's Ferry at different times.[38]

There is some evidence to indicate that the railroad camps developed some economic structure of their own, apart from the construction companies. A report in 1885 lists twenty-five shop employees, which suggests that various companies in Victoria ran branches in the camps under the management of employees. Furthermore, Chinese stores in the towns along the right of way probably also served the railway workers.

Apart from the economic structures of work and commerce, there appears to have been little organization among the Chinese railway workers. There was no union; no secret society lodges operated among them, so far as we know; no locality or clan associations were represented. The reason for this is probably the transient nature of the population. A comparison between the figures on immigration during the years of railway construction and the actual numbers engaged in the work at any particular time suggests that there was a rather high turnover. This is not surprising, for the conditions of work and life were far from satisfactory. Accidents were frequent, with many more Chinese than whites as victims, a fact that manifests the racist approach of the railway company. The company even issued accident figures that excluded the Chinese. On one occasion, for instance, the Yale *Sentinel* reported that there had been no accidents for almost three months, during which time Henry Cambie recorded four accidental deaths of Chinese on his stretch of the construction in a single month.[39] Lee states that many died from sheer exhaustion at the hard work and long walks between camp and work site. "Others perished in rock explosions or were buried in collapsed tunnels, or they drowned in the river after falling from an unfinished bridge. In 1882, in the Fraser Canyon, a collapsing tunnel buried a dozen workers at one time."[40] It is not surprising that white foremen were occasionally attacked by Chinese workers who had become incensed at their carelessness.

Not only work, but living conditions, too, caused much suffering and some deaths along the railway. So many died at Yale during the first year that the townspeople feared a smallpox epidemic, although the real villain was scurvy. The Yale *Sentinel*, probably the most sympathetic paper to the Chinese at the time, decried their living conditions and the lack of concern or medical attention provided them by their employers. "Here in British Columbia along the line of the railway, the Chinese workmen are fast disappearing under the ground," it reported in 1883.

> No medical attention is furnished nor apparently much interest felt for these poor creatures. We understand that Mr. Onderdonk declines interfering, while the Lee Chuck Co., that brought the Chinamen from their native land, refused, through their agent Lee Soon, who is running the Chinese gang at Emory, to become responsible for doctors and medicine.[41]

Lee Tung-hai records an epidemic in 1883 that killed more than 200 Chinese workers at Port Moody.

Winter, in particular, brought hardships to the Chinese. So suddenly transferred from the warm climate of Guangdong to the interior of British Columbia, they were ill-prepared for the continental winters that even the Victoria Chinese did not have to face. The Chinese at Port Moody suffered extreme hardship during the winter of 1882-83, when the supply ships were unable to get through the ice on Burrard Inlet. When the work was completed in the Fraser Canyon during the winter of 1883-84, the contractors, with a callousness that seems incredible today, fired Chinese workers at the work site, leaving them, as Berton writes, "to scrabble for pickings in the worked-out bars of the Fraser or to exist in near destitution in the dying towns along the completed track." It is no wonder they joined the Chinese Benevolent Association as soon as it was established.

Today, the Chinese in Canada have a saying that a Chinese worker died for every foot of railroad through the canyons. While this is, of course, an exaggeration, Lee estimates that at least 600 Chinese died during railroad construction, more than four for every mile.[42] This is probably a conservative estimate, since it is based on Onderdonk's testimony to the Royal Commission. In 1891 the Chinese Consolidated Benevolent Association (CCBA) of Victoria arranged for the collection of more than three hundred unidentified corpses from the Fraser and Thompson canyons; they were returned to China for decent burial by the CCBA.

EARLY CHINESE COMMUNITIES

By the 1880's, Chinese settlement patterns in western Canada were becoming established. The railroad greatly affected the distribution of Chinese communities on the mainland of British Columbia. Previously, gold had been the major attraction, and Chinese had therefore been found mainly along the Fraser Canyon and in the Cariboo. After 1881 large communities grew sequentially at the railroad camps near Yale, Lytton, Savona's Ferry, and Kamloops. By 1890, however, Yale had diminished considerably in size, since the railroad to Vancouver destroyed its importance as a river port. In the Cariboo, Keithley and Quesnel Mouth continued to be the major centres of Chinese settlement throughout the 1880's and 1890's, having replaced Barkerville in the early 1870's.

It seems safe to estimate that by 1880 the Chinese in British Columbia numbered about 3,500, of whom over 2,000 lived in Victoria, the only Chinese community of that size in Canada at the time. Victoria was a qualitatively different community from any of the others. With the possible exception of New Westminster, all the other centres comprised mainly miners and labourers. In Victoria, on the other hand, businesses and domestic servants each accounted for about a quarter of the Chinese population and a likely estimate is that over 75 per cent of the Chinese companies and 85 per cent of Chinese domestic servants in Canada were concentrated in Victoria at that time. Victoria was still the metropolis of the province in 1880, containing most of its commercial offices and almost all of its wealthy citizens. Naturally, the Chinese community in Victoria contained most of the Chinese businessmen, as well as serving the wealthy white citizens of the city.

At this period, three sorts of communities can be identified. One type was found in those places where a large number of Chinese worked for non-Chinese companies. The largest enterprise was, of course, railway construction, but there were similar communities at the coal mines in and near Wellington, at the sawmills in Burrard Inlet, near the fish canneries in New Westminster and Skeena, and on the farms at Harrison, Clinton,

Cache Creek, and 150 Mile House. Most of these communities included one or two Chinese merchants, prostitutes, and such service occupations as barbering.

A second type of Chinese community consisted of a core of commerce and service for a large body of independent Chinese miners. This form of community was found in the Cariboo, in the Okanagan, at Lytton, and at Lillooet.

The third type comprised the communities where there were several occupations serving the white population, including servants, tailors, vegetable-sellers, cigar makers, and the like. These communities also included services for the Chinese population itself, such as doctors, barbers, teachers, and prostitutes, and they manifested the major concentrations of Chinese retail businesses. Victoria was the largest such community, but New Westminster and Nanaimo repeated its economic structure. Vancouver later emerged as one of this type as well. Almost all of the unmarried women were in these communities.

Research by Dr. David C.Y. Lai has provided interesting evidence from the archives of the Chinese Consolidated Benevolent Association (CCBA) in Victoria concerning the distribution of the Chinese in British Columbia in 1884. Using the books of stubs from receipts issued to Chinese by the CCBA at the time of its founding in 1884, Lai was able to show that there were Chinese communities of 100 or more in at least fifteen centres and that Chinese numbered in the tens in another eight towns. One cannot get accurate totals for each Chinese community from these lists, for although the CCBA expected every Chinese to pay dues, in fact the stubs of only 5,056 receipts were extant at the time of Lai's study, representing about one-third of the Chinese then in British Columbia. Nevertheless, they provide a valuable indication of the distribution and, in particular, of the provenance and surnames of the Chinese in Canada at the time.[43]

Table 4 in the Appendix, adapted from Lai, indicates the counties of origin for some of the Chinese in Canada in 1884. Almost two-thirds were from the Sze-yap (*Siyi*, "four counties") district, one-third of those from Toi-san alone. Sze-yap and Sam-yap (*Sanyi*) together accounted for over four-fifths of the Chinese in Canada. Of counties with smaller representations in Canada, several exhibited concentrations in particular centres in British Columbia. While the distribution in Victoria more or less matched the overall proportions, Lillooet and the Thompson River manifested heavy concentrations of Chinese from Poon-yue, while the Cariboo towns held predominantly Sze-yap Chinese. In particular, more than three-quarters of the Chinese in Quesnel Mouth came from Hoiping. Almost half of the Chinese in Kamloops were from Tsang-shing, a county with low representation elsewhere in Canada. Similarly, more than half of the Chinese in Lytton came from Sun-wui. Sixty per cent of the Chinese in Nanaimo came from Toi-san.

It has usually been assumed that most of the railway workers came from Toi-san, for the major labour contractors were Toisanese. However, the proportion of Toisanese at Savona's Ferry (which, in 1884, was a railway camp and held the largest body of Chinese outside Victoria) was less than the proportion for the province as a whole, 19.2 per cent compared to 22.9 per cent. Furthermore, those towns where the proportion of Toisanese was high are not associated with railroad construction, but with mining: Quesnel Forks, Nanaimo, Dog Creek, Stanley. It is clear from this distribution that the large proportion of Toisanese among the Chinese in Canada preceded the railway era and cannot be attributed to the practice of recruiting labour through Toisanese contracting companies. The largest groups among the workers at Savona's Ferry were from Yin-ping (20.0 per cent); the Sze-yap districts provided 68.8 per cent of the workers, a higher proportion than that in the total list.

The receipt stubs of the CCBA studied by Lai indicate a wide range of surnames, the most prevalent being Zhou, Li, Huang, Chen, Lin, Liang, Ma, and Wu. However, no single name accounted for more than 11 per cent, nor were these surnames spread evenly throughout the province, but were concentrated in certain places. Nearly half the Chinese in Nanaimo were named Ma, and almost a quarter of those in Yale had the surname Li. The most striking concentration, combining both surname and locality of origin, was to be found in Quesnel Mouth, where two-thirds of the Chinese were named Zhou and came from Hoi-ping County. (It is not surprising that the major trading families in Quesnel had used given names as surnames, for the family name would not have distinguished them from each other. The Hoys and the Keans were all originally named Zhou.)

Among the Chinese in Canada at this time there were very few women. Chinese emigration to Canada followed the same pattern as that to Southeast Asia; it was usually that of single males who sent back remittances to families in China. Thus, there were less than 160 Chinese women in all British Columbia in 1885, of whom seventy were listed as "Prostitutes" in the report by the Chinese consulate in San Francisco to the Canadian Royal Commission on Chinese Immigration. Commissioner Gray carefully points out that many of the "prostitutes" were living "as concubines, that relationship being among them [the Chinese] deemed no offence, and no discredit."[44] The Consulate General's report lists fifty-five married women and thirty-three girls (seven children also are listed without distinguishing sex). Women comprised only 1.2 per cent of the Chinese population, giving a sex ratio of about 1 to 82 at that time.

The presence of even a few children raised the question of their education. The first Chinese school in Canada was not established until 1899. Prior to that time the "private schools" among the Chinese in Victoria "were no more than a group of children taught in accounting and in writing letters by a shop-keeper after working hours," according to Lee. However, the Chinese consulate's report lists eight teachers in Canada in

1884, four of them in Victoria and the others in New Westminster (2), Wellington, and Nanaimo. Lee believes these were hired privately by the wealthier businessmen as tutors for their own and relatives' children. Such schools prepared the few children present for careers in China or for potential assistance in family businesses in Canada. Some Chinese children, also, it is reported, were attending Canadian schools in 1881.

Thus, by 1885, after twenty-five years of immigration there was a Chinese population in Canada of over 10,000. It was a population limited to British Columbia, but one with some occupational diversity, as indicated in Table 13 in the Appendix. Not surprisingly, the Chinese in Canada had already begún to organize themselves.

NOTES

1. Margaret A. Ormsby, *British Columbia: a History* (Vancouver, 1958), p. 141.
2. Cheng Tien-fang, *Oriental Immigration in Canada* (Shanghai, 1931), p. 33.
3. Lee Tung-hai (David T.H. Lee), *Jianada huaqiao shi* (Taibei, 1967), p. 59. (Henceforth cited in this and subsequent chapters as Lee Tung-hai.)
4. Vancouver City Archives, MSS 33, vol. 1.
5. James Morton, *In the Sea of Sterile Mountains, the Chinese in British Columbia* (Vancouver, 1973), p. 7.
6. *Daily Colonist*, 28 March 1861.
7. Lee Tung-hai, p. 60; F.W. Howay, *British Columbia from the Earliest Times to the Present* (Vancouver, 1914), II, p. 16.
8. Seto Ying-shek, interview with Willmott, 5 May 1962. The two major Chinese companies in Victoria during the first two decades of Chinese settlement were managed by Wong Tien from Poon-yue County and by Lee Chong from Tsang-sing County. (Letter from Lee Tung-hai to Harry Con, 26 October 1977.) Charlie Cho, interview with H. Con, 25 March 1973.
9. Quoted in Charles P. Sedgwick, "The Context of Economic Change and Continuity in an Urban Overseas Chinese Community" (M.A. thesis, University of Victoria, 1973), p. 9.
10. Lee Tung-hai, p. 81.
11. Morton, *Sea of Sterile Mountains*, p. 8.
12. Lee Tung-hai, pp. 89-90.
13. Morton, *Sea of Sterile Mountains*, p. 12.
14. Sedgwick, "Context of Economic Change," p. 12.
15. William J. Trimble, *The Mining Advances into the Inland Empire, a Comparative Study of the Beginnings of the Mining Industry in Idaho, Montana, Washington and Oregon, and the Southern Interior of British Columbia; and the Institutions and Laws Based upon that Industry* (Madison, Wis., 1914), p. 140.

16. Howay, *British Columbia*, pp. 74, 567-8.
17. Mary Ann Snowden, "Chinese Settlement in British Columbia, a Process of Segregation and Integration" (M.S. thesis, Cariboo College, Kamloops, 1973).
18. From an address by Walter Moberly on the "History of the Cariboo Wagon Road," presented 5 March 1908 to the Vancouver Art Historical Society (Vancouver City Archives, Knowlton Papers, vol. 1).
19. Richard Byron Johnson, *Very Far West Indeed* (London, 1872), p. 79.
20. Robert Edward Wynne, "Reaction to the Chinese in the Pacific Northwest and British Columbia, 1850-1910" (Ph.D. thesis, University of Washington, 1964), pp. 134, 126.
21. W.E. Willmott, "Approaches to the Study of the Chinese in British Columbia," *B.C. Studies*, 4 (1970), p. 44.
22. Lee Tung-hai, p. 63.
23. *Report of the Royal Commission on Chinese Immigration* (Ottawa, 1885), p. 59. (Henceforth: *1885 Royal Commission*.)
24. Bruce Ramsey, *Ghost Towns of British Columbia* (Vancouver, 1971), p. 48.
25. Moberly, "History of the Cariboo."
26. Lee Tung-hai, p. 68.
27. Trimble, *Mining Advances*, p. 58.
28. Lee Tung-hai, p. 65.
29. Wynne, "Reaction to the Chinese," p. 142.
30. Morton, *Sea of Sterile Mountains*, p. 27.
31. *1885 Royal Commission*, p. xxiii.
32. Pierre Berton, *The Last Spike, the Great Railway 1881-1885* (Toronto, 1971), pp. 185, 194.
33. Vancouver City Archives, H.J. Cambie, letter to J.M.R. Fairbairn, 4 September 1923.
34. *Ibid.*
35. Morton, *Sea of Sterile Mountains,* p. 94; Lee Tung-hai, p. 127; see also *1885 Royal Commission*, p. 84. On Kwong On Wo and Yip Sang, see *Biography of Yip Sang* (*Yeh Chun-tien xiansheng chuanji* (Hong Kong, 1973?), pp. 5 (English section), 11 (Chinese section).
36. *1885 Royal Commission*, Gray's report, p. v.
37. Berton, *The Last Spike*, p. 205. The one diary known to exist, that of Dukesang Wong, is being prepared for publication by his granddaughter, Wanda Joy Hoe. A popularized summary has appeared as "The Golden Mountains of Dukesang Wong," in *We are Their Children. Ethnic Portraits of British Columbia* (Vancouver, 1977), pp. 31-40. We are indebted to Ms. Hoe for supplying us with a copy of this volume.
38. Vancouver City Archives, ad. MSS 292.
39. Berton, *The Last Spike*, pp. 204, 201.
40. Lee Tung-hai, p. 131.
41. Berton, *The Last Spike*, p. 203.

42. Lee Tung-hai, p. 131.
43. David C.Y. Lai, "Home County and Clan Origins of Overseas Chinese in Canada in the Early 1880s," *B.C. Studies*, 27 (1975), p. 10.
44. *1885 Royal Commission*, p. 363.

THREE

Early Chinese Organizations

Chinese social organizations made their appearance in British Columbia at an early date. The contrasting way of life of the Chinese in the rural settlements and their compatriots in the cities led to the emergence of two distinct kinds of organization: the secret societies of the mining districts, and the *jiefang*, or "street associations," in Victoria. For the first two decades, until about 1876, they developed quite separately.

The first secret society, founded in Barkerville in 1863, was the Hong Shun Tang, a branch of the same secret society already active in California. This was one of the societies known collectively as the Hong Men Hui, or Hong societies, originally established in China during the seventeenth or the eighteenth century. These societies were necessarily secret because they opposed the rule of the Qing dynasty. Lee Tung-hai states that the Barkerville society was established by Huang Shengui, who came from California and was a member of the Hong Shun Tang even before he left China. According to Lee, it spread with the Chinese miners moving north from California through Montana and Idaho, thus missing Victoria altogether.

The original building of the secret society was destroyed by the fire that swept through Barkerville in 1868, therefore the present building dates from about that time. Restored in 1962, it now carries plaques and signboards donated by the Chinese Freemasons Headquarters in Vancouver. Some are thus anachronistic, but one plaque, obviously much older than the rest, carries the characters *Hong Shun Tang*, the original name of the association. Another has the characters *Yixing Gongsuo*, a name that was used for the Hong-men societies throughout North America at the end of the nineteenth century.

A set of rules pertaining to a secret society was discovered in Quesnel Forks in 1960. This document uses the name Zhigongtang (Cheekung-tong) association and indicates that it was "originally established in Quesnel Mouth in 1876."[1] The date and place imply that there is a discontinuity between the Barkerville Hong Shun Tang and the subsequent

Cheekungtong (CKT) established at Quesnel Mouth, although it is possible that the rules refer to the establishment of a separate branch of the same society.

Because the discovery of such a body of rules is a rarity, the document is worth quoting at some length; it sheds light on the nature of Chinese community organization in the Cariboo mining towns and those that subsequently developed in Cassiar and the Kootenay.

> It is said that a well-organised society is ruled by reason and that the security and harmony of society depend on the cultivation of harmonious sentiments. The nation treats peace and prosperity as matters of paramount importance; the cangue is moistened by rain. In a hostel a friendly relationship among the lodgers is of paramount importance; the gentle breeze is important on a sea voyage. . . . The purpose in forming the Cheekungtong is to maintain a friendly relationship among our countrymen and to accumulate wealth through proper business methods for the benefit of all members. Thus, those who do mental work and those who do physical work are devoting their strength to this common goal.

> Recently rumours and slander about our organisation have been spread increasingly abroad. Fortunately, in the face of danger, our comrades have held on to the truth firmly and unflinchingly, have carried on the work with steadfastness of heart, and have relied on self-confidence in the face of slander . . . it is high time to clarify the constitution and regulations [of this society] . . . so that our organisation does not have an abortive development.[2]

There follows the constitution of the society, comprising twenty-four clauses adopted at the 1882 conference at Quesnel Forks. The following are the most significant to an understanding of the society's role in community organization:

Regulations of the Society

4. No member will be permitted to act for outsiders to collect debts from Society members. Anyone who uses force to collect bad debts on behalf of outsiders and is convicted through evidence will be subject to punishment without clemency.
6. When new businesses are opened by the Society and helpers are needed, only members who have paid dues and have seniority in the Society are qualified for these posts. Any competition or struggle for these posts among members will not be permitted.
9. Members who collaborate with outsiders and use the name of the Cheekungtong to threaten others for financial gain may be punished.
10. Members in good standing may ask the Society for assistance in cases of urgent need. . . . Those who fail to register and do not

pay membership dues must submit 30 dollars supplementary fees when requesting the assistance of the Society in disputes.

12. This Society (Tong) was originally founded at Quesnel Mouth in 1876, and in 1882 it was established in this town. Since then no other Tongs have been formed. Anyone who intends to form a new Tong and create trouble will be prosecuted.

13. Members, no matter whether they are living in town, in mining areas, in ports, or in cities must maintain fair practices in business. Anyone who uses an advantageous position in business to oppress our countrymen will be brought back for punishment in accordance with the constitution if a complaint is made and evidence presented.

14. Members . . . must follow a policy of first come, first served when selling or buying businesses or mines. Anyone who does not follow this regulation will be punished in accordance with the regulations if a complaint is made and evidence presented.

15. Members . . . will not be permitted to reduce wages or to spread slander against each other in order to compete in hiring. Anyone committing these acts will be punished if a complaint is made and evidence presented.

20. Any dispute or mutual suspicion among members should be settled in the Society in accordance with reason. Those who persist in quarrelling with one another or who appeal to the courts either create more trouble and expense or damage friendships.

24. Criticism must be made only in the Society's meeting. Anyone who makes criticisms behind the scenes or utters slander against other members outside the meeting will be sentenced to 21 stripes.

It seems likely from these rules that the Cheekungtong was the major, probably the only, Chinese association in these mining communities, and that it undertook political and welfare functions for the community as a whole. Chinese were discouraged from taking cases to the Canadian courts, and most disputes, whether of a civil or criminal nature, were settled by the secret society. Even behaviour in brothels and gambling houses was regulated by the CKT. Furthermore, it is apparent from regulation 6 that the Society itself undertook economic enterprises, although we do not know the nature of these.

The CKT also served as a hostel in Quesnel Forks, and a third set of regulations relates to this function. From it we learn that the hostel provided staples such as tea, salt, fuel, and candles, the cost of which was divided equally among the lodgers each week. Cooking was done individually, however, according to an agreed schedule for use of the kitchen. Daily chores of chopping wood and fetching water were rostered, and lodgers were expected to stay less than a week. "All those who stay in this hostel should look after each other," states the first rule. "Friendly relations and kindness among lodgers are most precious." But at the end

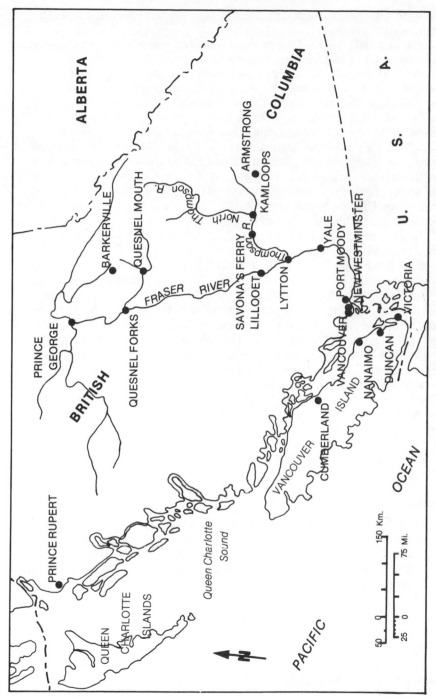

B.C. Nineteenth and Early Twentieth Centuries

the hostel regulations insist that "actions against these regulations will be prosecuted."

Yale, although it served the railroad workers, was also a centre for the Chinese miners still panning along the lower reaches of the Fraser Canyon, and its community organization resembled the other mining towns more closely than the railroad camps. The Cheekungtong was probably established in Yale in 1882, for in that year the *Inland Sentinel* reported that a Chinese "temple" was being built. The temple was opened the following April in a great ceremony that was attended by Chinese visitors from Victoria and New Westminster. Later in 1883 the CKT appears among the Chinese signatories on a donation to the fire brigade after a particularly disastrous fire had caused $50,000 damage to Chinese businesses. In August, 1883, according to the *Inland Sentinel*, a hall was built by the Chinese Freemasons Lodge, which at the time had over sixty members under the leadership of Chung Gim, Chung Yeh, and Ming Tehe. In January of 1884, the Grand Master of the lodge officiated at a Chinese wedding between the merchant On Lee and his bride, newly arrived from China.[3] This suggests that in Yale, as in the mining towns of the Cariboo, the CKT alone provided the Chinese community structure.

The first form of organization to emerge in the cities was a "street association," *jiefang*. A *jiefang* was established by mutual consent of the major Chinese companies in a city; if one company predominated, it was the logical leader, but in many cities the companies undertook in rotation to house its headquarters and provide its active leadership. It was often fairly informal, representing nothing more than temporary co-operation for a specific issue or project.[4]

In Victoria, the *jiefang* type of organization that enabled joint community action among the various Chinese business houses almost certainly centred upon the Kwong Lee Company, by far the largest Chinese trading company in the town. There is direct as well as inferential evidence for this. In March, 1864, when the Victoria business community was collecting money for a reception for Arthur E. Kennedy, the new governor of the Colony of Vancouver Island, the following letter appeared in the *Daily Colonist*:

> If the collectors appointed to receive donations for the governor's reception fund will call at Messrs. Kwong Lee & Co's Store on Cormorant Street, they will receive upwards of one hundred dollars contributed without solicitation by the Chinese residents of Victoria as a mark of loyalty to our Gracious Queen.
>
> – Richard Hall, Sin Shang

The reception committee acknowledged a donation of $103 from the Chinese a few days later.[5]

The signatory of this statement, Mr. Hall, also appeared as the interpreter for the Chinese a few days later when the three major companies – Kwong Lee, Yan Wo Sang, and Tai Soong – presented a petition to the new governor upon his arrival. The title "sin shang" (*xiansheng*) suggests Hall was Chinese, as does the language of the English translation of the petition. Left out of the formal welcoming celebrations, the Chinese took the initiative in April to lay before Governor Kennedy their grievances against the previous governor, Douglas, and their hopes that they would be treated more justly at his hands. Their specific requests were that Victoria should become a free port, without import tariffs on silk, tea, rice, and sugar from China, and that Chinese merchants from California should receive favourable treatment from the colonial government.[6]

The *jiefang* in Victoria were associated in those early years of Chinese settlement with a number of projects, such as the establishment of the Jubilee Hospital (to which the Tai Soong Company was a generous contributor), and the setting up of a house to store bodies for five years or so, prior to the shipment of the bones of the deceased back to China.

The various trading companies also played an important role in maintaining contact between the immigrants and their relatives in China. They arranged remittances to China and transported mail. A series of letters in the British Columbia Provincial Archives written by a man in Guangdong to his father in Victoria and recently discovered by Mr. Charles Sedgwick gives evidence of this arrangement. In one letter, the man mentions four stores in Victoria that carried mail: Tai Soong, Wing Cheung, Fook Sum, and Tai Cheung. This particular family used Tai Soong for most of their transactions, for the son acknowledges both mail and remittances transferred to him by the company. Unfortunately, there is no indication in these letters of the particular district in Guangdong whence they were mailed; otherwise, it might be possible to infer which companies handled mail for a specific district in China. We know that some time later each of several major Chinese companies in Vancouver was responsible for transactions with a specific district in China, and it is altogether likely that this was the case in early Victoria as well.

Besides the *jiefang* there was the Cheekungtong (CKT), founded in Victoria in 1876 by members from Seattle who came north to propagate their association in Victoria. The original founders were Lam Lip-fong (Lin Lifang), Chu Hee (Zhao Xi), Yip Wai-pak (Ye Huibai), Lee Yew (Li You), and Chan Yew (Chen Yao). We do not know which of these men came from Seattle and which were already residents of Victoria. It appears that the secret society lodge in Victoria had little to do with those in the Cariboo at this time. Not until the late 1880's did a regional structure emerge linking the various branches in British Columbia, and not until 1919 was a Canada-wide convention of the Cheekungtong held.

At about the same time as the Cheekungtong, the first locality associations were founded in Victoria. At first, groupings of men from the same village or small district came together to form co-operative boarding houses, called *fangkou*, where men from the mainland could live while in

Victoria. Gradually *fangkou* from the same county grouped together to form a "benevolent hall" (*shantang*) for that county. The purpose of these benevolent halls was to arrange the transportation of remains back to China and to raise subscriptions in times of calamities in the home county in China. According to Lee, these *shantang* were branches of those already established in San Francisco, and they were rather informal at this time, being *jiefang* without clearcut structure or buildings. When something needed doing, "the members gathered in one of the shops belonging to a member; after the problem was resolved, they dispersed."[7] Lee states that there were ten such *shantang* in Victoria in 1875 ("at the beginning of Guangxu") representing the following nine counties in China: Sun-ning (later Toi-san), Sun-wui, Heung-san (later Chung-san), Hoi-ping, Yin-ping, Poon-yue, Tsang-sing, Nam-hoi, and Sun-dak. The tenth grouped Hakka from various counties and was the first to become a formal locality association in 1872, entitled the Yan Wo Tong (Ren He Tang). It is not unusual for minority groups among overseas Chinese communities to band together into an appropriate association to protect their interests against the majority, whose interests are often served adequately by co-operation among the dominant business houses. The small number of Hakka and their linguistic isolation from the Cantonese comprising the rest of the Chinese population may well have led them to consider an alternative association earlier than other sub-groups in the community.

Meanwhile, several new associations were emerging among the Chinese in the capital city of Victoria, and a somewhat similar situation was developing in the other centres of that type, namely New Westminster and Nanaimo. The large number of Chinese flowing through Victoria may well have initiated these developments, for while the merchants could control the resident population, the many labourers and miners who spent their winters in Victoria during 1881-84 no doubt produced major problems for the leaders of the resident community.

At the time, Victoria Chinatown was booming. Fifteen opium dens and eleven hotels served the Chinese transients and residents; three companies were playing Cantonese opera, and there were numerous other places of amusement. These activities were supported, not only by the transient railway workers, who came through Victoria in both directions throughout the construction period, but also by the buoyant condition of Chinese business in Victoria itself.

While the Chinese economy in Victoria was experiencing this boom, however, many Chinese were suffering serious deprivation. During the winter of 1883-84, in particular, as more and more Chinese were dismissed from the railroad construction companies and found themselves destitute in various towns along the right of way, the suffering of ordinary Chinese workers must have contrasted markedly with the lives of the wealthy merchants in Victoria. Many of the unemployed drifted into Victoria's Chinatown, increasing its social problems.

All these circumstances led the merchants in Victoria to seek advice in organizing a community-wide Chinese association. In March of 1884 they wrote to the Chinese consul-general in San Francisco, Huang Cunxian, asking him to take the initiative in establishing a Chinese association in Canada. Part of their concern was the discriminatory legislation that had just been introduced in the B.C. legislature. The fact that they were seeking a Chinese consulate in Victoria as well as an all-embracing association indicates that the growing threat of discriminatory actions towards the Chinese community was as important as the social problems within Chinatown in motivating Chinese merchants towards the establishment of the Benevolent Association.

According to Lee, the Chinese consulate in San Francisco responded by sending Huang Xiquan to help the merchants organize an association. During his stay in Canada, Huang Xiquan collected information on each of the Chinese centres in British Columbia, which was later presented to the Royal Commission on Chinese Immigration, set up in 1884.

Huang Xiquan was also responsible for drafting the regulations of the Chinese Consolidated Benevolent Association of Victoria (CCBA). The association was inaugurated in June, 1884, when a body of regulations was adopted and officers elected. Prominent among the original sponsors were Li Youchin (Lee Yau Kian) of Guong An Long, Li Tianpei (Lee Tin Poy) of Lian Chang, and Li Yide (Lee Yick Tack) of Tai Yuan, three of those who gained the most from labour contracts with Onderdonk. Li Youchin was elected the first president of the Association, and both the others to its Board of Trustees. Huang Ruichao (known as Wong Soy Chew) was elected treasurer, and the other trustees were Ma Xu (Mar Sau) and Xu Chuanli (Chu Lai). The two secretaries were Feng Chinchun (Kum Shoong) – who had also been among the original sponsors of the Association – and Won Alexander Cumyow (Wen Jinyou), who, being fluent in English, was able to serve as interpreter for the Association.[8]

Cumyow had spent his childhood in New Westminster, where his father ran a business, and during the railroad period was himself briefly the agent of Kwong Lee at Yale until 1884, when he moved to Victoria after visiting Montreal, New York, and San Francisco. He grew up learning English as well as two Chinese languages (Cantonese and Hakka), and so was able to perform the important function of interpreting between the Chinese and white communities, first as English-language secretary of the CCBA and later as court interpreter in Vancouver, which position he held from 1888 until 1936.

Before the CCBA held its inaugural meeting, the organizing committee issued a statement to all Chinese in British Columbia on April 10, 1884, appealing for contributions of two dollars per person to assist the committee in founding the Association and in campaigning against discriminatory legislation. The statement requested contributions before October 3, but the receipt books of the CCBA indicate that they were still arriving through 1885 as well. In all, over 5,000 men paid their two dollars, representing about a third of the Chinese population in Canada at the time. Returns were remarkably high from the mainland, from both railroad and mining centres. This indicates either that the Victoria merchant elite held considerable power in these communities or that there was present a strong desire for an all-Chinese association even in centres remote from the capital. Probably both factors contributed; commercial ties could have been mobilized for this collection, but there may well have been growing concern about both discrimination and the lack of cohesive Chinese organization. The fact that about 1,500 railroad construction workers paid their contributions, despite their being the least permanent residents, indicates the extent of their dissatisfaction at the time.

The purpose of the CCBA was stated clearly in its constitution:

> This association has been established in order to express our feelings of unity, to undertake social welfare, to settle disputes, to aid the poor and the sick, to eliminate evils within the community, and to defend the community against external threat.[9]

The preamble legitimates the CCBA by documenting its mandate from the Chinese consul-general in San Francisco, who in turn, of course, represented the Qing Emperor. This attempt to provide the CCBA with authority to supervise all other Chinese associations did not succeed, however, for the Cheekungtong, which opposed the Qing dynasty, never accepted its supervision, although the locality and clan associations did at the start. Furthermore, when a CBA was later established in Vancouver, probably in the early 1890's, it was largely independent of the CCBA in Victoria. Nevertheless, the CCBA served as the top of the political structure of Victoria's Chinese community from its inception until long after the turn of the century.

The CCBA bought a property at 558 Fisgard Street on the site of a small temple. There it built a three-storey brick building, which was still standing in the 1970's. For many years, the top floor was used as a temple, with the ornately carved altar, altar tables, screens, and images that are now located in the hall of the Chinese Public School at 636 Fisgard Street. The first Chinese public school was organized by the CCBA in this building.

From the thirty-seven regulations included in the 1884 constitution, we can gain some insight into the structure of the CCBA and its place in the Chinese community of Victoria. The regulations assume that all Chinese should become members by paying the two-dollar subscription, and there are fines imposed upon those who refuse as well as a repeated injunction that the Association will not serve those who have not paid. In later years the CCBA became restructured as a federation of associations, but in the nineteenth century it began as an individual membership association, the officers being elected at an annual general meeting held at the middle of December. Candidates for the presidency were to be prosperous businessmen of good character. All offices were honorary, with the exception of the General Secretary, who was paid an honorarium of $120 per annum at the start, but became full-time a few years later. Provision was made in the constitution for the appointment of an English-language secretary as well.

The temple was looked after by a caretaker, who tendered for the job. His chief source of income was donations from worshippers rather than his salary paid by the Association. This was one of three temples in Victoria in the 1880's, the others being the temple of the Yan Wo Society (Hakka) and the sacred hall of the Cheekungtong.

The CCBA provided aid to any paid-up member who was "insulted, beaten, robbed or owed money" by non-Chinese, as well as providing rewards for the capture of non-Chinese who had killed a Chinese, and legal aid to Chinese unjustly accused of criminal or bad behaviour by a non-Chinese. Furthermore, the CCBA attempted to protect the Chinese community from its own gangsters by prohibiting any assistance to a convicted Chinese without the permission of the Association.

Perhaps a more important function of the CCBA was settling disputes among Chinese. Although there is no indication of the nature of disputes brought to the CCBA, Article 14 indicates something of the procedures involved.

> ARTICLE 14: When a Chinese asks the Association to arbitrate in a dispute with another Chinese, each party may be represented by no more than three persons, not including those called as witnesses. No weapons may be brought into the association rooms. Accusations must be made in the presence of the accused. Bickering or fighting is not permitted. Even if one of the two parties is not happy with the decision, he must leave peacefully, without insulting his adversary or the conciliators. Otherwise, he will be expelled from the Association and handed over to the police.

As to welfare, the Association provided aid to any man over sixty who could not afford his return fare to China, both by donation and by organizing a collection. Furthermore, the Association ran a home for the sick and poor who lacked the means of support, and it also paid for the burial of anyone dying in poverty and without relatives.

The final article in this section of the constitution relates to a social problem that exercised missionaries in Victoria, namely prostitution and "slavery."

> ARTICLE 20: If anyone informs the Association that a young girl has been kidnapped and sold in this city, the buyer will be forced to set the girl free. The Association will look after sending her to the Tung Wah Hospital in Hongkong, which will inform the family. In case the girl has no family, the Tung Wah Hospital will arrange for her to marry a decent man.

39

It is difficult to establish exactly what other associations existed among the Chinese in Victoria at the time the CCBA was founded. Certainly, locality associations were operating in Victoria even before this time, probably as *jiefang*. It is possible that some had become formal associations by the mid-1880's, for the exhumation and washing of human bones for shipment back to China was a well-established practice in Canada by 1883, much to the consternation of some of the white citizens.[10] None is mentioned as donating to the CCBA after its founding, however, which strongly suggests that they were still merely *jiefang*. Lee Tung-hai supports this view, for he states that the *shantang* handled the shipment of remains to China at this time, and that the first locality association in Victoria was not established until 1893, when the people from Sun-ning (later Toi-san) built a hall on Cormorant Street for the Sun-ning Yu Hing Tong, later to be called the Toi-san Ningyung Wuikuan. Li Yingsan became the association's first chairman.[11]

Almost a decade before the Toi-san locality association opened its hall, the Chinese from Poon-yue County organised a Victoria branch of their San Francisco-based locality association about 1886. The association in San Francisco, established early in the 1850's, was called the Chong Hoo Tong, and its strength in Canada was based on the prominence of the Tai Soong Company in Victoria, whose founder and president was Huang Tianlu (Wong Tin Louis), himself from Poon-yue County. Tai Soong Co., therefore, became the headquarters of the *jiefang* for Poon-yue people, and even after the branch of the Chong Hoo Tong was established in 1886, Tai Soong's many branches in British Columbia provided a network for this association throughout the province.

While the Chinese Consolidated Benevolent Association was the first formal community-wide Chinese association in Canada, Nanaimo developed a unique community structure in the shape of a land company, the Wah Hing Shat Yip Kungsi (Huaxing Shiye Gongsi). In the late 1870's the coal mines had attracted over 1,000 Chinese to the Nanaimo area. In 1881 local Chinese merchants established the Wah Hing Company, which bought land on Princess Street and leased it out to Chinese companies and individuals to build stores and houses. Prior to that, Nanaimo's Chinatown had been located near the port, not far from where the CPR wharf is now, but rising rents had forced the Chinese to move. In 1908, the Wah Hing Company bought a piece of land to the west of the city where a new Chinatown was built.[12]

Thus by the 1880's the number of Chinese organizations was growing. This development did not go unnoticed among the small minority of whites who were agitating fiercely for the exclusion of all Chinese. This was to be the beginning of a continuing battle the Chinese in British Columbia would have to fight.

NOTES

1. Stanford Lyman, W.E. Willmott, and Berching Ho, "Rules of a Chinese Society in British Columbia," *Bulletin of the School of Oriental and African Studies*, XXVII, 3 (1964), pp. 530-1.
2. *Ibid.*, pp. 534ff.
3. Quoted in Andrea Laforet, "Folk History in a Small Canadian Community" (Ph.D. thesis, University of British Columbia, 1974), pp. 162-4.
4. W.E. Willmott, "Some Aspects of Chinese Communities in British Columbia Towns," *B.C. Studies*, 1 (1968-69), p. 34.
5. James Morton, *In the Sea of Sterile Mountains, the Chinese in British Columbia*, p. 24.
6. Matthew Macfie, *Vancouver Island and British Columbia* (London, 1865), pp. 386ff.
7. Lee Tung-hai, p. 203.
8. *Ibid.*, p. 176; see also David Chuen-Yan Lai, "The Chinese Consolidated Benevolent Association in Victoria: Its Origins and Functions," *B.C. Studies*, 15 (1972), p. 55.
9. Lee Tung-hai, pp. 179-86.
10. Morton, *Sea of Sterile Mountains*, pp. 104ff. Morton mentions (p. 35) that in 1871 arson destroyed a "Chinese Dead House" on Store Street where fifty bodies awaited shipment to China; we have no record of what organization this morgue represented.
11. Note that Lee Tung-hai, p. 204, gives it as Cumberland Street, but this is probably an error in transliteration.
12. David Tom, interview with Willmott, 17 March 1962. The resulting Chinatown, along Pine and Hecate Streets, was unique in several ways, situated as it was on top of a hill overlooking a residential part of Nanaimo and built entirely of wood, rather like the set of a western movie; it was called "cowboy town" by many Chinese and non-Chinese. Unfortunately, it was destroyed by fire on 8 October 1960 (Lee Tung-hai, pp. 83-4).

FOUR

Rising White Opposition

Relations between Chinese and white in British Columbia and Vancouver Island were cordial during the 1860's and most of the 1870's. Anti-Chinese agitation was limited to a few politicians in Victoria, New Westminster, and Nanaimo until 1878, and their attempts to develop support for their racist proposals did not receive enthusiastic support from wide circles in British Columbia. This is not to say that the Chinese did not experience prejudice and discrimination, for sporadic incidents of violence were recorded right from the start. Nevertheless, the *Victoria Gazette*, owned by two Californians and printing the kinds of anti-Chinese slogans and articles that were popular south of the border, found itself out of step with the general trend of tolerant thinking in Victoria and closed down in 1859.[1] Racism in British North America was less able to find expression in discriminatory laws and this legal situation may well have prevented in Canada some of the excesses of persecution that the Chinese suffered in California and other western states.

Under the Franchise Act, 1859, the Colony of Vancouver Island permitted only British subjects to vote for the seven members of the House of Assembly. But in 1861, an "act to enable Aliens to Hold Real Estate" gave aliens the same rights of ownership and alienation of property enjoyed by British subjects in the colony, and the Aliens Act of 1861 provided that "Aliens resident for three years within the Colony who shall take the Oaths of Residence and Allegiance shall have all the rights of British Subjects."[2]

Nevertheless, the first attempt at discriminatory legislation against the Chinese in Canada occurred only two years after their arrival. In 1860 the House of Assembly of the Colony of Vancouver Island proposed a poll tax of $10 to be levied on each Chinese in the colony. The measure was opposed by Amor de Cosmos and other leading citizens of Victoria, however, who argued that the presence of the Chinese was good for business. "Our prediction is," wrote de Cosmos in the *British Colonist*, "that while British Columbia profits directly from their labour, in-

42

directly our [Vancouver Island] commercial prosperity is assured."[3] Accordingly, the tax was dropped. In opposing the 1860 proposal to tax the Chinese, however, de Cosmos indicated the extent of his own anti-Chinese prejudices, which were quite typical of his day:

> They may be inferior to Europeans and Americans in energy and ability; hostile to us in race, language and habits and may remain among us as a Pariah race; still they are patient, easily governed and invariably industrious. . . . Hereafter, when the time arrives that we can dispose of them, we will heartily second a check to their immigration.[4]

Such prejudice was manifested in incidents of discrimination, persecution, and even violence when Chinese and white came into conflict. In August, 1859, the *Colonist* printed a report from its correspondent in Fort Yale, which indicated that racist incidents were not uncommon along the Fraser River.

> The Chinamen in the Little Kanyon (five miles above Yale) have occasional conflicts with their white neighbours, in which John is invariably worsted. The white men aver that the Celestials have pursued a more aggressive policy in jumping claims while the owners were in town buying provisions, pulling up stakes and tearing down notices, and behaving in an insolent manner generally, thereby meriting a sound trouncing.

A description of prejudice, discrimination, and violence is provided by a British traveller, R. Byron Johnson, who toured British Columbia in the 1860's:

> It is the fashion on the Pacific Coast, to abuse and illtreat the Chinaman in every possible way . . . he is treated like a dog, bullied, scoffed at, kicked, and cuffed-about on all occasions, his very name is made a slang reproach; and yet, withal, he betrays no sign of meditated revenge, and pursues his labours calmly, and is civil and polite to all. . . . Even in the matter of religion, a score on which Americans claim to have particularly tolerant views, he is insulted to a pitch that would not be endured by a person of any other nationality.

It has been suggested that the first prospectors used violence to keep the Chinese out of the Cariboo until 1862.[5] Certainly an incident is recorded of two Chinese being shot dead in 1861 by white miners in Cayoosh. However, the useful services the Chinese provided by opening restaurants, vegetable gardens, laundries, and other amenities desired by bachelor miners precluded their complete exclusion from the gold-mining areas. Furthermore, there are recorded instances of Chinese and white miners together working the same claim or co-operating to build a common flume to service adjacent claims, indicating that relations were relatively cordial in the goldfields. This cordiality depended on the willingness of the Chinese to accept the inhuman treatment meted out to them by the whites. Sometimes, however, they found it intolerable; as early as 1861, some Chinese were leaving British Columbia because of white hostility.[6] Amor de Cosmos described this hostility in the *Colonist* and called upon the citizens of British Columbia and Vancouver Island to treat the Chinese as equals.

In the Cariboo, unlike the Fraser River or the Kootenay, gold came primarily from deep mining, for which a company had to control sufficient capital to build a mine-head and dig for some time without any returns. As gold mining became less lucrative, beginning in 1864, antagonisms developed between white and Chinese labour in the Cariboo. In 1869, when the Chinese workers at a mine on Williams Creek struck for better conditions, the owners hired white scabs and broke the strike.[7] That same year the buildings of Kwong Lee in Quesnel Mouth were burned out, killing ten Chinese employees.[8]

Meanwhile, similar antagonism was building in the coal-mining region of Vancouver Island, and for the same reasons. By 1871 Chinese numbers had risen to over a hundred, and this began to worry some of the leading citizens in Victoria, whose sights were turned towards the promised railroad from eastern Canada. Nanaimo was held up by the *British Colonist* as an example of the dangers of Chinese labour's replacing white's, although it was rather contradictorily claimed that a white worker was the equivalent of two Chinese. Not surprisingly, the most outspoken leader of the anti-Orientalists at the time was Arthur Bunster, the first MP for Nanaimo. He was closely followed by John Robson, editor of the *British Columbian* and the first MLA for Nanaimo.

In 1867, one year after the two colonies of Vancouver Island and British Columbia were merged, the Aliens Ordinance replaced the three separate laws relating to aliens. The crucial clause in the new law reduced the period of residence from three years to one year before application for naturalization could be made. The prescribed procedures for applying for naturalization involved declarations of residence and character, an oath of allegiance, and court appearances, none of which appeared to discriminate in any way against Chinese. Furthermore, the right of aliens to own and sell real estate was reconfirmed by the law.[9]

By this time, however, public opinion was moving in another direction, and even the *British Colonist* was beginning to sound anti-Chinese. Having favoured Chinese immigration in 1865 and praised the Chinese for their diligence and trade, it had turned around by 1867 to chastise the striking Chinese workers at the Nanaimo collieries as unworthy of residence in the colony. By 1871, the voices raised against the Chinese were even more strident, both inside the provincial Parliament and without.

One of Arthur Bunster's first actions in the B.C. Legislative Council in

1871 (before he was elected to the Canadian Parliament) was to promote a bill "imposing a poll tax of $50 per head per annum on all Chinese engaged in any occupation in this colony." When the assembled representatives greeted this proposal with laughter, Bunster, a rather coarse speaker, told them that "It's going to be a test question at the next election – see if it ain't. . . . I want to see Chinamen kept to himself [sic] and foul diseases kept away from white people. . . . Why when I drive . . . past the hovels, the stench is enough to knock me off my seat. . . ."[10] He claimed that the Chinese did not pay taxes and that they pushed white people off the sidewalk with "their smelly baskets." Interestingly, Amor de Cosmos mildly supported Bunster, pointing out that the Chinese were interfering with white trade; nevertheless, the bill was withdrawn without a vote.

In 1871, British Columbia entered Confederation and its Legislative Assembly became a provincial parliament. One of its first moves was to pass an Act to amend the Qualification of Voters Act which would disenfranchise Chinese and Indians in provincial elections. The Lieutenant-Governor of the province, Joseph Trutch, was of the opinion that this Act might contravene the British North America Act, so forwarded it to the Governor General of Canada for his advice.[11] The Deputy Minister of Justice presented his opinion, in which the Prime Minister, John A. Macdonald, concurred, that the legislation did not contravene the British North America Act, and that it was within the powers of a province to amend its own constitution, including changing its franchise.

The issue at this time was entirely a matter of the Indian franchise, and the Chinese were not mentioned in the correspondence. Nevertheless, there must have been some delay in the legislation, for it was not until late 1875 that the Chinese were removed from the voters lists of British Columbia. Eight Chinese voted in a Lillooet by-election in 1874, and ninety-two Chinese voted in the Victoria municipal elections in August of the same year, although it was later shown in court that some of their names had been added to the list after the successful mayoral candidate had paid their taxes for them. Chinese were prevented from exercising their vote by other than legal means, however, as in the first Nanaimo municipal elections in January, 1873, when they were physically barred from the polling stations.[12] The *Colonist* applauded the rednecks:

> True, the Act does not exclude these people; but so sensible were the Freemen of Nanaimo of the impropriety, the degradation of allowing these heathen slaves (as the great bulk of them undoubtedly are) to stand side by side with themselves at the Ballot box and have an equal voice in the management of affairs which they little understand and in which they have still less interest or sympathy in common, that they, with one accord, decided to exclude them.

Shortly thereafter, in May of 1873, the first Anti-Chinese Society was established in Victoria. It called for restrictions on Chinese immigration, and pointed to the dangers of increasing immigration from California due to the persecution of Chinese there.[13]

A Qualifications and Registration of Voters Act was passed by the British Columbia legislature in 1875, by which it became illegal to grant the franchise to any Chinese and all Chinese names were to be deleted from the voters' list. Failure to comply with the provisions of this act carried a $50 fine or one month's imprisonment. Although this Act would have serious consequences for them, at that time the leaders of the Chinese community did not appear to have reacted to this disenfranchisement.

A major concern of the anti-Orientalists was the possibility that the promised railway from eastern Canada would be built by Chinese labour. To forestall this, John Robson presented a resolution in the provincial legislature in 1872 to prohibit the hiring of Chinese on any public works. The motion was defeated on the grounds that it interfered with free enterprise. The following year the newly formed Canadian Labour Union, in its Toronto convention, passed a resolution opposing the importation of convict labour or contract labour "receiving lower wages than usual." The resolution was not couched in racist language, but presented a purely economic argument against the competition of cheap labour. At the time, the only trade union west of Ontario was the Shipwrights and Caulkers Union (established in Victoria in 1862), which faced no competition with Chinese. The first loud voices raised against Chinese labour in Canada were not those of workers, but of politicians and businessmen in Victoria and New Westminster, who saw their future prospects enhanced by the immigration of larger numbers of white workers who would patronize their shops rather than Chinese businesses.

Meanwhile, Arthur Bunster's voice was being heard frequently in the Dominion Parliament. In 1878, he tried to introduce a bill forbidding the hiring of any labourer for the railroad who "wore hair longer than 5½ inches." The bill was obviously aimed at preventing Chinese from working on railroad construction, and Prime Minister Alexander Mackenzie rejected the bill out of hand. The issue of Chinese immigration was simply of no interest to anyone in the eastern provinces at the time.

In Victoria, on the other hand, anti-Chinese expressions were becoming more frequent. Although Robson's first attempt to ban Chinese labour had failed, the Victoria City Council agreed in 1875 to Noah Shakespeare's proposal that no Chinese labour be hired on city works. In 1878, legislation was unanimously passed by the provincial parliament prohibiting the employment of Chinese on public works. Two days later the legislature introduced what amounted to a head tax on the Chinese. Several provisions of this act are important. It excused Chinese from assessment and school taxes on the grounds that these were difficult or impossible to collect. In their place, "in order . . . that a more simple method should be adopted for the collection of taxes from Chinese," the act stipulated that "every Chinese person over twelve years of age shall take out a licence every three months, for which he shall pay the sum of ten dollars, in advance." Employers were required to provide a list of the Chinese in their employ and were liable to a fine of up to one hundred dollars per Chinese employee for failure or falsification. Furthermore, employers of Chinese without licences were also subject to the same fine, and it was their responsibility to keep the licences of all Chinese in their employ.[14]

Any Chinese unwilling or unable to pay for a licence was liable "to perform labour on public roads or works" at a rate of fifty cents per day. Paradoxically, the legislature had just passed the act preventing Chinese from being hired on public works projects.

This iniquitous tax law was given second reading in August, 1878. The Chinese in Victoria reacted immediately. They engaged a lawyer, Mr. A. Rocke Robertson, who helped them draft a petition to the Governor General after the act was passed on August 12. The petition asked the Governor General to disallow the act on three grounds: (1) it applied to "children over twelve," whereas other provincial taxes were paid only by residents over eighteen; (2) it was not graduated according to ability to pay, but was "a large and arbitrary amount payable by poor and rich alike"; and (3) it applied only to Chinese, "many of whom are British subjects."[15] The petition was signed by ten Chinese merchants, including Kwong Lee.

At the same time, the Victoria Chinese leaders sent petitions to the newly appointed ambassador from China to Great Britain, Guo Songtao, and to the Chinese ambassador to the United States, Chen Lanbin. Ambassador Guo protested to the British government, who forwarded his protest to Ottawa.[16]

Chinese political action was not limited to petitions and letters. Several merchants refused to pay the tax, including the directors of Tai Soong, Sam Gee, On Hing, and Tai Yoon. Accordingly, as the law provided, the Collector proceeded to seize goods and chattels from a number of companies on September 16, whereupon all the Chinese businesses closed their doors. The following day, the entire Chinese community went on strike: stores closed, Chinese workers did not report to work at hotels or boot factories, and all the 200 Chinese domestic servants stayed away from their places of employment. The strike lasted for five days, and it demonstrated a level of community organization among the Chinese that took the rest of the city completely by surprise. Anti-Chinese activists, like the editor of the *Daily Colonist*, hoped that the strike would prove the city could get along without Chinese, but instead it succeeded in forcing the government to return the impounded goods. Meanwhile, Tai Soong's manager, a Mr. Huang, was granted an injunction by Justice John Hamilton Gray against the public auction of his goods, on the grounds that the new tax law was unconstitutional.[17] On the basis of the B.C. court decision and recommendations from his Minister of Justice,

47

the Governor General of Canada disallowed the law on October 28, 1879.[18]

Of course, not all whites in British Columbia were as opposed to the Chinese immigrants as were the members of the provincial Parliament. The nine canneries, for example, protested to the Governor General when the Act was passed, pointing out that they used Chinese labour in the canneries because none other was available and that the presence of Chinese cannery workers permitted the development of fishing.

On September 1, 1878, the Workingman's Protective Association was organized in Victoria, under the leadership of Noah Shakespeare. Avowedly racist, this association aimed at:

> the mutual protection of the working class in B.C. against the great influx of Chinese; to use all legitimate means for the suppression of their immigration; to assist each other in the obtaining of employment; and to devise means for the amelioration of the condition of the working class of this province in general.[19]

A petition sent to Ottawa also demanded that no Chinese be hired to build the railroad. Although the WPA attracted several hundred supporters in Victoria and soon established a branch in New Westminster, it was destroyed by political infighting and disappeared before the end of 1879, when it became the Anti-Chinese Association, still under Shakespeare's leadership. But while it operated, it wielded considerable influence and created a number of incidents, such as the cutting of Chinese prisoners' queues in the various jails as a "health measure."[20] According to one source, nine Chinese prisoners who refused to have their heads shaved were "hosed" until they acquiesced.

The actions of the WPA provided the MPs for British Columbia with the support they needed to push their anti-Chinese cause in Ottawa. When Amor de Cosmos called on Sir John A. Macdonald in January, 1879, he was able to argue that there was strong opposition to Chinese in British Columbia, thus neutralizing a letter sent to the Prime Minister a few weeks later by the B.C. senators, all of whom opposed the anti-Chinese actions of their provincial legislature. Amor de Cosmos then presented to the House a petition with 1,497 signatures demanding the restriction of Chinese immigration, the exclusion of Chinese labour from railway construction, a tax on all resident Chinese, the disenfranchisement of British subjects of Chinese extraction, and the exclusion of Chinese from leasing Crown land and from working on Canadian ships or any ships in Canadian waters.

Since there was no anti-Chinese agitation in any other province, Macdonald could not support the members from British Columbia, even though his own seat was in Victoria at the time. Accordingly, he suggested the setting up of a select committee to study the question. Alexander Mackenzie, the leader of the opposition, while expressing some sympathy with the plight of British Columbia, stated that ". . . the principle that some classes of the human family were not fit to be residents . . . would be dangerous and contrary to the Law of Nations and the policy which controlled Canada." Nevertheless, a select committee was established under the chairmanship of Amor de Cosmos, and it duly reported in May, 1879.[21]

During the two months it sat, the Select Committee heard several witnesses, all from British Columbia, only two of whom, Senator Cornwall and Edgar Dewdney, expressed any sympathy whatsoever for the Chinese population in their province.

Despite the virulence of its anti-Chinese tone, several points in the report are revealing of white attitudes at the time. Bunster claimed that three Chinese workmen were equivalent to two whites, and that the Chinese earned $1.35 per day compared to a white labourer's $2 per day. One witness accused the Chinese of introducing a "more virulent form" of syphilis than any other immigrants. Mr. Barnard, who ran the mail stage from Yale to Cariboo, made the most telling comment of all: "The fact is, gentlemen, the Chinese are too smart for us. They will beat us wherever they get a foothold. Q: That is the greatest objection to them on the part of the white population? . . . I think it is."[22]

The Select Committee had expected that its report in 1879 would produce some legislation in Ottawa, but it went more or less unnoticed throughout the country because of the long-delayed start on construction of the railroad across Canada. Even a request from the B.C. legislature to the Dominion government in 1880 to restrict Chinese immigration, to authorize a provincial head tax on the Chinese, and to prevent their naturalization was ignored by the Dominion government, for, as Sir John A. Macdonald told the members from B.C., if they wanted the railway they would have to accept Chinese construction workers.[23]

In Victoria, the arrival of large numbers of Chinese en route to the construction sites in the Fraser Canyon provided the occasion for racists like Noah Shakespeare to incite antagonism. Stepping beyond his authority, he even tried to collect the school tax from each Chinese worker as he stepped off the ship. Conditions in Victoria's Chinatown were crowded and unsavory, causing repeated unfavourable comment in the newspaper.[24] By 1882, the rate of immigration was alarming B.C. politicians. Amor de Cosmos predicted in the House that there would be 24,000 Chinese in Canada by August and that by the end of the year they would outnumber the 30,000 whites in British Columbia. Macdonald was sufficiently concerned to ask for a report from Onderdonk, who wrote to explain that no more than 6,000 Chinese were working on the railroad at the time. Onderdonk extolled the virtues of the Chinese as construction workers, pointing out that their obligations to family and friends made them thoroughly reliable, unlike the white workers, who tended to desert the construction sites as soon as they received their pay.[25] Nevertheless, Macdonald agreed with the members from B.C. "in preventing the permanent settlement of Chinese and Japanese," for he believed they were "an alien race" that could not be assimilated into Canada. His election campaign in 1882 was based on the racist slogan "Canada for Canadians." Macdonald opposed restrictions, however, arguing that "a permanent degradation of the country by a mongrel race" was not yet a danger because the Chinese would not settle.

By this time, anti-Chinese editorials were appearing in eastern papers such as the Toronto *Telegram*, the Toronto *World*, the Toronto *Globe*, and the Ottawa *Herald*, calling for restrictions on Chinese immigration. Meanwhile, the United States Congress passed the Chinese Restriction Act in May, 1882, which gave encouragement to the growing anti-Chinese movement in Canada. This act excluded "Chinese Labourers" for ten years unless they had been in the United States by November, 1880.[26]

During 1883, there were several incidents of violence involving Chinese. In February, Chinese workers at Maple Ridge formed a vigilante crowd to force the release of two Chinese under arrest for assault. In May, a Chinese construction gang at Camp 37 near Lytton, objecting to the firing of two of their number, assaulted the foreman and several other whites, inciting a retaliatory raid by twenty whites on their campsite that night. The whites burned down their cabins and brutally clubbed the Chinese, killing one, Ye Fook, and severely injuring several others. While the *Colonist* decried the violent reaction of the whites in the latter incident, it nevertheless used it to fan the flames of anti-Oriental sentiment in its leading articles.

Also in 1883, a major strike in the Dunsmuir mines at Wellington contributed to racial antagonisms. The Miners' Mutual Protection Association had been formed during a strike in 1877. In August, 1883, it asked for an increase in wages of twenty-five cents per ton of coal, no discrimination against union members, and the reinstatement of workers fired for union activity. Robert Dunsmuir rejected them out of hand, allowed the strike to begin, then evicted the miners from company housing and tried to import scabs from the south. This was typical of Dunsmuir, who had a reputation for anti-labour policies, in marked contrast to the Vancouver Coal Company that ran mines nearby at Nanaimo.[27] According to the manager of the Vancouver Coal Company, S.M. Robins, Dunsmuir had introduced several hundred Chinese workmen into his mines at Wellington "as a weapon with which to settle disputes" with his white workers,[28] for the Chinese were willing to work for $1.00 to $1.25 per day when the going rate for white labour was $2 to $3.75.[29] At the time of the strike, Dunsmuir had about 450 Chinese workmen, all above ground.

Since the Chinese workmen were not members of the Miners' Mutual Protection Association, they did not participate in the strike. Despite their successful exclusion of scabs, the union by November had dropped all its demands and "asked only that all Chinese employed at the mines be fired,"[30] but even this demand was not met, and the strike was completely defeated. In the provincial legislature Dunsmuir suggested that he would be willing to replace Chinese labour with white children if the minimum age were dropped from sixteen to fourteen. One year later, he pointed out to the Royal Commission on Chinese Immigration that Chinese unskilled labour was an asset to the province, since it freed white workers for more skilled jobs. By that time Chinese were working underground as well, and their number had risen to over 600.

Incidents of violence and the Wellington strike allowed the B.C. legislature to take an ever stronger line against Chinese immigration. It introduced three drastic acts in the legislature: An Act to Prevent Chinese from Acquiring Crown Land, An Act to Prevent Chinese Immigration, and The Chinese Regulation Act. The first and third of these acts were declared *ultra vires* by the B.C. Supreme Court; the second was disallowed by the Governor General. And there, for the time being, the matter rested. But not for long.

NOTES

1. Robert Edward Wynne, "Reaction to the Chinese in the Pacific Northwest and British Columbia, 1850-1910," p. 116.
2. *A Collection of Public General Statutes of the Colony of Vancouver Island – Passed in the Years 1859, 1860, 1862, and 1863* (Victoria, 1864), pp. 17, 95, 101.
3. Wynne, "Reaction to the Chinese," p. 121.
4. James Morton, *In the Sea of Sterile Mountains, the Chinese in British Columbia*, p. 10.
5. Keith Ralston, interview with Willmott, 15 June 1974.
6. Wynne, "Reaction to the Chinese," pp. 125, 136, 126.
7. *Ibid.*, p. 145.
8. Morton, *Sea of Sterile Mountains*, p. 23.
9. *Laws of British Columbia* (Victoria, 1871), pp. 305-7.
10. Morton, *Sea of Sterile Mountains*, p. 28.
11. *Correspondence, Reports of the Ministers of Justice, and Orders in Council on the Subject of Dominion and Provincial Legislation. 1867-1895* (Ottawa, 1896), pp. 1011ff.
12. Wynne, "Reaction to the Chinese," pp. 157ff.; Morton, *Sea of Sterile Mountains*, pp. 47-50.
13. Morton, *Sea of Sterile Mountains*, pp. 41ff.
14. *Statutes of the Province of British Columbia* (Victoria, 1878), pp. 129-32.
15. *Dominion and Provincial Legislation*, p. 1062.
16. *Ibid.*, pp. 1063-5.
17. Morton, *Sea of Sterile Mountains*, pp. 62ff.
18. *Dominion and Provincial Legislation*, p. 1067.
19. Paul Phillips, *No Power Greater: A Century of Labour in B.C.* (Vancouver, 1967), pp. 168ff.
20. Morton, *Sea of Sterile Mountains*, pp. 74, 65.

21. *House of Commons Journals, 1879*, Appendix 4.
22. *Ibid.*, pp. 9, 21, 39.
23. *Journals of the Legislative Assembly of the Province of British Columbia* (Victoria, 1880), pp. 20ff. See Morton, *Sea of Sterile Mountains*, p. 92, for Macdonald's reply.
24. Morton, *Sea of Sterile Mountains*, pp. 86, 88.
25. Wynne, "Reaction to the Chinese," pp. 353-6.
26. *1885 Royal Commission*, pp. 371-5.
27. Phillips, *No Power Greater*, pp. 7-8.
28. *Ibid.*
29. *1885 Royal Commission*, p. xvi.
30. Phillips, *No Power Greater*, p. 8.

FIVE

Growing Pains:
Discrimination and
Depression

The attempt on the part of the British Columbia government to pass a series of discriminatory acts manifested a degree of anti-Chinese feeling in the province which the Dominion government could ignore no longer. Accordingly, in July, 1884, it established a Royal Commission on Chinese Immigration. Two commissioners were appointed, one from the East and one from British Columbia. Dr. Joseph Adolphe Chapleau was Secretary of State of the Dominion government; he was joined on the Commission by Dr. John Hamilton Gray, a British Columbian and a Supreme Court judge. Nicholas Flood Davin, editor of the Regina *Leader*, was appointed secretary to the Commission.[1]

The appointment of Judge Gray to the Commission was not a popular move with the strongly anti-Chinese segments of Victoria, for it was he who had declared the Chinese Tax Act illegal in 1878, much to the disgust of the *Colonist* and others. Upon hearing of his appointment as commissioner, the *Colonist* protested, for it "did not think much of his . . . unbiased opinion." "He can in no sense be regarded as a representative of anti-Chinese element [sic] in the province nor as a representative of public opinion on the Chinese question." Noah Shakespeare boycotted the Commission hearings as did others in Victoria and New Westminster.

In Victoria, New Westminster, and Yale, the Commission heard from fifty-one witnesses, some of whom, like Onderdonk, submitted their evidence as written answers to a list of twenty-seven questions provided by the Commission.[2] Although almost all witnesses manifested prejudice against the Chinese, there was substantial disagreement among them as to what policy the government should follow.

The 400 pages of evidence appended to these reports shed more light on white reactions to the Chinese than upon Chinese conditions at the time. Only two Chinese witnesses were heard, both officials from the Chinese consulate in San Francisco, one testifying about the situation in the United States and the other providing useful information on the

Chinese in British Columbia. Many witnesses insisted that anti-Chinese sentiment was to be found among the working class rather than the upper classes, although several also blamed the "politicians" for fomenting it. For instance, W.C. Ward, manager of the Bank of British Columbia, stated that the agitation was "chiefly political, with a view to the labouring class vote."[3]

Two labour unions gave evidence. The Victoria lodge of the Knights of Labor could not testify as a society, for it was "not registered, but is a secret society," as its representative, Mr. F.L. Tuckfield, explained. The Commission included only a summary of his written statement in its Report. On the other hand, the Nanaimo lodge submitted a written brief that is reproduced with the other evidence. The other union submission was by the Nanaimo Trades Association.

In attempting to understand the nature of anti-Chinese agitation at the time, it is interesting to compare these three submissions. That from Victoria is a rabidly anti-Chinese statement, accusing the Chinese in extravagant language of filth and degradation:

> Vice, including prostitution and gambling, is abundant in those (Chinese) quarters. . . . They are a non-assimilating race. Their vices are most disgusting. They turn their sick out to die in the streets, and their lepers to fill our prisons. They control the labour market in this city . . . they are of no benefit to this country. . . . Our children must seek employment in other countries to make room for a race of cuckoos. . . . In fact, the results of our investigations brings us to the conclusion that the Chinese are a disgrace to a civilised community, and we beg that steps may be taken to stop the influx of Chinese to our shore.[4]

On questioning, Tuckfield admitted that the Chinese were clean in appearance, that he knew of only one case of leprosy, and that Chinese laundries did not appear to spread disease.

In marked contrast, neither of the statements from Nanaimo unions was expressed in racist terms, despite the fact that white workers in Nanaimo were in much more direct competition with Chinese labourers than any in Victoria. It was this competition that they brought to the attention of the Commission. Pointing out that the exploitation of British Columbia's resources was unfairly limited by government policy and Dunsmuir's power, the Nanaimo Knights of Labor politely asked the Dominion government to protect them against unfair competition from Chinese labour which was used by the big companies to keep wages down:

> It is unjust to place a few individuals, already too wealthy, in possession of nearly all the natural resources of the country, and thus beyond the reach of all competition, and at the same time expose us who are the producers of wealth and the source of all prosperity to the killing competition of a degraded race who are practically slaves!

As British Columbians we demand it is our right. . . . As Canadians, we demand it in the name of that grand national sentiment which it should be the aim of all true Canadians to foster and encourage. No universal national feeling can arise or exist in any country which allows its labour to become degraded.[5]

At another point in their brief, they stated that the Chinese, being single men, were able to live on very low wages:

They are thus fitted to become all too dangerous competitors in the labour market, while their docile servility, the natural outcome of centuries of grinding poverty and humble submission to a most oppressive system of government, renders them doubly dangerous and willing tools whereby grasping and tyrannical employers grind down all labour to the lowest living point.[6]

While other parts of their statement are not entirely free of racism, these quotations indicate that the Nanaimo lodge of the Knights of Labor considered the Chinese to be victims of an exploitative system rather than the root of evil. It was the Anti-Chinese Association in Victoria, led by Tuckfield and Shakespeare, not the trade unions, that provided the worst anti-Orientalism.

Summing up the evidence provided by the many witnesses, Judge Gray suggested that public opinion in British Columbia could be divided into three categories. One was "a well-meaning, but strongly prejudiced minority, whom nothing but absolute exclusion will satisfy." A second was an "intelligent minority, who conceive that no legislation whatever is necessary" because the problem would disappear of its own accord. The third category was "a large majority, who think there should be a moderate restriction" and a stricter enforcement of sanitary regulations.[7] Both commissioners clearly concurred with the "large majority," and both recommended legislation along those lines.[8] Gray, in particular, recommended that a head-tax of $10 be levied on each disembarking immigrant, whether man, woman, or child, to be collected from the ship. He also recommended the establishment of special joint tribunals (Chinese and white) and procedures to replace the Chinese associations in hearing cases and settling disputes within the Chinese community. A tribunal would be responsible for "an efficient system of registration of all Chinese resident in the Province, classifying their names, sexes, occupations, and places of residence as nearly as possible, once in every year."[9]

THE CHINESE IMMIGRATION ACT, 1885

While it did not respond positively to all of Gray's suggestions, the Canadian government was not slow to act on the Royal Commission's Report. On April 13, 1885, Chapleau, as Secretary of State, introduced into Parliament An Act to Restrict and Regulate Chinese Immigration into Canada, and it received royal assent from the Governor General on July

20, 1885. Parliament must have been willing to move with alacrity because growing anti-Chinese sentiments were now being expressed well to the east of British Columbia. The *Manitoba Free Press*, for instance, wrote in an editorial on July 2, 1885, the following warning to the government:

> If something is not done speedily it will be too late to consider whether the Pacific Province shall be given up to the Chinese or not. They will have solved the question by taking complete possession of it. The Celestial wave may be expected to roll eastward. The channel for it will have been cut by the Canadian Pacific Railway through the Rockies. Ten times more people than Canada now holds could be poured in on us from the teeming soil of China without being missed from that land.

This editorial illustrates how the building of the railway had suddenly brought the extent of Chinese immigration to the attention of eastern Canada in a new way. Previously, the problems of isolated British Columbia were of little concern to the East. Now the unification of Canada by the CPR made events on the West Coast more relevant to Manitoba and even to Ontario.

Anti-Chinese agitation increased in British Columbia while the bill was before Parliament. Dissatisfied from the start with the Royal Commission, some citizens of Victoria continued to call for sterner measures against Chinese immigration. On March 9 the B.C. Legislative Assembly again passed the same Act to Prevent the Immigration of Chinese that had been disallowed by the Governor General in 1884. The only concession was a clause permitting the re-entry of Chinese temporarily out of the country at the time the act became law. Not surprisingly, this did not make the act acceptable to Ottawa, and it was disallowed by the Governor General once again.

On May 5, a public meeting held in Victoria, chaired by the mayor, passed resolutions condemning both the Royal Commission Report and the Immigration Act. The meeting also called for all employers to boycott Chinese labour, and it passed the following resolution, which Noah Shakespeare forwarded to the Secretary of State in Ottawa:

> That the people of British Columbia have shown themselves patient and long enduring under grievous wrongs; that they have repeatedly petitioned the dominion government for redress; that they have held numerous public meetings to make known their wants and wishes; that the city council of Victoria has passed by-laws relating to the Chinese which [sic] the legislature of British Columbia has enacted laws which the Governor General acting on the advice of the Dominion ministry has vetoed; that every constitutional means has been resorted to and exhausted to obtain justice and without effect or beneficial result, on account of the ill-advised and misinformed partiality of the Dominion authorities in favour of the Chinese; and if

in consequence the people find themselves compelled to take the laws into their own hands as a last resort, and abate by forcible means a nuisance as they undoubtedly have the right to do, then the Dominion Government and the Judges of the supreme court should and must be held answerable for any rioting or even bloodshed which might unfortunately accompany a general uprising of the white labour classes in vindication of their just right against their natural enemies – the Chinese.[10]

At another meeting, it was decided to establish the Anti-Chinese Union, which seems to have replaced the Anti-Chinese Association at this time, and regular meetings were held to condemn Ottawa's inaction on the Chinese "problem."

This agitation in British Columbia and expressions of sympathy for it elsewhere in Canada had two small effects on the legislation introduced by Chapleau, both of them amendments in the direction of further restricting Chinese immigration. Whereas Chapleau had proposed a head tax of $10 per immigrant, the final wording of Section 4 stated that "every person of Chinese origin shall pay . . . on entering Canada, at the port or other place of entry, the sum of fifty dollars."

The other amendment had the effect of severely limiting the number of Chinese who could come to Canada on any single ship. Chapleau's original bill limited Chinese passengers to one for every ten tons of ship's tonnage, a measure which could be defended on the humanitarian grounds of preventing overcrowding. The final act, however, limited Chinese to one per fifty tons, a provision that was modeled on an anti-Chinese law adopted in Queensland, Australia, in 1874, and which made it impossible for companies to charter ships to bring large numbers of Chinese immigrants to Canada, a practice that had alarmed the citizens of British Columbia during the railway construction days of 1881-83, as we have seen.

The responsibility for assuring the collection of the head tax from Chinese passengers was laid on the captain of each vessel, who had to present a passenger list and the sum of payable fees to the port controllers before any of his passengers or crew could disembark. The penalty for defaulting or defrauding was the seizure of his ship, a fine of $500-$1,000, and possible imprisonment for each offence.[11] Exempted from the head tax were several categories of people, including diplomatic and consular officials, tourists, "men of science and students" who could present visas and proof of qualifications, and merchants. The act made it clear, however, that "merchant" did not include "any huckster, pedler [sic], or person engaged in taking, drying or otherwise preserving shell or other fish for home consumption or exportation."[12]

Part of the objection to Chinese immigration was expressed as concern over hazards to health that the Chinese were thought to represent. The new law provided in Section 9 that "no permit to land shall be granted to any Chinese immigrant who is suffering from leprosy or from any infectious or contagious disease, or to any Chinese woman who is known to be a prostitute."

Two new offices were established by the Chinese Immigration Act: Controller of Chinese Immigration and official interpreter. The Controller, although not specifically created by the law, was charged with keeping a register, issuing certificates of residence upon receipt of the head tax, and replacing these certificates with re-entry permits for those Chinese who wished to leave Canada temporarily. The appointment of an interpreter was provided for by Section 21:

> The Governor in Council may engage and pay an interpreter, skilled in the English and Chinese languages, at a salary of not more than three thousand dollars per annum, to reside in the Province of British Columbia, and may assign to him such duties as he deems fit.

When the law was promulgated, Won Alexander Cumyow, the English-language secretary of the Chinese Consolidated Benevolent Association in Victoria, applied for the position. His familiarity with Cantonese, Hakka, and English uniquely qualified him for the appointment. The *Colonist* supported his application, as did a petition among Victorians. The successful applicant, however, was the American missionary, John Vrooman, who spoke Cantonese and had experience as court interpreter in San Francisco before coming to Victoria to run the Chinese Mission School on Cormorant Street. He was opposed by some as too pro-Chinese because his references included a letter from the Chinese Consul in San Francisco, Huang Cunxian.[13]

Another interpreter acted informally in Victoria at this time; he was Yip Wing, who became official court interpreter in 1902, and whose son, Jack N. Yip, succeeded him in 1924.[14] Mr. Yip had originally come to Victoria in 1864, having left his home village in Hoi-ping in 1860. In 1877 he conducted a "Chinese lecture party" through the American northwest, and then embarked on a tour of Europe. After visiting his home in China, he returned to Victoria in 1880. Cumyow, on the other hand, was convicted of forgery at the end of 1885, although the evidence suggested "merely a rather loose method of practicing business."[15] He subsequently moved to Vancouver, where he became official court interpreter in 1888, a position he held until 1936, when his son, Gordon Cumyow, succeeded him.

Gray's report had included several recommendations for legislation that would have regulated the internal organization of the Chinese community. The Canadian government, however, did not wish to become involved with complicated intervention into the functioning of the Chinese community itself and did not include most of Gray's recommendations in this regard. Nevertheless, Section 17 of the Chinese Immigration Act is of particular interest:

> 17. Every person who takes part in the organisation of any sort of court or tribunal, composed of Chinese persons, for the hearing and

determination of any offence committed by a Chinese person, or in carrying on any such organisation, or who takes part in any of its proceedings, or who gives evidence before any such court or tribunal, or assists in carrying into effect any decision or decree, or order of any such court or tribunal, is guilty of a misdemeanor, and liable to imprisonment for any term not exceeding twelve months, or to a penalty not exceeding five hundred dollars, or to both; but nothing in this section shall be construed to prevent Chinese immigrants from submitting any differences or disputes to arbitration, provided such submissions be not contrary to the laws in force in the Province in which such submission is made.[16]

It is evident that this clause makes no change in the law, for the second half takes away everything that is not already illegal by provincial law. Nevertheless, the clause indicates clearly that the federal government recognized the political functions of the Chinese associations, for as we have seen, both the Cheekungtong (CKT) and the Chinese Benevolent Association (CBA) settled both civil and criminal disputes within the Chinese community.

The new law had an immediate effect upon Chinese immigration, which dropped in 1886 to 212 from the thousands that were entering during the early 1880's. In 1887, it was only 124, but the following year it began to rise, and by 1890 it was over 1,000 once again. Evidently, the imposition of a head tax and passenger restrictions disrupted immigration patterns without dampening demand, and new patterns quickly emerged to fit the new requirements.

THE GROWTH OF THE CHINESE COMMUNITY: VANCOUVER AND VICTORIA

Perhaps more significant than the new immigration law in changing the patterns of Chinese settlement in Canada was the economic depression that hit British Columbia following the end of railway construction. It was exacerbated for the Chinese, of course, by the sudden unemployment of thousands of Chinese workmen. Some of them moved to Victoria, but there was little relief for them in that city, for Chinese business was also badly hit. The end of construction also affected sawmills, machine shops, and provisioners, many of the last being Chinese companies. Kwong Lee, once the most prosperous Chinese company in Canada, went bankrupt in August, 1885, following a lengthy court battle between two brothers, Loo Chuck Fan and Loo Chou Fan, over its control. Just prior to that, Tai Chong Yuen also had closed its doors when it was fined $700 for failing to pay the provincial tax on a number of Chinese workmen contracted to the builders of the Esquimalt and Nanaimo Railway. Some Chinese left Canada; others moved eastward over the newly completed railroad and began to establish small Chinese settlements east of the Rockies. Calgary appointed its own controller of

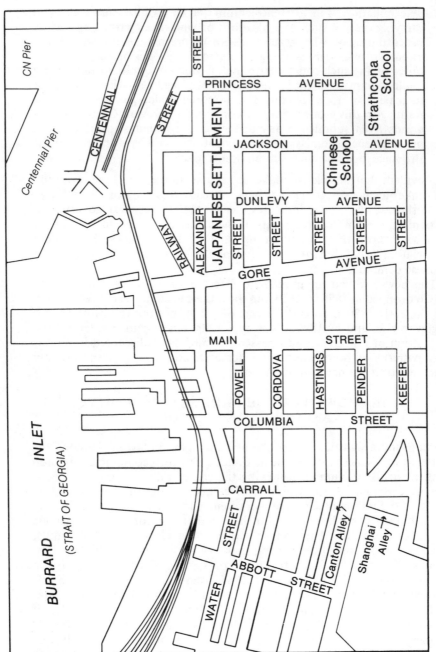

Vancouver Chinatown

Chinese immigration in 1886, indicating that Chinese had begun to settle in that city soon after the end of railway construction. In March, 1887, Lee Turn opened the first Chinese laundry in Medicine Hat; in 1889 a second laundry and a restaurant followed.

For British Columbia, the most significant change in settlement patterns was the rapid rise of Vancouver as a port and the consequent growth of its Chinese population. Small numbers of Chinese had worked as sawmill hands in Burrard Inlet for over a decade, for the 1874 Victoria *Directory* counted fourteen Chinese in "Moodyville, Hastings, and Granville." In 1884, the Chinese in Burrard Inlet comprised five merchants, ten store employees, thirty cooks and laundrymen, and one prostitute, as well as sixty sawmill hands. In Granville itself, which was closest to what later became Vancouver, only one Chinese grocer and two laundrymen were listed in the *British Columbia Directory* for 1884-85.

After it became known in 1885 that Vancouver would become the western terminus of the CPR the city grew rapidly, and increasing numbers of Chinese provided services to the growing population. Early in 1886 Chinese began to clear 160 acres of bush land beside the road to New Westminster for vegetable gardens. "This tract has been leased to them rent free for ten years," stated the *Vancouver News*, "on condition that they cleared and cultivated it. Every imaginable kind of vegetable is growing on the land. . . . Their market wagons can be seen daily, bringing vegetables of all descriptions to this city for sale. They supply private residences, hotels, and boarding houses, who depend almost entirely upon the Chinamen for their vegetable products."

By the time of the disastrous Vancouver fire of June 13, 1886, Chinese had begun to settle at the corner of Carrall and Dupont (now Pender) Streets, near False Creek's marshy extremity. Laundries and other Chinese business houses began to spread along Dupont Street towards Columbia. There was also a Chinese settlement further east on False Creek, which survived the fire. Vancouver was decimated, however, and "on the night of the 13th June a bare dozen (houses) marked the spot where that morning a prosperous city [of between five and six hundred houses] had existed."[17]

While the rebuilding of Vancouver provided considerable employment for the several hundred unemployed white workmen in the area, strong feelings against the unfair competition of Chinese labour continued to be expressed by the Knights of Labor, who emerged in Vancouver at this time. The first Canadian chapter of the Knights had been established in Nanaimo in 1883, followed by Victoria and then Wellington, and the rapid growth of Vancouver prompted the inauguration of a fourth chapter in Vancouver in June, 1886. R.D. Pitt, the Master Workman of this chapter, had run unsuccessfully for alderman in the first municipal elections the previous month, campaigning on a strongly anti-Chinese platform.

During the summer of 1886, the CPR let contracts to clear the area that would become the city centre of Vancouver. The land included a 350-acre piece, the Brighouse Estate, that stretched from what is now Burrard Street to Stanley Park and from Coal Harbour to English Bay. John McDougall bid $325 per acre to clear the Brighouse Estate at a time when most of the CPR contracts were going at $500. He then sub-contracted part of it to "a Victoria syndicate" for $150 per acre. These low bids were possible because the Victorians could hire Chinese labour at fifty to seventy-five cents per day, while the going rate for unskilled white labour was two dollars.[18]

Against such competition, the Knights of Labor were adamant that Vancouver should exclude all Chinese. They tried to organize a city-wide boycott of Chinese labour in November, 1886, threatening violence against those who did not comply. When the first Chinese arrived from Victoria in January to begin work on the Brighouse Estate, it was rumoured that 250 in all would be coming. At a public meeting on January 8, the Knights of Labor joined with several prominent business-men in calling for the exclusion of Chinese labour from Vancouver and their "return to the place from whence they came." They agreed to raise money to compensate Chinese sent away. The following day, a commit-tee of the meeting persuaded nineteen Chinese to leave their camp at Coal Harbour in return for a one-way ticket to Victoria. Several others were persuaded to leave the city for New Westminster during the next few days, causing what became known as "the expulsion of the Chinese."[19]

Anti-Chinese meetings were held regularly throughout January, 1887, and an extremist wing of the movement, known as "The Vigilance Com-mittee," posted notices threatening forcible evictions of Chinese and ad-vising citizens not to do business with them. On February 2 a public meeting, chaired by Pitt, agreed to form an Anti-Chinese League in the city when they heard that at least a hundred Chinese had entered the city that month.

Pitt then crossed the Georgia Strait to chair a meeting in Nanaimo two days later, where identical action was inaugurated. The Workingmen's Protection Association in Nanaimo had nominated a candidate in the provincial elections the previous year on an anti-Chinese platform, and although Dunsmuir had won the seat, the WPA had aroused sufficient anti-Chinese sentiment by the campaign that proposals to boycott Chinese business and exclude Chinese labour were being heard regularly in Nanaimo.

But it was in Vancouver, not Nanaimo, that the first violent incident occurred. When twenty-four Chinese arrived from Victoria aboard the *Princess Louise* on February 24 to clear the Brighouse Estate, a placard was carried through the streets of Vancouver: "The Chinese have come. Mass meeting in the City Hall tonight."[20] The meeting heard several speeches supporting unity between businessmen and workers on the issue. After the formal adjournment, someone in the audience called for "Those in favour of running out the Chinese tonight." The crowd responded with a roar and immediately marched through the snow the two miles to the Chinese camp at the western end of the Coal Harbour Bridge. Three or four hundred rioters roughly herded the Chinese outside and destroyed the camp, tearing down shacks and making bonfires into which they threw their belongings. The Chinese were kicked and manhandled, some of them even forced to take to the water to avoid injury and others chased onto the CPR right-of-way without shelter.[21] Following this, part of the mob returned to Vancouver and set fire to some of the Chinese buildings on Carrall Street, and a few went on to attack the Chinese shanties on False Creek. The following day, a crowd descended on Chinatown and forced the Chinese to leave for New Westminster in twenty-five drays and wagons.

The historians do not agree on the role of the police during the riot. According to a reliable account the chief of police and a superintendent arrived on the scene as quickly as they could after being informed that the meeting was marching on the Chinese camp. They protected the Chinese from the mob and succeeded in dispersing the crowd, although they were unable to prevent the destruction of property. Only three arrests were made, however, which the Attorney General in Victoria considered an inadequate response to lawlessness and riot. He promptly introduced into the provincial legislature a bill entitled An Act for the Preservation of Peace within the Municipal Limits of the City of Vancouver, which took police powers away from the city and placed them in the hands of the Provincial Superintendent of Police.[22] The provincial police brought thirty-six special constables from Victoria to Vancouver on March 2. By that time, most of the Chinese in Vancouver had left for either New Westminster or Victoria, leaving only five laundrymen in the city. However, by the end of February, another twenty-four Chinese workmen had arrived to clear the Brighouse Estate.

The Chinese did not leave the matter there. On March 7, Yung Chung filed a claim for damages through John Boultbee. The following week, Thornton Fell filed a similar claim on behalf of several Chinese. Fell later asked the Council to provide police protection to the Chinese working once again on the Brighouse Estate, and in April he and Boultbee filed the particulars of the Chinese claims.[23]

SOCIAL PROBLEMS IN CHINATOWNS

After the "Victoria specials" arrived, the Chinese began to return to Vancouver. By the middle of the month, "eighty Chinese were working on the Brighouse Estate and ninety were at other locations in the city."[24] The Chinese labour force on the Brighouse Estate rose at one point to three hundred, but in July all but three were discharged because of the fire hazard, causing the population of Vancouver's emergent Chinatown to rise rapidly.

By the end of 1887, Dupont Street included a number of Chinese businesses and several opium dens and brothels.[25] *Henderson's Directory* listed thirty-two Chinese businesses in Vancouver, comprising fourteen Chinese laundries, three "general stores," seven "merchants," five grocers, a shoemaker, a contractor, and a "Chinese store." One grocer and one general store were also listed as labour contractors. Among the merchant houses was the Sam Kee firm at 110 Dupont Street, founded by Chan Doe Gee. Chan, who had become one of the three leading Chinese merchants in Vancouver by the beginning of the twentieth century, was known by his shop's name, which was the custom at the time. "Sam Kee" later moved his place of business to 48 Dupont Street, from there to 433 Carrall Street, and still later to 147 Keefer Street.

The nineteenth-century Vancouver directories provide a clear indication of how the Chinese were concentrated in Chinatown. In 1890, twelve of the fifteen laundries were scattered throughout the city, but all the other Chinese companies were found on either side of Dupont Street between Carrall Street and Westminster Avenue (now Main Street). In that one block were seven general merchants, five grocers, four tea merchants, three barbers, three laundries, an opium factory, a butcher, a pin-maker, a tailor, and a "Chinese store," as well as six "Chinese dwellings."[26] There were two Chinese missions in Vancouver at the time, one at 114 Dupont Street (at the southwest corner of Westminster Avenue), run by the Chinese missioner, Lim Yik Pong, and the other at 329 Seymour Street, run by a Miss England.

Much of the missionary activity in the final decades of the nineteenth century was directed against the major social problems experienced by Chinese in the growing Chinatowns. Although the missions had few converts in that period,[27] they drew attention to some of these problems among the wider public, as well as mitigating their worst effects for some individual Chinese, by providing sanctuary for young women, material aid for destitutes, and English classes for workers. From the point of view of the wider Canadian society, opium, prostitution, and gambling were the serious problems, but from the point of view of the Chinese themselves, the living conditions in Chinatown were far more serious. Overcrowding, the lack of refuse collection, and unhealthy sewage disposal were all health hazards, especially in Vancouver.

Unlike the Chinatown in Victoria, which was built during the boom period of the gold rush and included many brick buildings, Vancouver's Chinatown comprised only wooden buildings, many of which were shoddily built. Furthermore, its location at the marshy extremity of False Creek did not lend itself to solid construction, and many shacks were raised on piles over ground too wet for foundations. Some of the shacks were "dilapidated and filthy," and the surrounding land was saturated with "manurial refuse and garbage," for the houses on Dupont Street were not on the sewer.[28] Many Chinese suffered serious overcrowding which further exacerbated the unhealthy living conditions.

These miserable conditions lasted for a decade in Vancouver. In 1896, a municipal by-law was passed requiring sanitary conditions in all laundries, and that same year a sewer was built on Dupont Street. Four rows of shacks that had been built over the swamp were destroyed and the land filled to raise it to street level. The health inspector sensed an immediate improvement in the health of Chinatown's inhabitants, but even in 1899 a Vancouver newspaper was complaining of unsanitary conditions in Chinatown's laundries and boarding houses.[29] In 1899, Vancouver passed a Lodging House By-Law aimed at removing the worst of Chinese housing conditions.

Not surprisingly, pulmonary tuberculosis was the major cause of death for the Chinese in Vancouver. In 1899, Chinese accounted for eighteen of the forty-seven deaths by tuberculosis, whereas they accounted for one ninth of the city's total mortality. Of the fifty-seven Chinese deaths in Vancouver in 1899 and 1900, thirty-seven, or 65 per cent, were from pulmonary tuberculosis. As the health inspector stated in his report of 1900, "Overcrowding, absence of ventilation, and cellar life are three elements, the elimination of which would render sanitary efforts, in this portion of the City, a less puzzling and serious problem."[30]

Conditions in Victoria's Chinatown were somewhat better. For one thing, the site was not so swampy, although garbage created a problem. Overcrowding in the boarding houses caused some concern among non-Chinese, although usually this issue was raised by the anti-Chinese racists rather than by those seeking to improve conditions. Leprosy became a burning issue for a short time in 1891, when two "leperous" Chinese were brought to Vancouver from New York by the CPR. Although it was discovered later that one of them did not have leprosy, the two Chinese became the centre of a flurry of concern in Vancouver, including some notice in the newspapers. The two Chinese were isolated, first in a CPR shack and later on D'Arcy Island.[31] Later in the week the following advertisement appeared in the *Daily News Advertiser* (11 November):

BEWARE:

LEPROSY! LEPROSY! LEPROSY!

One Leper let loose in Chinatown. See Dr. Carroll's advice to Town Council. Why not patronise the CYCLONE LAUNDRY, the only White Laundry in the city. P.F. Ryan and Miss Della Morris, proprietors, 912 Richard St. Branch cor. Cambie & Water Sts. Telephone 346

The Vancouver Trades and Labour Council unanimously passed a resolution condemning the federal authorities for permitting "Mongolians to pass the boundary without passing a medical examination" and asking the City Council to resolve the matter rapidly.[32]

65

Another issue that was seen as a health problem by anti-Orientals at the time was the Cantonese custom of exhumation. The Chinese buried their dead in separate sections of the cemeteries in Victoria and Vancouver, then after seven years exhumed them, cleaned the bones, and shipped them to the Tung Wah Hospital in Hong Kong, which distributed them to the various villages of destination. This practice, so strange to the non-Chinese residents of Canada, roused some emotion. The *Colonist* had this to say in 1883:

> Those whose sense of decency is rather susceptible are cautioned against visiting the old cemetery unless they would turn sick with disgust and horror. . . . [The Chinese] practice their heathenish rites even within the most sacred . . . precincts, [which] turns religious liberty into license and in the prosecution of their ghoulish work of resurrecting the bodies of their dead countrymen, scraping their bones and burning the refuse flesh in their cemetery furnace (or altar), mayhap neglect or deem it unnecessary to re-fill the graves with earth, which consequently expose to view the boxes and coffins from which the bodies have been taken. Worse than this, there can be seen portions of queues and matted hair attached to sundry planks which have been torn off the coffins and are lying strewn about.

Such lurid accounts fed the fires of anti-Orientalism that produced legislation a year later making exhumation more difficult. When the CCBA in Victoria tried to establish their own cemetery in 1889, neighbouring residents prevented the move, until in 1901 the CCBA finally established a Chinese cemetery at Harling Point. In December, 1890, "a number of Chinese" in Vancouver requested through John Boultbee that a small piece of land adjoining the present cemetery "be set aside exclusively for the purpose of their dead," and they offered to "clear, grub and fence it" themselves. The Council agreed to the request.[33]

A somewhat more substantial problem, but one that caused far less anti-Oriental expression at the time, was an outbreak of smallpox in 1892. The *Empress of Japan* arrived at Victoria in April with one case of smallpox among its 530 Chinese passengers. With typically racist logic, the health officer quarantined all the Chinese in tents at Albert Head and permitted all the white passengers to proceed to their destinations. Smallpox was subsequently reported in Victoria, Vancouver, Howe Sound, Nanaimo, Moodyville, and Hastings, and several people died of the disease. In Vancouver several houses were burned because smallpox victims had lived in them, and W.A. Cumyow, who was then official interpreter, wrote to the City Council asking it to provide a "pest house" where Chinese could be quarantined. The Council referred the matter to the Board of Health, which promptly arranged for one to be established on Deadman's Island in Coal Harbour.[34] When the *Empress of Japan* arrived on its next trip in June, another case was discovered and immediately transferred to the new "pest house."

In Calgary, too, small though its Chinese community was, anti-Chinese sentiment developed early, and it focused upon questions of health. In 1892 a carrier of smallpox was discovered living in one of the Chinese laundries. Three people died of the disease. Four Chinese were placed in quarantine for a short time but did not develop the disease. When they were released, however, a mob of three hundred angry whites descended upon the local Chinese laundries, destroying some and terrorizing the occupants. Local authorities did nothing to stop them. The North West Mounted Police were called in to disperse the riot and the Chinese were under police protection for several days thereafter. The *Calgary Herald* supported the rioters, but the *Tribune* denounced them and demanded punishment of the leaders. The *Winnipeg Free Press* also defended the Chinese. The local leaders of the anti-Chinese movement included a city councillor and an American member of the Anti-Chinese League who had recently arrived from the West Coast. The two had established a branch of the League, to which the mayor and one other councillor had subscribed. The clergy, however, opposed the League, petitioning the City Council to condemn the rioters and to punish the leaders.[35]

While exhumation, leprosy, smallpox, and unhealthy living conditions undoubtedly created problems, all of them were used by the anti-Chinese movement to fan exclusionist sentiment and they, therefore, assumed unrealistic proportions for the non-Chinese Canadians in the West. The Royal Commission on Chinese and Japanese Immigration reported in 1902 that there were very few infectious diseases among the Chinese. In 1900, for instance, of the 183 reported cases in Vancouver, only six were found in Chinatown, and none of the others could be traced to Chinese.[36] Like everyone else, the Chinese suffered illness – and more than others when it came to pulmonary tuberculosis – but they were not the source of virulent infection the anti-Orientalists claimed they were. Only two instances of Chinese bringing diseases into Canada were reported to the Commission, the smallpox epidemic mentioned above and an outbreak of typhoid in Rossland in 1896, which reportedly spread from a Chinese laundry in that city.[37]

Another charge against the Chinese was that their community was "depraved" because of the pervading presence of such vices as prostitution, opium addiction, and gambling. The extent of these three practices, like that of infectious diseases, was exaggerated by the exclusionists, although all three undoubtedly existed in Chinatowns at the time. We know from the census undertaken by Huang Xichuan in 1884 that there were prostitutes in several Chinese communities in Canada. Seventy seems a surprisingly low number, however, for a population of almost 10,000 single male adults.[38] Nevertheless, by 1880 Victoria's Chinatown had a reputation among non-Chinese as a red-light district, suggesting that Chinese prostitutes had a clientele beyond the Chinese community. "No decent person now thinks of venturing into that locality," the *Colonist* proclaimed at the end of 1881. "The Chinese cyprians reign supreme in their quarter and solicit customers with an effrontery which cannot have escaped the notice of Superintendent O'Connor and his aides." There is an implication in this statement that the Victoria police were turning a blind eye, and such was certainly the case in Vancouver a few years later. There, the police were accepting $8 a week as protection money from Chinese prostitutes on Dupont Street. In Victoria, however, Chinese houses of prostitution were constantly being raided by policemen during 1886-87.[39]

Dupont Street was the red-light district of Vancouver during the 1890's and early twentieth century, but not merely because of its few Chinese brothels. It is clear from city directories and archives that non-Chinese prostitutes worked in establishments along Dupont Street in the blocks between Carrall and Main, and they, too, were mentioned in the police investigation of 1889. The unsavoury reputation of Chinatown was based, therefore, to some extent upon non-Chinese activity in the quarter.

Another issue from which the anti-Orientalists made political capital was opium. Prior to 1908 the importation, manufacture, and use of opium was not illegal in Canada, although there was agitation for its prohibition throughout the 1880's and 1890's. Perhaps its increasing use by non-Chinese strengthened the prohibition forces.

The suggestion that opium first entered Canada with the Chinese railway workers in the early 1880's[40] is contradicted by the fact that the drug was imported for at least a decade before that. Nevertheless, the rapid increase in the number of opium factories in Victoria from one to twelve during 1881-84 suggests that the Chinese railway workers were probably a significant market. On the other hand, the peak period of imports was between 1885 and 1894, during which time they averaged over fifty-four tons per year. The price of opium rose accordingly, from seven or eight dollars a pound in 1871 to fifteen in 1888.[41] One source attributes this great increase to the opening of the CPR and the consequent possibility of shipping opium to the eastern provinces and states from factories in Victoria.[42] The decline in imports after 1894 has not been explained; it may be due to the emergence of alternative routes through Europe to the eastern seaboard of North America or alternative sources of opium in the Middle East. Several of the opium dealers were already in financial straits by 1889, and one closed that year.

There is no way of knowing just how much opium was actually imported into Canada at that time. The anti-Orientalists claimed it was being smuggled in large quantities, and in 1891 the licence inspector in Vancouver suggested he should be given extraordinary powers of entry without warrant in order to seize the large amounts of contraband opium that he suspected then existed in the city.[43] Vancouver issued its first opium licence at the end of 1888, an additional one in 1889, and these two licence holders, Hip Tuck Lung and Wing Sang, were the only licensed dealers in the city.

Opium was not limited to Chinese, of course, for there were many users of the drug among the whites in North America. The Royal Commission of 1884 interviewed a young white woman, Emily Wharton, who at the age of twenty had been smoking opium for four years. When asked why she smoked opium, she replied, "Because I must; I could not live without it . . . partly because of the quiet enjoyment it gives, but mainly to escape from the horrors which would ensue did I not smoke." Miss Wharton testified that in San Francisco she had known "some of the first people visit opium houses and many respectable people do the same here [Victoria]."[44] There is no way of knowing, apart from the volume of opium imported, how many whites used the drug, but it is apparent that the Chinese themselves did not consider it a social problem of any magnitude. Indeed, as late as 1895, the two Chinese merchants in Vancouver requested the City Council to lower the opium licence fee. Outright condemnation of opium-smoking by Chinese was not heard from Chinese in Canada, except among the small minority of Christians, until the famous Chinese statesman, Li Hongzhang, called upon the Chinese to cease gambling and opium-smoking during his visit to Vancouver in 1896.[45]

By the turn of the century, white attitudes toward the drug had become strongly negative, and police raids on opium dens became more frequent, with the obvious result that police reported "an increasing number of places used by opium smokers in Chinatown."[46]

Unlike opium, which was in the hands of commercial enterprises, gambling was organized by various Chinese associations in the nineteenth century. Accepted by the Chinese as a normal form of recreation, gambling was condemned by the missionaries as one of Chinatown's major vices. There is no way of determining, of course, the extent of the practice, and the frequent references by missionaries and anti-Orientalists alike to its damaging effects upon the community may reflect their own ideological commitments more than they reveal the extent of the "vice." Very few persons were convicted of gambling offences prior to 1900. Indeed, during the five years (1879-84) reviewed in the 1885 Report of the Royal Commission, only twelve Chinese were brought to court in Victoria for infractions of the gaming laws, ten in 1879 for playing a prohibited game, fantan, and two the following year for possession of an illegal game. The archives of the Attorney General's Department in British Columbia include information on only two cases during the nineteenth century, in 1895 and 1896, and one in 1901.[47] In general, it is safe to conclude that gambling was not considered a problem by the Chinese and that the amount of publicity it received was due primarily to the efforts of the exclusionists, in some cases augmented by missionary concern.

The establishment of the Chinese Consolidated Benevolent Association had been inspired by concern among Chinese leaders about social problems within Chinatown during the railway construction period, and the growing anti-Chinese agitation. These two concerns were soon to be joined by another, which gradually became dominant as the nineteenth century drew to a close. This was the political situation in China itself, where the Qing dynasty was rotting from within and threatened from without, causing the emergence of conservative, reformist-liberal, and revolutionary trends within Chinese politics. These trends were reflected in overseas Chinese communities around the world, and Canada was no exception. While traditionist associations were founded in the emerging Chinese communities and continued to be established in Victoria, they were soon joined by a new kind of association, that dedicated to supporting a particular political tendency in China.

NOTES

1. For reaction to the commissioners, see James Morton, *In the Sea of Sterile Mountains, the Chinese in British Columbia*, pp. 112-13, 121.
2. *1885 Royal Commission*, pp. 69ff.
3. *Ibid.*, p. 103.
4. *Ibid.*, p. 68.
5. *Ibid.*, p. 159.
6. *Ibid.*, p. 156.
7. *Ibid.*, Gray's report, p. cii.
8. *Ibid.*, Chapleau's report, p. cxxiv; Gray's report pp. lxxvi-lxxix.
9. *Ibid.*, Gray's report, p. lxxxix.
10. Cited in R. Sampat-Mehta, *International Barriers: Aliens, Immigration, and Citizenship in Canada* (Ottawa, 1973), p. 34.
11. *1885 Chinese Immigration Act*, sections 4, 5, and 7.
12. *Ibid.*, section 4. An amendment in 1887 provided this exact wording, according to Sampat-Mehta, *International Barriers*, pp. 37-8.
13. Robert Edward Wynne, "Reaction to the Chinese in the Pacific Northwest and British Columbia, 1850-1910," p. 376.
14. *Vancouver Province*, 27 June 1934. Note that the *Province* gives the date of Yip's appointment as court interpreter as 1904, but the record of *Rex v. Ah Wooey* in 1902 refers to the "chicken oath" being administered by Yip Wing.
15. Morton, *Sea of Sterile Mountains*, p. 136.
16. *1885 Chinese Immigration Act*, p. 47. A similar act, apparently copied from this one, was passed in Newfoundland in 1906.
17. *Vancouver News*, 27 July 1886.
18. Alan Morley, *Vancouver: From Milltown to Metropolis* (Vancouver, 1961), p. 93.
19. Patricia E. Roy, "The Preservation of the Peace in Vancouver: the Aftermath of the anti-Chinese Riot of 1887," *B.C. Studies*, 31 (1976), p. 48.

20. *Vancouver News*, 25 February 1887.
21. Accounts of the riot are available in Roy, "Preservation of the Peace in Vancouver," pp. 50-1; Morton, *Sea of Sterile Mountains*, pp. 149-52; and Morley, *Vancouver*, pp. 93-4. All these are based on the description in the *Vancouver News* of 25 February 1887. Unfortunately, no account from the Chinese point of view has survived.
22. Roy, "Preservation of the Peace in Vancouver," p. 51.
23. Vancouver City Archives, Council Minute-Book no. 1, pp. 274, 280, 294, 319.
24. Roy, "Preservation of the Peace in Vancouver," p. 53.
25. Morley, *Vancouver*, pp. 90-1; see also Vancouver City Archives, Annual Report of the Vancouver Board of Trade, 1889.
26. *Henderson's British Columbia Directory* (Vancouver, 1906), p. 57. *Williams' B.C. Directory, 1891* (Victoria, 1890), pp. 133-6, 160.
27. *Report of the Royal Commission on Oriental Immigration, 1902* (henceforth, *1902 Royal Commission*), p. 40.
28. Vancouver City Archives, "Incoming Correspondence," vol. 17, 1885 Health Inspector's Report, McLean letter to City Clerk, 15 November 1900, pp. 3-4.
29. "More Shacks Will Go," *Vancouver Province*, 13 November 1899.
30. McLean letter to City Clerk, 15 November 1900, pp. 1-6. The causes of death among the Chinese in 1900 were: tuberculosis, 19; bronchitis, 1; pneumonia, 1; cancer, 1; heart disease, 3; heart failure, 1; rheumatism, 1; Bright's disease, 1; hernia, 1; accidental, 1; typhoid, 1; gangrene, 1; total, 32.
31. *Vancouver News-Advertiser*, 6, 7 November 1891.
32. Vancouver City Archives, City Clerk's Incoming Correspondence, vol. 4, pp. 4585-7.
33. Vancouver City Archives, City Clerk's Incoming Correspondence, vol. 3., *ibid.*, Council Minute Book no. 4, p. 169 (29 December 1890).
34. *Ibid.*, pp. 39, 86.
35. Howard Palmer, "Anti-Oriental Sentiment in Alberta, 1880-1920," *Canadian Ethnic Studies*, II (1970), p. 33; J. Brian Dawson, "Chinese Urban Communities in Southern Alberta, 1885-1910" (M.A. thesis, University of Calgary, 1976), pp. 10-19. There is evidence that the American had been active in the Brighouse Estate riot in Vancouver five years earlier.
36. *1902 Royal Commission*, p. 297.
37. *Ibid.*, p. 29. See McLean letter to City Clerk, 15 November 1900, p. 7.
38. *1885 Royal Commission*, p. v, and Appendix C, pp. 363-6.
39. Morton, *Sea of Sterile Mountains*, p. 141.
40. For example, G.E. Trasov, "History of the Opium and Narcotic Drug Legislation in Canada," *Criminal Law Quarterly*, IV, 3 (January, 1962), p. 274.
41. Cecil Clark, *Tales of the British Columbia Provincial Police* (Sidney, B.C., 1971), p. 50.

42. Charles P. Sedgwick, "The Context of Economic Change and Continuity in an Urban Overseas Chinese Community," p. 57.
43. Vancouver City Archives, City Clerk's Incoming Correspondence, RG 2 Al, vol. 4, p. 3958.
44. *1885 Royal Commission*, pp. 150-1. See also Vancouver City Archives, City Clerk's Incoming Correspondence, vol. 17, for raids in 1901.
45. Morton, *Sea of Sterile Mountains*, p. 179.
46. Vancouver City Archives, City Clerk's Incoming Correspondence, RG 2 Al, vol. 17, p. 1313: 13 May 1901 from Robert Marrison, Health Inspector.
47. Public Archives of B.C., Attorney General's Files, Register of Depositions.

SIX

Between China's Politics and Canada's Restrictions

Political contacts between the Canadian Chinese and the government of China went back to the late 1870's. Victoria's Chinese leaders, in particular, sent many letters to Guo Songtao, the Chinese ambassador to Britain, and his successors, Zeng Jice, Xue Fucheng, and Luo Fenglu. Petitions from the Victoria Chinese frequently were sent through Huang Cunxian, the Chinese consul-general in San Francisco, to the Chinese minister in Washington, who then forwarded them to the Chinese minister in London. Although there is little direct evidence, these diplomatic representations may have softened somewhat the effects of legislation upon the Chinese of British Columbia.

The first major political figure from China to visit Canada was the famous Li Hongzhang. In 1896 Li was out of favour in China as a consequence of his handling of the Chinese side of the Sino-Japanese War and subsequent treaty negotiations. Encouraged to take a trip around the world, Li was en route back to China via North America. Before leaving England he had received a petition from the Victoria CCBA asking for a Chinese consulate in Canada and also requesting that he negotiate with British officials concerning the entry tax on Chinese immigrants to Canada. At the time, B.C. labour organizations were proposing that this tax of $50, already seen as burdensome by the Chinese, be greatly increased. Li discussed the matter in London and departed for the United States. He then crossed into Canada and, after a brief pause in Toronto, took the train to Vancouver.

His arrival in Vancouver was a major event for that city, not to mention the Chinese communities for miles around. A crowd of 6,000, including representatives of Chinese communities as distant as Seattle, Portland, and San Francisco, turned out to welcome him. Li was driven from the station under a ceremonial arch constructed by neighbouring Chinese communities. Before sailing to Victoria and back to China, he received government dignitaries and Chinese leaders and departed to the accompaniment of booming cannon salutes and rattling firecrackers.

While in British Columbia he discussed the tax matter, and his representations may have delayed for a time the proposed increase.[1]

With Li's visit, the politics of China reached Canada. Defeat by Japan in the recent war had shocked the Chinese political world to its roots. Proposals for the radical reform of the Chinese government, military, and economy now began to be voiced. Under the patronage of the young Emperor, a group of such reformers, led by Kang Youwei and Liang Qichao, seemingly achieved power in the summer of 1898. For three months the Emperor issued an amazing series of reform edicts embodying their proposals for constitutional government with representative assemblies, government encouragement to industry and commerce, and fundamental educational changes. The real power, however, resided with the Empress Dowager, who soon ousted the reformers into exile under threat of their lives, sent the Emperor back into retirement, and, for a time, reversed the reform edicts.

While Kang's group sought reform within a constitutional monarchy, Sun Yat-sen's reaction to the defeat by Japan was to promote revolution, which would replace the Qing dynasty with a republic. Sun's early efforts at revolution were abortive and he fled into exile in 1895. Thus, by 1899 both reformers and revolutionaries were in exile, seeking bases overseas from which to launch their efforts for change in China. For the next dozen years, until the Revolution of 1911, Kang, Liang, and Sun became itinerant orators, organizers, and fund-raisers, going wherever there were overseas Chinese communities of any size. Since Canada had a substantial Chinese population by 1899, it became an important stopping place for all three of these political figures.

Kang Youwei visited Canada three times: in 1899, 1902, and 1904. During his first visit he established the first North American branch of his reform association in Victoria. Fearing for the fate of his imperial patron at the hands of the Empress Dowager, he named it the Emperor-Protection Association (Bo Wong Wui), although the English title, Empire Reform Association, correctly reflected the broad aims of this group. Between 1899 and 1903 some 103 branches of the Empire Reform Association were established in the Western Hemisphere. The largest number were in the United States, especially in the Northwest.

Kang's association attracted the support of the older, more prosperous Chinese merchants in Canada.[2] Most of these men had resided in North America for many years and so were conversant with the strengths and weaknesses of Western societies. Some were interpreters for the Immigration or Customs services or for the courts. They were, in other words, a rather cosmopolitan elite, in favour of modernizing China through selective borrowing from the West. This, they believed, should be done through progressive reform within the framework of a constitutional monarchy, rather than by revolution.

During the first several years after 1899 the Empire Reform Association enjoyed some support in Canada from the Cheekungtong (CKT).[3]

Although the leaders and members of the CKT were small merchants and labourers, who lacked the polish and scholarly interests of the richer merchants, their political interests overlapped those of Kang and his supporters. Accordingly, the CKT leaders were for a time allies of the Association.

By Kang's third visit in 1904, there were twelve Canadian branches of the Empire Reform Association and a reported membership of 7,000.[4] Their interest in Chinese politics was intense. At the height of the Boxer Movement in 1900, when Western missionaries and diplomats in China were besieged by the anti-Western Boxer troops and foreign military forces were being dispatched to rescue them, Won Alexander Cumyow, secretary of the Empire Reform Association in Canada, announced to the Vancouver press that his group was ready to send Overseas Chinese troops, including some from Canada, to accompany the relief forces. The idea was that these would punish the Empress Dowager for backing the Boxers and rescue the Emperor from her clutches. There is no indication that such an expedition was sent.

The Empire Reform Association did not confine its activities to the Chinese communities in Canada. During his 1899 visit Kang Youwei met Prime Minister Laurier, attended a session of the Dominion Parliament, and was received by the Governor General and the Speaker of the House of Commons. During his 1904 visit, he travelled from Montreal to Vancouver, where he was interviewed at the Hotel Vancouver and subsequently entertained by a group that included the Japanese and American consuls and other non-Chinese.

Like Kang Youwei, Liang Qichao was of interest to white political and business leaders who saw the Reform movement as a hopeful indicator of improved trade and political relations between China and the West. The Chinese reformers, in turn, were interested in obtaining the goodwill and support of Canadians and Americans of influence. During his only visit to Canada in 1903, Liang Qichao was the guest of honour at a dinner in Vancouver which was attended by business and political leaders from British Columbia and from the nearby state of Washington. Liang expressed hopes for closer relations between North America and a reformist China, and toasts were proposed to the mutually beneficial relations of Britain, the United States, and China.[5] Liang also visited Ottawa, where he attended a session of Parliament. After a brief visit to Montreal, he left Canada for the eastern United States. Liang's account of his North American trip is a fascinating source of information about Chinese immigration and employment at the turn of the century.[6]

The Empire Reform Association enjoyed its greatest prosperity in Canada during the period 1899-1911. Its headquarters were established jointly in the branches at Victoria, Vancouver, and New Westminster, with branches set up following Liang's 1903 visit in Toronto, Ottawa, and Montreal.[7] Calgary had a branch by 1910; Medicine Hat apparently had a branch by 1911, with a restaurant as its meeting place.[8]

75

By 1905 the Empire Reform Association was flourishing in Victoria and Vancouver. In each city the Association sponsored a Chinese school, the Oikwok Hoktong, or Patriotic School. Both of these schools were established about 1900, and the Vancouver one was the first recorded Chinese school in that city, although the CCBA had established the Lequn Yishu in Victoria the year before, the first Chinese public school in Canada.[9] In Vancouver the Association also sponsored a newspaper, the *Yat Sun Bo* (Daily News).

But its prosperity was to be short-lived. Internal dissension was part of the problem. A company had been formed by the Association to promote investment in western China. After many shares had been sold in Canada, the company collapsed, amidst accusations of mishandling of funds. Meanwhile, shortly after 1905, competing political groups of revolutionary persuasion began to appear and to woo the CKT away from its loose alliance to the reformers. By 1911 the *Yat Sun Bo* had ceased publication and the Empire Reform Association had passed its peak.

Sun Yat-sen visited Canada three times: in 1897, 1910, and 1911. On his first two visits his activities were confined to fund-raising in Vancouver and Victoria. By the time of his second visit, revolutionary sentiment had begun to develop among Canada's Chinese. In Victoria a radical youth group had formed, the Chi-chi She, or "Sworn-oath" Society, devoted to the cause of revolution in China. Among its founders were Seto Ying-shek (Seto More), Wu Shang-ying, and Chu Chi-ngok.[10] By 1910 a branch of Sun's T'ung-meng Hui, or Revolutionary Alliance, was being secretly formed in British Columbia. Meanwhile, a newspaper war raged in Vancouver's Chinatown. Shortly after the reformers' *Yat Sun Bo* began publication, the bilingual *Wah Ying Yat Bo* (Chinese-English Daily News) had appeared. Originally Christian in ownership and interest, it gravitated into the hands of the Empire Reform Association briefly and then to the CKT, before it disappeared in 1908. In 1907 the CKT also founded its own paper, the *Tai Hon Bo* (to be known as the *Tai Hon Kung Bo*, or "The Chinese Times," after 1914, and still publishing in the 1970's). Revolutionary sentiment found expression first in the *Dai Luk Bo* (Mainland Times), published in Vancouver in 1908-1909. Then, when Feng Tzu-yu, a follower of Sun Yat-sen, became editor of the CKT's *Tai Hon Bo*, he turned that paper in the direction of the revolutionary cause. This was in line with the growing support for Sun among CKT members, whose North American Grandmaster, Wong Sam-duck, had endorsed Sun's cause. During Sun's second and third visits, therefore, the newspaper war in Vancouver was between the reformers' *Yat Sun Bo* and the CKT's *Tai Hon Bo*.[11]

As Chinese politics came to Canada, so did modernized Chinese schools, and the two were not unrelated. We have no information about the curriculum in the two schools founded by the Empire Reform Association at the turn of the century, but it seems likely that they would have included some modern content.

After 1901 the idea of reform became widely accepted in China and even the Empress Dowager sponsored it. After 1905 modern schools began to be established in China and in 1908 an educational commissioner from China, Liang Qingkui, inspected Chinese schools in B.C. and offered suggestions and Chinese government financial assistance for improvement. His arrival came in the midst of a school crisis. The B.C. government's Department of Education had decided that students should be racially segregated. The Chinese of Victoria, where the largest number of school-age children were located, were searching for ways to provide adequate instruction for their children in both traditionally Chinese and modern subjects. The Lequn Yishu, located in the old CCBA building, was too small for the fifty-plus students it served. The segregation crisis of 1907-1908 suggested that the burden of educating the Chinese children might become even heavier if public facilities were to be no longer available.

In response to the segregation crisis, the Victoria CCBA raised funds throughout Vancouver Island's Chinese communities to hire a lawyer to protest the proposed segregation. The protest was successful and there were funds remaining. Under the leadership of Lim Bang and the Immigration interpreter, Lee Mongkow, these funds were devoted to building a new CCBA building large enough to house an adequate Chinese school. The new school, subsequently named the Chinese Public School (Wahkiu Hokhao; Huaqiao Xuexiao), was completed and opened in 1909. With Lee Mongkow as principal for the next decade, the Victoria Chinese Public School established a reputation as one of the best Chinese schools in Canada. It has survived to the present.[12]

ORGANIZATIONAL GROWTH IN CANADA

The period from 1884 to 1911 also witnessed the earliest formal establishment of Chinese benevolent associations, district and clan associations, and Chinese chambers of commerce, particularly in the more developed communities of western Canada. The date of the founding of the Chinese Benevolent Association of Vancouver is traditionally given as 1889. At that date, however, Vancouver was still a very small city, and although several of Victoria's prosperous Chinese firms would shortly establish branches or move their operations to Vancouver, in 1889 Victoria was still the only Chinese community with several prosperous merchants of the kind likely to found a CBA.[13] We know that the Vancouver CBA was registered as an association under the B.C. Societies Act in 1906. We also know that a petition was sent to Li Hongzhang in 1896 from the three CBAs at Victoria, New Westminster, and Vancouver. It would seem, therefore, that at some time between 1889 and 1896 the Vancouver CBA was informally established, perhaps with some assistance from Victoria, and formally registered only in 1906. Differences in names of those who were the founding members would reflect differences in leadership as between the informal period of the 1890's and the date of formal establishment, 1906. In any case, by 1911 there were at least three Chinese benevolent associations, those in Victoria, New Westminster, and Vancouver.

District organizations were also emerging in rudimentary form in Victoria. One of the earliest of these, the Chong Hoo Tong, had acquired a Vancouver version between 1900 and 1911.[14] Another, the association of natives of Toi-san County, had formed the Toi-san Ning Yung Yu Hing Tong in Victoria in 1893, followed by a branch in Vancouver by 1912. But even this association remained somewhat in a *jiefang* stage, in that its Vancouver branch had no regular headquarters of its own until some time after 1911.[15] Like all district associations, its major distinctive function was that of collecting the bones of deceased members and shipping them to China for final burial. Since Toi-san natives were the most numerous group among the Chinese in Canada, the Ning Yung Yu Hing Tong undertook to co-ordinate collection and shipment for all districts.

Clan associations had many of the same welfare functions that district associations did. They provided lodging facilities, assistance in obtaining work, recreation facilities, relief when needed, and financial aid towards burial. Despite the term, members were not necessarily related to one another. Chinese believe that all Chinese of the same surname must be related, however distantly, in some way. Hence, a common surname becomes a useful basis for forming welfare associations. At some time between the 1880's and 1911 clan associations began to emerge in Victoria and Vancouver. The Lim Sai Ho Tong traces its founding in Victoria to 1908.[16] Others of the earliest known clan associations, such as the Lee Long Sai Tong, the Lung Kong Kung-So, and the Chee Duck Tong, probably were in existence in Victoria before 1911 and perhaps in Vancouver as well.

Merchants' associations, or "chambers of commerce," began to appear in 1900. The Zhaoyi Gongsuo and the Gongyi Gongsuo, both of which were organized in both Victoria and Vancouver around 1900, were of this type.[17] Although these occupational associations no doubt had local reasons for their existence, their emergence at this particular moment was probably influenced by Chinese politics. Associations of this kind were appearing in China and among Overseas Chinese in other countries, with some encouragement from the Chinese government, which hoped thereby to mobilize merchant opinion at home and abroad on its side.

Although other Chinese communities were becoming important, only Victoria's had a Chinese hospital before 1911, the Taiping Fang, established in 1885. Ten years later it had become too small, and a two-storey building took its place. This institution, named the Chinese Hospital, was the first such in Canada, and predecessor to those later to be established in Vancouver and Montreal. The Victoria Chinese Hospital was administered by the CCBA. Until the 1940's the Chinese community provided all of its financial support, although with much difficulty. Thereafter, it received financial aid from the city.

Chinese cemeteries appeared in several western Canadian towns and cities between the 1880's and 1911. By 1911 there were Chinese cemeteries in several B.C. localities: Victoria, Duncan, Nanaimo, Cumberland, Prince George, Vernon, and Kamloops. Across the Prairies, Chinese cemeteries could be found at Calgary, Edmonton, Moose Jaw, Regina, and Saskatoon.

From the 1860's to the 1890's Chinese temples devoted to various popular deities were established both in association halls and in separate buildings. By the early twentieth century most of these had fallen into disuse and disappeared, as the buildings they were in were diverted to other uses. The Tam Kung temple of the Hakka people in Victoria is the only remaining temple of that era.[18]

RESTRICTIONS TO GROWTH, 1900-1910

According to the census there were 17,312 Chinese in Canada in 1901. Official records cannot be taken entirely at face value, however. During the years 1891-1900, official net immigration was 15,915, yet according to the census the Chinese population had grown by less than 8,000 in that decade. It is clear that several thousand Chinese left Canada unofficially during the 1890's, probably crossing the border into the United States. American officials complained of this phenomenon at the time and throughout the subsequent decades into the 1950's.

Between 1889 and 1901 immigration from China, which had dropped off somewhat in the late 1880's, had greatly increased and was averaging over 2,000 arrivals per year. Undoubtedly, continued difficulties in China and apparent opportunities in Canada spurred the increase in arrivals. Another factor was surely the inauguration of the Canadian Pacific steamship lines between South China and Victoria and Vancouver. The "Empress" vessels were to become a regular part of Canada's West Coast scene. Along with the Blue Funnel steamers, they brought most of the Chinese to Canada during the next two decades. They also employed many Chinese as crew members. Although Chinese had begun to move east across Canada in the 1880's and 1890's, the clear majority were still in British Columbia in 1901.

In the decade 1901-11 Vancouver began to pass Victoria as the commercial centre of British Columbia and, thereby, as the preferred residence of B.C.'s Chinese. The 1906 CCBA census shows 6,000 Chinese in each city. In the 1911 official census each city shows about 3,500.[19] Shortly after 1900 Vancouver's Chinatown centred as before on the intersection of Dupont (later Pender) and Carrall Streets. But major stores and associations were now found not only on those two streets but also on the nearby Shanghai Alley and Canton Alley.

New Westminster had had an important Chinatown since the 1860's.

As the "jumping-off place" for Chinese activities in the interior of B.C., New Westminster had become known to the Chinese as "*yi-fao*," or "second port-city," in relation to Victoria. The extension of the CPR to Vancouver meant the decline of New Westminster's Chinatown, although in 1906 New Westminster's Chinatown, by the CCBA's figures, still had 2,000 inhabitants—about the same number as Nanaimo, Cumberland, and Duncan.[20] The fortunes of these last three Chinese communities were closely related to the coal-mining operations on Vancouver Island. Cumberland, in particular, enjoyed a boom and a large influx of Chinese miners around 1899.[21]

At the turn of the century Chinese were entering new occupations. In the main, Chinese-owned businesses before 1900 had served the needs of the Chinese community, rather than white customers. By 1900, however, the Chinese were establishing more businesses of their own, many of which served a large white clientele. Laundries were the pioneer institutions as the Chinese migrated across the country. Chinese-owned vegetable gardens also appeared near Vancouver and other cities, but the really new business was the Western-style restaurant, which could be found especially in the prairie towns.[22]

The Chinese society of 1900 was made up of a small elite of well-to-do merchants, a larger group of small merchants, and an even larger body of labourers. The well-off merchants were usually engaged in import-export trade between China and Canada. Some of them had their wives and children with them. Indeed, the only complete families present in the Chinese communities were those of well-to-do merchants. Small merchants, especially those who operated restaurants, might hope some day to become wealthy. But in the meantime neither they nor the labourers had their complete families with them.

The general absence of families in the Chinese communities raises the question of whether the Chinese in Canada came as sojourners, not intending to settle permanently. There certainly was a tradition in coastal South China of migration overseas with the idea of making enough money to return to retirement in comfort in one's native locality, where one could buy land, build a large house, and live in prestige and ease. That dream continued down to the 1940's, although we do not know how many Chinese from Canada realized it. After 1949 the land reform and other policies of the new Communist government made it impossible to buy land and live at ease as before in China. It could be argued that during the period of formal discrimination against Chinese in Canada, 1875-1947, racist rejection forced the Chinese to be sojourners and to think in terms of returning to China. Although there is no doubt of the rejection, the point may not be easy to prove. During the period before outright discrimination, 1858-1875, there were very few families among the Chinese in Canada. There were not many more during the period 1875-1904, when discriminatory taxation was still moderate. In fact, the largest influx of families, such as it was, occurred between 1904 and 1923, when the financial and other disabilities of being in Canada were at their highest. What that indicates is that the problem is more complex than simply "racist rejection" or "sojourner mentality."

Secondly, the decision whether or not to settle permanently depended partly upon financial status. Wealthy merchants could not only afford to have families in Canada and to take them back to China, if they all wished to retire there; they also had such heavy investments and complex involvements that success in Canada was no longer simply a means to an end, if that had been the original idea, but had become an end in itself. At some point a wealthy merchant would have to make a decision about settling permanently in Canada, in a way that a small merchant or labourer would not have to do.

The third point is that sojourning or settling also depended upon personality. There is no doubt that there were adventurous Chinese among the small merchants and labourers who, given a chance and a modicum of prosperity and acceptance, would have preferred to settle in Canada, just as there were others who were truly sojourners, wishing only minimum involvement with the Canadian environment while they made enough money to retire to China.

The question is complicated by the fact that in Canada, as in other places where Chinese immigrants have settled, their tendency to send home remittances, to make repeated trips back to China, and perhaps to retire there has been used as a rationalization for discriminatory taxation and other unfair measures. The usual argument was that the Chinese contributed nothing, except perhaps their labour, and thus sent money out of the country rather than spending it within the country. Finally, having exploited the host country, they returned to China. Taxation, then, was seen as a way of forcing some of the earnings of the Chinese to be spent in the host country.

From the standpoint of the individual Chinese, the burden was staggering. He was often prepared to accept employment for less than the going wage in order to obtain work. Sedgwick's comparative wage table for Victoria in 1902 shows that in most occupations wages paid the Chinese workers were about half those paid to white workers.[23] It is likely that these ratios were typical of at least British Columbia. Whether or not he planned to retire to China, a single Chinese in Canada usually felt obliged to send remittances to relatives there. However open-minded he might be about staying in Canada, he was viewed by government, after 1885, as a sojourner who should have to pay extra for his opportunity to make money in Canada. Given the burden involved in paying remittances and discriminatory taxes out of an income that was already smaller than that of other workers in comparable jobs, it is hardly surprising that Chinese were noted for working harder and for being more frugal than other workers. They had to be so. And it is perhaps understandable, given these strains, that often any surplus income left to a Chinese after all those demands might go at the gambling table, leaving him stranded in Canada whether he wished to be or not.

During the 1890's labour groups and politicians in British Columbia continued their efforts to exclude, or at least restrict, Chinese immigration, and to limit the occupations open to those Chinese who were in Canada. At almost every session the B.C. legislature passed laws of this kind. Those not concerned with immigration attempted to prohibit the use of Asian labour (by this time there were also significant numbers of Japanese in British Columbia) on public works or specifically the employment of Chinese in the underground part of mining work. The immediate rationale for the latter legislation was the Nanaimo Coal Mine explosion of 1887 which killed 200 persons. This disaster was blamed on the Chinese who were working underground in that mine at the time. Besides this legislation, government and private groups in B.C. bombarded Ottawa with petitions for federal laws excluding or severely limiting Asian immigration.

Ottawa's response was to refuse the petitioners' requests and to disallow most of the legislation. In the first place, the legislation was *ultra vires* the provincial legislature. Second, much of it violated rights established for Chinese or Japanese subjects by treaties between their countries and Britain. Finally, the Dominion government argued that some of the legislation was contrary to imperial interests. For example, a proposed act requiring immigrants to be literate in English was ruled *ultra vires* on the grounds that it would also rule out immigrants from other parts of the world whom the government might wish to attract.[24]

In response to pressures from British Columbia, Ottawa passed the Chinese Immigration Act of 1900, which went into effect January 1, 1902. Like the 1885 Act it limited the number of Chinese who might be brought to Canada to one person for every fifty tons cargo per ship. The main difference between this Act and the one of 1885 was that the entry head tax was to be raised from $50 per person to $100, and that the province was to receive one-half.

The $100 head tax was much less than the $500 figure British Columbia had wanted. Agitation from the West continued, so in 1901 Ottawa struck a Royal Commission to investigate oriental immigration.

The Commission reported that the Chinese were paying little in the way of taxes and tried to avoid taxation whenever they could. In consequence it recommended the denial of the right to vote. Concerning the possible effects on Canada-China trade of any greater restrictions on Chinese immigration, the report concluded that there would be no damage, since the United States' Chinese Exclusion Law had had little effect on U.S.-China trade.[25]

In 1903 the Dominion Parliament enacted a new Chinese Immigration Act, which established a head tax of $500 on each Chinese immigrant. There were six classes of persons who were exempt: established merchants and their families (the definition of which was not clearly made, leading to abuses), diplomats, clergymen, tourists, students, and men of science.

Dominion government attitudes toward restrictions on Chinese immigration during this period illustrate a major problem the Chinese would confront for the next forty years. China's perceived weakness in the international arena made restrictions on Chinese immigration more readily possible than might be true of immigration from elsewhere. Although trade with China had been a consideration in the disallowances, by the late 1890's imperial interests in Asia had clearly become more important relative to Japan than to China. After Japan's victory over China in 1895, it was clear that she was the major regional power in Asia. Britain now moved toward an alliance with her, which was formalized in 1902. Thus, although Japanese immigration to Canada had greatly increased during the 1890's, and many in British Columbia favoured restrictions on all Orientals, it was clear that federal legislation against Japanese immigration would not be possible.

One of the B.C. measures not disallowed forbade the employment of Chinese on projects involving Crown lands within the province; another removed the municipal franchise from the Chinese. We have seen that the provincial franchise was taken away from the Chinese earlier. Because Dominion voters' lists followed provincial ones, the Dominion franchise was thereby removed. With disenfranchisement at the municipal level, the process of removal of the vote was completed. And since eligibility for certain professions in British Columbia, such as law, pharmacy, and chartered accountancy, depended upon being on the voters' list, Chinese were automatically ineligible.

For a brief moment it appeared that there was a chance for native-born Chinese to have the vote. In 1900, Tomey Homma, a Canadian-born Japanese, challenged the B.C. Provincial Elections Act of 1895, which denied the vote to persons of Asian ancestry. Although Homma won in the courts, the case went to the Privy Council, which, in 1902, reversed the courts' decisions. Japanese Canadians could not vote; Chinese Canadians could not either.[26]

British Columbia was not alone in removing the franchise from the Chinese. In Saskatchewan the Elections Act of 1908 disenfranchised the Chinese who lived in that province. The Chinese were hardly a demographic threat; in 1911 there were but 957 Chinese in a total Saskatchewan population of 492,432. Alberta, too, discussed the possibility of disenfranchising its Chinese. There was little support for the idea, however, and it was not pursued.

Federal legislation to reduce the flow of Chinese immigration enjoyed only limited success. As critics of the 1900 Chinese Immigration Act predicted, raising the head tax from $50 to $100 was no deterrent, and immigration levels remained as they had been for the few years previous. In fact, in 1903 they went up to 5,000 arrivals, the largest ever for a single year. Alarmed at this inflow in light of the unemployment situation at the time, the Victoria CCBA telegraphed the Governor of Guangdong Province asking that he prohibit for a time all emigration from his jurisdiction to Canada.[27]

We do not know his response, but it was probably the Immigration Act of 1903 rather than any efforts of his that brought a momentary pause in Chinese arrivals. At this point, the law of supply and demand asserted itself. Chinese were deemed by many whites to be a necessity for certain kinds of occupation. Now it seemed they were to be in short supply. Accordingly, the wages those already in Canada could earn increased and with it the ability of those Chinese to pay the $500 head tax for relatives or non-related Chinese to come.[28] By 1907 Chinese immigration was once again on the upswing.

In early 1907 the B.C. legislature had passed for the fourth time a "Natal Act" – named for its South African model – by which a language test would be applied to prospective immigrants. All previous versions of this had been disallowed at the federal level. This time, the Lieutenant-Governor, James Dunsmuir, refused to sign the bill, thereby provoking the wrath of many residents of the province. Dunsmuir was a member of the family of wealthy coal mine operators that had become famous for using Asian labour extensively in their business operations and thereby restricting or countering wage demands from white labour.[29]

Newspapers in the province were full of this question as they were of the arrival of increasing numbers of Asians during the early part of 1907. Anxieties tended to focus upon Vancouver. As a port of entry and the fastest growing urban centre in British Columbia, Vancouver had become the destination for much of the new Asian immigration. By 1907, one report by city officials estimated that one-sixth of the city's population was Asian.[30] All of the foregoing provided the background to the Vancouver riot of that year.[31]

In the summer of 1907 a branch of the Asiatic Exclusion League had been founded in Vancouver. Similar organizations had existed before, but the foundation of this one was particularly ominous. On the evening of Saturday, September 7, a well-publicized rally of the League took place. A parade to the City Hall, where the rally was to be held, accumulated an estimated following of 5,000. On arrival at City Hall Lieutenant-Governor Dunsmuir was burned in effigy, while a packed audience listened to speakers call for a "White Canada," and one representative from nearby Bellingham, Washington, described how 700 East Indians had been chased out of that community.

The Vancouver City Hall was located between the Chinese and Japanese quarters. At some point during the evening, part of the crowd outside City Hall moved towards Chinatown. On Carrall Street near Hastings someone threw the first stone at a Chinese storefront window. Soon the crowd had moved up and down Carrall and adjacent streets of Chinatown leaving no windows unbroken. The Chinese, apparently caught by surprise, did not offer resistance, but withdrew to the backs of their buildings, barring doors where possible.

The mob now moved on, past City Hall to the centre of Japanese settlement on Powell Street. Forewarned, the Japanese armed themselves with knives and bars, extinguished all lights, and waited. As the mob surged down Powell, rocks and pieces of wood were thrown down from the roofs of buildings by the Japanese defenders. Discouraged by this resistance, the mob returned to Chinatown by 11 p.m. By then city police and firemen were able to prevent further violence.

On Sunday, Powell Street was patrolled by the Japanese and hence was inaccessible to curious outsiders. Chinatown was not, and sightseers could examine sidewalks that were inches deep in shattered glass. On Monday, as the Japanese went on a work strike for half a day and held a mass community meeting, the Chinese boarded up their store fronts and withdrew their services for a full day, greatly inconveniencing all those whites who depended upon them for domestic service, laundry, cheap produce, restaurant cooking, or mill work. Hardware stores reported a large volume of gun sales to Chinese. A cargo of guns and ammunition consigned to the prominent merchant Sam Kee (Chan Doe Gee) was confiscated from the inbound B.C. Electric Interurban from New Westminster. There was some discussion of a unified defence effort by the Chinese and Japanese. Apparently no real collaboration took place.

But there was to be no more violence. Amazingly, no one had been killed, although two stabbings had been reported and several people were injured by flying glass. The property damage was, of course, considerable. Twenty-four persons were brought to trial on various charges. One was sentenced to six months in jail. Several others had to pay fines of from $50 to $105.

The 1907 riot was a shock to the city. Newspapers and public figures universally deplored it. Even the Asiatic Exclusion League, or at least a prominent but unidentified member of it, deplored the fact that "the mob . . . broke loose." But this event, he pointed out, would force the authorities in senior governments "to recognize the fact that British Columbia people will not permit this country to be made a dumping ground of yellow cheap labour."[32]

One Vancouver newspaper, blaming the riot on "a few young men and boys," was concerned with the bad publicity the riot would create for the city.[33] Another paper took a strong stand for law and order and the protection of the property of all persons, whatever their race.[34] Again, the riot was blamed on a minority – in this case, a "gang of hoodlums."

Whether the rioters intended to attack Asian individuals as well as their property may never be known. One intriguing bit of evidence, in the form of a report that during the violence Asians often moved about the crowds unmolested,[35] suggests that property destruction may have been the limit of the mob's conscious intentions. Certainly, the majority of the citizens of Vancouver deplored this resort to violence. Yet it is probably a safe assumption that Vancouver Liberal MP R.G. MacPherson spoke for the majority of white British Columbians in saying:

> B.C. is to be a white man's country. The majority of the residents are utterly opposed to the present flinging wide the gates to Asiatics. If the Government does not step in and put a stop to the already humiliating condition of affairs there will be another little episode like the one which occurred in Boston harbor when the tea was thrown overboard.[36]

Robert Borden, leader of the Conservatives, probably spoke for an even larger group of Canadians in saying that British Columbia had to be "a British and Canadian province, inhabited and dominated by men in whose veins runs the blood of those great pioneering races which built up and developed not only Western but Eastern Canada."[37]

No doubt there were some white British Columbians who were caught in between – neither industrialists wishing cheap Asian labour nor white labour wishing an end to Asian wage competition, but persons who saw both the needs of the provincial economy and those of white labour.[38] Mayor Bethune of Vancouver, himself a member of the Asiatic Exclusion League, issued a statement regretting the riots. He and the City Council then moved to block a forthcoming meeting of the League.[39]

At the federal level there was immediate action. In response to a protest by the Japanese consul in Vancouver, Prime Minister Laurier immediately replied with a message to the Mayor of Vancouver:

> His Excellency the Governor General has learned with the deepest regret of the indignities and cruelties to which certain subjects of the Emperor of Japan, a friend and ally of His Majesty the King, have been victims and he hopes that peace will be promptly restored and all the offenders punished.[40]

One month later, Laurier cabled his regrets to the Emperor of Japan, assuring him that efforts would be made to prevent recurrence of such an event. No similar expressions of regret were sent to Chinese authorities. China had as yet no consular representation in Canada, and if there was a Chinese protest to London it apparently went unheeded.

Assuming compensatory responsibility for the riot damage, the Dominion government appointed its Deputy Minister of Labour, W.L. Mackenzie King, as Commissioner to assess losses sustained and to make recommendations for federal compensation. King arrived in Vancouver in late October. After eleven days of hearings he recommended awards to Japanese claims totalling over $9,000. Although the claims filed amounted to over $13,000, King was praised by the Japanese consul for his generosity.[41]

While assessing Japanese claims King became aware of contract arrangements by which Japanese immigrants had been brought to Canada. Wishing to investigate this further, he proposed a second commission with this objective. Ottawa agreed, and King remained in Vancouver through November for this purpose. Although he had examined only Japanese claims in his work for the prior commission, King included Chinese and East Indian immigration in his report for the second commission.

Not until the middle of 1908 did King return to Vancouver to investigate Chinese claims for damages during the 1907 riot. If his approach to Chinese claims might be called leisurely, it was in the end generous. The Chinese award of almost $26,000 included almost everything requested by the Chinese claimants. On only one type of claim did King balk: that was for compensation for lost business to some opium dealers. That opium was legally traded and used by the Chinese in British Columbia and had been since the beginning was a shocking revelation to King. Within a few days' time the Dominion Parliament passed a bill outlawing it. The effect upon Chinese business in Victoria, where much of North America's opium was processed and sold, was disastrous; the abolition of the opium was as much responsible for the stagnation of Victoria's Chinatown as was the competitive economic growth of Vancouver.

Another outcome of the Vancouver riot of 1907 was the mission of Rodolphe Lemieux, Minister of Labour, to Japan to negotiate an agreement that would restrict Japanese migration to Canada. The arrangement he negotiated, the so-called "Gentlemen's Agreement" of 1908, was a device by which Japan would undertake to limit certain classes of emigrants to Canada. The general categories of permitted immigrants were to be: returning residents and their families, servants of established Japanese residents of Canada, students, merchants, tourists, agricultural labourers under contract to Japanese owners of farm land in Canada, and labourers for specific projects under contracts approved by the Canadian government. An informal limitation of 400 was to apply to only the last two of these classes.

Nothing further had been done about Chinese immigration. The annual intake of Chinese immigrants by 1907-1908 was again over 2,000 a year. At one point, the Vancouver Chinese "Board of Trade" (Chamber of Commerce) attempted, as the Victoria CCBA had tried before and was to do again later, to discourage such large numbers of immigrants, in the face of employment difficulties and white hostility. If their effort had any effect, it is not indicated in the immigration statistics.

By 1910 rumours of an immigration scandal in British Columbia resulted in the appointment of Mr. Justice Denis Murphy of Vancouver as a commissioner to investigate alleged irregularities in the handling of Chinese immigration. The commission uncovered the complicity of a Customs interpreter and some government figures. But aside from the political ramifications of the scandal, the main result of the commission's investigation was to tighten up Chinese immigration administration somewhat. Its effect upon the flow of Chinese immigration apparently was negligible.

NOTES

1. Lee Tung-hai, pp. 263-70; Victoria *Daily Colonist*, 15 September 1896; Vancouver *Province*, 19 September 1896.
2. Lee Tung-hai, pp. 275-89; Wu Xianzi, *Zhongguo Minzhuxianzhengdang dangshi* (San Francisco, 1952), pp. 25-7. We are indebted to Dr. Jung-pang Lo for making available a copy of Wu's volume.
3. Lee Tung-hai, pp. 276, 287.
4. *Ibid.*, p. 282. Either the 7,000 figure is inflated or the membership included more than prosperous merchants. It is not possible that there would be 7,000 prosperous merchants in a community numbering only 28,000 in 1911. An estimate that 35 per cent of the Chinese in Canada joined the Reform Association shortly after its foundation, based upon a Reform Association source, is found in Eve Armentrout-Ma, "A Chinese Association in North America: The Pao-Huang Hui from 1899 to 1904," *Ch'ing-shih wen-t'i*, IV, 9 (November, 1978), p. 91.
5. Vancouver *World*, 3 April 1903, in University of British Columbia Library, Special Collections Division, Cumyow Collection, Box 1-5.
6. Liang Qichao, *Xin Dalu yuji* (Taibei, 1967), pp. 226-34.
7. Wu, *Zhongguo*, pp. 25-7.
8. J. Brian Dawson, "The Chinese Experience in Frontier Calgary," in A. Rasporich and H. Klassen (eds.), *Frontier Calgary: Town, City and Region 1875-1914* (Calgary, 1975), p. 138. Howard Palmer, "Anti-Oriental Sentiment in Alberta, 1880-1920," p. 54, n. 69.
9. Guan Qiyi, "Jianada Huaqiao jiaoyu shilue," *Weiduoli Zhonghua Huiguan tekan*, Part IV, p. 17; Chen Kwong Min, *Meizhou Huaqiao tongjian* (The Chinese in the Americas) (New York, 1950), p. 419.
10. Lee Tung-hai, pp. 347-50, 298; W.E. Willmott, "Approaches to the Study of the Chinese in British Columbia," p. 49.
11. Lee Tung-hai, pp. 347-50; Feng Tzu-yu, *Huaqiao geming zuzhi shihua* (Taibei, 1954), pp. 69-70, 83.
12. Lee Tung-hai, pp. 332ff.; Lim Bang, "Weishi Zhonghua Huiguan zhi yange ji Huaqiao Xuexiao chuangli zhi yuanqi," *Weiduoli Zhonghua Huiguan tekan*, Part IV, pp. 1-2; Li Zhenxiung, "Benxiao xiaoshi," *ibid.*, Part III, pp. 54ff. The 1907 segregation proposal was not the first such proposal in Victoria. See W. Peter Ward, *White Canada Forever* (Montreal, 1978), p. 62.
13. Lee Doe Chuen (comp.), *Quan-Jia Zhonghua Zonghuiguan gaikuang* (Inside the CBA) (Taibei, 1969), p. 26. See also Lee Tung-hai, pp. 194ff.; Yue Yun, "Yungaohua Zhonghua Huiguan chengli niandai zhi kaozheng," *Jianada Weiduoli Zhonghua Huiguan chengli qi shi wu, Huaqiao Xuexiao chengli liushi – zhounian jinian tekan* (Victoria, 1960), Part V, pp. 3ff.
14. *Yu Shan Zonggongsuo luocheng jinian ce* (Vancouver, 1949), pp. 3-4; Charlie Cho, interviews with H. Con, 17, 22, 25 March 1973.
15. *Quan-Jia Taishanyiqiao dierjie kenqin dahui tekan* (Taibei, 1975),

pp. 130-1; Chan Kung Yung and Ng Lun Ward, interviews with H. Con, 26 March 1973.

16. *Yungaohua Lin Xi Ho Zongtang Jiumu Gongsuo bazhounian jinian dahui zhuankan* (Vancouver, 1941), p. 102.

17. Lee Tung-hai, pp. 208-9.

18. *Ibid.*, pp. 219-26.

19. Lee Tung-hai, p. 33; *Census of Canada*, 1911, II, pp. 372-3.

20. Lee Tung-hai, p. 33.

21. *Ibid.*, p. 489.

22. Cheng Tien-fang, *Oriental Immigration in Canada*, p. 169.

23. Charles P. Sedgwick, "The Context of Economic Change and Continuity in an Urban Overseas Chinese Community," Appendix III, pp. 206-7. A survey made in British Columbia in the early 1930's concluded that "the average earnings of the Chinese are lower than the average earnings of Whites in the Province." W.A. Carrothers, "Oriental Standards of Living," in H.A. Innis (ed.), *The Japanese Canadians* (Toronto, 1938), p. 274. Note the explanation on pp. 291-2.

24. Cheng, *Oriental Immigration*, pp. 64-5; Robert Edward Wynne, "Reaction to the Chinese in the Pacific Northwest and British Columbia, 1850-1910," pp. 396-7.

25. Cheng, *Oriental Immigration*, pp. 67-70.

26. Ken Adachi, *The Enemy That Never Was: A History of Japanese Canadians* (Toronto, 1976), pp. 53-5. Ten years later the Chinese unsuccessfully tested the B.C. Elections Law as far as the Supreme Court of Canada. See Morris Davis and Joseph F. Krauter, *The Other Canadians* (Toronto, 1971), p. 64.

27. Lee Tung-hai, p. 490.

28. Toronto *Globe*, 21 September 1907; Cheng, *Oriental Immigration*, pp. 73-4.

29. James Morton, *In the Sea of Sterile Mountains, the Chinese in British Columbia*, pp. 102, 107, 118, 162-3, 178, 188ff., 196-7; Adachi, *The Enemy That Never Was*, p. 72.

30. *Calgary Herald*, 14 September 1907.

31. The following description of the 1907 Riot is based upon Adachi, *The Enemy That Never Was*, Chapter 3; and Howard S. Sugimoto, "The Vancouver Riots of 1907: A Canadian Episode," in H. Conroy and T.S. Miyakawa (eds.), *East Across the Pacific* (Honolulu, 1972), pp. 92-126. Another account and additional references are found in Ward, *White Canada Forever*, pp. 67-70, notes 49-50.

32. Vancouver *Province*, 9 September 1907, quoted in Sugimoto, "The Vancouver Riots," p. 102.

33. Vancouver *World*, 9-12 September, quoted in Sugimoto, "The Vancouver Riots," p. 102.

34. *Vancouver News-Advertiser*, 8 September 1907, quoted in Sugimoto, "The Vancouver Riots," p. 101.

35. Sugimoto, "The Vancouver Riots," p. 99.

36. Quoted in Adachi, *The Enemy That Never Was*, p. 77.
37. *Ibid.*, p. 79.
38. Toronto *Globe*, 21 September 1907.
39. Sugimoto, "The Vancouver Riots," p. 107.
40. Quoted in *ibid.*
41. *Ibid.*, pp. 108-9; Adachi, *The Enemy That Never Was*, pp. 80-1.

PART TWO

1911-1923

SEVEN

Expansion and Diversity

Following the Murphy Commission report,[1] the Chinese communities dropped from the headlines in Canadian newspapers. Nevertheless, in relative obscurity, significant growth was taking place. By 1911 there were Chinese living in every part of Canada, with the exception of the Yukon and the Northwest Territories. Of the approximately 28,000 Chinese known to be in the country, almost 20,000 (or 70 per cent) were still living in British Columbia.[2]

With the completion of the CPR in the 1880's, however, Chinese had begun to move eastward. By 1911 there were over 1,700 living in Alberta – mostly in Calgary, Edmonton, and Lethbridge – with smaller numbers in places such as Medicine Hat, Red Deer, Fort Macleod, and Canmore. In Saskatchewan, Moose Jaw was initially one of the largest settlements, with over 160 Chinese and over twenty businesses by 1911. Other settlements were made in Regina, Swift Current, Battleford, and Saskatoon. In Manitoba, Brandon and Winnipeg were the major Chinese settlements, totalling together some 900 persons.[3]

Even before the railway was completed there were a few Chinese in Toronto, probably numbering 100 or more by the 1890's. Toronto grew rapidly during the first decade of the twentieth century and its Chinese population grew with equal rapidity. By 1910, of the 2,800 Chinese recorded as living in Ontario, at least 1,000 of these were in Toronto, and a Chinatown section of the city was identifiable in the area of Queen and King Streets, East and West. Elsewhere in Ontario, small Chinese communities were scattered in towns such as Kingston, London, Hamilton, Sudbury, Timmins, North Bay, Windsor, and Ottawa.[4]

Like Toronto, Montreal had a few Chinese inhabitants before the completion of the CPR. There is evidence of a few Chinese registered for language study at a Montreal Catholic school in 1863.[5] But as late as 1881 there were no more than seven Chinese in all of Quebec, probably all in Montreal. By 1912, however, the Montreal Chinese community had reached a size of 1,000, comparable to Toronto's. Montreal also served

91

as both a departure point and a supply base for emigrants to the Maritimes, who were not numerous enough to establish Chinatowns of their own and hence continued to draw on Montreal for supplies and news of China and Chinese affairs.[6]

By 1911 there were over 200 Chinese settlers in the Maritimes and Chinese had begun to settle in Newfoundland in the 1890's. Immigrants to Newfoundland rarely arrived via Canada. Instead they came direct from Hong Kong or Europe, or else through New York in bond. Their numbers were small; as late as 1922 there were only about seventy or eighty Chinese in St. John's. The Chinese Immigration Act of 1906 of Newfoundland was similar to Canadian legislation; it required a head tax of $300 and placed a limit of one Chinese passenger per every fifty tons' weight per ship.[7]

In both Vancouver and Victoria, where the Chinese communities had become well-established, Chinese were moving into a variety of occupations. They were to be found working as tailors, jewellers, photographers, shoemakers, and in other trades that served both the Chinese community and white society. On the fringes of these cities there were also Chinese produce-growers and shingle-mill workers.

Outside of British Columbia, however, Chinese were found almost exclusively in the laundry, grocery, and restaurant businesses.[8] In Alberta, for example, while a few found jobs as miners, most Chinese became laundrymen and cooks. Secondary occupations included grocery operators, suburban market gardeners, and domestic servants. The directory listings for Calgary in 1911 are typical of the small-scale, single male nature of Chinese enterprise in Canada at that time. It appears that there were at least 314 small stores (groceries, restaurants, laundries, and tobacconists) operated by the 482 males and three females who, according to the census, comprised Calgary's Chinese population.[9]

In Winnipeg by the 1890's there were eleven laundries on King, Princess, James, and Main Streets. Winnipeg's Chinese colony is of particular interest because of the early dominance of people surnamed Lee from the county of Hok-san in Guangdong. The Lees excluded all other Chinese from Winnipeg, and it was not until after 1910 that their monopoly was broken.[10]

A similar situation developed in the Maritimes, where immigration was dominated by a few surnames, who tended to monopolize the few occupations that were open to Chinese, thereby preventing the settlement of other Chinese. In this kind of situation it sometimes happened that two surname groups in a given settlement would bring with them to Canada a long-standing clan or lineage feud from China. This was to be a source of the violence that has plagued Chinese communities in Canada.[11]

In many communities the earliest organization was the Cheekungtong (CKT), whose members took it with them as they migrated across the country. In many localities all or most of the job opportunities open to

Chinese were monopolized by the CKT, so that if one wished to work in those towns it was necessary to become a CKT member.

Nevertheless, apart from these few restrictive communities, by 1911 most Canadian cities with a significant Chinese population had established Chinatowns, which provided the services appropriate to a Chinese population large enough to need Chinese restaurants, Chinese groceries, and other Chinese businesses. There were Chinese laundries in or near Chinatown that served a non-Chinese clientele, but there were also Chinese laundries well outside of Chinatown, which were also the places of residence of their operators and workers. This was not surprising, since Chinese hand laundries and, to a lesser extent, Chinese-operated grocery stores and Chinese-owned restaurants that served Western food were conveniences to white society only if they were conveniently located in relation to their customers. Whatever their feelings about large groups of Chinese, white neighbourhoods, in the interests of convenience to themselves, could easily tolerate the existence of individual laundries with live-in Chinese, just as they could accept individual Chinese living in white households as servants. Chinatown served as both a Chinese city within a Western city and as a supply and service base for Chinese individuals and businesses scattered in many parts of the city.

However, the tolerance of whites for occasional Chinese residents outside of Chinatown did not extend to instances when a Chinese laundry or restaurant was believed by neighbourhood ratepayers and merchants to be detrimental to property values or to the neighbourhood environment.[12] In most instances the criticisms levelled against laundries were that they were unsanitary. In Calgary, Lethbridge, and Fort Macleod there were by-laws aimed at restricting or eliminating their operation in certain areas. Calgary's Chinatown was forced to change location twice between 1900 and 1910 because urban expansion made the property occupied – but not owned – by the Chinese desirable for other uses. Only in 1910 and only by buying property, did the Chinese succeed in establishing what was to be a permanent Chinatown, and only then after prolonged discussion with whites, who found the crowded Chinese rooming houses (*fang-kou*) unhealthy and agreed to the proposed location because the Chinese were unwelcome everywhere else.[13]

Hostility to the developing Chinatowns was also fed by lurid accounts of opium and white-slave traffic. Typical of these sentiments is this 1911 description of Toronto's Chinatown in the muckraking newspaper, *Jack Canuck*:

> Are the Chinese stores, laundries and restaurants, so thickly abounding on King, Queen and York Streets, which these unfortunate girls are alleged to frequent, "dens"? If so why the tolerant attitude of our Morality Department towards them? . . .
>
> One need only stroll through the above mentioned blocks and notice the throngs of Chinese lounging in the streets and doorways

to realize that the "Yellow Peril" is more than a mere word in this city.

In 1907, even the reputable Toronto paper, the *Globe*, had published an editorial on the "Asiatic Peril to National Life." Asian immigrants could never become good citizens of Canada, it argued, because the Asian intellect was incompatible with Anglo-Saxon democracy. Hence, the presence of a large number of Asians could only lead to "national decay" through making it impossible for Canada to develop and sustain its "national character." It was, the editorialist concluded, as great a mistake to create Chinatowns in the West as it was for Westerners to establish Western colonies in the Chinese treaty ports. The two sides and their institutions and intellects were hopelessly incompatible. In Montreal, too, anti-Asian expressions appeared early. In 1899 the *Gazette* had written:

> John Chinaman is too much with us, not only in Montreal, but in all the cities and large towns of Quebec and Ontario. He displaces Christian labour, and is in no sense a welcome or desirable addition to our population.

The Chinese did, however, have their defenders, particularly among the Presbyterian and Methodist missionaries, who often attempted to make their mission buildings into centres of Chinese community life and provided dormitory facilities for young Chinese men. In the small Chinese community of Edmonton, for example, they were active spreading both their faith and their language, the latter through courses in English. In Montreal, also, Presbyterian missionaries to the Chinese community supported the latter in protests against discriminatory legislation. A notable instance was a protest against a Quebec tax law aimed at Chinese laundries. Like other missionaries, however, they were critical of gambling and what they considered the various other social evils of the Chinese community.

A NEW GENERATION

During the period 1911-14 the annual rate of Chinese immigration was higher than it had been at any time since 1904. The findings of the Murphy Commission concerning methods of illegal immigration seemingly had no effect upon immigration rates; the general trend towards prosperity in Canada apparently did. From a level of 2,000 entrants per year in 1910, the annual rate advanced to levels of 5,000 to 7,000.[14] The really significant development, however, was an increase in the number of women. Up to 1911 the Chinese population had been essentially made up of adult males and teen-age boys, the latter coming over to work with their fathers, uncles, or brothers. After 1911 there were many more women and, with them, many more small children, particularly in Vancouver, which had replaced Victoria by 1911 as the largest and most dynamic Chinese community. A missionary report of 1919 noted that there were 210 families in a Vancouver Chinese population of 6,000. This may be compared with 150 families in the older Victoria community of 3,000 persons and only thirty-five families in the younger Toronto community of 2,100.

This comparatively large influx of children and the maturation of the small number of merchants' children born in the 1890's added up, by 1915, to a small but visible new generation of Chinese either born in Canada or brought here at an early age.[15] In 1915 the Victoria Chinese school was able to graduate its first full high school class, a group of twelve, including both boys and girls. By 1920 the school had an enrolment of about 100, about the same as that of the Vancouver Chinese Public School. Despite the larger size of the Vancouver community and the greater influx of children there after 1911, Victoria held its own in school registration, probably because it was an older, more settled community, having more well-established merchants and thereby more families that were established earlier than Vancouver did.

The earliest Chinese-Canadian university students now began to appear. The University of British Columbia was barely established when Susan Yipsang, a daughter of the pioneer merchant Yip Sang, enrolled in 1914-15. Whether she was the earliest Canadian-born student of Chinese background at a Canadian university is not certain, but she certainly must have been the first woman student of such a background. Other Chinese-Canadian students quickly followed and by the middle 1930's eleven students of Chinese background had graduated from the University of British Columbia.

Besides the new generation of Chinese Canadians there were now students coming from China for study at Canadian universities. The first of these attended McGill as early as 1906. Some others, including the Kuomintang activist Chan Sue-yan, who was a part-time student, found their way to the University of British Columbia. The significant thing is that some of these visiting students became active in Chinese-Canadian community affairs, allying themselves with the new generation of Canadian-born Chinese.

There now were also young Chinese individuals, recently graduated from mission schools in China, coming to Canada not to study but to aid in missionary work among the Canadian Chinese. Chinese of this kind already knew English and possessed some of the cultural skills needed to become leaders in Canadian Chinese communities. A good example of this type of person is Mak Tso-chow (T.C. Mark), who arrived in Toronto about 1914. He was the founder of the Toronto Chinese school, working closely with the Reverend Ma T.K. Wou, who had come from China to Victoria some years earlier. T.C. Mark joined a group of young Chinese who had founded the Chinese Christian Association in Toronto which, for the next ten to fifteen years, was to be the most effective spokesman for the community interests of Toronto's Chinese.[16]

The presence of young Chinese trained in China proved to be a leavening agent in Canadian Chinese communities. So did the ideas that came from China at this time. It was a time when youth in China were speaking out on political issues affecting their country. The May Fourth Movement, an amorphous intellectual and political development that extended from 1915 well into the 1920's, began with student and other youth reaction to the humiliating experience of Japan's Twenty-One Demands of China. It grew into a vast movement that involved all major cities in China and stimulated great intellectual activity in universities and high schools as well as a wide range of political activity.

The May Fourth Movement was fuelled partly by Chinese students returning from advanced study in the West. At the same time the small number of Chinese students who came to Canada brought with them some of the intellectual and political ferment of the May Fourth era. They found a ready response among the younger generation of Chinese Canadians and in the 1915-23 period speech-making by young Chinese Canadians became a common phenomenon.[17]

Missionary influence on the new generation was substantial. Apart from a few isolated clergymen working in British Columbia, Protestant missions among the Chinese had not begun in earnest until the 1880's and the Presbyterians and Methodists were especially active. They aimed their activities particularly at young men in the Chinese communities. Most missionaries viewed gambling and opium smoking as Chinese community vices which originated in lack of alternative activities for Chinese during their non-working hours. The goal of the missionaries was to prevent younger men from engaging in these activities by providing other activities and residential accommodations that were physically removed from such vices. Typically, each Protestant mission, besides its street preaching, took organized youth activities as a major obligation and provided dormitory space for young men whenever its physical premises would permit. These and other church activities proved to be attractive to many young Chinese Canadians.[18]

YMCA organizations were particularly popular. Typically, a mission would spawn a YMCA almost as soon as the mission itself was organized. The YMCA movement had come to Canada in the 1850's, shortly after its foundation in England. By the 1880's it had reached China where, after 1911, it was enjoying its period of greatest popularity. In China the identification of the YMCA with secular features of Protestant Christianity – the social gospel; social services of all kinds; a positive, forward-looking, modernizing optimism – evoked a ready response among the new, urban, middle class of business and professional people and intellectuals.[19]

In Canada, these same features appealed to idealistic young Chinese Canadians who were concerned about both their own community and the future of China. Of perhaps even greater appeal was the fact that in Canada, as in China, YMCAs were organized and run largely by young Chinese themselves, not by their missionary mentors. The desire for autonomy of some Christian Chinese in Canada is very evident in the various independent associations they established. In Montreal, strong-minded young men broke away from the leadership of Reverend Chan Nam Sing and formed their own Young Men's Christian Institution (YMCI).[20] In other places YMCIs or "Chinese Christian Associations," with varying degrees of autonomy, were founded, mostly under the leadership of young men who wished to reduce missionary tutelage and to exercise more of the leadership themselves.

In Vancouver a separate congregation, the Christ Church of China, was established in 1911, breaking away from a Presbyterian mission con-gregation. Made up of Chinese of all ages, many of them Christians before their arrival in Canada, it was to have a long and distinguished history under several volunteer ministers.

Christ Church of China is remarkable in several respects. Although it began as a Presbyterian offshoot, it developed as a self-consciously ecumenical Protestant body, drawing for its membership and financial support from Chinese adherents of all Protestant denominations. Its leaders were lay preachers and Chinese ministers – often retired from ac-tive service – who served in rotation. It maintained itself this way over many decades. A major reason for its existence, according to one of its leaders, was to demonstrate to the Chinese of the 1911-23 era that there was no necessary contradiction between acceptance of the white man's religion and maintenance of one's autonomy and cultural identity.[21]

One attraction of the missions, YMCAs, and Christian Associations was that they provided lessons, usually in the evenings, in the English lan-guage. To a young, ambitious Chinese a workable knowledge of English was the key to success in Canadian society and, in some respects, a key to a leadership position even within the Chinese community.

In Toronto Christian influence was particularly strong. Protestant missionaries had begun work among Toronto's Chinese by the 1880's. In 1905 the Chinese Presbyterian Church was established. Fifteen years later missionary work in Toronto and in other parts of Canada east of Manitoba was administratively organized into the Eastern Canada Mis-sion, headed by energetic leaders like W.D. Noyes and A.E. Armstrong, and with its headquarters in Toronto. Toronto was also the headquarters of the Canadian Presbyterian missions and, later, United Church mis-sions to China. Toronto's new generation of young Chinese were, therefore, in touch with church leaders of experience, stature, and in-fluence beyond that of most missionaries working among the Chinese in other parts of Canada.

In British Columbia the arrival of a new, politically conscious genera-tion was signalled by the founding of the Chinese Canadian Club, or Tong-yuen Wui (literally: "common-origin association"), in Victoria in 1914 and in Vancouver soon after. Despite the name, membership was not limited to Canadian-born Chinese. Foon Sien, for example – a later leader who was born in China and came at an early age to Canada – was a

97

member. The Chinese Canadian Club represented the new generation as we have defined it: persons born in Canada, others born in China but coming to Canada when very young, and China-based mission-assistants and students in Canadian schools. It emerged in Victoria and Vancouver during World War I and it was recognized during the early and middle 1920's as one of the major associations in the Vancouver-Victoria Chinatowns.

The new generation provided some new leaders, but they were just beginning to emerge as such by about 1920. Their relationship to the older generation was quite unlike that of the Japanese-Canadian *nisei* vis-à-vis the *issei*. In the Japanese case the *issei* maintained control over Japanese communities until the onset of World War II when, unable to cope with relocation, they simply lost it overnight to the *nisei*.[22] In the Chinese case, there was no challenge or break. Some of the new generation of Chinese Canadians were as different from their elders, and as Canadianized, as the Japanese *nisei*. But there was no single issue like the crisis of World War II to challenge the generations. Instead, some members of the new generation moved into leadership positions in the 1920's alongside their elders. Among the leaders of the 1920's there were also relative newcomers from China who, although young, were not as Canadianized as were the members of the new generation.

NOTES

1. The details of this commission's findings may be pursued in *Report of Mr. Justice Murphy, Royal Commission Appointed to Investigate Alleged Chinese Frauds and Opium Smuggling on the Pacific Coast, 1910-11* (Ottawa, 1913); Public Archives of Canada (PAC), Immigration, RG 76, vols. 120, 121, file 23635, part 2: Public Archives of British Columbia (PABC), Attorney General's Files, David C. Lew Letterbooks, 1907-1908; and January, 1911, issues of the Vancouver *Province* and the Vancouver *World*.
2. *Census of Canada*, 1911, II, pp. 340-1.
3. *Ibid.*, pp. 162-9; and Huang Jin (ed.), *Wanguo jishin bianlan* (International Chinese Business Directory) (San Francisco, 1913), pp. 1372-7, 1383.
4. Paul Levine, "Historical Documentation Pertaining to Overseas Chinese Organizations" (M.A. thesis, University of Toronto, 1975), pp. 78-83; Gordon Taylor, conversation with Johnson, Willmott, and Wickberg, 19 June 1974; Gary Kenneth Lawrence, "The Windsor Chinese Community," reprint from Chinese Students Association, *University of Windsor Magazine* (December, 1976), pp. 1, 4; Seto Chong-yim, interview with H. Con, R. Con, and Wickberg, Ottawa, 5 June 1973; *Census of Canada*, 1911, II, pp. 372-4.

5. Rev. Thomas Tou, "A Brief History of the Chinese Mission and its School," *Mandike Zhonghua Tianzhutang chengli wushi zhounian jinian tekan, 1822-1972* (Montreal, 1972), p. 25.

6. Gordon Taylor, conversation, 19 June 1974.

7. Memorial University of Newfoundland, Chinese Student Society (comp.), "Chinese Community in Newfoundland" (St. John's, 1977?), pp. 17-24.

8. Charles P. Sedgwick, "The Context of Economic Change and Continuity in an Urban Overseas Chinese Community," Chapters V-VI; Huang Jin (ed.), "International Chinese Business Directory," pp. 1354-85.

9. J. Brian Dawson, "The Chinese Experience in Frontier Calgary," pp. 133, 136.

10. Gustavo de Roza, *A Feasibility Study for the Redevelopment of China-town in Winnipeg* (1974), pp. 61-4; and C. Millien, E. Woo, and R. Yeh (eds.), *Winnipeg Chinese* (Ottawa: Secretary of State, 1971), pp. 8-13.

11. For a spectacular example of these problems, see Public Archives of Newfoundland, files on Wo Fen Game murder case.

12. Examples are found in Vancouver City Archives, City Clerk's Incoming Correspondence, RG 2 A1, vol. 31, pp. 24604-5; vol. 30, p. 24218; vol. 35, p. 26525; vol. 15, pp. 11766-7.

13. Dawson, "The Chinese Experience," pp. 134-40.

14. R. Sampat-Mehta, *International Barriers: Aliens, Immigration, and Citizenship in Canada*, p. 82.

15. This group, though small, is the true second generation. However, with the influx of immigrants after 1947, a large, more prominent second generation of Chinese grew up, and the term "second generation" is also applied to them. Whenever possible we have tried to indicate which group is being referred to in the text.

16. *Jianada Dulangdu Zhonghua Jidujiao Qingnian Hui, jianlou baogao* (Toronto, 1927), pp. 2-3; and "Memoirs of Anna Ma," typescript (ca. 1973).

17. See issues of the *Chinese Times*, 1915-1923, especially those of August-September, 1919.

18. "Religious and Missionary Survey," UCCA, Presbyterian Church, British Columbia, 1888-1925, Box 3, letters to R.P. MacKay from missionaries in British Columbia, 1917-1924.

19. Shirley Garrett, *Social Reformers in Urban China. The Chinese Y.M.C.A., 1895-1926* (Cambridge, Mass., 1970), Chapters 2, 4-6.

20. See *Mancheng Zhonghua Jidujiao Qingnian Hui jinxi jinian tekan* (Montreal, 1961); and UCCA, Presbyterian Church, Montreal, 1894-1925, Box 6.

21. "Religious and Missionary Survey," UCCA, Presbyterian Church, British Columbia, 1888-1925, Box 3, Duncanson to Armstrong, 16 July, 10 September 1914; Rev. Lum Jo-yin, interview with Willmott, 13, 20 July 1961. In the missionary correspondence it is said that the new congrega-

tion was founded by "the more substantial Chinese." Subsequent membership, however, seems to have come from all classes. Rev. Lum Jo-yin, interviews, Vancouver, 13, 20 July 1961.

22. See Adachi, *The Enemy That Never Was: A History of Japanese Canadians*, Chapter 7 and after.

EIGHT

Revolution in China, Organization in Canada

CHINATOWN POLITICS

Between 1911 and 1923 two major political events pulled at Canada's Chinese. These were the 1911 Revolution in China and the First World War. The 1911 Revolution pulled them towards China; World War I pulled them in the direction of Canada. The 1911 Revolution generated great excitement in Chinese communities abroad. It held great promise for China's modernization, strengthening, and, after years of humiliation, recovery of the world's respect.

Although Overseas Chinese had always been tied to China by personal links, their political ties began to appear only in the 1870's. At that time the Qing government recognized the value of the Overseas Chinese as a source of funds and began granting honorary titles to major contributors of funds. By the 1890's wealthy Overseas Chinese could purchase offices in the Qing bureaucracy. Shortly after 1900 the Qing government encouraged the leading Chinese businessmen overseas to organize Chambers of Commerce, which were supposed to work closely with similar bodies then being formed in China and, through them, with the Qing government. The *quid pro quo* for Overseas Chinese funds was protection of their overseas interests. Investigating commissions were sent out to determine the conditions under which Overseas Chinese lived and consulates were established where possible to protect Overseas Chinese lives and properties.[1]

In the case of Canada, Li Hongzhang's visit of 1896, which included discussion of the condition of the Canadian Chinese, and the visit of a Qing educational commission in 1908 were evidences of this concern. Funds were made available to assist in constructing a new building in Victoria to house an expanded school, to be called (so the donor government hoped) The Great Qing School. As it turned out, the Victorian Chinese organizers of the school called it the Chinese Public School.[2] Another evidence of Qing concern for the Chinese in Canada was the establishment of a consulate-general in Ottawa in 1908. A Vancouver consulate, subordinate to it, was established shortly after.

From the 1890's to 1911 Qing government efforts to woo the Overseas Chinese became more urgent in competition with those of Chinese reformers and revolutionaries in exile who had scattered to Chinese communities around the world. The reformers and revolutionaries competed against each other as well as against Qing-sponsored activities. The result of this rivalry was greatly to intensify the political aspects of Chinese community life in Canada. If before these communities had been only mildly political, they now became exceedingly so. From the 1890's it became clear that China was entering a period of drastic changes in the direction of modernization. In whose hands would those changes take place and under what political forms? Would the Qing dynasty somehow stay on top, providing continuity and stability, or would there be a revolution with a new form of government as well as a new group of power-holders? It was a time of great political uncertainty. The revolutionaries preached the overthrow of the Qing dynasty, not merely to make way for republicanism, but because the Qing was alien in origin, a Manchu group, whose political dominance over the Han Chinese was symbolized in the queue hairstyle required of all Han Chinese males as a mark of submission. Cutting off one's queue became a symbol of revolt and in the decade before 1911 in Canada, as elsewhere in Overseas Chinese communities, there were Chinese who removed their queues, other who kept theirs, and still others who either hid a retained queue under a hat or else kept a false queue to fasten on in moments of danger or indecision.

Whatever the political outcome might be, the role of the Overseas Chinese in the hoped-for new, modern, prestigious China was bound to be important. A strong China would be able to protect their interests as a weak China had not and could not. There could be no $500 head tax applicable only to Chinese among all immigrants to Canada if there were a strong, modern China. A strong, modern China would provide the prerequisites of prosperity for relatives at home and better investment and retirement opportunities when they returned to China.

Thus, whether in terms of immediate interest overseas or long-term interest in their future in China, the Chinese in Canada had good reason to become involved in Chinese politics. So long as their opportunities in Canada were restricted and so long as many saw their futures as being tied to China, this was inevitable. There was also patriotism that went beyond self-interest – a patriotism born of pride in Chinese civilization and one's identification with a country once the most powerful and now seemingly helpless, exploited and despised by other countries as a "mere geographic expression," not a modern nation.

We have seen that during his visits to North America before 1911 Sun Yat-sen had sought CKT support for his proposed revolution and an alliance between the CKT and his own loose political organization, the

T'ung Meng Hui. At one point Sun and his lieutenant, Feng Tzu-yu, had formally become CKT members, thereby gaining introductions and access to CKT circles. Sun's third visit in January, 1911, was much more exciting than his two previous ones had been.[3] His daily lectures at the Chinese theatre on Canton Alley drew packed audiences of 1,000 or more each time, including many who were not sympathetic to the cause or revolution. Sun, in a letter to the CKT headquarters in San Francisco, expressed it this way:

> Since I arrived in Vancouver on the 8th, I have been royally received by all. Every day I lecture at the [CKT] hall or the theatre to audiences of 2-3,000. Even though it rains heavily there is enthusiasm unprecedented in Vancouver. If people feel this way, the success of the Revolution is inevitable.[4]

Sun and leading CKT figures in Vancouver, like Chen Wenxi, Liu Rukun, and Chin Fashen, quickly established a fund-raising bureau. But as Feng Tzu-yu pointed out, rank and file members of the CKT, the most likely contributors, were mostly labourers and could afford only small contributions. The quickest way to raise large amounts would be if the CKT headquarters in Victoria could be persuaded to mortgage its headquarters building. The Victoria headquarters agreed to the idea, but the money thus derived fell short of the $10,000 hoped for. Accordingly, Lim Bang and two other Victoria merchants pledged $1,600 and another $900 was borrowed from a Canadian bank. Other branches of the CKT responded readily. The Montreal, Ottawa, and Toronto branches raised HK $40,000, of which $10,000 came from mortgaging the Toronto branch's building and $4,000 from mortgaging the Montreal branch's building. The Vancouver branch contributed HK $20,000. CKT branches in smaller British Columbia communities produced HK $10,000. Altogether the amount raised exceeded HK $100,000, or Can. $35,000.[5]

While Sun was in Toronto, the abortive Huang Hua Kang Uprising broke out at Canton, on March 29, 1911. Sun was upset at the news, knowing that the revolutionaries were ill-prepared. As he feared, the revolt failed and was ruthlessly suppressed by the Qing government. Of the many executed, seventy-two bodies were recovered and later enshrined as revolutionary martyrs. Some years later a monument to these martyrs was built. On it are inscribed the names of cities and towns in western Canada and the Chinese organizations in them that contributed financially to this unsuccessful uprising.[5]

Revolution finally did come to China in October of 1911. The Qing dynasty collapsed and a republic was established in its place. Once again, merchants both within China and overseas helped pay for the Revolution.

The fall of the Qing dynasty did not usher in a millennium of stability and modernity in China. Instead, the next several years were ones of factionalism, division, and violence, which was reflected in the life of

Chinese communities in Canada. The Republic had been established through a compromise between the republican supporters of Sun Yat-sen (mostly South Chinese) and the conservative, North China-based backers of the militarist president, Yuan Shikai. Two years of struggle followed between a parliament bent on representative government and a president inclined toward dictatorship. Soon after 1911, Sun's associates founded another political party, the Kuomintang (KMT) which soon came to dominate the parliament and provided the strongest opposition to Yuan Shikai. Yuan dismissed parliament in 1915 and until his death a year later ruled as dictator. A North-South division now appeared. Yuan's ex-commanders and other warlords struggled over North China and, from Peking, claimed to rule the whole country. In the South, other warlords refused to acknowledge them and in Shanghai and Canton, Sun Yat-sen, in alliance with regional and local militarists, established "southern" governments, which also claimed legitimate rule over all of China.

In Canada these events exacerbated existing conflicts and introduced new ones, expecially in the largest Chinese communities of Victoria and Vancouver. The KMT set up a branch in Canada known as the Chinese Nationalist League. Prominent among its organizers were the founders of the earlier Chi-chi She, Seto Ying-shek, Chu Chi-ngok, and Wu Shang-ying. Seto was a leader in education and in CBA affairs in Victoria and Vancouver. Chu was to be for many years editor of the CKT newspaper in Vancouver. Wu later became a high-level official in various governments in China. The Kuomintang established a newspaper in Victoria, the *New Republic* (*Hsin Min-kuo Pao*), which was affiliated with the Kuomintang newspaper, *The Young China* (*Shao-nien Chung-kuo Ch'en-pao*), of San Francisco. The CKT reacted to these developments with resentful anger. CKT leaders had understood that Sun Yat-sen had promised rewards in the form of offices and influence in the new republic to CKT adherents, in exchange for their contributions to the 1911 Revolution. Instead, they had received only an expression of thanks. The upstart Kuomintang was acting as if it were the progenitor of the Chinese Revolution. The resentment of CKT leaders in Canada and the United States toward Sun and the Kuomintang seems to be the origin of the CKT-KMT friction, which was intense during the period 1911-1923 and reappeared periodically over the next several years.[6]

The Empire Reform Association also opposed the Kuomintang for reasons that seem as much related to personalities and political competition as to matters of political principle. After the disappearance of the Chinese Empire in 1912 this association had adopted the name Constitutionalist Party, or Xianzhengdang (XZD), and had continued to take Kang Youwei and Liang Qichao as its leaders. Kang's and Liang's political manoeuvres in China usually put them in positions opposed to those of Sun, and their followers consistently opposed Sun's party. In Canada the Constitutionalists (XZD) tended to oppose what they saw as the radicalism and trouble-making activities of the Chinese Nationalist League.

It was difficult for anything to remain apolitical in Canada's Chinatowns. In an age when force seemed to be the only effective means of political action in China, the Canadian Chinese were finding themselves drawn in the direction of violence in Chinese politics. When Yuan Shikai had attempted to make himself emperor in 1916, a brigade of Overseas Chinese from Canada set out to help stop him. In the preceding year military units had been formed in Vancouver, Edmonton, Saskatoon, Lethbridge, and Victoria. A unit of over 200 men embarked for China. Yuan died before they arrived, but the unit was sent to Shandong province where it remained for several months. When Sun Yat-sen established his "southern" government at Canton in September, 1917, part of this group went to join him; the remainder returned to Canada. Some of the former eventually became part of Sun's bodyguard detachment and, after Sun's burial in 1929, two served as honour guards at his mausoleum for some years.[7]

At the same time, aviation units, which Sun Yat-sen was to use in various ways after 1917, began training under Western instructors at Esquimalt, B.C., and at Saskatoon.[8] Money also continued to come to Sun from Canada. Of an estimated Mex. $11,962 sent by Overseas Chinese to Sun Yat-sen in 1922, Canada's contribution was $2,258 – almost 20 per cent, and second only to that from San Francisco.[9]

Violence appeared again in the murder of Tang Hualong in September, 1918. Tang was a political figure previously associated with the Northern (Peking) government who was travelling in North America. In Victoria he was shot and killed by a young man said to be a member of the Kuomintang, although the Kuomintang implication was later called into question.[10]

Between 1911 and 1917 the Kuomintang had grown to a position of some importance in Canadian Chinese communities. In some places there were Kuomintang schools and KMT members sat on executive boards of local Chinese Benevolent Associations. But the Kuomintang's position was precarious. The various consular officials of China in Canada represented first the Yuan government and later various Northern (Peking) governments. They would hardly be sympathetic to supporters of Sun Yat-sen, and, in fact, they sometimes attempted to persuade Canadian government officials that Kuomintang adherents were violent radicals whose activities were dangerous to the stability and orderliness of Canadian Chinese communities and thereby threatened Canadian security and the Canadian war effort.[11] There is evidence that the Canadian government accepted at least some of these arguments. The office of the Chief Press Censor, established in 1915 as a wartime measure, monitored telegrams sent and received by various Chinese organizations. It was particularly concerned about possible KMT efforts to communicate with Germany. By early 1917 the Northern (Peking) government in China was moving China into World War I on the side of the Western Allies against Germany. This would make China and Canada allies, hence the concern that the Southern government supporters, the Kuomintang, might be intriguing with Germany. No evidence of such intrigue has been found. Information furnished by the consulate, however, was cited as one factor in the eventual decision to outlaw the KMT.[12]

In November, 1918, the Kuomintang, three related organizations (the *New Republic* newspaper, the Min Sing Reading Room, and the Kwong Chow Min Kuun Association), and the Chinese Labour Association (Zhonghua Gongdang) were all banned by the Canadian government and some of their leaders imprisoned. The war was ending, however, and the proscription lasted only six months. Both the KMT and the Labour Association were in operation again by the summer of 1919.[13]

ORGANIZATIONAL GROWTH

The political violence of these years was accompanied by organizational growth in Chinese communities across Canada. The decade 1911-23 witnessed a proliferation of organizations probably unmatched in any previous decade. The reasons were many: the appeal of Chinese politics; the opportunity to participate in the economic and educational modernization of China; the growth in size of various Chinese communities in Canada; the new occupations into which Chinese had begun to move; and the new leadership emerging in these communities. All of these developments produced a number of organizations whose reference was China and several others that were responses to restrictions on the opportunities of Chinese in Canada.

Let us consider the various kinds of organizations that were found in Chinese communities during this decade. There are four basic types of association characteristic of Overseas Chinese communities everywhere: the community-wide body, the fraternal-political association, the district association, and the clan association. The community-wide organization attempts to control the community internally while representing it externally to the host society and government. Typically, it is an "umbrella" organization, in the sense that it usually represents, in one way or another, all the organizations in the community. It therefore occupies the organizational apex in the community. The fraternal-political association is usually concerned with the local welfare and recreational needs of its members, but more specifically with politics, whether in China or the host country. Its membership cuts across lines of kinship or place of origin. The district association, whose members are from the same county or sub-county locality in China, is concerned with the welfare and development of that county and the well-being of county residents overseas. The clan association's membership is based upon a common surname or small group of surnames whose bearers are considered to be related to one another. Its interests and functions overlap those of the district association. By 1923 representatives of each of these types of organization were found in Canada's Chinese communities, and there were other types of organization as well.

By 1923 community-wide organizations mostly in the form of Chinese Benevolent Associations had been established across Canada, in Victoria, Vancouver, Winnipeg, Toronto, and Montreal. In 1919, Ottawa, with a small Chinese population of only 300-500, had formed a "United Chinese Association," under the leadership of Hum Quon and Wong Xianying, which functioned much like a CBA.[14] The Saskatoon Chinese community, which had expanded rapidly in this decade, had an informal association of what were then the leading organizations in the community: the Kuomintang, the Youth Association, and the Overseas Chinese Reading Room.[15] Kingston, with a Chinese community of only 100, had a CBA, but its existence was precarious and short-lived. Since half of the members of the community were Kuomintang adherents, KMT decisions tended to be community decisions.[16] There were many communities across Canada in which either the Kuomintang or else the Cheekungtong dominated. In the case of Kingston, and perhaps in similar cases of one-party domination, organization of a CBA might be the minority's way to make itself heard. If so, the existence of all such CBAs was likely to be precarious.

In Toronto the CBA was not the unquestioned spokesman of the Toronto community. In particular, the Chinese Christian Association, or Young Men's Christian Institute, founded around 1910, immediately interested itself in the affairs of the community as a whole – non-Christians as well as Christians. Its leaders represented Toronto not only at meetings of eastern Canadian Chinese community-wide organizations, but also of youth and other organizations in the eastern and northern United States, where contacts were made and information exchanged about comparable community problems, such as immigration policy and legislation.

Montreal's "CBA," called the Chinese Association of Montreal, was established in 1914 in specific response to the agitation of an association of white owners of mechanized laundries against Chinese hand laundries. The Chinese Association was organized and financed through the efforts of the CKT, the Constitutionalist Party (XZD), and six clan associations, and the subscriptions for its foundation were paid by 600 stores.[17]

In Winnipeg the task of organization was more difficult. There were 1,000 Chinese in that city and many stores supported the idea of a CBA with contributions. Political friction, however, seems to have been the reason for the delay in founding the association from 1917, when first proposed, to 1919.[18]

Co-ordinating organizations, such as the CBAs, attempted to control the community internally by mediating disputes while speaking for it ex-

107

ternally to Canadian government and society. Although they assumed a representative character, they were usually in practice led by the more powerful and influential businessmen in the communities where they existed. Still, some form of representation in elections seems to have been emerging as a principle during this period. In Montreal, for example, the CBA executive was chosen to represent occupations. In Edmonton, where a CBA was not established until 1932, the three most important executive positions were to represent the three dominant clan associations, the Mah, Wong, and Gee, but the remainder of the executive board of about fifty was to be elected in a way that would represent minority surnames and other associations.[19] In Vancouver, what had been an unstructured system of voting became, by 1918, election based upon district association-nominated representatives as electors.

The Vancouver system illustrates both the development of the community to a size where diverse interests could not be represented in the old way, and also the effect of the dynamic Kuomintang upon the local political scene. For many years before 1911 the major Chinese merchants in Vancouver, most of them members of the Constitutionalist Party (XZD) and its predecessor, the Empire Reform Association, had been electing and re-electing themselves to the executive of the Vancouver CBA. After the Revolution the Kuomintang and its predecessor, the T'ung-meng Hui, began a drive for voters. Appealing to clan associations and, through them, to surname sentiment, in the 1912 election the T'ung-meng Hui elected twelve members to the twenty-man board. Where the XZD had hitherto dominated the board, they elected only one member.[20]

The Kuomintang continued the T'ung-meng Hui's efforts. During the tenure of Tsang Shak-chun, a Kuomintang leader, as chairman of the executive, there were many proposals for a change in voting from direct election to a system of electors representing district associations. The proponents of this system were mostly representatives of district associations, who perhaps desired to counter the Kuomintang's appeal to clan associations. The new system was accepted and in 1918 the first election using the electoral body was held. According to the new system, each of the major district associations was to nominate members of an advisory council as follows:

FIVE REPRESENTATIVES EACH:
Toi-san (Sun-ning); Poon-yue; Heung-san (Chung-san); Sun-wui

FOUR REPRESENTATIVES EACH:
Hoi-ping; Yin-ping

TWO REPRESENTATIVES EACH:
Nam-hoi; Sun-dak; Tung-koon; Tsang-shing; Hok-san; Sam-sui; Sun-on; Fa-uen.

Besides serving as an advisory body, these forty-four representatives were to elect the executive and supervisory committees of the organization. The Vancouver CBA thus became representative of the district associations. However, this did not simply mean district association control over the CBA. District association representatives often were also active members of clan associations and other organizations as well. In time, too, the CBA allowed for other interests to be represented by reserving several council seats for "at-large" representation.[21]

The emergence of several CBAs in individual Chinese communities across the country and the growing possibility of restrictive immigration legislation aimed at the Chinese raised the question of what body, if any, could and should speak for all the Chinese communities and all the CBAs. As early as 1916 the Vancouver CBA, on the basis of the size of the Vancouver Chinese Community, had asserted its right to do so, and had attempted to convene a cross-Canada meeting to discuss a Saskatchewan law that threatened Chinese interests. Again, in 1923, the Vancouver CBA attempted to call a national meeting to discuss proposed immigration legislation. It is not clear whether other CBAs accepted this conception, but in practice it mattered little because when the crisis came in 1923, the speaking was done by an *ad hoc* representative organization in which the key role was played by members of the Toronto community.

The Kuomintang burst onto the Canadian scene immediately after the 1911 Revolution. Within two years there were KMT branches in all major and minor Chinese settlements in British Columbia and Alberta, and in nine locations further east. In terms of strategy there were two major distinctions between the KMT and its competitors, the CKT and the XZD. First, the KMT systematically attempted to establish branches all the way across the country, paying considerable attention to eastern Canada. By contrast, the XZD seems to have had no branches east of Montreal and the CKT, although influential in membership terms all the way across Canada, also did not establish branches east of Quebec until after 1920. The KMT was also strong in the West, but it set about very early attempting to establish a weekly newspaper in Toronto, the *Shing Wah* (established 1916), where it sent some of its most able men; and it maintained branches eastward all the way to Halifax and St. John's. Second, where the CKT and XZD, despite their international membership and linkages, relied upon Chinese already in Canada for their executive positions, the KMT recruited some of its leadership from China and elsewhere outside of Canada.

It is clear from the quality of the KMT cadre assigned to Canada from elsewhere that Sun Yat-sen saw Canada as potentially very important to the support of his revolution, at least between 1911 and 1923. In early 1915, Sun dispatched Lin Sen and Wong Bock-yue, an American-born Chinese, to Montreal and the Toronto area to stir up patriotic sentiment for resistance to Japan and against the government of Yuan. Lin, who was head of the general branch of the KMT in the United States at the time, was later to become a revered political figure in China and eventually president of the country during the war against Japan (1937-45).[22]

Another outside KMT notable was Ch'eng T'ien-fang, who while study-ing at the University of Toronto served as head of the Toronto branch of the KMT and chief editor of the KMT's Toronto newspaper, the *Shing Wah*. After 1926 Ch'eng returned to China where he embarked upon a distinguished career as an educator and diplomat.[23]

A major figure in western Canada was Chan Sue-yan (Ch'en Shu-jen), who was Director of Party Affairs for Canada and the United States be-tween 1916 and 1922. Chan had come to Canada as a protégé of Feng Tzu-yu. With his base in Vancouver and Victoria, he served as editor of the KMT's western newspaper, *The New Republic*, published in Victoria, and as vice-principal and teacher at the Party's Chinese Public School in Vancouver. Chan also enjoyed a distinguished career in China after leav-ing Canada. From 1932 to 1948 he served as head of the Kuomintang government's Overseas Chinese Affairs Commission.[24]

Not all leaders came from the outside. Tsang Shak-chun, the other ma-jor figure in the West, was a Canadian resident. He established the Chinese Public School in Vancouver and served as its first principal. He served on the Vancouver CBA executive and in 1918 engaged in verbal dis-putes with the consulate and its supporters. At one point, it is said, he felt sufficiently threatened to maintain a personal bodyguard.[25]

Once established across the country, the KMT began to hold regional and national conferences. It also participated in all-North American meetings. Within Canada, the first Eastern Canada Conference was held in Toronto in 1916. In the following year the first All-Canada Con-ference took place at Vancouver. Although the KMT had no formal head-quarters, Vancouver served as a kind of nerve centre of its activities. It was at this point that the government declared the KMT an illegal organization: Chan Sue-yan, Tsang Shak-chun, and forty other leaders were arrested and put on trial. Some received prison sentences of one year, but were released on probation for that period. The trials revealed that the party had reached a membership variously estimated at 5,000 and 8,000, with over fifty branches. Branch offices were now closed and documents in them and in related organizations were confiscated.[26]

During the eight-month ban from September, 1918, to May, 1919, the KMT survived by continuing to hold informal meetings, operating out of business firms rather than as a political party. In February, 1919, an eastern Canada meeting was held at which major branches from Kingston, Toronto, Hamilton, Ottawa, and Montreal were represented. By June, 1919, the crisis had been weathered and the organization was free to operate as a political party again. By late 1919 a central headquar-ters was finally established, and within a few years the new headquarters building at Gore and Pender Streets in Vancouver had been completed. An all-Canada conference opened it. Meanwhile, in eastern Canada, the practice of eastern regional conferences continued.

For the Cheekungtang the decade was one of expansion of its inter-national activities and its relations with white Canadian society. Between

1885 and 1914 the CKT had reached its greatest size in Canada: over forty branches and 10-20,000 members.[27] Despite membership competition from the KMT during this period, the CKT maintained the same number of branches in 1923 and probably about the same level of membership. Meanwhile, it went through an interesting development. Once the Qing dynasty was overthrown and republican government had been nominally established in China, the CKT became an open political party. Within a short time it had been registered as such in both China and Canada. It thus became the Zhigongdang (or Zhigong political party), rather than the Zhigongtang (or Zhigong Society). By 1920 it had begun to call itself the Chinese Freemasons.

The Canadian Chinese Freemasons now became active participants in the international conferences that the CKT had begun to call. These meetings concerned themselves with creating constitutional structures for international liaison among national organizations and branches and the establishment of linkages in China at such places as Hong Kong, Canton, and Shanghai. Before 1923 the CKT in Canada had also begun the practice of frequent all-Canada conferences.[28]

As it began to emerge as a political and welfare organization, the CKT began to reach out toward white society. One example of this was the CKT's purchase of Canadian government bonds during these years. A second was its effort to create friendly and co-operative relations between some of its western Canadian branches and the white Masonic lodges in those localities. From Winnipeg to Victoria Chinese Freemason lodges invited members of the Masonic Order to attend their initiation and other ceremonies. As it turned out, no permanent bonds were established between the Chinese and the white Freemasons.

Internally, the Freemasons created a new organization of part of its membership, the Dart Coon Club. In the atmosphere of political violence that typified these years, Freemason leaders in the West saw a need for an "inner circle" of members whose loyalty and ability to keep association secrets were unquestionable. This had become an issue because it was still possible for a member of the Freemasons to be also a member of the KMT, and many were. Of more importance, the Freemasons needed a fighting arm, just as many other associations had at the time. The Dart Coon Society was to fill that job. Its martial arts skills were naturally accompanied by athletic activities and a dragon-dance team. By 1923 it had branches in Victoria, Vancouver, Cumberland, Nanaimo, Kamloops, Cranbrook, Calgary, and Winnipeg.

The Xianzhengdang, meanwhile, was in general decline. Unlike the Freemasons, the XZD had long manifested an interest in white society. As early as 1902 white speakers addressed meetings of the association. Individual members of the organization, as successful Chinese businessmen and language interpreters for white organizations, were frequently fluent in English and had many white associates. But these affiliations did not prevent the continued decline of the organization. Indeed, it is possible that they hastened its decline, since XZD leaders were probably the most assimilation-prone among Chinese leaders.

The XZD also was plagued by internal problems. Even before 1911, scandals associated with the party's investments in modernizing schemes in China and personal rivalries among leading members had weakened party unity.[29] Moreover, after 1908 the XZD increasingly lost the support of the CKT (Freemasons), which was being wooed by Sun Yat-sen and Feng Tzu-yu. Since both the Kuomintang and the CKT wished to overthrow the Qing dynasty while the XZD continued to support it, the KMT-CKT alliance was a more natural association. After 1911 the CKT moved toward political modernity. It no longer needed to look up to the XZD as its political mentor. In the opposition to the KMT which developed after 1911, the CKT was fully capable of acting in its own right as a political party and, if anything, the XZD would have to follow its lead. Finally, the popularity among Canadian Chinese of the cause of revolution in China further reduced the attractiveness of the XZD, which seemed too much tied to the old regime.

The XZD continued to exist, with headquarters in Vancouver and a particularly strong branch in the conservative Chinese community in Montreal. A new constitution was written in 1916 and all-Canada meetings were held in 1917 and 1918. But it was becoming clear that its fortunes were likely to depend upon those of the Freemasons and indeed Tom Yee, a leader of the Toronto Freemasons, proposed an alliance in 1921.[30]

Although the KMT, Freemasons, and XZD were the major political associations, there were also quasi-political bodies such as "reading rooms" (*shubao she* or *yuebao she*), several of which had been established in Vancouver by 1923. Reading rooms established in the 1911-23 period contained newspapers and books and their premises might serve as meeting halls for ordinary affairs of the association that founded them or for speech-making sessions on political issues relating to China or Canada. The Chinese newspapers of the period make frequent reference to "speech days" at reading rooms. That some of the reading rooms were, or became, clan associations is apparent from their names and later information about them.[31] But the political side of the reading room is equally apparent from the provisions of the early Chinese Republic for the election of Overseas Chinese representatives to the Chinese Parliament. Those representatives were to be chosen by CBAs, Chambers of Commerce, and reading rooms in the countries of Overseas Chinese residence.

It is surprising that in general there were so few district associations with branches across Canada. During this period only one district association had established formal branches in several locations across the country. That was the Toi-san Ning Yung Yu Hing Tong, representing the district of origin of the largest number of Chinese in Canada, which had spread east at least as far as Toronto. In Vancouver, and in

112

Victoria, there were more district associations than elsewhere, perhaps reflecting greater sub-ethnic diversity in those two communities. Vancouver had associations representing all four counties that made up the Sze-yap region of Guangdong, that is, Toi-san, Hoi-ping, Yin-ping, and Sun-wui. The Yue San association represented natives of Poon-yue in the three-county (Sam-yap) part of Guangdong. The Shon Yee Association was formed by the majority of those from Heung-san (Chung-san) county and the Fook Sun Tong by the remainder of the Heung-san people. Segmentation had produced the Hoi Ngai association and the Shar Duey Mutual Society, representing a sub-county locality in Sun-wui county.[32]

Since the district associations took the home district or county as the point of reference, appeals from home districts for disaster relief or for investment in various modernizing projects might have been expected to have stimulated the growth of district associations in Canada. There does appear to have been concern in Canadian Chinese communities for such local projects, but that does not seem to have produced a proliferation of district associations in Canada.

Two modernizing projects in home districts are particularly noteworthy for their scale and the sustained interest that was shown in them. Between 1911 and 1920 discussions were begun between school officials from Toi-san and Toisanese in Canada about the possibility of building a large, modern high school in the home district. By the early 1920's, after many fund-raising campaigns, the new high school was a reality. Essentially the work of Canadian Chinese of Toi-san origin, this school was said at the time to be the most modern high school in all of China. On a more modest scale and at a slightly later date, natives of Hoi-ping, apparently stimulated by the Toi-san example and acting through fund drives led by the Hoi-ping Kwong Fook Tong, their district association, raised enough money to build a modern high school in their home district.

Clan associations were more numerous than district associations. By 1923 Vancouver, with twelve district associations, had twenty-six clan associations. Toronto, with two district associations, had ten clan associations. Calgary had only one district association but six clan associations. Nine clan associations apparently had chapters from Vancouver to Ontario. Many associations were established informally and met infrequently long before they had a hall of their own. They might use as their headquarters the store of the wealthiest merchant member of the association. Or they might hold their meetings in the CBA.[33] It also appears from the names used by some clan and district associations that they began as lodging places for members. Note, in this connection, the name *bitsuey* (*bieshu*) used for the association of Wongs from Toi-san in Vancouver and the term *fong* used by three of Toronto's clan associations. *Bitsuey* were sometimes originally subordinate to other, larger associations. The use of the term often indicates segmentation.

Associations were funded in a variety of ways. Among the methods used were: foundation or share subscription money; membership dues, usually quite small; and exit fees, levied on any member who returned to China. Those associations who owned their own building could also obtain a regular income from renting out the lower floors to businesses or to other associations. Finally, a lucrative though dangerous source of income was gambling. There were periodic police crackdowns on gambling, and there were always persons in the community who, for personal or political reasons, were prepared to inform. Gambling and illegal immigration were the two most vulnerable areas for Chinese individuals and associations by the 1920's. Anyone wishing to "do in" a personal enemy or a competitive association could use information to authorities as a potent weapon. Informing, or suspicion thereof, might lead to battles between associations, as in Montreal in 1922.

Diversity played a large part in the development of associations in Chinese communities. Trade associations were found in Vancouver in larger numbers than elsewhere, not merely because the community was the largest in Canada, but also because the occupational structure of Vancouver's Chinese community was more diversified than those elsewhere. The greater contact that Vancouver and Victoria had with China may have added a stimulus to the formation of labour unions in those two B.C. cities, since the labour movement was just getting under way in China. Indeed, the Chinese crewmen on the Canadian Pacific steamers that ran from China to B.C. had organized a union of their own by 1922.[34]

Most of the trade associations were organized in reaction to white attitudes or policies. The Vancouver Chinese Chamber of Commerce was organized in 1922 to protest proposed limitations on Chinese business activities.[35] The Vegetable Retailers and Shingle Mill Workers Associations came into being during the 1914-19 period because of existing or proposed measures or policies that discriminated against Chinese in relation to whites in the same occupations.[36]

The presence of youth in the Chinese communities was another stimulus to the formation of associations. Youthful political interest led not only to youth organizations but stimulated the growth of reading rooms and theatrical activities. Theatres had already existed in the larger Chinese communities. Growing concern about home districts and about China in general led, after 1911, to the development of benefit performances to raise money for disaster relief or other China-oriented projects which, in turn, stimulated the development of theatre groups. Youth were particularly active in these projects.

New leadership also had something to do with association development. When Montreal's Chinese found their laundry interests threatened in the 1890's they turned to white missionaries for leadership. When a similar thing happened fifteen years later they handled the problem themselves by forming a CBA. The existence of so many associations after 1911 suggests a substantial number of persons wishing to be leaders. It is well-established in the literature that Overseas Chinese holding positions as community leaders owe it to their leadership of several key associations within their communities.[37] Since everyone who wishes to become a community leader may not be able to become a leader of the existing associations which occupy the key positions, there is some encouragement for newcomers to found new associations they may lead. There surely were more prospective leaders in Canadian Chinese communities by 1911-23 than earlier. Population growth, occupational diversification, the appearance of the small "new generation," with its useful English skills, and the much greater availability than before of night courses in language and speech-making all would work in this direction.

NOTES

1. The foregoing general discussion of late Qing (Ch'ing) policy toward Overseas Chinese is based upon the following: Yen Ching-hwang, "Ch'ing's Sale of Honours and the Chinese Leadership in Singapore and Malaya (1877-1912)," *Journal of Southeast Asian Studies*, I, 2 (September, 1970), pp. 20-32; Michael Godley, "The Late Ch'ing Courtship of the Chinese in Southeast Asia," *Journal of Asian Studies*, XXXIV, 2 (February, 1975), pp. 361-85; Lea E. Williams, *Overseas Chinese Nationalism: The Genesis of the Pan-Chinese Movement in Indonesia* (Glencoe, Ill., 1960); and Edgar Wickberg, *The Chinese in Philippine Life, 1850-1898* (New Haven, 1965), pp. 209-36.

2. Lee Tung-hai, pp. 324-30.

3. Sun's visits to Canada are discussed in Lee Tung-hai, pp. 240ff., 301ff., and in the various writings of Feng Tzu-yu. On the third visit, see particularly Feng's *Zhonghua Minguo kaiguo qian geming shi*, 2 vols. (Taibei, 1954), II, p. 163.

4. Translation by Edgar Wickberg from the quoted original in Lee Tung-hai, p. 243.

5. Sources disagree about the size of the Canadian Chinese contribution. A figure of Hong Kong $63,000 is found in Yen Ching Hwang, *The Overseas Chinese and the 1911 Revolution* (Kuala Lumpur, 1976), p. 311, and in Chun-tu Hsueh, *Huang Hsing and the Chinese Revolution* (Stanford, Calif., 1961), p. 86. A Chinese-Canadian source, Lee Tung-hai, presents a figure of "over $100,000" (Hong Kong dollars). Lee Tung-hai, pp. 240-51. See also sources cited in note 8 below.

6. For the CKT version, see Wong Sam-duck, *Hongmen geming shi* (n.p., 1936); and Lin Honggong, *Jianadaren fadong Xinhai Geming zaocheng minguo*. The KMT interpretation is found in the writings of Feng Tzu-yu.

7. See account in Lee Tung-hai, pp. 308ff.

8. *Ibid.*; Chen Kwong Min, *Meizhou Huaqiao tongjian*, p. 477; PAC, Exter-

nal Affairs, RG 25, Annual Registers, 1922; *Chinese Times*, 12 May 1922.

9. C. Martin Wilbur, *Sun Yat-sen. Frustrated Patriot* (New York, 1976), p. 307, n. 51.

10. Lee Tung-hai, pp. 315-18. Compare the account in Chen Kwong Min, *Meizhou*, pp. 424-5. See also PAC, Governor-General, RG 7, G21, vol. 239, file 348A.

11. See *Chinese Times*, 1914-1918; PAC, Chief Press Censor, RG 6, E 1, vol. 37, file 168; and several files from the United Church of Canada Archives.

12. PAC, Chief Press Censor, vol. 86, file 246-1/246-2, Sherwood to Chambers, 27 September 1918.

13. *Ibid.*, Report of Special Chinese Operator #220, September, 1918; *Chinese Times*, 1, 29 May 1919. For the further development of the Labour Association, see *ibid.*, 5-7 August 1920.

14. *Chinese Times*, 27 February 1919; Fong Sau But, Seto Chong Yim, Ham Hung Tip, interviews, Ottawa, 5 June 1973.

15. *Chinese Times*, 9 September 1918.

16. Kingston KMT, *Jianada Qingshitun Zhongguo Guomindang jiuzhou jingguo dangwu* (Kingston, 1924), Prefaces and p. 149.

17. *Chinese Times*, 6 February 1914. But note a reference to a "Chinese Association" at 336 Lagauchetière in an unidentified English-language newspaper of 1909, found in PAC, RG 76, file 827821, part 2.

18. See *Chinese Times*, issues of 1916-1919.

19. Ban Seng Hoe, *Structural Changes of Two Chinese Communities in Alberta, Canada* (Ottawa, 1976), pp. 182-4.

20. Feng Tzu-yu, *Huaqiao geming zuzhi shihua*, pp. 73-4.

21. See *Chinese Times*, especially issues of 23 June, 7, 15 August 1918; 16 December 1921.

22. Chen Kwong Min, *Meizhou*, p. 421; Lee Tung-hai, p. 308; Howard L. Boorman (ed.), *Biographical Dictionary of Republican China*, 4 vols. (New York, 1967-71), II, p. 380. Two other well-known KMT cadres who came to Canada at that time to organize anti-Yuan efforts were Hsia Chung-min and Ma Chao-i. See Lee Tung-hai, p. 308.

23. Boorman, *Biographical Dictionary*, I, p. 289. Ch'eng's reminiscences of his stay in Canada are found in his *Ch'eng T'ien-fang caonian huiyilu* (Taibei, 1968), pp. 58-68. Another editor of *Shing Wah* during the 1920's was Huang Chi-lu, later Minister of Education in the KMT government on Taiwan.

24. Boorman, *Biographical Dictionary*, I, pp. 234-5. For more information about Chan, see UCCA, Presbyterian Church, Box 3, Thomson to MacKay, 26 December 1918; PAC, Chief Press Censor, *passim.*; *Victoria Times*, 4 March 1919.

25. *Chinese Times*, 1917-1918; Lee Tung-hai, pp. 334-5; Feng Tzu-yu, *Huaqiao geming zuzhi shihua*, p. 74; *Zhongguo Guomindang diyiersan-*

sici quanguo daibiao dahui huikan (1934), reprinted in Shen Yun-lung (ed.), *Jindai Zhongguo shiliao congkan*, di 98 ji.

26. Kingston KMT, *Jianada Qingshitun, passim.*; *Chinese Times*, 18 December 1918; Victoria *Colonist* and *Victoria Times*, October, 1918-April, 1919; PAC, Chief Press Censor, file 168-A, vol. 2; *ibid.*, volume 37, file 168, Daniels to Chambers, 6 July 1917; Vancouver *World*, 20 August 1917.

27. Lee Tung-hai, p. 234. As of 1924 the CKT-related organizations claimed a worldwide membership of 2,000,000 in some 400 branches. Canada, therefore, represented at most 1 per cent of the membership and about 10 per cent of the branches. *Chinese Times*, 10 March 1924; *ibid.*, 21 December 1915; Lin Honggong, *Jianadaren fadong*, pp. 23-31; Lee Tung-hai, pp. 243-52.

28. See *Chinese Times*, issues of 1918, 1919, 1923. The first all-Canada conference was held in Victoria during December of 1919. See *Chinese Times*, December, 1919, for details.

29. Feng Tzu-yu, *Huaqiao geming kaiguo shi*, p. 109; and Lee Tung-hai, pp. 251-6.

30. *Chinese Times*, 26 March 1921.

31. W.E. Willmott, "Chinese Clan Associations in Vancouver," *Man*, LXIV, no. 49 (1964), p. 35.

32. Shar Duey's existence is recorded in *Chinese Times*, issues of 1920-1923, and its forty-second anniversary was celebrated in 1962. *Ibid.*, 3 December 1962.

33. See references in *Chinese Times*, 1914-1937.

34. *Chinese Times*, 30 January 1922.

35. *Ibid.*, 4, 20 March, 5 April 1922. It is not clear what if any relationship this new association may have had with the "Chinese Board of Trade" that existed in 1908-09 and the earlier Gongyi and Zhaoyi associations that were present around 1900. The Zhaoyi gongsuo may have been an exclusively Sam Yap merchant guild. Eve Armentrout-Ma, "A Chinese Association in North America," p. 99.

36. *Chinese Times*, 11 March, 20 August 1919; 13 August 1918.

37. G.W. Skinner, *Leadership and Power in the Chinese Community of Thailand* (Ithaca, N.Y., 1957); W.E. Willmott, *The Political Structure of the Chinese Community in Cambodia* (London, 1970); Karin Straaton, "The Political System of the Vancouver Chinese Community: Associations and Leadership in the Early 1960's" (M.A. thesis, University of British Columbia, 1974).

NINE

Unfinished Bridges: World War One and Its Aftermath

World War I had important effects upon the Chinese-Canadian communities. During the first three years of the war (1914-16) unemployment was severe. One missionary report estimated that 70-80 per cent of Vancouver's Chinese were jobless in 1916.[1] The Chinese met this situation with self-help. The wealthy supported the poor, sometimes directly, sometimes through associations. The CBA, the CKT, and various other associations provided relief for the needy. These associations, and particularly the Victoria CCBA, encouraged jobless Chinese to return to China and would-be immigrants to refrain from coming.[2] Indeed, the immigration rate dropped sharply in those years, from about 3,000-4,000 per year to about 1,000 per year or less. Certain government rules also were suspended; normally, a Chinese visiting his homeland had to return to Canada within one year or lose his right to tax-free return. Now, the government provided one blanket extension after another until finally it announced that all Chinese otherwise eligible to return had until twelve months after the formal declaration of peace to make it back.[3]

These extensions of leave were not just a way of preventing the jobless from returning; they also recognized the fact that many were stranded in China because British shipping had been commandeered for military purposes. The shortage of shipping also meant shortages and high prices for foods imported from China and other parts of Asia. The combination of high food prices and high unemployment was recognized as a community problem. In Vancouver and Victoria import companies were formed by the CBA and other associations with the objective of providing imported food – especially rice – at moderate prices.

As the war continued the Chinese found themselves supporting both China's modernization and Canada's war effort. On one hand they elected representatives to the Chinese parliament, provided relief and defence funds for China, and purchased Chinese government bonds. On the other hand, they bought Canadian government bonds and participated in Victory Loan Drive parades.[4] The Chinese of Vancouver contributed well over $100,000 to the war effort in bond purchases. At the same time, as "aliens" they were required by Canadian security legislation to register, and monitoring and censorship of their communications were established as legitimate forms of surveillance.

Although no Chinese were drafted for military service, a small number volunteered for infantry service as enlisted men (no officers were commissioned) and a few lost their lives. Service in the war led to agitation for the vote, a movement led by CBAs and particularly the Chinese-Canadian Club of Victoria-Vancouver. In 1919 the Commons considered granting the federal franchise to Chinese, Japanese, and East Indians. At this point, the 515 Canadian-born and naturalized Chinese of Victoria wrote to the government, pointing out that they owned real estate and were taxpayers and that the naturalization papers held by 400 of them stated that they were endowed with all rights, powers, and privileges of citizens. Despite this petition the Dominion Elections Act legalized what had hitherto been only custom: Chinese and others who lacked the provincial franchise would continue to be without the federal voting right.[5] In British Columbia, the residence of the largest number of naturalized and Canadian-born Chinese, and hence the place where the largest number of likely voters lived, 200 sympathetic whites petitioned for the provincial franchise on behalf of the Chinese. They argued that they were Canadian-born, that their parents had been naturalized, that they were educated in British Columbia, and that some of them had served in the war. Even these qualifications apparently were insufficient; the petition was unsuccessful. The Chinese of British Columbia and Saskatchewan, regardless of citizenship, remained without the franchise.

In 1917 the Northern (Peking) government took China into the war on the side of the Western allies. Unable to contribute troops, China provided 50,000 coolie labourers for service behind the lines in France. These crossed Canada en route to Europe and were photographed in British Columbia in 1917.[6] On their return at war's end, they again crossed Canada in sealed railway carriages, being let out long enough for muster and picture-taking in British Columbia, before the Canadian Pacific and Blue Funnel steamers took them back to China. A few expressed a desire to remain in Canada but apparently they were not allowed to do so.[7]

When China became Canada's ally, the Chinese consuls in Canada were able to use this new relationship against the KMT. In Vancouver, the city government had already given the local consul the right to decide which Chinese groups could hold street-corner meetings. After China entered the war, the consuls urged demonstrations of friendly relations with Canada and participation in the Canadian war effort. When the CBAs, the CKT, and the XZD complied but the KMT did not, because it opposed the Northern government and all of its policies, consuls could point this out to the Canadian government as an example of the KMT's unreliability in the war effort and possibly subversive character.[8]

World War I brought whites and Chinese together in some ways, but not in others. Their relationship was mixed: co-operation in some ways, friction in others; efforts to bridge the gap accompanied by Chinese cultural nationalism and white rejection of the Chinese.

In the final two years of the war, the Chinese employment situation improved. A manpower shortage developed, especially on farms, and the economy of the country had improved sufficiently so CBAs and other associations now began to encourage Chinese to immigrate. Chinese communities prospered and annual immigration figures reached levels of up to 4,000. At the end of the war the Chinese population approached 40,000. Nevertheless, in a total Canadian population of almost 9 million this amounted to only .45 per cent. This in itself was hardly an occasion for alarm among whites. It was the increase in the rate of immigration beginning in 1917 and, above all, the movement of Chinese into new occupations, especially in British Columbia, that created concern. Veterans returning from the war found the economy depressed and jobs difficult to get. It was now argued by some that jobs opened to Chinese and other Asians during the manpower-shortage years of 1917-18 should be turned over to veterans. Vancouver area sawmills, for example, employed 900 East Asians out of 2,200 workers. Over 2,000 Chinese worked in the 150 shingle mills in and around Vancouver. There were proposals that veterans be trained to replace at least some of these Asian workers. There was white concern also about Asian landownership and farm operations in rural areas near Vancouver and Victoria, and the numerical and geographical expansion of Chinese produce-sales and grocery stores.[9]

Even older Chinese occupations, such as the operation of inexpensive restaurants serving Western-style food, especially in small towns, were brought under attack. Perhaps this was in reaction to an expansion of Chinese-owned restaurant operations, but this is not clear. The opposition took two forms: proposals to exclude Asians from the restaurant business, and laws in some provinces that would make it illegal for white women to work in Chinese restaurants and other small businesses run by Chinese. Saskatchewan, Manitoba, Ontario, and British Columbia enacted laws which, where enforced, struck hard at small Chinese restaurants by denying them the services of white waitresses.[10] The first of these laws appeared in Saskatchewan in 1912. The occasion was an alleged physical assault by a Chinese restaurant owner upon a white female employee. There is no doubt that some moral concern, whether exaggerated or not, was part of the background of this law and similar ones in other provinces. But the fact that these laws usually applied only to Chinese restaurant owners, and that simultaneously there were efforts in British Columbia, Manitoba, and Ontario to exclude Chinese from the restaurant business, suggests that economic reasons were paramount.[11] The Chinese restaurant serving Western-style food at inexpensive prices was found especially in small towns across the Prairies. It was usually operated by a single Chinese man. If he needed help it was difficult for him to get it at rates suitable to his inexpensive operation. The $500 head tax made it almost impossible for a person of his resources to bring in members of his family from China. The cheapest Canadian labour available was that of young women.[12]

In Saskatchewan the Chinese fought this legislation through the provincial and federal courts, and even appealed it to the Privy Council in London. Their efforts were only partly successful, but in time this law and its successor simply lost any effectiveness because they were only sporadically enforced.[13] For example, after a flurry of discussion in Toronto during the late 1920's, when the mayor began to enforce Ontario's long-dormant law, the question seems to have disappeared. Indeed, it has been said that after 1930 everywhere in Canada laws of this kind were either nullified or ignored.[14] That is not quite the case, as we shall see later.

White agitation in major Canadian cities also focused on the moral, public health, and safety conditions in Chinatowns. For some years there had been concern over the health and safety conditions of Chinese boardinghouses (*fangkou*). That gambling was a major business in Chinatowns, and that it could and often did lead to crime and violence, was well-known. Prostitution was also known to exist, with some of the same consequences. Opium sales, possession, and use had been illegal since 1908, but opium continued to be readily available and widely used in Chinatowns. Given these conditions, it was inevitable that there would be proposals to "clean up Chinatown." One proposal, in Vancouver, was to start all over by establishing a new Chinatown on Franklin Street, well to the east of the existing settlement. Presumably, if this did not result in an eradication of the evils of Chinatown it would at least remove them from the sight of business people and others in the centre of the city. Although some Chinese made preliminary property acquisitions, the project was abandoned because it was felt that the city offered inadequate compensation for the old property.

By the end of the war the white vision of Chinatown as a blighted area had become fully developed. Especially in Vancouver, letters to newspaper editors about the evils of Chinatown became frequent. The newspapers joined in with sensational reports. The lurid fiction piece, *The Writing on the Wall*, published by the *Vancouver Sun*, touched every nerve of white racism, catered to every white anxiety and fantasy. Omniscient Chinese criminal lords used opium to enslave white girls as prostitutes, while planning the reduction of British Columbia to the Oriental will.[15] To be sure, not everyone in white society read books of this kind, let alone allowed himself to be preoccupied by their subject matter. But the rising white concern and indignation about the unhealthy side of Chinatown is unmistakeable. The Vancouver City Health Department held inspections in Chinatown. A minimum of 400 cubic inches of breathing space per person was established for buildings in that city. The Vancouver CBA was advised that the small Chinese hospital, long housed

121

within the CBA building, did not meet health standards and must be moved. An arrangement was made with the Catholic Sisters of the Immaculate Conception, who operated St. Joseph Hospital, so that the Chinese hospital could be given space and facilities within that institution.[16]

In Vancouver the city police, with church encouragement, began in 1918 what were probably the biggest gambling raids up to that time. The problem was not small. One Chinese group claimed that there were over forty dens employing 700-800 persons, and that over 3,000 Chinese (plus an untold number of non-Chinese) were regular gamblers. During 1918 some 1,000 arrests of gamblers were reported, with what immediate results we cannot be certain.[17]

Opium problems were greatest in British Columbia partly because Victoria and Vancouver were the major ports for illegal opium importation. In 1920 the RCMP assumed responsibility for enforcing drug laws in British Columbia, replacing the provincial police. Two years later the federal government strengthened its narcotics legislation by giving itself the power to deport, subject to a review hearing, any alien found guilty of a drug offense. Immigration records of the middle 1920's show that during that decade there was a small but steady flow of Chinese deportees under this law, the number averaging seventy-eight per year.[18]

Some of those who clamoured for changes in Chinatown were Chinese business leaders, especially those who were Christians. In 1921 a Chinese Anti-Drug Association was established, and in the following year leading Chinatown merchants met several times to consider possible reactions to the revelations about drug, health, and gambling conditions.

MISSIONARY EFFORTS AND ATTITUDES

The missionaries, both white and Chinese, took Chinatown and Chinese communities as their responsibility, and were much concerned about the social evils they saw there. Missionaries usually knew the Chinese communities better than any other white Canadians. To understand their perspectives on the Chinese it would be well first to outline the results of their efforts by the early 1920's.

Before 1923 most of the Christian missionary work was in the hands of the Presbyterians and Methodists. The first church to open a regular mission to the Chinese in Canada was the Methodist Church, which appointed John Endicott Gardiner as part-time missioner to the Victoria Chinese in 1885. Prior to that, the Methodist Home for Chinese Girls was established at Victoria in 1883 to provide refuge for young women escaping the servitude of prostitution or of unwilling marriage contracts. Gardiner, born of missionary parents in Canton, was well suited to the task of preaching to the Chinese in Victoria, since he spoke Cantonese fluently and was moved by a burning hatred of the vices and secret societies he believed blighted their lives. He came from San Francisco in 1885 to act as interpreter at a trial in Victoria, and, as one contemporary remarked, "Touched by the inhuman wrongs and sufferings of these poor creatures, he began the Christ-like work of rescuing them and for some time carried it on at his own expense."[19] In 1888, Gardiner became a full-time missionary for the Methodist Church and worked in Vancouver before opening a church in Victoria in 1891. The Presbyterians opened a Chinese school in Victoria, and a mission followed in 1900.

Three well-known Chinese missionaries in Canada were Fong Dickman (Fong Dak Man) and two brothers, Chan Sing Kai and Chan Yu Tan. Dickman was converted by Mrs. Monk (daughter of the Rev. Ebenezer Robson) at New Westminster; the Chans were born into a Christian family in China. Chan Sing Kai worked for the church in Hong Kong for eight years before coming to Canada in 1888. He was successively in charge of the missions at Vancouver, New Westminster, and Victoria. His brother, Chan Yu Tan, took over the Vancouver mission in 1896, when Gardiner retired to San Francisco. One of Chan Yu Tan's converts was Kwan Mow Lung, who later worked for the bilingual Chinese newspaper, the *Wah Ying Yat Bo*, when Fong Dickman and other Christians commenced publication in 1906.

By the turn of the century, there were Methodist missions to the Chinese in Victoria, Vancouver, Nanaimo, and New Westminster. Further east, the Presbyterians were active in Montreal and Toronto, running both schools and missions in each city.

Anglican missionary activities were modest before 1920 and Roman Catholic efforts in the same period, even in Montreal, were informal and ancillary to other work. In Toronto and Winnipeg the enterprise was interdenominational; further west, Methodists and Presbyterians worked separately. In terms of the number of converts, the results of this work were modest. Published statistics for the whole country are lacking before 1931, but from information about individual communities it seems likely that at most 10 per cent of the Chinese in Canada were Christians by 1923.[20] Some of the Chinese who were converted became missionaries in Canada themselves; other Chinese missionaries were imported from Canton, where they had trained in church schools. Canadian Chinese converts sometimes went to their home districts as missionaries; missionaries from Canton were assigned to Canada and those already serving in Canada were reassigned to Guangdong.

Among the notable Chinese ministers in Canada during this period were Ma T.K. Wou in Toronto and Mah Seung, who served in Cumberland, B.C., and later in Winnipeg. Reverend Fong Dickman was active over many years in Alberta and British Columbia. Ng Mon Hing, a pioneer Chinese minister, was best known for his many years in Victoria, where young political activists in his congregation reportedly chafed at his insistence upon the full gospel, as opposed to the social gospel. Some of the earliest practitioners of Western medical science in Chinese communities in Canada were also products of Protestant missionary efforts. Young men like Edward Gung (Gung Bong-yue) and Philip Chu were trained as physicians in Ontario universities and assigned to British Columbia as medical missionaries.

It has been argued that Canada's Protestant missionaries to the Chinese were different from many white Canadians in believing the Chinese were assimilable. Assimilation – "Canadianization" – may have seemed the only way they could see to keep the Chinese in Canada from having bad effects upon Canadian culture. Hence, while working for the conversion and social betterment of the Chinese, the missionaries assumed a white Canada, one which could only be preserved by limiting the number of Chinese allowed into the country and by assimilating the relatively small number of Chinese who were already present.[21]

It might be more precise to say that the missionary position was ambivalent. On the one hand missionaries were sympathetic to the plight of the Chinese in the face of discriminatory legislation and popular attitudes. They were also prepared to recognize the value of certain aspects of Chinese culture that did not conflict with Christianity, and the likelihood that these would be retained. On the other hand, however, they found some aspects of Chinese culture to be the sources of the evils in Chinatown and utterly irreconcilable with Christianity. While committed to the task of changing the Chinese in certain ways, they apparently did not see it as necessary to change them in every way. Nor did they seem to welcome intermarriage. Hence it might be more accurate to say that they favoured integration rather than assimilation.[22]

The issue of gambling was one in which this ambivalence appeared quite readily. Although some missionaries ardently campaigned against it, several others, while deploring the effects of gambling and attempting to isolate their converts from it, recognized that it was often a major source of support for the associations to which the members of their congregations belonged. If the missionaries opposed clan and district associations, or saw them as necessarily in opposition to their own efforts, it is not apparent from the documents at hand.[23]

In sorting out their attitudes toward the Chinese and Chinese culture, the missionaries, because of their special task and experience, faced a much more subtle and complex problem than did most white Canadians. In the 1911-23 decade many missionaries saw themselves as locked in a battle with the political associations of the Chinese communities, especially the KMT and the CKT, for the loyalty of the community's younger generation. One missionary saw the temptations and vices of Chinatown in terms of high unemployment and lack of other forms of recreation. Idle young men, who crowded the streets, were not allowed in white theatres and drifted to gambling halls unless the churches could provide alternative forms of recreation.[24]

But the real issue of contest lay not in recreation but in cultural orientation. The new generation appeared at the time when Chinese nationalism, rapidly developing in China itself, was being implanted in overseas Chinese communities. Chinese nationalism found expression in overseas Chinese schools, including those in Canada, where the Chinese national readers were used and where interest in building China and in reviving Chinese culture was stressed. From a missionary perspective, Chinese schools could be seen as competitors to missionary schools. To the missionaries, education in English was linked to the idea of stimulating interest in Christianity and Canadianization. Where Christian groups established schools that also included Chinese language study, they looked for principals and teachers (T.C. Mark is an example) who could teach Chinese studies in ways that did not conflict with Christianity.[25]

Some missionaries complained that the KMT and the CKT were now setting up English classes or English-Chinese schools as a counter-attraction in order to lure students away from Christian schools and Christian influence. It was not merely the nationalist content of the Chinese schools that bothered the missionaries. The Confucian content of some was, if anything, more repugnant. Nationalism diverted interest in Canadianization, but might still be harmonized with Christianity. But a dose of Confucianism as an antidote to Christianity was more than missionaries could tolerate. Indeed, it appears that some Chinese schools, and other youth-directed efforts, were a direct reaction to missionary night schools – an attempt to do the English-teaching and the recreational work themselves, without the Christian inducements, and thereby reclaim for Chinese culture the youth who might have defected otherwise. In one community, Cumberland, B.C., which must have been a "hardship" post for missionaries, an exasperated, almost paranoid missionary reported that the local CKT was enrolling twelve-year old boys as members of their society in order to frustrate his efforts to "save" them.[26]

Cumberland deserves more than passing notice. When the coal mines opened on Vancouver Island, Cumberland quickly developed a large Chinatown made up almost exclusively of miners. Although it was destined to disappear completely by the 1960's, the Cumberland Chinatown was for many years one of the largest in Canada and as late as 1921 retained a population of almost 1,000. The CKT, by this time called Freemasons, clearly dominated the Cumberland Chinatown. Half the Chinese population were members, and the town's commercial resources, including the lucrative gambling business, were said to be Freemason assets. Missionaries found Cumberland a trying post. Both the Freemasons and the KMT were agreed on the need to keep teaching the young and many other organized activities in Chinese hands. Occasionally, some member of the community would send a daughter to the mission school; but he sent his sons to Chinese-run classes.[27]

Still, there was no necessary incompatibility of Christianity and Kuomintang membership. In fact, since both appealed to young, idealistic Chinese for some of the same reasons – their forward-looking, modernist ideals – many church members were also KMT members. Missionaries and church leaders who wished their members to remain non-political found it a problem that some of their young members were involved in the radical politics of the KMT. The attractiveness of the KMT to young Christians, noted by church leaders at the time, did not mean that all idealistic Christians joined that Party. The CKT, also, was attractive, as it became a modern political party with social welfare dimensions. Community leaders in Toronto like Mark Moon and the physician, Dr. Henry Lore, were both leading Chinese Christians and leading members of the CKT.[28]

One of the greatest problems for Christian missionaries and Chinese ministers was the anti-Christian wave that swept into Canada from China as part of the May Fourth Movement. The intellectual side of the May Fourth Movement was characterized by widespread criticism of Confucianism as a system of thought said to be unsuited to the demands of twentieth-century nationhood. Instead, it was hoped, China would recreate its civilization, minus the major Confucian component. On this and related issues, there was no consensus in China. Debates between cultural conservatives and radicals raged over the nature of China's "cultural essence" and the problem of "recreating civilization." Nationalism was at fever pitch. Christianity was caught in a cross-fire. Politically, it was popularly associated with foreign imperialism in China, which was by this time the major target of Chinese nationalism. Culturally, it was caught between the conservative pro-Confucians and the radical anti-Confucians.

Anti-Christian tracts appeared widely in China and, as so often happened, what went on in China was echoed in Canada. One such placard, issued by the Anti-Christianity Society in Vancouver's Chinese community, illustrates the sentiments of many young Chinese intellectuals of the day.

<blockquote>

The Religion of Jesus: Not worth one Cash – the
Source of Ten Thousand Evils

This religion obstructs the progress of science. It deceives men and confuses their ideas. . . . Now at the present the educated people in our country already know that it is poison. . . . We are afraid that our overseas brothers do not yet know the poison of Christianity, but still think it a good religion which exhorts men to do good. They do not know for what reason our country resists it. . . .

A. Christianity is a deceiver of the people
   The blue sky is only filled with air. . . . There is nothing else but emptiness. . . . What kind of heaven is there? What is God? What kind of demonology is this to frighten the people? It is only fit for dark ages to frighten the ignorant. But in this present

</blockquote>

generation it is not fit to be allowed to remain, to obstruct the progress of the world and science . . . if the Bible were true Jesus would have power over Heaven and Earth and everything in them. Those who belong to him would all be perfectly good. . . .

B. Christianity is not equality
Many say that Christianity preaches the virtue of equality. Look at the Bible. It says woman is made from the rib of man. . . . Is this to be called equality? We have four classes: scholars, farmers, workmen, merchants. From morning to night these do exceedingly hard work. . . . Christian ministers only talk nonsense for three or four hours a week and have plenty to eat and wear. . . . Is there any equality in this?

C. Christianity is not love
Although I am not in favor of polytheism, still I think Christians ought only to preach their own doctrine and not resist others. . . . At present wherever their preachers go they open their mouths only to revile polytheism. . . . The Christians and the Mohammedan Turks fought for 178 years. . . . How can this be called love? Christianity not only exerts its strength to oppose other religions but is divided in itself. Europe had thirty years of war and distress. . . .

D. Christianity brings harm and misery to China
The Governments of every country train a lot of tramps to preach and build churches. They secretly measure and make maps of China and prepare to invade her. . . . Why do the uncivilized governments of all the Powers spend so much money every year for the establishment of Christianity in China?[29]

In terms of number of converts, the Christian missionary effort among the Chinese in Canada could not be considered a success by 1920. But twenty years later the percentage, at least, was much higher. By 1941, of 35,000 Chinese in Canada, approximately 10,000 claimed to be Christians. This increase is less significant than it may at first appear. It should be understood in the light of changes in federal immigration policy in 1923, which cut off all new immigration and encouraged some Chinese already in Canada to return to China. The Chinese population of 1941 was smaller by 12,000 persons than that of 1921, reflecting deaths and departures and a dearth of new immigrants. Those most likely to remain in Canada were the Christians, thereby raising their proportion of the total. There is no evidence of a surge of interest in Christianity between 1920 and 1940.

What is more significant is the geographical distribution of these Christians. Despite the fact that half of the Chinese in Canada lived in British Columbia, only 1,400, or about 8 per cent of the total Chinese population of B.C., were Christians in 1941. In Ontario, however, where the Chinese population was about one-third that in British Columbia, almost half of the Chinese population was Christian. And the Ontario Christian population of 2,500 accounted for over 40 per cent of the total Christian Chinese population of Canada. The concentration of successful Presbyterian and United Church effort in Ontario is what accounts for most of the difference.[30]

These statistics may help us to understand some differences we can observe between the Chinese communities that had emerged as opposites to each other by 1921: Toronto and the two B.C. communities, Vancouver and Victoria, whose leadership and institutions were broadly shared. In Vancouver-Victoria community leadership continued to be in the hands of associations established without white assistance in the late nineteenth century. In Toronto the role of missionaries and Chinese Christians in forming leading associations and of Christian Chinese in playing leadership roles in the community is apparent from the start.

Chinese in Ontario, unlike those in British Columbia, could vote and could practise as lawyers, pharmacists, and accountants. Since this was the case, we might find that in Toronto opportunities for upward mobility were better and that there was a much more common association of church membership with social mobility than in British Columbia. The suggestion is that greater opportunity in eastern Canada may have meant greater interest in Canadian life on the part of eastern Canadian Chinese, including an interest in Christianity as one important dimension of Canadian life shared by most Canadians. Church membership may also have been a means of making personal and business contacts in white society which would enhance one's chances of professional success.

EDUCATION AND CHINESE MILITANCY

The churches played an important role in education, but neither missionary-run nor Chinese-run schools could provide all of the educational facilities Chinese parents wanted. Chinese children appeared in the public schools of British Columbia by the last decades of the nineteenth century, but even by 1923 they amounted to only 1.4 per cent of the total school population of the province.[31] Many of the Chinese students were overage for the school grade to which they were assigned. That is hardly surprising, considering that the usual age of arrival from China was in one's early teens, and few such immigrants had had much education – least of all any training in the English language. There was some concern in Victoria and Vancouver about the social or moral effects of assigning teen-agers to the same classrooms as small children. There were also pedagogical arguments against the practice. The British Columbia Department of Education tended to view the overage Chinese student with his language problems as a detriment to the progress of others in his grade.

The possibility of segregated education for Chinese students had been discussed in Victoria as early as 1901, and a brief attempt at it was made in 1904-1905, abandoned apparently because Chinese parents would not send their children to a segregated class. Once again the issue surfaced, in 1907-1908, this time in both Vancouver and Victoria. The provincial Department of Education proposed an achievement examination which, if implemented, would have disqualified many Chinese students from attending classes at any level. This proposal was not put into effect, but there was partial segregation in both cities during these years, which was enough to hasten the Victoria CCBA's efforts to provide its Chinese school with some English-teaching facilities.[32]

In 1922 the matter came forward again. In Vancouver most school principals did not consider it necessary, and the CBA was able to negotiate non-implementation. In Victoria, however, the school board was determined to put all Chinese students into segregated facilities. Specifically, it proposed to put all 240 students into a flimsy building the Chinese derisively nicknamed the "chicken coop."[33]

The reaction of the Chinese community was one of determined resistance. Segregated facilities implied neglect or inferior instruction. Indeed, the quality of the proposed physical facilities confirmed suspicions of inferior instruction. It was observed by the Chinese that this ruling applied to no other immigrant group – certainly not to the Japanese. It also lumped native-born Chinese Canadians, who had attended missionary kindergartens where English was used, with teen-agers newly arrived from China, and the Board did not respond to parents' challenges to publish student standings that would demonstrate whether or not all Chinese students were lagging behind. As an "economy measure," another explanation given by the Board, this action seemed to be "economizing" at the expense of one group defined in ethnic terms. The Chinese, as one letter from the community pointed out, paid in real estate taxes double what it cost the city to educate their children. Moreover, many Chinese had also paid the head tax, half of which went to the province of British Columbia.[34]

One member of the Chinese Canadian Club chided white Canadians for saying Chinese could not assimilate while not giving them a chance to do so. In theatres Chinese (if allowed in) were required to sit by themselves in corners. The British heritage of fair play was supposed to be alive in British Columbia, yet Chinese were not allowed to vote and thus to participate in the society. Even in religion, he said, Chinese had learned not to take the missionaries literally. Will there be, the writer asked, segregated Heavens, and will St. Peter demand a $500 head tax from the Chinese?[35]

Chinese parents and teachers, responding to the segregation attempt, formed an association to boycott the public schools, establish and run their own alternative schools, and collect funds for agitation against the segregation policy. For over a year the dispute dragged on. The school board offered a compromise which would provide segregation within the same building, but the Chinese parents and children rejected it. Finally, the city backed down to the extent of proposing that not all Chinese were to be segregated in separate classrooms – only those who were indeed behind in their work. On that basis, the parents and children accepted the terms and their year-long boycott came to a victorious conclusion.[36]

The determination to resist, evident in this school strike, speaks for the frequent militancy of the Vancouver and Victoria Chinese communities in their external relations during these years. We have already noted that nationalism in China was influencing the Chinese in Canada. Given China's military and political weakness, the most effective weapons of Chinese nationalism were usually the boycott and the strike. The Chinese in Canada also adopted these measures.

Strikes became a major weapon of organized Chinese groups in Canada against perceived injustices or measures detrimental to their interests. The period 1911-23 is marked by the formation of several militant unions and strikes became common, especially after 1918. As early as 1916, the Chinese Labour Association (Zhonghua Gongtang) had been organized. By 1918 it had 500-600 members. Strikes were concentrated in the lumber industry, where a large proportion of the B.C. Chinese employed in white industries were found. The first major strike was in the sawmills of Vancouver and New Westminster, where the Chinese went out in an attempt to shorten their working day from ten to eight hours, in line with that of white workers in the same trade. The success of this strike was no doubt encouraging to other Chinese workers. Unions were organized among the Chinese workers of the Vancouver-area shingle mills and several strikes took place during 1918-20.[37]

Chinese produce hawkers in the Vancouver area also organized themselves into a union and withdrew their services for a period of about three months, beginning in November, 1919. Ever since 1909 the Vancouver City Council had been under sporadic pressure to take some kind of action against Chinese produce hawkers who, it was believed by some, controlled too large a share of the vegetable retailing with adverse price effects for the consumer. By 1918-19 when City Council decided to act, the Chinese itinerant produce hawker with his shoulder pole, walking through the neighbourhoods of Vancouver, was beginning to be replaced by the Chinese-owned truck, operating from central produce distribution stations in a few parts of the city.[38] The by-law of 1919 proposed that the Chinese, who were presumed to be making profits at least twice those of other dealers, be required to pay a licence fee twice that of other dealers. Through the summer and early fall the Chinese continued to sell but paid no more than the usual tax. When the city pressed the issue the Chinese withdrew their services. In this case, the strike was unsuccessful and the Chinese hawkers by early 1920 were accepting the payment of a $50 licence fee, as compared to the $25 fee paid by all non-Chinese.

These strikes reflect not just the growing militancy of the Chinese but the post-war dislocations, which included wage reductions and work layoffs. These and other unhappy economic conditions were frequently blamed upon the Chinese. The reaction of the Chinese was clear: they were prepared, where feasible, to resist being made the scapegoats, and to do so they organized unions when they could. The Chinese militancy we see here strikes us with particular force because what has been much more widely publicized is the use of Chinese as strike-breakers in the coal mines of Vancouver Island only a few years before the unionism we are discussing here. The strike-breaker episodes, in turn, have encouraged a popular image of the Chinese as passive and accepting, never militant. An awareness of the militancy of Chinese activity during the 1911-23 period should revise that view. Indeed, it is clear that militancy was not a new development in Canadian Chinese communities in 1911.

NOTES

1. UCCA, Presbyterian Church, Box 3, R. Duncanson to A.E. Armstrong, 26 January 1916. Compare the estimate of 40-50 per cent in Lee Tung-hai, p. 493.

2. *Chinese Times*, 1914-1916; and David Chuen-yan Lai, "Chinese Attempts to Discourage Emigration to Canada: Some Findings from the Chinese Archives in Victoria," *B.C. Studies*, 18 (1973), pp. 33-49. See also Vancouver *Province*, 26 July 1913 and 5 February 1914, in PAC, RG 76, file 23635, part 3, with enclosure from the "Chinese Board of Trade Guild, Victoria." All of these sources indicate that before the European war began the CBAs of Vancouver and Victoria and the Vancouver consulate were urging Chinese to refrain from emigrating to Canada.

3. "Report of the Chief Controller of Chinese Immigration, W.D. Scott," in *Immigration and Colonization, Annual Report*, 10 George V, A.1920, House of Commons, *Sessional Paper 18*, pp. 20-1.

4. *Chinese Times*, 1914-1918; Vancouver *Sun* and Vancouver *Province*, 13 November 1917. On the method of electing representatives to the Chinese parliament, see PAC, RG 25, volume 1133, file 477. *Chinese Times*, 12 November 1919. Cf. Morton, *Sea of Sterile Mountains*, p. 233.

5. *Chinese Times*, 27 September 1919. See House of Commons, *Debates*, 26 September 1919, pp. 661-681, for viewpoints of MPs; Adachi, *The Enemy That Never Was*, p. 105.

6. See photos in Ma Qing (ed.), *Yimin Jianada bidu* (Hong Kong, 1977).

7. *Chinese Times*, 28-29 November 1919; 23 February 1920.

8. *Ibid.*, 8 May 1915; 15 August 1917; 4 November 1918.

9. See *ibid.*, 28 February, 11, 19 March, 20 October 1919; *Victoria Times*, 12 October 1922; Toronto *Sunday World*, 25 November 1922, in PAC, RG 76, file 729921; W. Peter Ward, *White Canada Forever*, pp. 123-7.

10. *Chinese Times*, 30 March 1917; 22 March 1918; Lee Tung-hai, pp. 358-9.

11. On the Saskatchewan case, see *Chinese Times*, 22 March 1918; Chen Kwong Min, *Meizhou Huaqiao tongjian*, p. 477; "Project Integrate: An

Ethnic Study of the Chinese Community of Moose Jaw," Report of a Summer O.F.Y. Project, Moose Jaw, 1973, p. 10; Lee Tung-hai, pp. 358-9. On moral concern, see R. Sampat-Mehta, *International Barriers: Aliens, Immigration, and Citizenship in Canada*, p. 67; and PAC, RG 25, vol. 1524, file 867, Gordon and Elliott to Lapointe, 24 September 1928. But note in the same file a clipping from an Ontario labour publication of 1928 which says that "Labour has long sought this regulation and it expects the Ontario government to enforce the law."

12. There is little doubt that the Chinese saw these measures as attempts to oust them from the restaurant business. See PAC, RG 25, vol. 1142, file 308, Consul-general Yang Shu-wen to Sir Joseph Pope, 4 February 1914. See also several references in the *Chinese Times*, 27 November to 21 December 1923.

13. PAC, RG 25, vol. 1524, file 867; Vancouver City Archives, City Clerk's Incoming Correspondence, vol. 75, Yang to Oliver, 4 April 1919; *Yungaohua Huiguan luocheng tekan*, p. 1.

14. One source says these laws were cancelled by the various provincial assemblies after 1931. Lee Tung-hai, p. 359. However, one notes as late as 1937 discussion of a Vancouver law which might be enforced. *Chinese Times*, January-February, 1937; and Vancouver City Archives, City Clerk's Inward Correspondence, RG A1, vol. 216, Vancouver Mothers' Council to Mayor and City Council, 29 September 1937. For other references to these laws, see *Chinese Times*, 17 November 1925; 25 February, 1 September, 2 October 1928; PAC, RG 25, file 867; and *ibid.*, G 1, file 379.

15. H. Glynn-Ward [Hilda Glynn Howard], *The Writing on the Wall*, with an introduction by Patricia E. Roy (Toronto, 1974).

16. Vancouver City Archives, City Clerk's Incoming Correspondence, vol. 75, Health Committee Meeting, 31 March 1919; *Vancouver Daily World*, 3 March 1923. It is of interest that one survey of 1922 showed that of 103 owners of Chinatown properties in Vancouver, forty-three were not Chinese. *Ibid.*, 6 February 1922.

17. Vancouver City Archives, City Clerk's Incoming Correspondence, vol. 71, 1918: S.Y. Chen *et al.*, Petition to the People of the City of Vancouver; UCCA, Presbyterian Church, Box 3, correspondence of 1917-1918; *Chinese Times*, 14 December 1918.

18. PAC, RG 76, file 831196, Jolliffe to P. Reid, 20 October 1923, attachment: Statement showing deportations by nationalities under the Narcotic Drug Act, from 1 April 1921 to 31 January 1929. A general report on opium and other narcotic use in British Columbia is found in RCMP Archives, RCMP HQ file 1922-HQ-189, Q-1, Wroughton to Commissioner, 20 May 1922. On problems of enforcement, see R. Bassett, "Enforcement of the Opium and Narcotic Drug Act, 1920-1940," unpublished manuscript, RCMP Headquarters, 1972.

19. S.S. Osterhout, *Orientals in Canada* (Toronto, 1929), pp. 74-8, 80-8.

20. "A Religious and Missionary Survey of the Chinese," UCCA, typescript, 1919; Osterhout, *Orientals in Canada.*

21. W. Peter Ward, "The Oriental Immigrant and Canada's Protestant Clergy, 1858-1925," *B.C. Studies*, 22 (1974), pp. 40-55.

22. PAC, RG 76, file 82782: Ottawa Christian Workers to Stewart, 11 April 1923; Montreal Chinese Mission to Stewart, 17 April 1923; MacKay to Stewart, 23 May 1923.

23. Gordon Taylor, conversation, 19 June 1974. For more on missionary views, see "Religious and Missionary Survey"; Osterhout, *Orientals in Canada*; and files in the United Church Archives previously cited. See also references cited concerning the 1923 Chinese Immigration Bill.

24. UCCA, Presbyterian Church, Box 4, R.G. MacBeth, "Social Centre for Chinese in Vancouver," 30 September 1921.

25. For the "competitive" interpretation, see *ibid.*, Duncanson to Armstrong, 16 January 1916 (Box 3); Colman to MacKay, 3 March 1924 (Box 6); and Smith to MacKay, 22 March 1924 (Box 6).

26. *Ibid.*, Colman to MacKay, 3 March 1920 (Box 4). See also Colman to MacKay, 22 June 1923 (Box 5).

27. "A Town's Ghosts Wait for the End," *Canadian Magazine*, 6 January 1966, pp. 9-11; T.W. Paterson, "Cumberland's Ghosts," Victoria *Daily Colonist*, 17 September 1967.

28. Gordon Taylor, conversation, 19 June 1974.

29. UCCA, Presbyterian Church, Box 5, 1922.

30. *Census of Canada*, 1941, I, Table 52; Table 23, p. 552.

31. W.A. Carrothers, "Oriental Standards of Living," in C.H. Young and H.R.Y. Reid, *The Japanese Canadians,* ed. H.A. Innis (Toronto, 1938), pp. 213-14; *Chinese Times*, 8 January 1921. In 1921 there were 490 Chinese students in the Vancouver city schools. *Ibid.*, 20 October 1921. All were in elementary school. The Victoria figure usually cited is 240 (thirty-three of whom were in high school). *Ibid.*, 28 November 1921; *Victoria Times*, 12 October 1922.

32. Ward, *White Canada Forever*, pp. 62-4. Sampat-Mehta, *International Barriers*, p. 59; Lee Tung-hai, p. 357. In 1907 there were ninety-eight Chinese students in Vancouver. Two attended high school; nearly all of the others were students at either Central Elementary School or Strathcona Elementary School. In the same year there were forty-four Chinese boys and six Chinese girls in Victoria's public schools. PAC, RG 76, Accn. 70/47, Box 60, file 729921.

33. Lau Kwong-joo (Joseph Hope), "Weifao Huaqiao sanian fendou shiji," *Weiduoli Zhonghua Huiguan tekan*, p. 6; *Chinese Times*, 20 October 1921; Lee Tung-hai, pp. 357-8.

34. *Victoria Times*, 12, 21 October, 2 November 1922; 8, 30 January 1923.

35. P. Lee to editor, *Victoria Times*, 17 October 1922.

36. Lee Tung-hai, p. 358; *Chinese Times*, 4 September 1923; Ward, *White Canada Forever*, pp. 127-8.

37. *Chinese Times*, 28 March, 13 April, 8 June 1918; 5, 7, 11 March, 1, 9, 10, 26 April, 16 July 1919.
38. *Ibid.*, 14 January 1915; 12 December 1918; 11 September 1923; Vancouver City Archives, City Clerk's Incoming Correspondence, RG A1, vol. 69: Copy of a Resolution Passed by the Council of the City of Vancouver on 13 August 1918.

TEN

An Act of Betrayal: The 1923 Legislation

White hostility toward the Chinese grew in the post-war period, no doubt partly fuelled by increased Chinese militancy. The Chinese still constituted less than 0.45 per cent of the total Canadian population, but they were concentrated in British Columbia where, in Vancouver, for example, their numbers had increased by 80 per cent since 1911.[1]

Of course, some whites had business or social dealings with Chinese and did not subscribe to the more virulent anti-Chinese sentiments. White labour in British Columbia, long among the leaders in anti-Chinese agitation, began to recognize the power of organized Chinese labour. In Vancouver in 1917 white workers joined Chinese workers in a strike, and other white unions discussed Chinese membership or support for their policies. Business also began to see some advantages to alliance rather than discriminatory legislation. In Montreal, faced with a new tax, Chinese and white restaurant owners joined forces to oppose it.[2] Quite apart from the interests of various economic groups, individuals could and did form friendships across the colour line and there were communities that had "pet" Chinese, for whom everyone else felt affection and whom almost nobody would hurt.[3] But British Columbia and the rest of Canada were still a long way from willingness to accept as equals large numbers of Chinese, close at hand and in competition for jobs.

For their part, the Chinese maintained a mixture of separateness and integration. Those Chinese who worked for white employers in mills, mines, and the like were thrown into a work situation with whites, and thereby into direct comparison with them. They also became eligible for some employee benefits such as worker's compensation. The widespread use of worker's compensation by B.C. Chinese labourers reminds us that the notion that the Chinese community "always takes care of its own" and that Chinese did not require or use public services until the Depression of the 1930's is just that – a notion, and a mistaken one. It is clear that when put in a white employment context, as they were in B.C., the Chinese were prepared to rely on Chinese versions of white institutions –

Chinese labour unions – and to co-operate with white groups on matters of mutual interest, rather than to rely exclusively upon CBAs and other Chinese-style associations to protect their interests.

In some ways, Chinese cultural practices helped maintain a certain distance between themselves and white Canadians. It continued to be the practice to disinter and send the bones of deceased Chinese back to their home districts in China for final burial, and some communities had set up their own cemeteries for this purpose. But in many localities there were no Chinese cemeteries, and the Chinese made use of sections of the white cemeteries.

White society's limits on Chinese activity also shaped the ways in which Chinese used white institutions. In British Columbia, where Chinese could train as lawyers but not practise, those Chinese who could afford it were not averse to seeking the best white counsel when they had recourse to the courts – witness Sir Charles Tupper as defence counsel for Chan Sue-yan.[4] But many more Chinese who were less affluent and unable to speak English needed the services of interpreters with some knowledge of the law. Thus there developed *ad hoc* arrangements by which the Chinese professional or semi-professional could offer his services. A case in point is David C. Lew of the Vancouver community, who had trained in law but could not be admitted to the bar, and so was attached to a white law firm, so he could interpret for and give advice to clients.[5]

Brokerage roles of this kind can be one basis for community leadership; and in these years many of the Chinese leaders owed their positions largely to the brokerage function they were able to perform. One of the most influential roles was that of official interpreter for government departments, particularly the Immigration Department, and for the courts. But for all his influence and access to white officialdom, an official interpreter was in a vulnerable and sometimes dangerous position – besieged with offers of bribes, a prime suspect for both white and Chinese communities whenever there was a hint of immigration fraud.

It was immigration fraud and the supposed loopholes in immigration policy that most exercised whites. Current immigration policy allowed merchants and their families exemption from the head tax and freedom to move in and out of the country. But the qualifications for "merchant" status were not clearly defined, leading to labourer immigration in the guise of merchant immigration.[6] Existing legislation and policy also allowed Chinese to enter the country exempt from the head tax as students. Educators and government officials argued that Chinese educated in the United States were carrying back to China positive impressions of that country. Since these students, it was argued, were future leaders, their favourable attitudes would create favourable consequences in trade and diplomacy. Canada, it was said, should follow the American example.[7] A loophole existed because of the political situation in China. Chinese intending to go to Canada as students or merchants were supposed to be certified as to their educational or financial background by the Chinese government and the British consul. In fact, the government of China recognized by Canada – the one in Peking – did not control the Canton area where most emigrants to Canada originated. The British consul in Canton routinely approved applicants presented by the Canton government, making little if any efforts to verify their status. There were no Canadian immigration officials in Canton or Hong Kong to investigate.

The well-known existence of Chinese immigration abuses led to public and governmental proposals to change policies. Those proposals went beyond merely closing loopholes by more careful definition or administrative rearrangement; they included suggestions that the present policies of selective exclusion and application of the head tax to most of those not excluded be replaced by general exclusion and abandonment of the head tax.

Public clamour for exclusion appeared in concert with public complaints about the Chinese in general. In Vancouver especially, proposals for exclusion were part of a general campaign against the presence (and presumed excessive profits) of Chinese in certain occupations and against the many evils, actual and imagined, of Chinatowns. There is no doubt that this campaign was stimulated by post-war economic dislocations: a general economic slump, factory layoffs, jobless war veterans, and so on. As always in trying times, visible minorities were made the scapegoat.

Economic, cultural, and moral issues were lumped together. When the Victoria Chamber of Commerce and the Vancouver Board of Trade called for Oriental exclusion in 1920, they also called for school segregation. That school segregation was as much a moral as an educational issue is evident from the expressed concern that older Chinese students were a bad moral influence on their younger white classmates. Age differences aside, there was also the anxiety, as expressed by a Vancouver school trustee, about the future of a white Canada if his daughter were seated next to a Chinese boy.[8] In 1921 the Vancouver Board of Trade, on the subject of excluding Orientals from landholding, spoke of the importance of doing everything possible to "retain British Columbia for our own people."[9] The B.C. Board of the Retail Merchants of Canada, in a letter to Prime Minister King, said: "To us, it is not merely a question of competitive merchandizing, aggravated by a lower standard of living. It is in fact a struggle of far deeper significance in which home, family, and citizenship considerations outweigh mercenary motives. . . ." A Vancouver judge explained why he regularly rejected Oriental applications for citizenship: "the question is whether or not this country of ours is to be filled up with Orientals from across the Pacific. . . . When I die I want to leave a country a fit place for my children to live in."[10]

Besides the Chambers of Commerce and veterans' organizations, farmers' groups, labour unions, and certain city councils and ratepayers associations joined the cry. The newspapers did their part, notably the *Vancouver Daily World*, which found anti-Chinese articles a useful antidote to sluggish circulation in 1921. By 1921 these groups had managed to bring their concerns to government at both provincial and federal levels, and anti-Orientalism became an issue in the federal election of 1921. Each of the two major parties accused the other of being favourable to Orientals and each denied the charge by attempting to pin it upon the other. Although it is difficult to know how important the issue may have been for the average voter in B.C., anti-Orientalism was obviously popular enough to encourage candidates to bring it up.

It might be inferred from this that only the whites of British Columbia had a negative view of the Chinese and other Asians in their midst, or were concerned about some of the economic and cultural implications of the presence of a Chinese population in Canada. As we have seen, such was hardly the case. Other parts of the country, with far fewer Chinese residents, discriminated against Orientals. In Toronto, for example, labour groups supported the anti-Oriental proposals of their British Columbia colleagues, and their publications included the notion that Asian immigrants had not only lower living standards but lower ideals. *Maclean's, Saturday Night*, and *Jack Canuck* told their readers that the Chinese were an inferior race. Allowed to enter Canada in great numbers, given a chance to intermarry, they would only pollute and weaken Canada. As early as 1907 *Saturday Night* suggested that the Chinese in that city be kept moving so that no Chinatown could be established. Indeed, Toronto's Chinatown, like Calgary's, took some time to form in a fixed location. It was not until after 1915 that a stable Chinese business and residential area emerged in Toronto.[11]

The result of this mounting anti-Oriental sentiment was a campaign for a change in the federal legislation governing immigration of Orientals. In the spring of 1922, two Members of Parliament, H.H. Stevens of Vancouver and W.G. McQuarrie of New Westminster, introduced a resolution in favour of the exclusion of Chinese. The motion also had considerable support among other members in the House. As well, the Department of Immigration and Colonization was aware that the immigration policies were not working as had been intended. It was therefore not difficult for the Mackenzie King government to be persuaded of the need to tighten the law.

Although there was as much concern about the Japanese as about the Chinese, it was politically impossible to pass an anti-Japanese exclusion law. Japanese immigration was covered by the secret "Gentlemen's Agreement" of 1908, by which Japan undertook to restrict the number and kind of its emigrants to Canada. Until 1922, Britain and Japan were partners in the Anglo-Japanese alliance, which was then replaced by a multilateral arrangement, with Britain and Japan among the members. Relations with Japan, therefore, were those of two major powers to one another and were defined in Canada as involving "imperial interests."

China, of course, was in a different category. In 1923 it was still what it had been since 1900, the "sick man of Asia," and in no position ever to be an equal partner to an alliance with any of the Powers. An exclusion law that applied to the Chinese in Canada was, therefore, possible to pass with only mild concern about "imperial interests."

The Canadian government had, to be sure, taken some cognizance of the Chinese government's interests and expressions. In 1915 the Chinese consul-general had presented a draft "Gentlemen's Agreement" to regulate Chinese immigration to Canada. In 1922 the King government again negotiated briefly with the Chinese consul-general, Dr. Chilien Tsur. Tsur's government made it clear that it accepted the idea that some restriction might be necessary, but that it wished to negotiate for an expansion of the rights of those Chinese already in Canada. It agreed with the idea of abandoning the head tax, which had long been a humiliation since it applied to no other immigrants than the Chinese. But above all, it wished that changes be made in the form of a treaty between the two countries, not as a piece of legislation in the Canadian Parliament.[12]

When King began negotiations with the Chinese government in the summer of 1922, Chinese communities across the country, with encouragement from Consul-General Tsur, organized to present their views on what a new treaty ought to include. Since the Canadian government had shown interest in developing Canada's trade with China, it was suggested that two separate treaties on immigration and trade might be in prospect. In Vancouver and Victoria the CBAs and Chambers of Commerce took the lead, along with the Chinese Canadian Club, in organizing study committees, holding public discussion meetings, and soliciting public response to a list of questions about the treaties that was published in the Chinese newspapers. In other Chinese communities, the procedure probably was similar.

In September the Chinese Labour Association of Vancouver and its affiliated bodies, the Chinese Shingle Workers Federation and the Chinese Produce Sellers Group, presented a strong five-point response. (1) Chinese labourers should have unrestricted opportunity to visit China as other foreign labourers had to visit their native lands. If the two-year leave period could not be extended by a general rule, the Chinese consul should have the right to negotiate individual extensions. (2) Chinese immigration should receive treatment equal to that given the Japanese. Chinese merchants and students should be treated like the citizens of Canada's "most-favoured" trading partner. (Japan was allowed a quota said to be 500 labourers per year.) A similar quota should be set for Chinese labourers which should bear the same percentage relationship to the Chinese population the Japanese quota bore to the Japanese population. This quota should be constant, regardless of fluctuations in the Canadian economy. (3) All Chinese now in Canada and those to come in the future should have the right to bring their families. If there should be fear of dependents becoming public charges, there could be a rule that a Chinese must have saved a certain amount of money before being allowed to bring in his family. (4) The health examination given only to steerage class passengers (most Asians) is degrading and unnecessary. (5) Immigrants should be granted the freedom to hold any kind of job whatsoever.[13]

In January of 1923 the Vancouver study group, headed by Seto More (Seto Ying-shek), presented a four-point proposal. (1) The present law, with its head tax and various restrictions, should be abolished. (2) If all other countries' laws prohibit the immigration of labourers, then it is acceptable for Canada to follow suit, but every other class should be allowed to enter freely and once in Canada should be protected. (3) Chinese already in Canada should enjoy the same rights as other foreign residents. (4) Chinese already in Canada but lacking head tax certificates should be allowed to remain.[14] This last proposal touched a matter of great concern to the Chinese. The head tax certificate, containing the bearer's picture, was the only proof an immigrant had that he had paid his head tax and was legally in the country. It had to be available for presentation upon demand to RCMP constables and Immigration officials. Not all Chinese had certificates; some because they were illegal immigrants, others because they had arrived in the Gold Rush or CPR construction days before the head tax certificate system was established. The proposal was for a "let bygones be bygones" policy.

Consul Tsur attempted to soften anti-Chinese sentiment by speaking to white Canadian groups. He offered improved Canada-China trade as a *quid pro quo* to Canadian acceptance of Chinese immigration. China, he said, was now becoming prosperous, and hence a good market for Canadian goods. The more prosperous China became the less need there was for Chinese to go overseas to Canada and elsewhere seeking livelihood. Hence, Chinese immigration would not increase greatly. Concerning drug use in Chinatowns, he reminded his listeners that it was Westerners who introduced opium to China. Increased tobacco consumption might overcome opium use, and British and American tobacco companies in China were making efforts to bring that about. The Chinese government and merchant circles were, he said, well aware of the treatment of the Chinese in Canada, including the current attempt to segregate Chinese school children in Victoria. They might choose to retaliate in ways that would impair the development of Canada's trade with China. Canadian missionary work in China was also hampered by the treatment of Chinese in Canada. How, Chinese in China asked, could Canadian missionaries preach a religion of love when Canadians in Canada treated the Chinese there in an unloving, discriminatory way?[15]

The point about trade was probably the strongest of the Chinese arguments. Canada's interest in expanding its China trade had reached the point of sending a Trade Commissioner, Dr. J.W. Ross, to Shanghai, where he was supervising a display of Canadian products. Persons inside and outside of government pointed out that the Chinese were masters of the boycott and a boycott of Canadian goods might very well be extended to British goods. Britain's trading pre-eminence in China was already being threatened by the Americans, who were making good use of the sympathies of young Chinese leaders who had studied in the United States. Debates about allowing Chinese students into Canada were thus very much to the point.[16]

In March, 1923, Tsur presented a twelve-point proposal to Mackenzie King. (1) Guarantees of rights, livelihood, and property of the citizens of each country who resided in the other country. (2) Abolition of the head tax. (3) Abolition of all special entry facilities for Chinese coming to Canada. (4) Right of all Chinese ministers of religion, students, and merchants to have unrestricted entry into Canada, regardless of the time or other relevant legislation. (5) Chinese of those categories to be able to bring their families to Canada. (6) The two governments to agree on an annual quota for appropriate classes of immigrants. (7) Chinese children to study in classrooms with whites, not in segregated facilities. (8) Chinese admitted under the quota to be established to be free to work in any government or corporate enterprise. (9) In accordance with the "most-favoured" principle, abolition of existing facilities for special medical examinations when nationals of either country enter the other country. (10) Chinese born in Canada, besides having the rights of other foreigners in the province where they are born, also to have the vote. (11) Import duties on Chinese goods to be the same as those on goods from other countries. (12) Chinese boats carrying Chinese goods and Chinese merchants to receive "most-favoured" treatment in Canadian ports.[17]

By this time the House of Commons was discussing a Chinese Immigration Bill which would virtually terminate further Chinese immigration. The government had decided against handling the matter by treaty because the Peking government did not control Canton and the other South China emigration areas and so could not enforce any agreement. The legislation that was finally introduced in 1923, therefore, contained the following provisions: (1) the head tax was abolished; (2) students below university age were no longer admitted; (3) only four classes of immigrants were to be allowed to enter. These were university students, merchants, native-borns returning from several years of education in China, and diplomatic personnel. University students were to be allowed in the country only for their period of university study. Diplomatic personnel might stay for several years, but they were not numerous and not really a part of the Chinese communities. In terms of the regular membership of those communities, merchants were the only group to be allowed as new immigrants. Merchants could bring in their families, but only on appeal to the Minister of Immigration on an individual-case basis and only for short terms, which had to be renewed. The definition of "merchant" was made carefully, so as to exclude operators of laundries and restaurants, retail produce dealers, and the like. It could include only those of substantial capital engaged in export-import trade between China and Canada. Following practice since 1921, a Canadian immigration officer was to be stationed in Hong Kong to visa all applications of those who claimed merchant status.

Responding to the proposed bill, which would have such a devastating effect on Chinese immigration, Chinese communities across the country began to form committees to seek the defeat of the bill, or, failing that, its amendment. In Vancouver and other large communities there were theatrical performances to raise funds. And it was common practice to assess each owner of a business a fee of $2 and each ordinary member of the community a contribution of $1.

In April the editor of the Freemasons' newspaper proposed strategies for dealing with the bill. He began by quoting a saying: "A weak country has no foreign policy." He modified that by suggesting that strong countries may use intimidation to gain their ends, but weak ones could only use things like public opinion. Since Consul Tsur represented a weak country he could do little with the Canadian government. It was up to the Chinese in Canada to make their case clear to Members of Parliament and the newspapers, representatives of possibly sympathetic groups, and Canadian society in general. Meanwhile, telegrams should be sent to influential groups in industry, commerce, and education in China and to Overseas Chinese in countries other than Canada, pointing out that the proposed legislation was insulting to China. Wires should also be sent to the British government and to British diplomats in China, stressing the point that this legislation was unreasonable and contrary to principles of international good will.[18] Similar strategies were proposed by the Edmonton Protest Association, and some were pursued.

By May, when the bill had passed Commons and the Chinese were trying to influence Senators to amend it, the mood of frustration and powerlessness was even more apparent. A *Chinese Times* editorial of May 17 noted the weakness and disunity in China and the divisions among the Chinese in Canada as forces making opposition to the bill difficult. There was still, however, a chance that public opinion, if sufficiently aroused on the side of the Chinese, might prevent passage. A few days later, the committee co-ordinating the Chinese opposition to the bill gave vent to its frustrations, saying that Chinese in Canada were treated as "slaves," as "insects," or as "beasts of burden." It was the Chinese who built the railroad that united the Canadians; now the Canadians wished to exclude them with an inhumane law. If the Canadian government tries to obtain a trade treaty with China, said the committee, business organizations in China must urge both the Northern and Southern governments in that country not to sign such a treaty unless the treatment given the Chinese in Canada be improved.[19]

By this time the Chinese communities were linked by a general headquarters for their effort to amend the bill. The Chinese Association of Canada was established with its offices in Toronto. Its executive committee represented several of the major Chinese communities across the country. Joseph Hope (Lau Kwong-joo) of Victoria was the head of the Chinese Canadian Association of Victoria, and past president of the Victoria CCBA. Y.N. Kwan was a prominent Methodist minister in Vancouver. The other members were Fairman Wong (Wong Fat-man) of Montreal and Lee Hong-yuey representing Winnipeg.

In the daily operation of the headquarters, the Toronto influence was strong. The association was housed in the building of the Chinese Christian Association of Toronto (YMCI) at 124 University Avenue. The president of the association was T.C. Mark. Ma T.K. Wou was vice-president. The English-language secretaries were also leaders of the Toronto Chinese Christian Association: Ing S. Hoan, George P. Mark, and E.C. Mark.[20]

On April 29 a large meeting of Chinese was held in Victoria Hall in Toronto to hear the concerns of various Chinese communities. Over 1,000 persons were reported to be in attendance. There were representatives from smaller Chinese communities in Ontario, such as Sarnia, Sudbury, Hamilton, Kitchener, North Bay, Windsor, and Kingston, and from Montreal, Ottawa, Regina, and Victoria. Shortly after, Toronto Chinese leaders and white supporters met at the King Edward Hotel in Toronto.

After these meetings the Chinese Association of Canada organized a representative committee to go to Ottawa to lobby against the bill. Here again, the influence of Toronto was evident. Of eight members, three were from the Toronto Chinese Christian Association (T.C. Mark, Ing Hoan, and E.C. Mark). The others were Joseph Hope, Ho Lem (Calgary), Hum Quon (Ottawa), and Fairman Wong and Reverend Lee Yuk-chin (Montreal).[21] They presented a long brief which proposed amendments to the bill. These would have recognized all Chinese now in Canada as legal residents and permitted families to join merchants already here and family migration of all future immigrants.[22]

Missionaries joined the Chinese in criticizing the bill and urging that it be amended. Reverend Noyes, the executive secretary of the Eastern Canada mission, Dr. MacKay, the secretary of the Presbyterian Church of Canada, and leaders of the Western Canada Presbyterian Mission to Orientals and the Methodist and Anglican Oriental Missions all wrote letters or sent telegrams urging amendment. Individual Chinese missions in Quebec, Ontario, and the Prairies also expressed their concern.

The bill's general exclusionist features were not opposed by missionary groups. Indeed, one group of missionary leaders suggested that cutting the flow of newcomers might make it easier to Canadianize and assimilate those already in Canada. Abolition of the head tax was also applauded.[23] The major concerns of the missionaries were to amend it in two areas. The unamended bill would make it difficult for Chinese ministers of religion and churchworkers to enter Canada, thus seriously limiting mission work in the Chinese communities. Their other objection was that the bill did not allow families to join those Chinese who were already here. This the missionaries considered both inhumane and harmful. The absence of families led to all the vices for which Chinatowns were criticized, and specifically to sexual immorality or intermarriage, both of which were considered undesirable.[24]

Appeals by the Chinese communities to Sun Yat-sen in Canton produced a response that had no effect on the proposed legislation. Sun and his colourful Canadian bodyguard, Morris "Two-gun" Cohen, cabled the Canadian government asking suspension of discussion of the bill. The Sun government in Canton, they said, had signed a railroad construction contract with a Vancouver firm, thus opening a new era of Sino-Canadian economic co-operation which should be discussed before passing such a bill.[25]

All these efforts succeeded only in amending the details of the bill. For example, illegal immigrants could pay $500 and be recognized as legal residents. Ministers and teachers might come in with individual-case permission of the Minister of Immigration. But these and other minor amendments did not greatly mitigate the legislation's central features, which were broadly exclusionist.

The result of the bill was that, barring a sudden expansion of China-Canada trade on a scale that would attract a great many new affluent Chinese merchants, Chinese immigration to Canada was virtually terminated. The Chinese hopes for a quota system were dashed. Any expectation that exclusion of further immigration would be accompanied by better treatment of those already in Canada also proved vain. Nothing was said about the franchise or about any laws or codes that restricted Chinese opportunity in Canada.

Why had the Chinese failed in their effort to oppose or seriously amend the bill? The Chinese themselves thought that China's weakness and disunity and their own divisions were basic limitations. Yet in their efforts to oppose the bill the Chinese in Canada created for themselves a unity much greater than they had ever had. They could not sustain it once the crisis was past, but the unified effort and the institutions used were to prove precedents when a second great crisis came.

China's weakness and division were undoubtedly important factors. But the terms of the Act, by allowing merchants engaged in China-Canada trade to continue to come to Canada, separated the issue of trade from those of general immigration and protection of all other Chinese in Canada. Trade could be encouraged while immigration was cut off, and Chinese business circles and the Chinese government need not feel it necessary to defend Chinese immigration in order to avoid damage to their other interests. If allowance for merchants and students had not been made, China's protests probably would have been more vigorous.

The other critical factor was absence of major support from anywhere within white society in Canada. Even if the Chinese in British Columbia and Saskatchewan had had the vote, it is doubtful that they could have prevented the development of a B.C.-led effort in Parliament towards exclusion. They simply were not sufficiently numerous, even had they been voters; and in other parts of Canada they were even less numerous. They had to rely upon white sympathizers and there were not enough of those willing to go far enough to defend their interests. Large employers of Chinese labour had earlier urged rescinding the Orders-in-Council that prohibited labourer immigration.[26] But on this occasion they apparently were not prepared to stand on the side of Chinese labour. The missionaries were sympathetic, but ambivalent. Other white Canadians were generally indifferent. In Parliament the united, non-partisan, anti-Oriental campaign by the B.C. members and the attitudes of indifference or doubt about capacity for assimilation of some eastern Canada members were enough to ensure passage of the bill.

Mackenzie King, who had had much more experience with Asians in Canada than most MPs, was aware that the Chinese felt it strange that they should be taxed in order to enter a country they were helping to build up. He wished to terminate the head tax as much because it was objectionable to the Chinese as because it was not effective at controlling Chinese immigration. He favoured Chinese university students because they might promote trade with China and because they would carry back to China some of Canada's "higher civilization."[27]

J.S. Woodsworth saw the problem in a larger context. He first pithily observed that great corporations had brought Asians to Canada as coolie labour, but now that the coolie labour had entered business and shown some success, business had turned anti-Oriental. He did not oppose exclusion, because the unemployment situation, he believed, required it. But the larger problem he saw as the absence of a minimum wage which, he believed, would prevent employers from attempting to undercut prevailing wages by bringing in coolie labour.[28]

Thus, no one stood up for the Chinese in Parliament. The B.C. members were supported by those in their province who felt threatened by the spread of Chinese farm operations, produce dealers, and grocery stores, and those who felt culturally threatened by the Chinese. The B.C. members were unanimous in their view and well-organized in their effort to produce anti-Oriental legislation.

The Chinese Immigration Act went into effect on Dominion Day, July 1, 1923. The Chinese marked the day as "Humiliation Day," refusing to participate in Dominion Day activities and closing their businesses, as they were to do every year thereafter until the "43 harsh regulations," as the Chinese called the Act, were replaced by a more favourable policy. The Act of 1923 had profound demographic and other consequences for the Chinese communities and, in fact, it ushered in a new era in their lives.

NOTES

1. See Appendix, Table 7.
2. *Chinese Times*, 6 February 1918.
3. S.S. Osterhout, *Orientals in Canada*, p. 92; Howard Palmer, "Anti-Oriental Sentiment in Alberta, 1880-1920," *Canadian Ethnic Studies*, II, 2 (1970), p. 40 and notes 69, 73; Vancouver *Province*, 22 November 1928, p. 1.
4. *Victoria Times*, 20 March 1919.
5. Vancouver *Sun*, 25 March 1924; PABC, Attorney General's Files, David C. Lew Letterbooks, 1907-1909.
6. See PAC, RG 76, Accn. 70/47, Box 60, file 729921: Commissioner to Cory, 22 April 1921; Cory to Jolliffe, 12 April 1921; Asst. Chief Controller to Cory, 8 December 1920; P. Reid to Cory, 28 April 1921; and P. Reid to Stewart, 6 May 1922. See also Sampat-Mehta, *International Barriers*, pp. 93-9.
7. Sampat-Mehta, *International Barriers*, pp. 82-6. Proposals of this kind were hardly new. For early examples of such, see PAC, RG 76, file 827821, part 2, Sir J.N. Jordan to Sir Edward Grey, 8 September 1908, and associated documents of 1908-09. For later discussion, see PAC, RG 25, vol. 1539, file 178; vol. 1599, file 333 (1930-31).
8. Ward, *White Canada Forever*, pp. 124, 62-3; Patricia Roy, "The Oriental Menace in British Columbia," in S.M. Trofimenkoff (ed.), *The Twenties in Western Canada* (Ottawa, 1972), p. 249.
9. Ward, *White Canada Forever*, p. 126.
10. Roy, "Oriental Menace," pp. 248-50.
11. K. Paupst, "A Note on Anti-Chinese Sentiment in Toronto," *Canadian Ethnic Studies*, IX, 1 (1977), pp. 54-9; Lao Bo, "Hostages in Canada: Toronto's Chinese (1880-1947)," *The Asianadian*, I, 2 (1978), p. 12.
12. PAC, MG 30, E 15, vol. 22: Loring Christie Papers, Subject Files, file 76.
13. *Chinese Times*, 7-8 September 1922.
14. *Ibid.*, 31 January 1923.
15. *Ibid.*, 31 January, 2 April 1923; *Victoria Times*, 29 January 1923.
16. *Victoria Times*, 29 January, 13 March 1923; see also PAC, RG 76, file 827821; and UCCA, Presbyterian Church, Box 5, MacKay to Smith, 23 May 1923. On this general issue, see *Chinese Times*, 17 October 1916; 17 April, 1 November 1919.
17. *Chinese Times*, 14 March 1923.
18. *Ibid.*, 23 March, 19, 23, 27 April, 7, 10, 15, 28 May 1923.
19. *Ibid.*, 22 May 1923.
20. PAC, RG 76, file 827821, part 9, Chinese Association of Canada to King, 12 July 1923.
21. *Chinese Times*, 16 May 1923.
22. PAC, RG 76, file 827821, part 7, Paterson to P. Reid, 18 April 1923; *ibid.*, part 8, P. Reid to Featherston, 18 June 1923; P. Reid to Dandurand, 21 May 1923; Proudfoot Petition to Senate, 7 May 1923; *ibid.*, part 9, Tsur to King, 31 May 1923.

23. *Ibid.*, part 9, Osterhout, Lascelles-Ward, and Smith to King, 3 April 1923.
24. *Ibid.*, part 7, Noyes to Stewart, 16 April 1923; Canon S. Gould to Stewart, 19 April 1923; Montreal Chinese Mission to Stewart, 17 April 1923; Ottawa Christian Workers to Stewart, 11 April 1923; Ellis to Stewart, 30 April 1923; Beech to King, 18 May 1923; North Saskatchewan Chinese Mission to King, 10 May 1923; MacKay to Stewart, 23 May 1923; UCCA, Presbyterian Church, Box 5, MacKay to Smith, 24 April 1923.
25. *Ibid.*, Sun to Minister of Interior, 17 May 1923; Cohen to Stewart, 6 May 1923.
26. *Ibid.*, file 729921, Scott to Niagara Falls Trades and Labour Congress, 21 August 1917.
27. House of Commons, *Debates*, 8 May 1922, pp. 1554-9.
28. *Ibid.*, pp. 1570-3.

PART THREE

1923-1947

ELEVEN

Humiliation and Tenacity: The Chinese Community after 1923

DEMOGRAPHY

The 1923 Chinese Immigration Act, by stopping further immigration, effectively ended the growth of the Chinese communities in Canada for the next twenty-five years.[1] Many older men retired to China; others lacking employment during the Depression were encouraged to return to China. These losses were not balanced by gains in natural growth. There were not enough Chinese women in Canada to produce substantial natural population increase. The demographic results of Canadian immigration policy as applied to the Chinese are readily visible in Table A.

TABLE A

Total Chinese Population, 1901-1941

Year	Total Chinese Population	As per cent of total Canadian population
1901	17,312	.32%
1911	27,774	.39%
1921	39,587	.45%
1931	46,519	.45%
1941	34,627	.30%

SOURCE: *Census of Canada*, 1911, II, p. 367; 1921, I, p. 353; 1931, II, p. 396; 1941, IV, p. 2.

In the 1920's natural increase offset the ending of immigration, adding 7,000 members to the Chinese population. After that, deaths and departures were dominant forces, and the population dropped even below the 1921 figure. It is not surprising that there were predictions that the Chinese population of Canada would eventually disappear.

Although the Chinese had been dispersing eastward across Canada during the first two decades of the century, the largest number still lived in British Columbia (see Table 5 in the Appendix). In the period after

1923, every province lost Chinese population, but western Canada more so than the East. It is likely that part of British Columbia's population loss was in the form of eastward migration, especially to Ontario. This trend was especially noticeable in Vancouver, which lost some 6,000 people (or half its Chinese population) during the 1930's. By contrast, the Chinese community in Victoria was remarkably stable. But when the coal mines of Vancouver Island declined as a source of Chinese employment in the 1920's, Victoria was also affected, as ex-miners came into the city looking for work. Vancouver and Victoria, unlike other parts of Canada, were much affected by seasonal labour conditions. A large percentage of their Chinese populations wintered in the city and did seasonal labour outside during the summer. In this the B.C. cities and the province of British Columbia were for the Chinese an area unlike any other in Canada.

British Columbia differed from the rest of Canada in another aspect – the male/female ratio. We have already seen that the Chinese population was predominantly one of single males. This unbalanced ratio, still marked in 1923, would decline over the next two decades because of the departure by death or retirement to China of older single men and the greater proportional importance of the Canadian-born Chinese population which, of course, had many more females in it than did the immigrant population. Nowhere was this trend more obvious than in British Columbia, which had more Canadian-born Chinese, and hence more Canadian-born females, than any other place.

The unbalanced sex ratios would suggest the possibility of intermarriage with white women in Canada. It is difficult to obtain information on this subject. Both in white society and in the Chinese communities intermarriage was socially disapproved of, at least up to the 1940's. It did occur, but how frequently is very difficult to determine. Regionally, the Prairies may have been an area of relatively frequent intermarriage because of the phenomenon of the isolated grocery store or restaurant operated by a single Chinese man.

The Chinese population was always one of the oldest among immigrant populations in Canada. The new or second generation growing up in the 1920's and 1930's was not large enough for there to be more than 10-15 per cent of the population as children at any one time. It is important to note, however, that with the virtual termination of new immigration in 1923 the character of the youthful population was greatly changed. By 1931 75 per cent of the Chinese teen-agers in Canada were Canadian-born, quite unlike the case in 1921, when immigrants formed the major proportion of the teen-age population. The disappearance of the teen-age immigrant helped raise the Canadian-language literacy rate in the Chinese population from 70 per cent in 1921 to 83 per cent in 1931. Some of this improvement was no doubt due to the deaths and retirements of several older men who were illiterate. Some of it may have reflected generally rising literacy rates in Canadian society as a whole.

The rate for Chinese teen-agers went up substantially, apparently because of the near-disappearance of immigrant teen-agers. Even the few teen-age immigrants who came in this period had higher rates of literacy than their previous counterparts, perhaps because, under the stricter controls of 1923, they were likely to be sons of genuine merchants and hence more likely to have had some previous contact with the English language than was the case for many of the pre-1923 immigrant teen-agers.

Ability to speak Canadian languages was also far from universal in the Chinese communities. In 1921, 32 per cent of Canada's Chinese were unable to speak English. In Quebec the number of French-speaking Chinese apparently was always small. In 1941, of 1,703 Quebec Chinese polled, only 10 per cent could speak French.

These changes, many of them consequent upon the 1923 legislation, resulted in a growing proportion of Canadian-born Chinese among the Chinese population. In 1921 only 7.5 per cent of the Chinese population was born in Canada; by 1931 it was 11.6 per cent. The largest number were always found in British Columbia; in almost any time period over 60 per cent of all Canadian-born Chinese lived in that province.

Along with the increase in Canadian-born Chinese, this period also saw an increase in naturalized Canadian Chinese. Here, though, the geographical differences are quite striking. From the beginning Ontario had a high rate of naturalization. While the national average was 4.8 per cent Ontario usually had 10-20 per cent of its Chinese population as naturalized citizens. Toronto, specifically, had a Chinese population that included 11 per cent naturalized Chinese in 1921 and 18 per cent in 1931. By contrast, B.C. and Vancouver/Victoria were always at the 2 per cent or 3 per cent level. To the extent that naturalization is an indicator of assimilation, we would expect the B.C. results to be as they are. Vancouver and Victoria had large, well-established Chinatowns, which provided services and environments that encompassed most of the needs of the Chinese who lived there. Many Chinese could get by with little contact with white society and little need to make any commitment to it. Of equal importance, in B.C. judges were more likely than elsewhere to refuse citizenship applications from Chinese.[2] Moreover, naturalization in B.C. did not cover the franchise or any other advantages.

The Maritimes were, in general, the opposite social extreme. Except for Halifax, there were no Chinatowns. Chinese were not numerous and those who decided to remain in Canada apparently were prepared to move toward assimilation. The rates of naturalization from New Brunswick and Prince Edward Island are very high, probably for that reason.

If we add the naturalized to the Canadian-born, we can see how the Chinese population was becoming more associated with Canada. By 1941, in those provinces where the largest numbers of Chinese were found, the proportion of the Chinese population that was either Canadian-born or naturalized had doubled between 1921 and 1941. In such communities, one-fourth to one-third of the members of the community were either Canadian-born or naturalized.

Another influence on the rate of assimilation was the spread of Christianity. The proportion of avowed Christians in the Chinese community rose from 16 per cent (7,600) in 1931 to nearly 30 per cent (10,000) a decade later. Again the regional spread is interesting. In the Maritimes, the majority apparently were Christians. Again, Vancouver and Victoria are exceptional. But even in Vancouver by 1941 20 per cent of the population was counted as Christian. Urban Ontario was a centre of Christian influence, with half the Chinese there being listed as adherents of that faith. The United Church was easily the leader throughout Canada. Almost half the Chinese church members were affiliated with it. Another 25 per cent were Presbyterians. Smaller proportions (about 10 per cent each) were Roman Catholics and Anglicans. Quebec was exceptional in the extent of Roman Catholic influence. Nearly 50 per cent of the Chinese Christians there were Catholics.

The geographical pattern of Christian influence among the Chinese seems to be similar to that of naturalization. Where there were the oldest and largest Chinese settlements – Victoria and Vancouver – the influence of Christianity was relatively slight. In other large but newer Chinatowns, such as those on the Prairies and in Ontario and Quebec, Christianity enjoyed an important minority position by the 1930's. In the Maritimes, Christians, by the 1930's and 1940's, were the majority.

The classifications "naturalized," "Canadian-born," and "Christian" are overlapping. Many of the Christians were Canadian-born or naturalized. We cannot add them up to give us an index of assimilation or integration. We can, however, say that by the 1930's and 1940's, due to Canadian immigration policy and to natural processes, the major Chinese communities looked very different from what they had in 1923. Large segments of each of these communities were Canadian-born or naturalized and large proportions were, or claimed to be, Christian.

During the 1920's and 1930's Chinese entered new occupations and increased their participation in some others where they previously had been only slightly involved. The broad trends in the most common occupations are visible from Table 14 in the Appendix. As before, the majority of Chinese workers were in the service industries. Most of the remainder were small commercial operators or labourers in extractive industries. In the Maritimes there were now Chinese longshoremen, truck drivers, construction workers, and a small group of professionals. In Quebec a few Chinese were owners of small-scale manufacturing enterprises. There were Chinese mechanics and machinists, and Chinese truck and taxicab drivers. In Ontario the same trends were visible and there were in addition some Chinese found in the building trades as carpenters, painters, and plumbers. Across the Prairies, agriculture and the service industries continued to be the loci of most Chinese activity, but Chinese had begun to appear in office work, mostly as clerks. All across Canada the most striking difference in the next two decades would be the much greater participation by Chinese women in the white sector of the economy. Many of them were textile workers, presumably in sweat-shop operations. But some began to appear in offices as well, as secretaries, bookkeepers, and clerks. Finally, the beginnings of a professional class emerged in the 1920's and 1930's. Architects, engineers, physicians, dentists, and bank managers started to make their appearance, more in eastern Canada than in the West, and hardly at all in British Columbia.

In British Columbia the most important occupational change was the expansion and diversification of Chinese interests in agriculture. Mechanization and declining production in mining operations sent many Chinese from small interior towns to Victoria or Vancouver, where many of them went into suburban agriculture or agriculture-related occupations. Chinese greenhouse operations expanded, and wholesaling was added to retailing as a Chinese activity. White reaction to this expansion was not long in coming and the Chinese met it by forming various agricultural associations to defend their interests.

The restaurant business continued to be important for the Chinese, and in the late 1920's and early 1930's there was a revival of interest, in some cities, in enforcement of by-laws prohibiting the employment of white women in Chinese-owned businesses. For the first time, laws of this kind were passed in provinces east of Ontario, specifically, in Quebec and in Nova Scotia. In Toronto and in Halifax Chinese restaurant owners organized associations to negotiate for non-enforcement, and it appears that everywhere enforcement was spotty.

LIFE PATTERNS

For the individual Chinese, particularly the aging single man, life during this period was one of insecurity and, above all, loneliness. For those who lived in Chinatowns with a developed associational life there was an opportunity for some variety in personal relationships. But for many laundrymen and restaurant operators in small towns or Chinese loggers and miners living together in bunkhouses, the only meaningful relationships were within the very small group that lived together. For those who did not join a white-sponsored church group or make their shops into centres of white community life, there was very little significant contact with individuals who were not Chinese. Cut off from white society by language, discrimination, and their own reluctance to become involved, they placed an enormous burden on each other and on their hopes for returning to China. As the years dragged on hopes of returning to China receded for all but a minority of the more successful Chinese. There was only the endless monotony of uninteresting work and the intensity of their relationships with each other. Perhaps it is not surprising that the most shocking crimes of passion seem to have occurred not in large Chinatowns, where murder was the outcome of politics or gambling rivalry, but in these lonely outposts on the Prairies or in the Maritimes.[3]

Loneliness, monotony, and hard work were the lot of the single Chinese male on the Chinese frontier in Canada. The Chinese house servant in a white household or the Chinese businessman with a family around him suffered less from these problems, but he, too, had to encounter discrimination. The experiences of these men are typical of many:

"You know those days: ching ching, Chinaman. . . . Every day, ching ching Chinaman; chop down tail. . . . Fight back? Chinese, we had to take it, that's all. . . ."

"In the '20s . . . everybody have very big problems. Why? Because they always want to send their families, to come closer with their families, to be together. But they can't, see? So every time . . . this is a very sad thing. . . . [In Montreal] they were mostly in laundry. . . . And these people were really working very hard, from the morning, 7:00, till midnight, 12:00. So that's why our church service was then usually in the afternoons. We have some members in laundry, they work so late they can't come to the service in the morning. That's why we make it in the afternoon."

"I came from Toi-san. My family is still in China. I always intended to go back, but I don't have enough money. I went back to China three times. . . . What was life like here? Oh, there was no transportation. I used to walk from Barkerville to Quesnel [B.C.]. I used to carry 200 pounds on this [shoulder] pole from Barkerville to Quesnel. There was good solidarity between everyone here, even between Caucasians and Chinese. . . . No trouble at all."

"They [whites] teased you by pulling your hair [pigtail]. They always sang in unison while doing this: "Ching Chong Chinaman, chop chop tail". . . . [some] were even worse. They threw stones at you. Aiya, things were really bad in those days [1907]. I was too scared to go out."

"I came to Canada August, 1913, landed at Victoria, B.C. In the old days we all come by ship. I came by the "Empress of India." It cost about $50.00 for the fare, third class from Hong Kong. It took about three weeks to a month to get to Victoria. . . . About a month after I landed at Victoria my uncle put me in school at the Chinese Benevolent Association to learn English. That lasted for only two weeks. My uncle thought that I should go to work instead of wasting time going to school. He said that Chinese came overseas to try to make money, not to get an education. My uncle was old; he was afraid that I'd get lazy by going to school, so he put me in a Chinese restaurant on Johnson Street in Victoria for about $5.00 a month, and sometimes I didn't even get paid. I worked 13-14 hours a day, 7 days a week. Those were the old days. No holidays, no nothing. I worked for the restaurant for about a year. Then a friend recommended me for a job as a houseboy in an English lady's home. She was a very nice lady and very good to me. . . . I lived there, ate there, and she taught me a little English. . . . I worked there for over a year. [Then] I worked around Chinatown, in a restaurant as a waiter and learned to be a cook. I left Victoria in 1919, then I went to Toronto working on the Great Lakes on the ships. I worked there for three years, then I went back to Victoria."

Q: When did you come to Canada? A: 1920. Q: So you were only 13 years old? A: I guess so. Something around there. I came on a Blue Funnel boat. It took 21 days . . . and when I arrived in Canada I was locked in Immigration for 19 days. Q: Here, or in Victoria? A: Here, in Vancouver, in the old building, behind steel bars, like a jailbird. . . . until they checked, because there were so many immigrants at that time.[4]

A typical pattern for a Chinese who came to Canada between 1911 and 1947 was to arrive as a teen-ager, sometimes with his passage arranged for by his father or uncle who had preceded him. Employment was miscellaneous and subject to frequent change in search of more income opportunity: laundry or restaurant work, houseboy jobs, rooming house or grocery store operation. After a few years in Canada a man in his early twenties would return to China to get married. There might be one or two later visits to father children. Otherwise, he remained in Canada, sent money to his family, but had little hope of bringing them to Canada to join him.[5]

Not all Chinese followed such a nomadic life. Some found suitable opportunities running restaurants or general stores in small towns on the Prairies. There they might fit in as trusted members of the local community. The Chinese-operated restaurant or general store might be the town meeting place where white men came to spend their idle hours. Its proprietor might be an informal banker, who accepted white men's money for safe-keeping, and made loans to those in need.

When the hotel closed down, he started his own restaurant and a store as well. . . . He always put in a bag of candy for the children with an order. He sold groceries, dry goods and kerosene. . . . He also bought furs and hides. . . . He acted as banker on Saturday nights; he often cashed cheques for hundreds, even thousands of dollars. Sometimes a customer would already owe his whole cheque, or most of it before he got it. . . . He kept many people from starving during the Depression.

Charlie was very well liked also; he too acted as a banker for many people. . . . He gave credit and helped where he could.[6]

Chinese who worked for several years as domestics for white families in large cities might also enjoy stable and affectionate relationships with their employers.

> My parents and other relatives and friends had Chinese cooks, who usually became almost members of the family and took the keenest interest in all family happenings, even acting pretty well as social secretaries in some cases, reminding their employers of what tea parties, etc., they should be going to on any particular day. At Christmas time in Victoria, a group of these cooks, who knew one another well, would congregate during evenings at one employer's house after another and have co-operative Christmas cake decorating bees. The results were fantastic, with stiff white sugar pagodas, etc. on the tops of the cakes.

The most stable life was that of the Chinese family. This could be quite conservative in terms of cultural practices and attitudes.

> I was brought up in a very traditional family. You know, I really could not say what religion we were – whether Buddhist or Confucian or Taoist, but it was very traditional. We would never think of contradicting our parents. We did not have any altar in our house, but every New Years we used to set the tables out to eat, then burn joss sticks and bow to our ancestors. . . . In the office where I work I am the only Chinese . . . and the others are always kidding me. But you can only go so far, and then you can't go any further. There is a barrier. You never know whether they are kidding or not.[7]

The barriers would remain for many years yet. After the discriminatory legislation the Chinese felt an overwhelming sense of betrayal and resentment. All they could rely on was each other. It is not surprising, therefore, that after 1923 organizational life would come to occupy an increasingly important place in their lives.

NOTES

1. This section is based on statistics contained in the censuses for 1921, 1931, and 1941.
2. For a general statement of naturalization certificate policy, 1915-1930, see PAC, RG 25, G1, vol. 1867, file 263, part I, P.C. 1378.
3. For example, Public Archives of Newfoundland, Wo Fen Game murder case, St. John's, 1922; and PAC, RCMP, RG 18, G1: Mah Hong murder case, Blairmore, Alberta, 1908; Lee Him murder case, Broomhead, Saskatchewan, 1914; Lee Noy murder case, Bankhead, Alberta, 1921.
4. The above quotations are from the authors' interviews in British Columbia. For other anti-Chinese verses, besides "ching ching Chinaman," see Ban Seng Hoe, *Structural Changes of Two Chinese Communities in Alberta, Canada*, p. 349.
5. *Ibid.*, pp. 271-5.

6. F.Q. Quo, "Chinese Immigrants in the Prairies," preliminary report to Secretary of State (Ottawa, November, 1977).
7. From the authors' interviews in B.C.

TWELVE

Organizations, 1923-1937

The initial Chinese reaction to the enforcement of the 1923 Immigration Act was one of resentment. The Act applied only to Chinese. Only Chinese were to be excluded and, of all aliens already present in the country, only Chinese had to register. Not only that, attainment of Canadian citizenship seemed to be more difficult for Chinese than for any other alien group. Some Chinese complained that other aliens could become naturalized rather simply, but Chinese had first to present evidence of registration in the special Chinese registration drive of 1923, then to submit to an investigation by the Immigration Department and provide information about their personal histories and conduct before being allowed to complete the usual naturalization formalities.[1]

Registration, like immigration processing of returnees, was a humiliating and difficult experience for the Chinese. The returnees were kept behind bars in the Vancouver immigration building and immigration clearance might take several days or even weeks, while quarantine was cleared or previous residence (and hence, right to return) verified. If the returnee were fortunate, a diligent immigration officer would locate a name in an early passenger list that roughly corresponded phonetically to the current rendering of the returnee's name and allow him admission. If not, there were suspicions, humiliations, and delays. The task was not easy for anyone. There were many cases of attempted illegal immigration. Many Chinese were semi-literate in English, had never standardized the romanized equivalents of their Chinese names, and were easily confused and intimidated by the situation. As if that were not enough, the names of the Blue Funnel steamships on which many Chinese came to Canada (some examples are: "Philoctetes" and "Proteselaeus") seemed to be fiendishly designed to defeat the comprehension and memory of both Chinese passenger and immigration agent.

July 1 was commemorated in Chinese communities across the country as Humiliation Day and the observance was probably more elaborate and more rigorously carried out in the first few years after 1923 than

157

later on. The observance in Vancouver in 1924 is a good illustration. Signs about Humiliation Day were widely posted. All Chinese-owned shops closed and although it was Dominion Day, Chinese did not fly flags. Amusement in public, such as strolling in the park or engaging in musical activities that might be heard on the street, was forbidden. Chinese were not to watch the Dominion Day parade. During the day there was a mass meeting at one of the Chinese theatres, at which several Chinese leaders, across the political spectrum, lectured on the Immigration Act and its humiliation of the Canadian Chinese. In Victoria the Chinese held their own Dominion Day parade. Several cars with signs calling attention to the humiliating aspects of the Act drove past the Parliament buildings and through several white neighbourhoods.[2] Seven hundred Chinese crowded into the Chinese Theatre to hear speeches. Among the speakers were old men who talked about their bitter experiences as CPR railroad construction workers: poor food, low pay, exposure to disease, and then, when the work was completed, abandonment in destitution.

Solidarity and community involvement show clearly the continued vitality of Chinese associational life, even in a community that was not able to replenish itself. But cutting off immigration from China did not mean cutting off the Canadian Chinese from China. Chinese in Canada continued to return for visits or, in the case of high-school-age students, for study. There was continued interest in the politics and welfare of home districts and in China generally. New policies by Canadian governments or white attitudes of hostility toward Chinese enterprise in certain fields continued to stimulate the development of trade and other associations to express and defend Chinese interests. Thus, the Chinese communities in Canada did not stagnate; they continued to change and to create new associations to meet their needs.

We can best understand developments in these communities by first looking at events of the period in China. In 1923, Sun Yat-sen, leader of the Kuomintang (KMT), in hope of reviving his revolutionary movement against the warlords, made an alliance with the Soviet Union, the terms of which meant also an alliance with the small Chinese Communist Party. These strategic arrangements were a source of disagreement and uneasiness among all participants. The KMT became divided: a "right-wing" group opposed what Sun had done, a "left" group supported it, and a "centre" group watched and waited. Sun's "Southern" government in Canton was now the staging area for a planned "Northern Expedition" to eliminate warlord rule and to unite and strengthen China under KMT leadership. At this critical juncture, Sun Yat-sen died of cancer, leaving behind no designated successor and only general instructions about the future.

As preparations for the Northern Expedition continued, the urban mass political movement, largely quiet since the May 4th, 1919 period, broke out again. Street demonstrations in Shanghai resulted in the May

30th Incident (1925) in which British-led police fired on demonstrators. The May 30th Incident became the May 30th Movement. Strike and boycott activity paralyzed the great port of Shanghai for weeks, and when a similar shooting incident occurred in Canton, the Movement spread to the south. Popular feeling was so strong against foreign privilege in China's major cities that the approach of troops of the Northern Expedition in 1926-27 was often the signal for mass assaults on foreign zones of residence and business establishments.

When in early 1927 the Northern Expedition forces reached the Yangtze River basin, the central part of China, the strategic alliance broke apart. Acting from a centrist position, Chiang Kai-shek, commander of the most important KMT troops, struck against the Chinese Communist Party and all left-wingers. The alliance of KMT and Communists came apart, and so did the KMT's alliance with Russia. When the Northern Expedition resumed, Chiang, with the support now of moderates and right-wingers, was clearly the KMT's leader. Through military success and negotiation he completed the Expedition, the country was nominally unified, and the KMT established a new government for all of China with Nanking as its capital.

The new unity was no more than nominal. The new government effectively controlled several provinces on the lower Yangtze River. The rest of the country could only be "governed" by negotiation with its local strongmen. Still, the KMT government was the most progressive government, the most modern in orientation that China had had, and it raised great hopes at home and abroad. Foreign business and governments found it to be a government that was trying to restore stability and unity and one under whom good trading prospects were in view.

Hardly had it settled into even its limited power when the Japanese invaded Manchuria in September, 1931. Chinese forces were driven out and southward to within the Great Wall. Popular indignation ran high in China, but Chiang, believing China was unready for opposition to the Japanese advance, temporized, while building up his forces and seeking domestic unification by military suppression of the Chinese Communists. Despite Chiang's orders not to resist Japanese military activities, the local 19th Route Army, headed by Cai Tingkai, independently fought the Japanese forces in and around Shanghai, and won the admiration of most of the world for their heroism. The Shanghai Incident of January, 1932, did not lead to all-out war between China and Japan. Instead, the Japanese advanced piecemeal, by demands and negotiations, into North China. Only in 1937 was Chiang ready to call off his campaigns to exterminate the Chinese Communists and to form a united front with them against the Japanese. At that point further Japanese probing resulted in the Sino-Japanese War of 1937-1945.

In Canada, developments in China added to the divisions and violence that plagued the Chinese communities. Across the country KMT members were divided along the lines of cleavage within the KMT in China. One

159

group supported the rightist "Western Hills Faction" in China; another group, by early 1927, was supporting Chiang Kai-shek. As the breakup of the alliance with the Soviet Union became imminent, the alternative to Chiang's government was one headed by Wang Ching-wei at Wuhan, where the Russian advisors and those Chinese most favourable to the alliance were headquartered. Some of the support for the Wuhan government came from those whose support was based as much upon Wang's claims to leadership and orthodoxy in terms of Sun Yat-sen as any favouring of the strategic alliance. In Edmonton, for instance, a pro-Wang Ching-wei association was established in 1927 and maintained its independence of the pro-Chiang Kai-shek group for a decade or more.[3]

The views of the "left" KMT (those who supported Wang's government) were expressed in Canada by the newspaper *Canada Morning Post* (*Jianada Zhongguo chenbao*), published in Vancouver from 1922 to 1929. The editor of this paper was Louie Ming-ha (Lei Ming-hsia), a political activist who had been sent to Canada by the KMT Central Committee some years before.[4] Funds had been raised in KMT branches across the country and the newspaper had been established under the direction of Louie, who had earlier served as an assistant secretary of the Canadian Branch of the KMT.[5] In August, 1927, Louie and an associate in the newspaper, Wong Yau-mui (Huang Yu-mei), were shot and killed in the newspaper offices. The assassin, a young man from Kamloops named Wong Suey-sang (Huang Jui-sheng) then, apparently, killed himself. A left-KMT newspaper in San Francisco said that "Western Hills" faction supporters were behind the murders. In Vancouver threatening letters from various persons were cited and the veteran leader, Tsang Shak-chun, was put on trial. But the case was dismissed for lack of evidence.

Outside KMT circles in Canada there were also strong reactions to events in China. News of the May 30th, 1925, Incident provoked strong responses, especially in Toronto, Vancouver, and Victoria. In Toronto a mass meeting of 1,000 persons voted to support the striking workers of Shanghai. In Vancouver, the CBA decided to lower its flag to half-staff at the death of Sun Yat-sen, sent wires of support to striking workers and student organizations, and raised over $29,000 in their behalf.[6] In Victoria 600 persons crowded into the CCBA headquarters on Fisgard Street to hear speakers propose that China boycott British goods and consider breaking relations with Britain. In speeches and in the resolution adopted by the meeting, their own concerns were linked to the events in China. One speaker proposed that Chinese in Canada form a single, comprehensive labour union, with subdivisions by kind of employment, such as domestics and industrial workers. With that kind of economic power, he argued, the Chinese could maintain themselves and protect their interests in Canada. The resolution sent to Shanghai demanded that no settlements with the Western Powers be made by Chinese representatives without including a repeal of the Canadian Immigration Law of 1923. It was reported that the meeting also interpreted the occasion as one in which to ponder China's humiliation and to teach the facts about that to the younger generation.[7]

The political divisions of 1927 in China were reflected in Canada. Not only was the Canada branch of the KMT divided within itself, the Chinese communities as a whole were of many minds. Once the KMT, under Chiang Kai-shek's leadership, had established itself as the likely unifier of China, there were new controversies. Under the KMT schools in China were to open each day with formal bowing by students to the portrait of Sun Yat-sen. Formal meetings of associations were to begin by reading Sun Yat-sen's Will, or final political statement. A flag similar to the KMT flag of red and blue with a multipointed sun in the centre was to become the national emblem instead of the older republican flag of five variegated stripes. Efforts by KMT supporters in Canada to enforce these changes often led to controversies over the next several years.[8]

When the Japanese invaded Manchuria, the Chinese communities held mass meetings, declared a boycott of Japanese goods, formed resistance organizations, and raised funds. The activities of the Victoria and Winnipeg communities are best known. In Victoria the CCBA called a mass meeting of the community at which an association to Resist Japan and Save the Nation was formed. A contribution of $4,000 was sent to aid Chinese troops fighting in Manchuria. Winnipeg also formed a resistance organization.

When the fighting spread to Shanghai in early 1932, the Victoria Resistance Association raised $20,000 for the armies of Cai Tingkai. They also appealed to white Canadians by circulating translations of the Tanaka Memorial, purportedly a Japanese master-plan for international conquest, and copies of *Two Years of the Japan-China Undeclared War* by the Cantonese political figure, Edward Bingshuey Lee. When the Institute of Pacific Relations convened its international conference at Banff in 1933, the Victoria organization wired the representatives of all countries participating, urging that they press Japan to withdraw its troops from Manchuria.[9] In other cities, such as Montreal and Ottawa, several Chinese organizations sent telegrams of support to Cai Tingkai and to the Chinese Chamber of Commerce in Shanghai.[10] In Vancouver the CBA, Freemasons, and various other associations were much engaged in fund-raising throughout February of 1932.

The brief defence of Shanghai in early 1932 proved to be quite memorable overseas. As late as January, 1937, the students of Mon Keong Chinese School in Vancouver and the executive of the Vancouver CBA commemorated the January, 1932, resistance at Shanghai with ceremonies and with shouted slogans of resistance to Japan.[11] Even in the 1970's the Vancouver CBA headquarters had a photograph of Cai Tingkai hanging on its wall.

The rise of the KMT to power in China by 1928 favoured the fortunes of the KMT in Canada. After 1928 the KMT in Canada did not have to face hostile consulates; instead, the consuls across the country represented a

KMT government. Moreover, communication between consuls and Canadian Chinese was now much easier. Previous consuls, representatives of Peking-based governments, were often northerners who did not speak Cantonese, the language used by Canada's Chinese. The KMT, by contrast, had begun as a Cantonese party, and Cantonese influence was still strong in 1928.

The new government took a more systematic interest than its predecessors in the economic and educational affairs of the Overseas Chinese. It organized an Overseas Chinese Affairs Commission, first as a bureau of the Department of Foreign Affairs, but shortly thereafter as an independent, cabinet-level commission. Chinese schools in Canada were encouraged to register with the Commission, studies of the economic condition of Canadian Chinese were sponsored, and Canadian Chinese were recruited as vice-consuls and supporting staff in the consulates across the country. Efforts were made to register all Chinese in Canada and to keep track of births, deaths, marriages, changes of residence, and deportations. It was reported that the consulates also were expected to assist and guide organizations and cultural activities.[12] By 1931 two Canadian Chinese, Wong Fat-man (Fairman Wong) and Chu Ping-shen, were among those named to sit upon the Overseas Chinese Affairs Commission in Nanking.[13]

The KMT government also revived Overseas Chinese representation in the occasional sittings of the Chinese National Assembly. In 1936 the practice was to select two Canadian Chinese. The selection process began with nominations from certain designated associations, in Vancouver the CBA, the Chamber of Commerce, the KMT Headquarters for all of Canada, and the KMT Branch Office for Vancouver. Similar bodies in other major cities presented nominees and a list of these, together with Vancouver's four nominees, was presented to the Consul-General in Ottawa, who chose six names to forward to Chan Sue-yan, who was now head of the Overseas Chinese Affairs Commission in Nanking. Chan would then select the two who would sit in the National Assembly.[14]

The KMT in Canada now entered a period of prosperity and growth, despite its persistent internal divisions. The high-water mark was reached during the 1930's and 1940's, when membership was estimated to range from 7,000 to 10,000, out of a Chinese population of 30-40,000. The headquarters at Vancouver supervised three divisions (zhibu): Eastern, Central, and Western. Under each division were various local branches (fenbu).[15]

The KMT was now making greater efforts to reach out to white organizations and leaders. An example is found in a report of the convention of the Western District of the KMT at the Empress Hotel in Victoria in 1928. The week-long meetings included a banquet to which the party invited the premier of British Columbia and his cabinet, the mayor and aldermen of the City of Victoria, the American consul, the heads of the

Chamber of Commerce and service clubs, members of the city school board, and business leaders. Party Secretary Lee Chee spoke of the organization's activities and hopes. Although claiming that 85 per cent of the Chinese in western Canada were KMT members, he explained that the process of registry of all Chinese, then in effect across the country, was to determine the identity of non-members, particularly Communists, so that they could be prevented from entering or re-entering China. It was also a part of the party's census of occupations, skills, and education of the Chinese in Canada, the objective of this being to select the most able to serve in the consulates.

The KMT's metamorphosis from conspiratorial party to established government party and the tighter links its government established with Overseas Chinese communities added new resources and new dimensions to leadership in Canada's Chinese communities. When Chu Ping-shen died in 1937 he had compiled a leadership history that would not have been possible a decade or so earlier. Besides being several times chairman of both the realty and charitable divisions of the Lung Kong Kung-so and serving on the executive committee of the KMT headquarters organization in Canada, he had served in China on the Overseas Chinese Affairs Commission, as a member of the National Assembly, and on the committee of the National Economic Reconstruction Movement of China.[16]

Meanwhile, the other major political-fraternal association in Canadian Chinese communities continued to be active. The Chinese Freemasons held numerous meetings, reorganized themselves administratively, and undertook new activities in Toronto. Between 1924 and 1937 there were seven national Freemasons conventions at Lethbridge, Toronto, Vancouver, Cranbrook (B.C.), Vernon (B.C.), Nanaimo (B.C.), and Winnipeg.[17] At the Lethbridge convention in 1924 seven jurisdictional districts were established for all of Canada, four in British Columbia, and one each in Calgary, Toronto, and Montreal.

The number of branches had continued to increase since 1919, when there were forty-eight, to a total of sixty-five by 1924. One of the new branches was at Halifax, thus extending the Freemasons' branches east of Quebec for the first time. But it is obvious, too, that forty-three of the sixty-five branches were in British Columbia. The Freemasons organization was still at its strongest in the West.

The new organizational form was supposed to allow for better communication between the national headquarters in Victoria and the various individual branches across the country. Each year the branches of each district were to elect a district supervisor, who would investigate the affairs of individual branches within his jurisdiction, reporting upon them to Victoria. The new constitution, which spelled out these administrative arrangements, also made it clear that financial relationships among the various branches were to be informal and mutually beneficial. Surpluses from some branches, according to these rules, might be drawn upon and applied to the needs of other branches. In 1929 the Victoria headquarters established an office in Vancouver, which then became *de facto* the national headquarters.

Besides these internal rearrangements, the Freemasons, by the mid-1920's, had entered what amounted to a formal association with the XZD, or Constitutional Party, in three cities of eastern Canada: Toronto, Ottawa, and Montreal. Liaison offices were maintained, formal celebrations by one usually involved the other, and certain projects, such as the Kwong Do school in Toronto, were jointly sponsored.[18] It appears that this collaboration was the result of the growing power of the KMT as compared to its two competitors and the declining strength of the XZD, which could do little on its own and was already collaborating with the Freemasons in China.

Canada's Freemasons also continued to participate in international meetings of their organization, as they had earlier in San Francisco and New York. At a third San Francisco meeting, the one held in 1923, six Freemasons – three from eastern Canada, three from the West, led by Low Chew-yuen of Vancouver-Victoria – represented Canada.[19]

These years also were marked by increased Freemason organizational activity in Toronto. In the mid-1920's a Freemasons' newspaper for eastern Canada, the *Hung Chung She Bo* (known in English as the *Chinese Times*, like its western Canada counterpart), was founded and at the same time a Toronto branch of the Dart Coon Club was established. These activities in eastern Canada may well have been a Freemason response to the growing influence of the KMT in that part of the country. Whatever the case, the Freemasons, besides these new organizations, could count upon active leadership in the East from such men as Tom Yee in Toronto and Pang Tong in Montreal.[20]

In the years immediately after 1923, the Freemasons expressed their goals in a convention document and in their newspaper. These included many objectives also held by the KMT. For China, the Freemasons sought democratic government, freedom of speech, and preservation of core values in Chinese culture. For Chinese overseas, they wished protection from discrimination and compensation to those who had bought bonds during the 1911 Revolution.[21]

In the 1920's and 1930's the Freemasons, no less than the KMT, sought white approval of their activities. The Fourth National Convention of the Freemasons in Vancouver during 1926 was well-publicized in the English papers of that city. A grandstand was erected on Pender Street so the public could watch exhibitions of martial arts. There were parades with lion dances and a closing banquet, to which the city's mayor, high officials, and prominent businessmen were invited. At the banquet Mayor Taylor spoke of the "peaceful progressiveness of the Chinese of Vancouver, instances of their kindness and integrity, and about the future of Vancouver as a link between East and West."[22] These were rhetorical themes that would be repeated and developed during the 1930's.

The KMT's rise to power in China upset the power balance in Chinese-Canadian politics. From 1923 to 1931 the largest Chinatowns in Canada – Montreal, Toronto, Winnipeg, Vancouver, and Victoria – were never far from political turmoil and struggle. There were several sources of controversy among associations, such as competition for female restaurant labour[23] and for gambling revenues. It is therefore not always possible to separate politically motivated struggles from those of other origins. In Montreal KMT and Freemason supporters engaged in a street fight with knives and sticks one morning in December, 1933. In an effort to mediate, the Montreal Chinese Association called a meeting of representatives of fifteen community organizations. At the meeting, which took place in the Chinese Hospital, a shouting match became a shooting match. Amazingly, no one was killed; but a dozen persons were injured and scores were arrested. At the time of these sanguinary incidents, an editorialist in the *Chinese Times*, writing from Ottawa, urged peace and co-operation. He pointed out that fighting undermined the purpose of the Chinese in coming to Canada – to make a living for themselves and their families in China – by creating a bad impression among whites and by wasting money on medical and court costs.

In Toronto the political controversies of 1924-25 became a newspaper war between the KMT's *Shing Wah* and the Freemasons' *Hung Chung* in late 1929, full of charges of slander, physical violence, and action in the courts.[24] In Winnipeg several business firms were terrorized in 1930-31 by the strong-arm tactics of the so-called "Five Tigers," who reportedly were bent on enforcing KMT hegemony in that city.[25]

In Vancouver-Victoria a year of Freemason-KMT controversy led to the formation of a Peace Preservation Society by disinterested association leaders in Victoria. Among those involved in negotiations were two non-partisans from Vancouver, the scholarly Seto Ying-shek and the respected businessman Lee Sai-fan.

The Chinese Benevolent Associations across the country were, among other things, supposed to be agencies of conciliation and mediation between disputing factions. It was, however, difficult for them to be so when they themselves were often the prizes of struggling factions. For example, in Winnipeg in the early 1920's, one group within the CBA of that city was accused by another group of using the organization's name to send telegrams of support to one faction in China.[26] This was neither the first nor the last time such charges would be made in Canadian CBAs. In the 1929 election of officers of the Vancouver CBA there were charges of irregular practices, such as self-nomination, and allegations that all candidates on the "at-large" list were either members of the KMT or of the Toi-san association, or both. In the early 1930's the Vancouver CBA was divided and unsettled by charges of involvement in illegal immigration.

In the middle 1930's there were charges that one group that controlled the Vancouver CBA had held no public meetings for sixteen months.[27]

The two major political associations, the KMT and the Freemasons, were not the only Chinese organizations to maintain their vigour during this period. It has been estimated that the Chinese communities in Canada increased their number of organizations by about 50 per cent during the 1920's and 1930's. The large and diverse Vancouver community is the hardest to be precise about. Not only did many associations rise and fall between 1923 and 1937, there were many others that existed in name only. Several processes were at work in the formation of new district and clan associations. Some represented surnames that for the first time were sufficiently well-represented to try organizing an association (e.g., Vancouver Ho association, Toronto Lim Sai Ho Tong, Calgary Lim Sai Ho Tong). Some represented segmentation by sub-district (e.g., Nam Ping Bitsuey, from the Hoi-ping Association), or segmentation by surname within a specific district (e.g., Wong Man Sing, Kuan Lung Sai). Some associations, however, were the result of consolidation or reorganization. For example, the Toi-san Ning Yung Yu Hing Tong was reorganized as the Toi-san Ning Yung Wui-Kuan during these years. The Lee association was reorganized in 1931, bringing together two or three previous bodies under the new name Lee-si Kung-so. Several clan associations established headquarters in Vancouver.

Reorganization and headquarters-establishment took into account the question of how to administer various functions that several associations had developed: local welfare, realty management,[28] self-defence, athletics, and such China-oriented activities as fund-raising for bandit suppression, emergency relief, and school construction. In Vancouver, where organizations were the most highly developed and where most headquarters units were located, there sometimes developed a cluster of organizations belonging to a given surname, as, for example, the Wong group of associations, which included Wong Kung Har, Wong Wun San, the Mon Keong School, and (after 1940) the Hon Hsing Athletic Club. Wong Kung Har Tong handled realty and education (it operated the Mon Keong School); Wong Wun Sun was responsible for welfare and defence.[29] The organizations related to the Freemasons, although not clan associations, offer another example of a cluster of associations with varying functions. The Hong-men group of organizations, of which the Freemasons (CKT) was a part, came to include the Freemasons (fraternal, welfare, and political affairs), Dart Coon, Freemasons' Athletic Club, and Freemasons' Realty.

In Vancouver two new labour unions were important during this period. The Western-style restaurant (Chinese) Kitchen Workers Union existed throughout the 1920's but collapsed in 1931. Besides attempting to improve employment conditions for its members, it organized disaster relief shipments to China and it sponsored member meetings at which there were lectures on Chinese nationalism and on the evils of warlords in

China. The Chinese Workers' Protective Association, founded in 1923, and in existence until the mid-1950's, was a left-wing organization with some fraternal affiliations with the Communist Party of Canada. During the early 1920's there were other labour organizations – short-lived as it turned out – such as the Chinese Labourers and Merchants Improvement Association and the Labourer's Intelligence Club.

The agricultural products associations in the Vancouver area reflect the development of Chinese enterprise in various aspects of that industry. In the mid-1920's, associations of farmers and hawkers and the older Chun Wah Commerce Association formed a federation of producers and sellers. By 1928 there was a wholesalers' organization, and in early 1937 the Vancouver Mainland Growers' Cooperative Association was formed.[30]

The appearance of Chinese women's organizations across Canada in the 1930's reflects the more active role Chinese women had begun to play outside the home. The Women's Movement in China had an influence and so, in all probability, did the Women's Movement in North America. Women in the native-born second generation were also a factor, as they found their way into new sectors of the work force. In 1924, in Cumberland, B.C., the Freemasons formed a women's group to study English. Similar phenomena were visible in the United States during this period.

The growing influence of youth in the Chinese community is apparent in the theatrical and sports associations. The former are especially important. Before 1923 theatrical groups had been used at times to raise funds via benefit performances and to stimulate interest in political causes. After 1923 these usages became so common in China as to stimulate the formation of new groups for this purpose in Canada. It is noteworthy that the names of many Canadian Chinese theatre companies contain such words as "arouse" or "awaken." Various groups – schools and fraternal-political associations, for instance – sponsored theatre groups.[31]

The establishment of headquarters units by several associations during this period reflects a general phenomenon of cross-Canada organizational linkage. The Freemasons organization held six cross-Canada conventions between 1924 and the middle of 1937. Freemason meetings in eastern Canada included as participants the XZD branches, with whom the eastern branches of the Freemasons had made an alliance. The Kuomintang also held six cross-Canada conventions between 1917 and 1937.[32] The Wong Association convened its first cross-Canada convention in 1922 and a second in 1929. The Toi-san branches across the country met together for the first time in the early 1930's.[33] Leaders and fundraisers from these and other associations frequently travelled across the country, visiting several branches, exchanging information, and soliciting support for various projects.

Available evidence suggests that the relationship between headquarters units and local branches was a loose one, in most associations, and that the headquarters could not compel acceptance of a policy or require participation in a given program.[34] Nevertheless, financial support for the establishment of new branches or projects was widely given. When the Freemasons established a new branch in Lethbridge, Alberta, in 1924, stockholders were recruited all over the country. The same thing happened when stocks were sold for a new Freemasons' newspaper in Toronto in the mid-1920's. Some projects received Canada-wide support that was not limited to members of the sponsoring organization. For example, when the Hoi-ping Association canvassed for funds to build a modern high school in the home district in China, it found contributors among non-Hoi-ping as well as Hoi-ping people in many parts of Canada. T.C. Mark and Ma T.K. Wou successfully raised funds on the Prairies for a Chinese school that directly benefited only the Chinese in and around Toronto.

Despite these growing linkages there was still no single organization at the apex of all the Chinese communities of Canada. The Toronto Headquarters organization of the committees that resisted the Immigration Bill of 1923 remained in existence for a time and could mobilize some support as a spokesman for Chinese interests, depending upon what those interests were and to whom the speaking was to be addressed. But it was the Victoria CCBA which set the pace and laid out the rules for the annual Chinese demonstrations and boycotts that commemorated the passage of that bill for many years after 1923.

NOTES

1. *Chinese Times*, 17 June, 6 November 1923.
2. *Ibid.*, 2, 4 July 1924.
3. Ban Seng Hoe, *Structural Changes of Two Chinese Communities in Alberta, Canada*, p. 88.
4. *Chinese Times*, 8 August 1927ff.; "Jianada Tebie Dangbu," in *Kuo Min Yat Po* (San Francisco), Sixth Anniversary Special Publication (1933?), pp. 79-80.
5. Kingston KMT, *Jianada Qingshitun*, p. 2.
6. *Chinese Times*, 16, 18 June, 9, 10 July, 26 September 1925.
7. Victoria *Colonist*, 4 July 1925.
8. See, for example, *Chinese Times*, 5 January 1931.
9. Lee Tung-hai, pp. 462-5.
10. *Chinese Times*, 16 March 1932.
11. *Ibid.*, 29 January 1937.
12. *Ibid.*, 13 September, 24 October 1928.
13. Lee Tung-hai, p. 497.
14. Vancouver *Sun*, 2 September 1936.
15. Chen Kwong Min, *Meizhou Huaqiao Tongjian*, p. 421.
16. *Chinese Times*, 21 May 1937.
17. *Programme of Second National Freemasons Conference, Lethbridge;*

Chinese Times, issues of August, 1925, November, 1926, September, 1928, November, 1930, August, 1932, October, 1937.

18. Fong Sau But, Seto Chong Yim, and Ham Hung Tip, interviews with H. Con, R. Con, and E. Wickberg, Ottawa, 5 June 1973; Ottawa XZD to *Chinese World* (San Francisco), n.d.; Toronto Liaison Office to XZD, San Francisco, n.d.; *Chinese Times*, 24 March, 15 April 1931.

19. *Programme of Freemasons San Francisco Constitutional Conference*, 1923.

20. Lim Hon Yuen, interviews with H. Con, 28, 30 March, 10, 20 April 1974; *Chinese Times*, 1923ff.

21. *Programme of Freemasons San Francisco Constitutional Conference*, 1923; *Chinese Times*, 2, 3 September 1925; June, 1926.

22. Vancouver *Province*, 29, 31 October, 2 November 1926.

23. See, for example, *Chinese Times*, 1 October, 14 December 1925.

24. *Ibid.*, 14 June 1924; 29-30 April 1925; 13, 14, 21, 23, 24, 26, 27, 30 December 1929. See also *ibid.*, February-March, 1927; 9, 21-24, 31 January 1930; 19 July, 25 September 1930.

25. *Ibid.*, 17 March, 29 April, 15, 19 May, 25 June, 11 October, 19 December 1930; 3, 7 February 1931. The only source available to us is the Freemasons' newspaper, the *Chinese Times*.

26. *Ibid.*, 29 December 1924.

27. Yungaohua Zhonghua Huiguan, *Yinian guanwu baogao* (1936-1937), Prefaces, pp. 1-4, Public Announcements, p. 1, Executive Committee Meetings, pp. 6-8; *Chinese Times*, 30 July 1934.

28. Several Vancouver associations developed real estate branches in the 1920's; for example, Chee Duck Tong, Lung Kong Kung-so, the Freemasons, Lew Mow Wai Tong, and the Shon Yee Association.

29. *Yun-fao Jianada Huang Jiangxia Zongtang zhangcheng* (Constitution of the Wong Kung Har Tong Headquarters, Vancouver, Canada, 1955); *Huang Yunshan Zonggongsuo dierjie Quan-Jia kenqin dahui daibiaotuan xiuding zhangcheng* (n.p., 1954) (Constitution of the Wong Wun San Society, 1954), both in University of British Columbia Library, Special Collections Division, Foon Sien Papers, Box 12.

30. The activities of Chinese agricultural associations are recorded in the *Chinese Times*, issues of 1924, 1925, 1926, 1928, 1930, and 1937. For details of the "Potato War," see the discussion in Chapter Thirteen.

31. It should be noted, however, that at least the professional theatrical bodies found it difficult to survive in the Depression years of the early 1930's.

32. Fong Sau But, Seto Chong Yim, and Ham Hung Tip, interviews with H. Con, R. Con, and E. Wickberg, Ottawa, 5 June 1973; *Chinese Times*, 12, 25 March, 21 October 1929.

33. Lee Tung-hai, "Ningyang Huiguan yuan-liu kao," *Quan-Jia Taishan dierjie dahui tekan*, p. 131. The first all-Canada meeting is also reported in the *Chinese Times*, 22-23 January, 17 February 1931.

34. Several examples are scattered through the issues of the *Chinese Times* in the 1920's and the 1930's.

THIRTEEN

The Maturing of
the Chinese Community and
the Depression

As we have seen, the 1920's and 1930's were characterized by a Chinese community static or declining in size but increasing in organizational activities. During this period, however, Chinese associations were faced with many difficulties. Some of these problems, such as the internal conflicts, were of their own making. The Chinese of Canada, whose philosophical heritage evoked the ideal of harmony, were anything but harmonious. They rarely could agree and they rarely could unite, except under emergency conditions. But many of the hardships they suffered, such as the privations during the Depression, were experienced by Canadian society as a whole.

Faced with the problems of the Depression, and an apathetic if not downright hostile white society, the Chinese organizations strove to look after their own, particularly in the areas of education, welfare, and social services.

Chinese schooling for the younger generation became a subject of increasing importance in these decades. Occupations open to Chinese in Canada continued to be largely those that did not require a knowledge of English and often did require skill in the Chinese language. Residence and social relations continued to be mostly with other Chinese. A Chinese education, therefore, was important. Its objectives were to ensure that the younger generation would be literate in the Chinese language and would understand and appreciate Chinese culture. Chinese schools in Canada were seen as sources of additional training for Chinese-Canadian youth, who were expected to attend the Canadian public schools as well. Chinese schools were supplementary and part-time institutions. Classes were held after public school concluded, from late afternoon to early evening.

At the high point of Chinese school development in Canada during the 1930's and early 1940's, there were, according to one survey, twenty-six Chinese part-time schools with forty-seven teachers in eleven locations across the country. Approximately one-third of these were in Vancouver.

Toronto and Victoria had more than one school each. The remainder were found in other major Canadian cities and in small towns in British Columbia. Other cities – Moose Jaw, London, Quebec City, and Halifax – tried but failed to establish schools that lasted. By 1941 it was estimated that approximately 1,500 students were attending Chinese schools.[1]

In some of the larger Chinese communities there were part-time Chinese public schools. In this case, "public" means that the teaching staff was salaried and that the local CBA contributed at least part of the support funds and exercised part of the supervision. "Private" schools were those operated by a church group, fraternal-political association, or clan or district association, often with unpaid teaching staff. In eastern Canada, where CBAs were not as well organized as in the West, "public" schools were often associated with a church group or, after 1928, the Kuomintang.

There was wide variance in facilities and in quality of instruction. The "public" schools at Victoria, Vancouver, and Toronto were recognized as comparable to schools in China by the Chinese government in the early 1920's. They could offer higher elementary as well as lower elementary coursework. Other schools were less well-developed, and nearly all of them faced problems of marginal funding, inadequate and depressing physical facilities, and uncertain academic standards. These problems caused many schools to collapse and others to seek affiliation with church groups or the KMT.

The curriculum and methods of most Canadian Chinese schools were rather conservative compared to those of Chinese cities of the 1920's and 1930's. Since in Canada Chinese school was on an after-hours basis and was supplementary to European-language school, Canada's Chinese schools did not duplicate coursework done in those schools, concentrating instead on Chinese language, literature, history, and geography. In China the iconoclastic May Fourth Movement had led to an educational revolution by 1922. A version of spoken Chinese, *baihua*, had become the basis of a new written language, which students learned to read and write in Chinese schools. The Mandarin dialect, in its Peking version, was also widely taught as the "national language." In Canada, once the initial waves of May Fourth had subsided, cultural radicalism vanished. *Baihua* was rejected in the Chinese schools in favour of a series of readers developed earlier that utilized a limited vocabulary, modern-oriented version of classical Chinese. Basic instruction was in Cantonese, not in Mandarin. In some of the private schools, instruction was even more conservative: the texts were the classics of Chinese education as used in the nineteenth century and the teaching methods also derived from that era. Despite the anti-Confucianism of the May Fourth years, most Canadian Chinese schools in the 1920's and 1930's formally adhered to the name and principles of Confucius.

Schools were supported by tuition, by fees assessed upon participating bodies, and by a deficit-covering subsidy from some association, usually

171

the CBA, that was the general supervisor or sponsor. Church-operated schools were found across the country. The United, Presbyterian, and Catholic churches were most active. In western Canada, where more Chinese children were found, churches sometimes sponsored kindergartens. Clan and district association sponsorship of schools was rare. The Yin-ping district association of Vancouver maintained a school in that city for a time. Of much greater importance was Mon Keong School, founded in Vancouver during the 1920's by the Wong association. This school quickly became one of the best in Canada and enjoyed a continued existence thereafter.

In China the new Kuomintang-led government, established in 1928, took a great interest in Overseas Chinese education. It encouraged Chinese schools around the world to register with its Overseas Chinese Affairs Commission, and it offered to supply teachers, textbooks, and general expenses. Some Canadian Chinese schools accepted this aid, especially during the Depression years. By 1934 at least three Canadian Chinese schools were supported in part by the Chinese government. Some others were at least registered with the Nanking government, and eventually there was also an association of Canadian Chinese schools, which was a branch of a worldwide association of Overseas Chinese educational institutions.[2]

By the late 1920's and the 1930's the churches, especially the Chinese United Church and the Chinese Presbyterian Church, had found that an increasingly familial community was one in which they could work most effectively. While not neglecting single men, the churches had always placed great stress upon activities for women and children. By the 1920's and 1930's a larger proportion of women and children than of men were Christians. While single men were usually not Christian, most families were, and by the 1930's, when many single men died or left for China, families became proportionally more important than before.

Churches were important in several other ways. By the 1930's many churches were led by Chinese ministers who were linguistically and culturally well-equipped to help both the China-born and Canadian-born members of their congregations. Chinese church ministers and members provided a significant portion of the community leadership. Besides supplying social services, Chinese churches sometimes served as meeting places for discussions of community problems, involving government officials as well as community leaders and members.

Hospital services for the Chinese also involved church workers, specifically, the Sisters of the Immaculate Conception, who operated the Chinese hospital in Montreal and, after 1923, St. Joseph's Hospital for Orientals in Vancouver. In Montreal the Chinese hospital began on an emergency basis during the influenza epidemic of 1918. The Sisters, who had been teaching classes in English and French to the Chinese for the previous few years, now turned their attention to this enterprise, with the

172

aid of some Chinese leaders who raised support for rent, food, and utility costs. Once the emergency had passed, the Sisters and the Chinese leaders decided to establish a small hospital for chronically ill single men who had no relatives to assist them. A building on Lagauchetière Street West was purchased in 1920 to serve as the hospital and the headquarters of the Chinese Association of Montreal. A hospital committee of the Chinese Association was nominally responsible, and funds were raised throughout the Chinese community on a regular basis to keep the hospital going. The regular operation, however, was entirely the work of the Sisters and physicians who volunteered their services. This hospital, which also included an out-patient dispensary, served Chinese in eastern Canada as a whole, including some from as far away as Halifax.

The early history of the Chinese hospital facility in Vancouver followed a somewhat similar course. When the new Mt. St. Joseph General Hospital was built in another part of Vancouver in the 1950's, the old building then became a home for aged Chinese.

Hospitals, like schools, were a regular concern of the Canadian Chinese communities. Not only did these communities maintain Chinese hospital facilities in Montreal, Vancouver, and Victoria; in smaller towns in western Canada there were various attempts to establish facilities, however modest, for the medical needs of Chinese in that region. It should also be noted that besides supporting private Chinese hospitals or dispensaries, Chinese communities in Canada also contributed to the support of public hospitals and made use of public hospital services.

The question arises as to how a small, far from wealthy, ethnic community such as the Chinese could support such a plethora of charitable and social institutions. One of the answers was through gambling – an activity that frequently drew much adverse attention from the white community. Opposition to gambling came not only from the churches but also from the business community. For example, merchants in Vancouver's Chinatown publicly complained that gambling had become so profitable and so many gambling houses had come into operation that building owners had raised rentals beyond the means of legitimate businessmen. They therefore requested a city campaign against gambling. But Canadian Chinese communities could take care of their own only as long as their associations had adequate income, and complete abolition of gambling would have jeopardized the welfare system. It may be, therefore, that there was an optimum level of gambling in the Chinese community – large enough to help support associational welfare activities and thus keep Chinese from adding to the burdens of Chinese churches and city welfare departments, but small enough to avoid economic and major moral problems. Perhaps it is not surprising that when the CBA's and hospitals' revenues began to dry up during the Depression years the sustaining device they resorted to was legalized gambling in the form of a public lottery.

MATURATION OF THE CBA AND OTHER ASSOCIATIONS

The role of the associations was pivotal in supporting many social and welfare activities in the community. The CBAs, in particular, tried to respond to the needs and concerns of the Chinese communities. The pledge of the Victoria CCBA's executive in 1925 is an example of an awareness of some of the issues concerning members of the community and a willingness to respond to them. The executive committed itself to work for: (1) unity within Canadian Chinese communities; (2) popular consciousness; (3) the establishment of Chinese high schools across Canada (there were none in 1925); (4) convocation of an all-Canada Chinese education conference; (5) continued support of the Victoria Chinese hospital; (6) publication of the CCBA's accounts.[3]

One of the concerns of the Chinese in Canada was repeal of the 1923 Immigration Law. CBAs across the country sponsored an annual Humiliation Day. Among other things, on that day, the Prime Minister of Canada could expect a telephone call from the Vancouver CBA asking him to work for the law's repeal.[4] The Vancouver CBA and the Victoria CCBA also made representations to China's delegates to international conferences of the Institute of Pacific Relations, in Hawaii (1927), and at Banff (1933), asking their assistance in publicizing the case against the 1923 Immigration Law.[5]

CBAs continued to protest against laws that adversely affected the Chinese and attempted to negotiate for their non-application or modification. Some examples of this are proposals in the B.C. legislature during 1926 that Chinese be forbidden to own real estate and that labourers, supposedly for safety reasons, be required to pass an examination demonstrating a knowledge of English. The idea of school segregation was revived from time to time in B.C. On occasion there were pressures to enforce specifically against the Chinese the 1920 law that forbade white women working in restaurants owned by persons of dubious morality. In 1935 the Vancouver city health department proposed that Chinese cooks working in Western-style restaurants be required to pass a physical examination at their own expense. In all such cases, the CBA protested and negotiated, often in co-operation with the consuls and with other Chinese organizations, with varying degrees of success.[6] Protest against proposed legislation was not the whole story; the CBA also warned Chinese businessmen to obey existing laws, such as city ordinances about closing hours for businesses.[7]

In the late 1920's and early 1930's the Vancouver CBA repeatedly negotiated with the city government for more police protection in the face of growing instances of robbery and vandalism in Chinatown. Although we have referred above to several instances of violence within the Chinese community, it is quite clear that there was also violence against the Chinese by outsiders, particularly during the Depression years, when poverty and frustration were widespread. A common news item through-out 1932, for example, is robbery of Chinese vegetable sellers, especially by young white men.

During these years the Vancouver CBA underwent some reorganiza-tion. At a mass meeting in 1925 it was decided to change the method of election to a combination of district representation and at-large election. The formula for district nomination was confirmed, but there were now to be twenty additional members of the CBA executive, elected at large. Nominations for these positions were to be made by Chinese business firms. The general public would then choose the twenty from the list of nominees so provided.[8]

Later, during 1925, the Vancouver CBA adopted a set of by-laws at a general meeting. This document notes that "All Chinese contributing to the Association shall be members during the current year of such contri-bution." There was to be an annual general meeting of all members, to hear a report and a statement of accounts by the Board of Managers. In between meetings, all books were supposed to be open to inspection of any member. These by-laws were not to be altered except at a general meeting and the Board of Managers was not empowered to contract loans or dispose of the Association's real property except by authoriza-tion at a general meeting. At such meetings, each member had one vote.[9] By 1927 there were over fifty persons involved in administering the af-fairs of the Vancouver CBA, and it was proposed and accepted that members of the large advisory council be given specific committee func-tions. Eight regular committees were to be established and staffed by members of the advisory council. The heads of these committees would join the managerial board to form an enlarged executive committee.[10]

Like the CBA, other organizations grew and changed during the years 1923-1937. We have space to discuss only two – the Toi-san district association and the Lim clan association – chosen as examples because of the availability of information about them. Since early in the twen-tieth century in Canada, Toi-san people had been the most numerous of any Chinese district. Perhaps it was their ubiquity and size that made it inconvenient or seemingly unnecessary for them to form a tightly organized multi-purpose association of their own at an early date. Ap-parently those of common surname relied upon clan associations for most of their needs.

Toi-san people did organize their own association very early, but until the 1920's its major function within Canada was to collect the bones of deceased Toisanese and send them back for final burial in the home district. The Victoria Toi-san association was in existence by the 1890's, and in Vancouver a Toi-san association was firmly in place by at least 1912. The most famous achievement of the Canadian Toi-san Associa-tions during their early years was their fund-raising for the Toi-san high school in the home district. Beginning in 1919, an estimated 9,000

Toisanese in Canada managed to raise over $250,000 in less than two years and made that high school essentially a Canadian Chinese contribution.[11]

The major organizational changes in this association came in 1931 with the first national convention of Toi-san associations, which was held in Vancouver. The eighty delegates voted to change the name of the Canadian Toi-san association from Ning Yung Yu Hing Tong to Toi-san Ning Yung Wui-kuan. This alteration recognized the change in name of the home district (to Toi-san),[12] which had taken place in 1914, and brought the Canadian bodies into conformity with the San Francisco general headquarters of Toi-san associations in North America. A second change was the formal establishment of the headquarters-branch system. Victoria was confirmed as the headquarters. Branches were confirmed at Vancouver, Calgary, Regina, and several small places in B.C. In fact, probably because of Depression conditions, attendance at this convention was limited to delegates from the West.

Finally, the convention created a constitution, which spelled out the functions and structure of the organization. The functions were to settle disputes between members and between members and outsiders; to assist members with immigration problems; to provide charitable services, for which the traditional $2 fee was to be collected from all members between the ages of eighteen and sixty who were about to leave for China; and to continue to care for bone-shipments. It was made explicit that the assistance of the organization would not be available to members who were breaking the law. Bone-shipments, which were to occur every seven years as before, might also include the remains of people from districts other than Toi-san, provided their district associations paid a fee to the Toi-san association. Despite its expanded functions, the association did not establish membership fees or annual dues, perhaps in recognition of Depression conditions. The $2 exit fee was its only levy.[13]

The Lim association represented one of the largest Chinese groups in Canada. Although not rivalling the Wongs, who are said to represent 20 per cent of the Chinese in Canada, the Lims, together with the Wongs, Chans, Lees, and Mahs, make up one of the five most numerous surname groups.

The Lim Sai Ho Tong was established in Victoria in 1908, and as Lim associations spread across the country the Victoria organization functioned, informally, as a kind of headquarters. Vancouver had its Lim Sai Ho Tong by 1914-15. In 1923, given the replacement of Victoria by Vancouver as the major centre of Chinese settlement and business, leaders of the Vancouver Lim association began negotiations towards formally establishing the headquarters in Vancouver. Victoria was reluctant and it took three years of diplomacy.

As the headquarters was being established and by-laws written, a group within the organization created a branch organization, the Lim Kow Mock Kung-so, which engaged in musical and other activities. The

Kow Mock organization also created what became perhaps the largest reading room in Chinatown.

In 1933, the two organizations, which had broadly overlapping membership, had found it expensive, in the face of the Depression, to maintain their separateness. They therefore merged, becoming an organization of over 600 members with the name Lim Sai Ho Tsung-tong Kow Mock Kung-so. Under the merger, the executive of the organization was to be elected by the whole membership and membership meetings were frequent: once per month.

The Vancouver headquarters' organization had an elaborate executive structure, much like that of the Vancouver CBA. Fifty or more persons might be part of the executive at any one time. There was an executive committee of seven, one of whom was standing committeeman. There were also nine bureaus, or functional committees, much like those in the CBA, each staffed with four to seven persons. The Victoria branch had an even larger executive because it had a council of forty-one persons. The council chairman and the branch chairman were the chief executives of the organization. There were also various bureaus and offices, for a total of almost seventy persons in the executive. By contrast, Toronto's executive numbered about thirty. There was a large executive committee of thirteen, with five alternates, and one standing committeeman. But there was no council and the functional committee structure was skeletal.[14]

Like many Chinatown organizations, the Lim association was much involved in fund-raising for China during the Sino-Japanese war of 1937-1945. But that did not prevent its acquiring a building of its own in Vancouver in 1941, which was subsequently remodelled. Rooms were rented to members at low rates, and other space was let out to business firms. To finance the purchasing of the building, shares of stock were sold across the country. Roughly two-thirds of the stock in the building came to be held by Vancouver Lims, the other one-third by Lim individuals and branches across the country.[15]

The Lim association seems to have been in adequate financial condition during the 1930's and early 1940's. Even before the building was acquired, the entry fee, the annual dues of $1, and extra contributions by the wealthier members apparently took care of all ordinary expenses.[16] By 1946, besides rental revenues from the building, the entry fee, which provided an endowment or reserve fund, stood at $5 per person, and the annual dues had been increased to $2.[17]

CHANGING WHITE PERSPECTIVES

Throughout the 1920's Chinatowns, especially the one in Vancouver, continued to excite the imagination of white society. The Janet Smith murder case is one example. The killing of a white servant girl in a fashionable Vancouver neighbourhood was blamed on a Chinese domestic. For a time the Chinese servant disappeared from sight, seemingly kidnapped. Eventually, he was brought to trial. Although some white organizations clamoured for punishment, the Chinese house servant was eventually acquitted. The case took over a year to bring to completion, with much consequent fund-raising in the Chinese community in support of the legal expenses of the accused.[18]

Although the English-language newspapers found the Janet Smith case exciting, a more serious development, from the Chinese perspective, was the murder of David Lew in Chinatown the evening of September 24, 1924. In death as in life, Lew was a subject of controversy. Born in China, the son of a well-to-do merchant who had already established himself in Canada, Lew was educated in the public schools of British Columbia. He had studied law but could practise it only informally as an assistant to white lawyers. In this advisor-cum-interpreter role he was in a position to influence cases at court in one direction or another. During the Murphy Commission hearings of 1911, Lew had been questioned extensively about his alleged involvement in an illegal immigration scheme. He was said to be widely knowledgeable about gambling affairs and gambling rivalries in Chinatown. In short, Lew was a man whose activities and stock of information inevitably had created many enemies and many possible assassins. The actual assassin was never brought to justice.[19]

The most important thing about the Lew murder was its timing. The newspapers were still full of the Janet Smith case and the suspicions about the Chinese houseboy. Shortly thereafter a murder involving Chinese at a shingle mill in nearby Port Moody added to the feeling of tension that was building up in Chinatown. English newspapers and police spokesmen contributed to Chinese anxieties with theories about tong wars involving imported "hatchet men." In the face of this the CBA and the consulate could only urge unity and calm.

White society was aware of at least some of the effects of civil war in China upon the Canadian Chinese communities. Discoveries of weapons in Chinatown led to theories in the press that these were to be sent to support one or another political group in China, and even to a supposition that they were part of a drugs-for-guns trade, by which Canada's Chinese supported their opium habit while also expressing their patriotism towards China.[20] It appears these theories were never put to the test of an investigation and charges.

Gambling was also a subject of white interest, partly because so many whites were attracted to Chinese gambling places. Police enforcement of anti-gambling by-laws was alternately rigorous and loose. After the David Lew murder it was sweeping and almost eliminated gambling in Chinatown for a time. Again, in the late 1920's, Vancouver was rocked by charges of payoffs from Chinese gambling operators to persons in high places in the city's government. The ensuing trials produced massive documentation and rigorous anti-gambling action for a time.[21]

Produce marketing became a contentious issue between Chinese and whites and between Chinese and government during the decade 1927-37. Federal legislation on marketing control gave rise to similar legislation in British Columbia. Many Chinese producers and distributors opposed the structure and practices of the B.C. Coast Vegetable Marketing Board, which this legislation established. They argued that having to sell their produce to the Board at quotas and prices fixed by the latter meant protection and profits for established wholesalers in Vancouver, but no profits for the grower and high prices for the consumer.

Although some white farmers agreed with the Chinese,[22] the question became a racial one because many white farmers and dealers disagreed and lumped this issue with their unhappiness at the rising power of Chinese farmers and wholesalers. Matters came to a climax in the so-called "potato war" of 1937. White vigilante groups posted on bridges leading into Vancouver intercepted Chinese vegetable trucks full of potatoes that had not been registered with the marketing board. There were incidents on the bridges, charges at court, and much activity in the newspapers for several days before the affair came to an end.[23]

An editorial in one of the Vancouver newspapers probably reflected views that were common in white society. Twenty years ago, it said, "John Chinaman" was willing to lease land and grow no more than what he could peddle. Now there were Chinese-owned corporations in the Vancouver area, led by Canada-born Chinese who claimed all the rights of citizens. They owned land, trucks, and warehouses; they used machines and cheap Chinese labour for production; and they had a large network of wholesale and retail outlets for distribution. Retail stores, it was said, were staffed by Chinese girls who were university graduates. How long, asked the editorial, before society would be completely dependent upon the Chinese for household necessities of this kind? The purpose of the marketing legislation, it said, was to reserve the produce industry for white Canadians.[24]

In spite of these sensational events, lurid stories, and long-established suspicions of the Chinatowns, in the 1920's and 1930's Chinese associations, both new and old, began to have new kinds of relationships with white society. By the 1920's Chinese soccer teams were a part of a local league in Vancouver where they held their own against white teams (much to the pleasure of a local Chinese newspaper). In the 1930's members of the Vancouver City Council for the first time held meetings with the Vancouver CBA in the latter's headquarters in Chinatown.[25]

Chinese participation in civic celebrations antedated 1923, but was much more extensive thereafter. The civic anniversaries of both Victoria and Vancouver were occasions of substantial Chinese contribution, particularly the latter. Reports of Chinese participation in Vancouver's fiftieth anniversary celebration in the summer of 1936 provided some indications that Chinese and whites in that city were beginning to move toward an accommodation with each other. A "Chinese village" was created adjacent to Chinatown, with a "Buddhist temple," pagoda, peasant cottage, and "mandarin palace." Chinese craftsmen did their work in public view, and a Chinese bazaar, Chinese magicians, and jugglers added to the amusement. A Chinese art collection was loaned to the city for the occasion. At the entrance to the "village," and symbolizing the co-operation of Chinese and whites, was an eighty-five-foot-high Chinese arch at the corner of Hastings and Carrall Streets. The Chinese had also chosen their first "Miss Chinatown" to participate with other neighbourhood beauty queens in the summer festivities.

Possibly changing white attitudes towards the Chinese and Chinatown were suggested by English-language newspaper reports. Vancouver had begun to discover its own "international" possibilities. A report of that city's Third International Festival in the previous year had spoken of the beauty of Mrs. H.H. Kung, wife of China's Minister of Finance, who had visited during the festival. It was noted that she was the sister-in-law of "the great Dr. Sun Yat-sen." An editorial during the Vancouver anniversary celebration observed that the "Chinese village" had called attention to Chinatown as a "permanent tourist attraction," and suggested that the city exploit it as such, as New York, San Francisco, and even London were doing.[26]

Vancouver was not alone in feeling a growing "internationalism" and a dawning curiosity about things Chinese. The academic study of China had begun by the 1920's at both McGill and the University of Toronto (although not yet at the University of British Columbia). At these institutions the study of China and the presence of Chinese students helped bridge the gap between Canada and China. At McGill Chinese studies were presided over by a distinguished scholar and political figure from China, Kiang Kang-hu. Kiang obtained a Chinese library collection for McGill which, unfortunately, was later sold to Princeton after Kiang's departure. While at McGill, Kiang interested himself in the affairs of the local Chinese community and, as a relative of the famous Liang Qichao, he was welcomed by the XZD political party.[27]

Canadian interest in China was more than academic. By the late 1920's several hundred Canadians staffed the Canadian mission fields of the United Church, the Presbyterian Church, the Anglican Church, and the Jesuit Order in China. Trade relations had also begun to develop. Toward the end of World War I the possibilities of wheat sales to China began to become apparent to Canadians. A trade commissioner was maintained for a time in Shanghai, and, beginning in 1926, trade missions were sent. The Kuomintang government, established in 1928, appeared capable of uniting China and its attitude toward foreign trade was encouraging. Finally, in 1931, the first Canadian consulate in China was established at Nanking, the Chinese capital, under the jurisdiction of the newly established Canadian legation in Japan.

In fact, trade had greatly expanded from the mid-1920's onward. Despite the emphasis in discussions on the possibilities of wheat trade, the Canadian cargoes sent to China were diverse in composition. Wheat, flour, timber, and fish were the largest items. But clothing, electric appliances, machinery, and foods of various kinds were also sold. Canadian life insurance and shipping companies were also said to be well-established in China.[28]

As some Canadians began to think of China and Chinatowns in more favourable ways, questions about rights and opportunities for Chinese in Canada once more surfaced. When Japanese-Canadian veterans of World War I were given the vote in 1931 the question of extending the franchise to all Orientals in British Columbia was briefly discussed in the newspapers. In 1934 J.S. Woodsworth, a leader of the newly founded CCF Party, expressed himself as in favour of enfranchising Asians in B.C. In the subsequent federal election of 1935, the CCF position became a major subject of Liberal and Conservative criticism in B.C. and was probably damaging to the CCF cause in that province. Indeed, the federal Liberals, who, years later, wooed and won much of the Chinese vote, on this occasion made vigorous use of the slogan "A vote for the CCF is a vote for John Chinaman."[29] In subsequent years, CCF people, among others, worked for Asian enfranchisement. But it was clearly not within reach during the 1930's.

Citizenship for Chinese had always depended heavily upon the whims of a district judge. If he refused to accept a petition from a Chinese there was little the Chinese could do. Events in China now made obtaining citizenship even more difficult. Once in power in that country, the KMT government reaffirmed in its 1929 Citizenship Law the principle of *jus sanguinis*, by which a child of a Chinese father born anywhere in the world was automatically a citizen of China. Two years later the Canadian government responded with an Order-in-Council (PC 1378) which required Chinese who wished citizenship to first obtain in writing the permission of the Minister of the Interior of China before being able to submit an application to the Canadian authorities. It thus became more difficult than ever to become a Canadian citizen.

DEPRESSION

As the Depression descended upon Canada, all the ambiguities of the white-Chinese relationship stood out in bold relief. Layoffs for the Chinese began with the closing of the shingle mills near Vancouver in 1929. As the number of unemployed Chinese swelled, the relief capacities of traditional Chinatown organizations were hard-pressed to meet the needs. The Vancouver CBA attempted to establish an employment bureau for Chinese seeking jobs in white-owned businesses. For several months, beginning in December of 1930, it provided food to needy Vancouver Chinese through several Chinatown restaurants. At one point, the Vancouver CBA even gave assistance to indigent Chinese in Calgary. But its resources were slight, compared to the task. Other Chinese organizations took up part of the responsibility, but before long welfare – and health, too – had become a major subject of co-operation between the Vancouver CBA and various public and private agencies outside the Chinese community.

As the crisis intensified the Chinese were forced to seek aid from white agencies. They were not always successful in obtaining it. For example: in 1933, about fifty Chinese led by two unidentified whites marched on Vancouver City Hall to demand unemployment relief, a demand which the mayor deflected by saying that the provincial government and the Anglican Church were already providing the necessary aid. In 1935 about twenty Chinese gathered on the steps of the B.C. Parliament building in Victoria to demand provincial aid after receiving nothing from the city of Victoria. They were sent back to the city welfare office.[30] When they had the assistance of Chinese business leaders or ministers, or aid from sympathetic white church workers, the Chinese could and did receive relief. But it was not necessarily at the same level as that given whites. In Alberta relief payments for Chinese were well below the rate for single white men. In January, 1937, about twenty jobless Chinese staged Calgary's first sit-down strike, on the tracks of a streetcar line, protesting that the provincial allowance to them of $1.12 per week, less than half that allowed whites, was insufficient to live on. A similar event occurred several days later. The striking Chinese were arrested on various charges and fined $5 each. Earlier, several Chinese had been evicted from basements in Calgary's Chinatown for sanitary reasons. Those who could, found free sleeping spots in a mission. The Supervisor of the Unemployment Relief Commission did not consider a housing allowance necessary because, as he put it, the Chinese "all live under more or less the same conditions, if on or off relief," and that they "do not give living conditions serious consideration."[31] Similar statements in British Columbia justified relief discrimination in that province.

In Vancouver the city contracted with the Anglican Church mission to the Chinese to operate a Chinatown soup kitchen and other facilities. There was much controversy surrounding the soup kitchen, which by 1935 was feeding an estimated 600 men.[32] Public funds in the amount of sixteen cents per man per day were allocated to the church in order to provide two meals per day. There were charges, mostly from organizations on the left, of corruption in handling the food money and, with or without corruption, claims that the food was insufficient in amount and so poor in quality as to contribute to the numerous deaths of Chinese from starvation and malnutrition-related diseases. It was clear that many Chinese were in very poor health before accepting food from the soup kitchen. But the deaths by starvation of well over 100 Chinese from 1931 to early 1935 and the presence of so many suffering from poor nutrition in the latter year encouraged these charges. An open meeting attended by over 1,000 Chinese was held and there were demands that the Chinese be put on the same relief basis – meal tickets and cash payments – as all other persons. It appears, however, that this was not done and the soup kitchen continued to operate as before.[33]

In Victoria the initiative came from the widow of the American consul, a woman who had had famine relief experience in China. Initially at her own expense and that of Chinese merchants, she opened a soup kitchen and reading room in Chinatown. Within a few months, various levels of government had assumed financial responsibility. Aid of various kinds came from the Anglicans and the Chinese Boy Scouts. For over three years this "relief room" served the destitute single men of Victoria's Chinatown; families were given food and clothing direct from the city. By 1935 many of the indigent single men had returned to China and those who remained were put on a new city program, ending the need for the "relief room."[34]

The plight of the Chinese during the Depression was of concern to the political left, ranging from the CCF to the Communist Party of Canada. *The Commonwealth*, the CCF's publication, called attention to Chinese complaints and riots over the food at the Vancouver Chinatown soup kitchen.[35] The Communist paper, *B.C. Workers News*, charged that Chinese were dying from the "slow starvation diet" given them at the soup kitchen, and asserted that although the government allowed sixteen cents a day per man for food, the soup kitchen meals were worth only about three cents.[36]

During the Depression, left-wing white labour seems to have expressed solidarity with the Chinese, seeing workers of all races as victims of class oppression under the capitalist system. For non-left white labour, however, as for white business and agriculture, the Depression exacerbated the competitive situation between themselves and the Chinese. White labour did not always take a competitive position. On at least one occasion there was, apparently, broad interest in the unemployment problems of the Chinese. In March of 1935, the left-wing Chinese Workers Protective Association, one of several Chinese organizations on the left in these years, and the Unemployed Workers Association held a joint open meeting, which was attended by over 1,000 Chinese. The meeting called for equal treatment in the employment and welfare of Chinese workers. Among those attending, besides members of the CCF and the Socialist Party, were members of the provincial labour union congress and individual unions.[37] On the other hand, the Seamen's Union repeatedly urged that Chinese seamen be fired and replaced by unemployed white seamen. Evidence of pressures on government from white labour and business may be seen in efforts in 1928-29 and in 1937 to modify and to enforce laws against white women working in Chinese restaurants, or Montreal's plan to increase the tax on hand laundries in January, 1932, from $50 to $200.

In June, 1932, the B.C. government published estimates of Asian employment and white unemployment, showing that a larger sum in welfare money was paid to the latter than the wages paid to the former, implying that the larger public welfare burden was due to Chinese occupation of private employment opportunities.[38] In the same spirit, the Vancouver city welfare committee suggested that shipping and rail companies help reduce the number of whites on welfare by replacing Chinese employees with whites.[39] It could probably be assumed that the dispossessed Chinese would be less likely to file for welfare than white workers would be.

In Vancouver Chinese cooks in Western restaurants were required to undergo a physical examination for infectious disease by a white doctor at their own expense. The Chinese saw this as a pretext to remove them from their jobs.[40] Vancouver's gaming house "income tax" was imposed for the first time during the Depression. Chinese-operated Western-style restaurants were refused the right to accept welfare meal coupons in Vancouver, leading the Chinese to form a short-lived restaurant association in opposition.[41] In 1931 the B.C. Minister of Finance announced that Chinese in that province who had hitherto claimed exemption from the provincial income tax of 1 per cent because they were supporting wives in China could no longer do so. Only if their wives were in B.C. could they claim this exemption. The irony, whether intended or not, was perfect. Most of the Chinese in B.C., excepting only a very few large export-import merchants, were legally unable to have their wives in B.C. The Minister indicated that the new ruling meant that "virtually all the Chinese workers of the province" would have to pay. "This is the first tax," he said, "with which the province has been able to reach the casual Oriental workers," who usually paid nothing into the provincial treasury.[42] Nothing was said about whether white casual workers were contributing to the treasury.

One government device for dealing with the problem of indigent Chinese on the welfare rolls was repatriation. During 1934 and 1935 the government of British Columbia paid the passage to China for several hundred impoverished Chinese who had agreed to go. The terms of the arrangement frequently included the understanding by the Chinese that he could return to Canada only after the passage of at least two years.[43] The B.C. government also persuaded the government of China to assume the custody of sixty-five Chinese mental patients, provided B.C. paid their passage to China.[44]

Did the Depression hit the Chinese harder than it struck white Canadians? It is difficult to answer that question, since Chinese would almost certainly be underreported in unemployment statistics, and in news reports of deaths by starvation or suicide. But it is possible to make some general comments. Many Chinese relied for employment upon their willingness to work for less than white workers demanded. To the extent that the 1928 minimum wage was enforced, the competitive advantage of Chinese labour was seriously reduced. That Chinese continued to be hired on less than minimum conditions is evident from a Port Alberni,

Chinese miners washing for gold near North Bend, B.C., in 1891.
(Courtesy Vancouver City Archives)

Chinese workmen on the CPR, 1880's. (Provincial Archives of B.C. #41770)

Fisgard Street, Victoria Chinatown, early 1890's. (Provincial Archives of B.C. #68226)

Dupont Street (now East Pender Street), Vancouver Chinatown, 1904. Note the shoulder-pole at far right. (Vancouver Public Library #6729)

Fish cannery work was one of the most important Chinese occupations. (Courtesy Vancouver City Archives)

Carrall Street, Vancouver Chinatown, after the 1907 Riot. At far left the pioneer firm Gim Lee Yuen, still in business today. (Vancouver Public Library #939)

Monument to the seventy-two martyrs
of the Huang Hua Kang Uprising of 1911 in Canton (Guangzhou).
On the stones are inscribed the names of Overseas Chinese organizations that contributed to this rising. Canadian Chinese communities figure prominently. (Graham Johnson)

The wives of merchants Ho Chong and Jeh Zhong, dressed here in Western style, ca. 1890's. (Courtesy Lillian Gee Wong)

Haw Chow Shee, second Chinese woman to come to Montreal, with her son and infant daughter, Avis Haw, who later married James Lee, a major figure in the Montreal Chinese community, ca. 1897. (Courtesy Mrs. James Lee, Prof. Douglas H. Lee, and Bernice Kwong)

A Chinese produce outlet in North Vancouver, 1910. (Courtesy Vancouver City Archives)

The pioneer merchant Yip Sang and his children, Vancouver, 1906. (Courtesy Gibb Yip)

A headtax certificate, required of Chinese immigrants to Canada,
1904-1923. (Edgar Wickberg)

Cumberland, B.C., Chinatown, ca. 1910. (Provincial Archives of B.C. #72553)

Some founders of the Chinese Christian Association of Toronto. Front row, left to right: E.C. Mark, G.T. Mark, Quan Chuck, and Lew Luke. Back row, left to right: Charles Lew, George P. Mark, Wong Poy, P.L. Quan, Reverend Ma T.K. Wou, Lem Yuey. (Courtesy Mrs. E.C. Mark)

Liang Qichao visits the Reform Association in Vancouver, 1903. Liang is standing in the centre. Several leaders of the association are present. W.A. Cumyow is third from the right. Note the differences in hair and clothing styles. (Courtesy Mrs. Hilda Cumyow)

The Chinese Nationalist League (KMT) holds its second national meeting at its new Vancouver headquarters building, Pender and Gore Streets, 1921. (Courtesy Vancouver City Archives)

The Cheekungtong in Kelowna, B.C., formally opens the meeting, January, 1920. The five-striped flag is that of the early Chinese Republic. (Courtesy Kelowna Dart Coon Club)

A Chinese-owned restaurant in small-town Alberta, ca. 1920's.
(Glenbow-Alberta Institute ND-2-111)

A restaurant, herbalists, and a miscellaneous goods store on Pender Street,
Vancouver Chinatown, ca. 1920. (Vancouver Public Library #20832)

Memorial procession in Montreal after Sun Yat-sen's death, 1925.
The Lee Long Sai Association group. Arthur Lee is at the front of the left column;
Roy Lee is at the front of the right column. (Courtesy Arthur Lee)

The Chinese Freemasons' lion-dance team performs in Toronto, ca. 1931.
Note the office of the Freemasons' newspaper, Hung Chung She Po, right rear.
(Multicultural History Society of Ontario #MSR 5639 #2)

The ceremonial structure erected by the Chinese of Vancouver as their contribution to that city's fiftieth anniversary celebration, 1936. Note in the background offices of the Toi-san Association and the Chinese Workers Protective Association. (Courtesy Vancouver City Archives)

The sixth graduating class of the Victoria Chinese Public School and their teachers pose in front of the school and the CCBA building, January, 1925. (Courtesy Guy Louie)

Toi-san County High School, originally constructed in the 1920's with money contributed by Canadian Chinese. (Graham Johnson)

The Montreal Chinese Hospital and the Chinese Association of Montreal (CBA). (Courtesy Montreal Chinese Hospital and Bernice Kwong)

*Chinese Canadian Engineer Unit (Force 136) at Camp Chilliwack, B.C., 1943.
All are from Vancouver and Victoria. This unit served in Southeast Asia.
Harry Con is second from the left in the back row. (Harry Con)*

V-J Day Parade in Toronto's Chinatown, August, 1945. (Courtesy Mrs. E.C. Mark)

Reverend and Mrs. Chan Yu Tan. Reverend Chan was a pioneer Chinese Methodist minister in western Canada. The picture was taken in 1939. (Multicultural History Society of Ontario #MSR 0551 #3)

Mon Keong School students and teachers celebrate the opening of the school, 1925, in front of the Wong Kung Har Tong building, Vancouver. (Courtesy Mon Keong School)

The Chinese Students Football Club of Vancouver, winners of the Brunswick Cup during the 1930's. (Courtesy Shupon Wong)

Vancouver CBA leaders, ca. late 1940's. Left to right: Consul Chu Chin-k'ang,
Leung Chup-kong, Foon Sien, Cho Mee-ding, Jimmy Seto (Seto Dip-yee).
(Courtesy Vancouver CBA, William F.W. Yee, President)

Douglas Jung campaigns for
M.P., Vancouver, late 1950's.
(Vancouver Public Library
#41618)

B.C., case of 1934. Three Chinese died at a sawmill near that city, reportedly from malnutrition-induced disease. Surviving Chinese workers claimed that during five months of work they had received no wages, and in the last month no food but rice and clams.[45] Chinese who took such employment risked not only their health, but the fury of frustrated white workers.

The employment opportunities for Chinese were more restricted than those for whites. The minimum wage law reduced their chances in the sawmills and canneries that stayed open during the Depression. In B.C. it had long been the law that Chinese could not work on public works projects or on Crown lands. Certain professions continued to be closed to those who were able to obtain higher education. Besides law, pharmacy, and accountancy in B.C., nursing, both in B.C. and in Alberta, generally refused to accept Chinese. Chinese graduates of normal schools frequently were not hired as teachers because of their race.

The Depression almost certainly reduced the amount of remittances that Canada's Chinese sent to relatives in China. Poor business conditions probably also reduced the amount that could be saved for one's return to China. To the poor but employed Chinese who were ineligible for the B.C. government's repatriation offer, the possibility of return to China must have seemed more remote than before. In other ways, the Depression seriously affected the Canadian Chinese. Prolonged depression meant the inability of Chinese associations to provide welfare at needed levels. That meant, for the Chinese, greater involvement than before in the public services of white society. And that, in turn, meant an increased awareness of what rights might be due them as residents or citizens of Canada. For a Chinese who could not return to China and whose needs could not be met by the "Chinese welfare system," there was no alternative but to resort to the Canadian welfare system and to learn its rules and the rights he could claim within it. The Depression also revived the highly competitive employment relationship between Chinese and whites. Pushed out of mines, canneries, and mills, the Chinese were most numerous in laundries, restaurants, and farm operations. Even there they were under pressure. To defend themselves they, and the organizations they relied upon, had to become more and more conversant with and involved in the rules of Canadian society.

NOTES

1. Lee Tung-hai, pp. 340-2. See also Gordon R. Taylor, "An Investigation of Chinese Schools in Canada" (M.A. thesis, McGill University, 1933), pp. 50-1.
2. Lee Tung-hai, pp. 342-3, 498; Chen Kwong Min, *Meizhou*, p. 435. For school associations in Vancouver in the 1920's, see *Chinese Times*, 7 June, 12 August 1926.
3. *Chinese Times*, 10 March 1925.

4. "Inside the CBA," in Lee Doe Chuen (comp.), *Quan-Jia Zhonghua Zhonghuiguan gaikuang* (Taibei, 1969), p. 33.

5. *Ibid.*, p. 15; Lee Tung-hai, pp. 496-8; *Chinese Times*, 17, 31 August 1933.

6. "Inside the CBA," p. 14; *Yinian guanwu baogao*, Correspondence and Executive Committee Meetings; Lee Tung-hai, pp. 496-8; Joseph Hope, "Wei-fao Huaqiao sanian fendou shiji," pp. 6-10; *Chinese Times*, 26, 29 March 1935.

7. See, for example, *Chinese Times*, 21 October 1938.

8. *Chinese Times*, 5 January 1925.

9. "By-laws of Chinese Benevolent Association," 4 April 1925, from PABC registry, published by the "Temporary Committee to Return the CBA to the Whole Chinese Community" in 1978.

10. *Chinese Times*, 19 May 1927.

11. Chan Kung Yung and Ng Lun Ward, interviews with H. Con, 26 March 1973; Huang Jisheng, "Jianada Yungaohua Taishan Ning Yang Huiguan shilue," in *Taishan Ning Yang Huiguan liushi zhounian jinian tekan* (1958), pp. 9-10; Lee Tung-hai, "Cuzi tanxin gonghua sangma," p. 41. A picture of the high school may be found in Chen Kwong Min, *Meizhou*, p. 429.

12. The Toisanese dialect rendering of the district name is Hoy-sun, hence the romanized name Hoysun Ningyung used by the Association. We have adopted "Toi-san" throughout in order to maintain dialect uniformity with other Guangdong districts.

13. Shouding, "Dui Wei-cheng Ning Yang Yu Qing Tang gaizu zhi shangque," pp. 6-14; Huang Jisheng, "Jianada Yungaohua," pp. 9-10; *Jianada Tai-shan Ning Yang Zonghuiguan zhangcheng*, 1932, Foon Sien Papers, Special Collections Division, University of British Columbia Library; Lee Tung-hai, "Ning Yang Huiguan yuanliu kao," p. 131; *Chinese Times*, 22-23 January 1931.

14. *Lin Xi Ho ba zhounian zhuankan*, pp. 99-104, 156-9, 160ff.

15. *Lin Xi Ho Zongtong kaimu jinian kan* (Vancouver, 1947), Section II, pp. 6, 8, 28-9, 32ff.

16. *Lin Xi Ho ba zhounian zhuankan*, pp. 109-10, 156-9.

17. *Lin Xi Ho jinian kan*, pp. 9, 11ff.

18. *Chinese Times*, 5 September 1924; 12 October 1925.

19. *Ibid.*, 25-30 September, 1-8 October 1924; 15-24 April 1925; PABC, David C. Lew Letterbooks, 1907-1909; Vancouver *Province*, 23, 25 October 1924; *Yu Shan Zonggongsuo jinian ce*, pp. 3-4; Charlie Cho, interviews with H. Con, 17, 25 March 1973.

20. *Chinese Times*, 20 September 1924. Related material is found in PAC, RG 25, vol. 1472, file 515; *ibid.*, vol. 1142, file 308. See also, RCMP Headquarters Files, 1921 HQ 189E-2, 1923 HQ 189E-1, 1929 HQ 189-3-E-1.

21. *Chinese Times*, 16 May, 9 July 1928; Vancouver City Archives, Transcripts of Police Investigation, 1928, 11 volumes.

22. Vancouver *Province*, 2 November 1936; 5, 9, 22, 29 March 1937.

23. *Ibid.*, 24 October, 3, 4 November 1936; 24 February, 23, 29 March, 29 May, 1 June 1937; Vancouver *Sun*, 7 November 1936; 17 February 1937; *Chinese Times*, 8, 29 January, 24 February, 1-9 March 1937.
24. Vancouver *Province*, 2 March 1937.
25. *Yinian guanwu baogao*, Executive Committee meetings and Summary sections, especially Summary section, p. 15.
26. Vancouver *Sun*, October, 1935; 13 July 1936. The last point was repeated in another paper in 1940. Vancouver *Province*, 6 July 1940.
27. Gordon Taylor, conversation with E. Wickberg, 13 June 1974.
28. Vancouver *Sun*, 22 January 1931.
29. Grace MacInnis, *J.S. Woodsworth, A Man to Remember* (Toronto, 1953), pp. 210ff. See also comments of Angus MacInnis in House of Commons, *Debates*, 11 February 1947, I, p. 337. For related material see *Chinese Times*, 14, 20 October 1933.
30. *Chinese Times*, 9 August 1929; 14 November 1933; 9 January 1935.
31. *Ibid.*, 9 February 1937; Ban Seng Hoe, *Structural Changes of Two Chinese Communities*, p. 93.
32. *B.C. Workers News*, 22 February 1935.
33. *Chinese Times*, 7 March 1935.
34. Victoria *Colonist*, 20 May 1932; 16 January 1935; *Victoria Times*, 24 December 1932; 18 June 1934. For information on welfare problems in Toronto and Windsor, see Paul Levine, "Historical Documentation Pertaining to Overseas Chinese Organizations," p. 92.
35. Quoted in *B.C. Workers News*, 8 February 1935.
36. *Ibid.*, 1, 22 February 1935.
37. *Chinese Times*, 3 March 1935.
38. *Ibid.*, 17 June 1932.
39. *Ibid.*, 6 February 1934.
40. *Ibid.*, 26, 29 March 1935.
41. *Ibid.*, 16 July 1935.
42. Vancouver *Province*, 4 May 1931.
43. Vancouver *Sun*, 28 December 1934; Victoria *Colonist*, 3 May 1935; *Chinese Times*, 27 April, 8 July 1935. Further discussion may be found in PAC, RG 76, file 827821, part 13, Jolliffe Memo, 31 January 1936.
44. Vancouver *Province*, 3 July 1930; *Victoria Times*, 11 February 1935. See also, PAC, RG 25, G1, vol. 1803, file 729.
45. *Chinese Times*, 23-26 January 1934.

FOURTEEN

Supporting the War against Japan

Of all the periods in the history of Canada's Chinese, the decade 1937-47 was the most exciting and momentous. It was the time when the Canadian Chinese made their most dramatic contribution to both China and Canada. Chinese communities in Canada also achieved perhaps the greatest unity they had ever known. What brought about these developments were the Sino-Japanese war, beginning in 1937, and the spread of the Second World War into the Pacific, beginning with the Japanese attack on Pearl Harbor in December, 1941. In the latter, Canada and China became allies, thereby linking the support of Canada's Chinese for both causes – China's and Canada's. The solidarity of the wartime effort evoked at least a temporary unity in the Chinese-Canadian communities. It also helped improve white Canadian attitudes towards Chinese Canadians and that, in turn, made possible, by 1947, enfranchisement of the Chinese in British Columbia and Saskatchewan, and major improvements for the Chinese in immigration policy.

When the Sino-Japanese War began in 1937 the Chinese government called, as it always did in moments of crisis, upon the Chinese residing overseas for financial assistance. And, as they always did, the Overseas Chinese, including those in Canada, responded magnificently. During the course of the war, 1937-45, there were fund drives for almost every conceivable military purpose. There were campaigns to buy airplanes or ambulances; collections for winter clothing for soldiers; fund-raising for medical supplies; collections for refugee relief and aid to war orphans; and, throughout the war, bond sales whose proceeds were used for general military purposes. Besides responding to these government-sponsored campaigns, the Overseas Chinese privately organized aid to their home districts and as individuals maintained, so far as they were able, the flow of remittances to relatives in China.

It is impossible to estimate the financial contributions of the Overseas Chinese to China between 1937 and 1945. One estimate holds that the Chinese in Southeast Asia alone – the largest group of Overseas Chinese and the biggest contributors of funds in the 1937-41 period – provided enough in remittances to relatives to maintain China's balance of payments during the first two years of the war, and a sufficiently high level of contributions to government to finance one-fourth of China's military expenses in the first year of the war.[1]

In the latter half of the war conditions changed greatly. As the Japanese took over much of Southeast Asia the Chinese there found it too dangerous to contribute to China's war effort and their financial support necessarily was greatly reduced. The burden now fell upon the Chinese in the Western Hemisphere. The Japanese conquest of Hong Kong made it almost impossible for Overseas Chinese anywhere to reach their home districts with relief aid and remittances. These remittances were vital to the income and maintenance of a large proportion of the families that lived in the home districts; many families received all or most of their income from relatives abroad. In the one district of Toisan, from which the majority of Chinese Canadians come, the absence of remittances and the presence of wartime economic conditions produced horrifying results: thousands died of starvation.[2]

How much did the Chinese in Canada contribute? Taking into account all kinds of financial contributions, the usual figure given is Can $5 million – or about $125 per capita. Although it is difficult to get at comparative figures, it is likely that the Canadian contribution was disproportionately great in relation to the representation of Canadian Chinese in the total population of Overseas Chinese. Organized contributions to causes in China were nothing new among the Chinese in Canada. They had had a long history of famine relief contributions, bond purchasing, and even aircraft financing. The scale of their contribution was now to be much larger than before. Organizations and individuals in Chinese communities across the country took part in this aggressive fund-raising. In Victoria, the "Resist Japan and Save the Nation" Association, formed in 1931, continued and enlarged its activities, becoming the co-ordinator of all forms of organized aid from that city's Chinese to China. The kinds of aid and the methods used in collecting it were as numerous and varied as anywhere in Canada. There were campaigns for military expense money, for direct aid to troops, for refugee relief, and for the purchase of ambulances and aircraft. Methods included pledges, bazaars, banquets, parades, tag days, theatrical performances, and campaigns to sell Chinese war bonds.

The Chinese in British Columbia joined American Chinese in Pacific Coast port cities in forming a network of opposition to Canadian and American shipments of scrap metal to Japan during the 1937-41 period. Their use of demonstrations at pier sites where scrap metal was being loaded for Japan was particularly effective at winning white sympathy. Some whites joined the demonstrators and at least one white organization, the CCF, supported an embargo on such goods.[3] Eventually, fears of riots at demonstration sites drove shipowners to stop taking such cargoes.[4] Fund-raising activities were another aspect of the war effort. After 1937 these assumed a greater scale than before, and during the eight-year period 1937-45 Victoria, with a Chinese population of only about 3,000, was able to raise Can. $750,000 for China's war against Japan.[5]

Vancouver's fund-raising efforts changed forms, emphases, and leaders several times during the course of the war effort. The Resistance Association that existed when the war began in 1937 continued as a fund-raiser for China's war effort until at least the end of 1943. Meanwhile, the CBA established an office for raising military expense money. By 1938, with the encouragement of the Kuomintang government in China, this office had been transformed into an association for the sale of Chinese war bonds, this being a major emphasis of Chinese government effort throughout the war. In a third stage (1944-45) the Bond-selling Association became the "Donate to Save the Nation" Association. New leaders accompanied each phase. In general, they represented the CBA, the KMT, the Freemasons, and the major businessmen in the Vancouver Chinese community.

As soon as the war broke out the Vancouver CBA and the Resistance Association urged a boycott by Chinese Canadians of all commercial dealings with Japan or with Japanese Canadians. It was acknowledged that such a boycott would not be painless for the Chinese Canadians, given established commercial relationships in agriculture, grocery stores, fish retailing, and hotel operation. Individual organizations, such as the Chinese Produce Dealers Association and the Chinese Farmers Association, pledged themselves to observe such a boycott. By November a formal boycott had been declared. Those who violated it were to be punished by fines, confiscation of property in China, and publication of their names in the newspapers. It was announced that 100 investigators would be hired to police the boycott, and the Chin (Chan) Association warned its members that any who might be beaten because they had violated the boycott would not be rescued or defended by the association.[6]

The Bond-selling Association was formed in Vancouver in late 1937 and early 1938. Its constitution required that each adult male in the Vancouver Chinese community purchase a minimum of Ch. $50 (about Can. $16) in Chinese war bonds.[7] Names of those who did not would be published in the Chinese-language newspapers, and those who wished to return to China had first to show the Chinese consulate that they had bought at least the minimum required amount of bonds.

As various fund-raising and other campaigns emerged from time to time, subcommittees of these Vancouver fund-raising organizations were created. For example, the Bond-selling Association had a subcommittee on Refugee Relief. The Liang-guang Refugee Relief Association was created in early 1939 to serve the home province of Canada's Chinese. At about the same time the Western Canada Branch of the Chinese Association for the Promotion of Aviation was organized to raise money for airplane purchases. In June of 1939 the CBA and the Resistance Association, in response to the "Spiritual Mobilization" campaign in China, formed a "Spiritual Mobilization" campaign in Vancouver, which collected funds for China.[8]

In general, organizational unity was achieved in Vancouver only late in the war. In 1940 the Bond-selling Association was reorganized to make it more representative of district and other associations, and to make its executive directly elected by member associations. The leadership of soliciting associations was sometimes mistrusted by the rank and file of Chinese. During the "One Bowl of Rice" Campaign of August-September, 1939, there were suspicions in Chinatown that the CBA leadership was mismanaging the funds collected. Feelings ran high because for poorer people real financial sacrifice was involved in giving to such campaigns. A crowd gathered outside the CBA one evening and would not be dispersed. CBA officials were accused of malfeasance and police who tried to break up the crowd were pelted with vegetables. Not until the early morning hours did the crowd dissolve. The CBA responded with soothing statements that the "CBA is your CBA" and criticism of it amounted to criticism of oneself.[9]

What the Chinese consulate in Vancouver saw as the real problem, however, was that there were many associations soliciting and sending aid, rather than a single, unified body. In 1942 the consul urged the five major soliciting associations, the CBA, Resistance Association, Bond-selling Association, Kuomintang, and Freemasons, to co-operate in creating a new, unified organization.[10] A "United Donate to Save the Nation" Association was formally created in July, 1942, but the five major soliciting associations continued to act independently as well. Finally, in April and May, 1944, a single "umbrella" organization, the "Donate to Save the Nation," was created for the last year of the war. Adding together all forms of monetary aid, Vancouver Chinese contributed an estimated Can. $1 million to China between 1937 and 1945.[11]

Vancouver was the collection centre in western Canada; Toronto filled that role in the East. Organizational unity came almost immediately in Toronto, although there were difficulties in holding together all groups. The influence of the Kuomintang and its government in China are much more apparent in Toronto than in Vancouver during this period. Toronto lacked a functioning CBA; the Chinese Christian Association performed some CBA functions, but could not claim to speak for the entire community on all questions. The Chinese Patriotic Federation of Ontario, which came into being in early 1938, drew its leadership from the Chinese Christian Association, the Kuomintang, the Freemasons, and other organizations.

Some groups had begun to form Resistance Associations by early 1937. But it was the arrival of the KMT Central Committeeman, Liu Wei-chih, that brought real organization to the top of the Toronto com-

191

munity. Liu began his organization in the Lung Kong Kung-so association, one of the wealthiest in Toronto and headed by a powerful local KMT member, Chong Ying.

Born in China, Chong Ying had come to Canada in 1910 at about fifteen years of age. He began as a clerk in the Kwong Hong Tai grocery-import store, which he later managed. He helped establish the KMT's newspaper, the *Shing Wah Daily News*, and by 1943 had become its executive director. As head of the local KMT he was the logical person to be the link between the Chinese government and its Toronto fund-raising activities. Recognition of Chong Ying as head of the Chinese Patriotic Federation (CPF) and its various subsidiary committees and campaigns was probably due as much as anything to his personal ties to the KMT Party and government of China.[12]

By February Liu Wei-chih had established the Chinese Patriotic Federation, which linked all Toronto organizations. Two years later the Resistance Associations in the larger Ontario towns and cities were brought into the Federation.[13] Throughout the war the CPF maintained its position as the single unifying fund-raising body in Toronto's Chinatown. It also enjoyed great continuity of leadership. A relatively small group of men occupied leading positions in the Federation year after year. Of this group, Chong Ying and E.C. Mark were particularly outstanding.

It was E.C. Mark who served as secretary of a major subcommittee that grew out of the CPF, the Chinese War Relief Fund. This organization was the result of white Canadian initiative. In December, 1941, a group of white Canadians who wished to aid China approached the CPF about creating a joint committee for fund-raising. The resulting committee listed prominent white Canadians as patrons and a few prominent whites and several leaders of the CPF as members. It was authorized by the Canadian government under the War Charities Act to solicit relief funds, first in Ontario and later throughout Canada.[14] The Chinese War Relief Fund, which provided medical and other aid to the wounded and the homeless, continued to exist beyond the end of the war. It was estimated that in the five-year period from December, 1941, to December, 1946, over $4 million was raised for this fund, mostly from white Canadians.[15]

Like other fund-raising organizations at this time, the CPF attempted to establish required minimum contributions and used public shame and the application of fines to elicit compliance. Its constitution gave it the power to coerce community members, bringing them to trial for non-compliance or even for criticism of the CPF. In the case of poorer members of the community, it was permissible for some member of the CPF executive to submit payment in their behalf. But those able to do so were required to comply.[16] These disciplinary pretensions by the CPF did not necessarily intimidate everyone. On one occasion a CPF fund-raiser was beaten by a crowd of 100 who were dissatisfied with his explanation of how he had used their contributions. He was compelled to apologize.[17]

In Montreal a Resistance organization was formed as soon as the war broke out in China. In the spring of 1938 Liu Wei-chih, having reorganized Toronto's fund-raising and other war-support activities, arrived in Montreal. He reorganized the local group into a united Chinese Patriotic League. Executive positions in the new body were to be allocated to the KMT, Freemasons, and the Chinese YMCI. During the course of the war this organization collected Can. $400,000 for the Chinese war effort.[18]

Of the leaders of Montreal's wartime efforts to aid China, the most outstanding was Frank Lee (Lee To-chan), who made the largest financial contributions.[19] Frank Lee had come to Canada as a teen-ager in 1910. He began as a laundry worker, learned English at a Sunday school, and by the late 1930's had established a prosperous restaurant, Montreal Chop Suey, Ltd. A consistently large supporter of the Montreal Chinese Catholic Church, Frank Lee was also active in the Chinese Benevolent Association and, in later years, led the fund-raising for a new Chinese hospital.[20]

Another leader was Gordon Yuen. Born in Victoria and married to a Victoria-born Chinese woman, Gordon Yuen settled with his family in Montreal in 1919, where he first managed a restaurant and then operated the Sang Yuen grocery store. Active in CBA and KMT affairs, he became most widely known as an interpreter, informal and official, at various levels of the court system. Like many Chinese community leaders, he volunteered great amounts of time and effort in times of crisis, such as participating in the struggle against the Chinese Immigration Bill of 1923, or housing (in his own home) people who were homeless because of Chinatown fires, or seeking outside aid for the community in moments of need.[21]

Winnipeg had had a National Salvation organization between 1931 and 1935. After July, 1937, it was revived as a fund-raising general office; then, under Liu Wei-chih's influence, it was renamed the Chinese Patriotic League. As was the case elsewhere, the Winnipeg league punished those who failed to make the minimum required contributions. The small Winnipeg community, of only about 700 persons, was able to raise, in this fashion, over Can. $130,000 during the war years. Of the major contributors, perhaps the best known was Charlie Foo (Au Foo), a KMT leader.[22]

In Calgary, as in several other places, the demands of wartime support activity were the impetus to the formation of the first community-wide association. In August a National Salvation Association was organized and by early 1938, when Liu Wei-chih arrived, it turned its attention to bond sales. There were campaigns for aircraft purchases to defend Canton during the bombing of that city and clothing collection drives during the winter of 1939.[23]

The National Salvation Association soon became the Pan-Alberta Anti-Japanese League with its headquarters in Calgary. Its goal was to

193

co-ordinate the efforts of the various fund-raising and resistance associations that had developed in cities and towns across the province. Thus, in Edmonton, Lethbridge, Medicine Hat, High River, and Blairmore there were associations which in theory at least were linked to a headquarters organization in Calgary.

The sanctions applied to Chinese who did not observe the directives of the Calgary-based league were, on paper, severe. Besides publication of names in Canadian Chinese newspapers, ostracism from the community was possible, and those who continued to have dealings with such persons might be regarded as "traitors." The names of all such persons would be reported to the Chinese consulates and their property in China might be subject to confiscation.[24]

One major problem for the Calgary-based league was how to keep Lethbridge in the organization. In Lethbridge, a community of 220, where KMT-Freemason rivalry was very strong and had made co-operation difficult, the community was at war with itself over whether to be part of the Pan-Alberta organization. Slightly less than half the population wanted an independent organization; about one-fourth wanted association with Calgary; the remainder were undecided. Violence and court action ensued, despite mediation attempts. The issue remained unresolved.[25]

In Edmonton, where there were about 400 Chinese, three-fourths of them turned out to hear Liu Wei-chih speak. The local Resistance Association established a boycott with a fine of $50 for any Chinese who broke it. The proceeds of fine-collection went in support of the war. As in other cities, the Edmonton Chinese were required to purchase minimum amounts of bonds or make minimum contributions in each fund drive. For example, in the drive for airplanes to defend Canton, a minimum contribution of $10 was established.

Regina established a Resistance and National Salvation Association in August, 1937. Its small Chinese population of about 175 observed the memorial days, wired the Chinese government to keep up the fight, and used tag days and other devices to solicit funds.

Saskatoon and Moose Jaw also established Resistance Associations and they, together with Regina's association, tried to expand the boycott, agitate against scrap metal shipments to Japan, and raise refugee relief funds. In the middle of the following year Saskatoon's organization became the headquarters for all Saskatchewan resistance organizations, a congress of which was held there in 1940. Though having only 300 Chinese residents, Saskatoon achieved fame for its high level of bond purchases in the early years of the war. Moose Jaw (Chinese population, 260) had much the same kind of reputation.

In the Maritimes, Halifax had a National Salvation Association by January, 1938, and had begun remitting funds to China. In Newfoundland by the 1930's the Chinese population had increased to about 200 and the first stable associations had been formed. These were two clan associations, the Au Tai Mee Club (1927) and the Hong Hang Society (Hong surname) (1932), both in St. John's.

In 1940 the Chinese consul-general from Ottawa visited Newfoundland. A Chinese War Relief Association was established and the sale of bonds was promoted. Further encouragement to maintain the effort came from the visit of another consul in 1943.[26]

The $5 million collected in all of Canada during the war years was sent to China in various ways. At the beginning all of it went through the Bank of China in New York. Later, until December, 1941, that bank's branch in Hong Kong could handle such shipments. Refugee funds often went directly to Madame Chiang Kai-shek.[27] Some funds, such as airplane-buying contributions for Canton, could be sent via the Bank of Canton's branch in San Francisco.[28]

Although most shipments of funds were collected by the major community-wide organizations, they were supplemented by smaller sums regularly collected and sent directly to China by such organizations as the Freemasons, Vancouver Chinese Chamber of Commerce, the clan associations, district associations, schools, and churches.

Schools and other youth organizations seem to have specialized in raising relief funds, while most of the military-related aid was collected by men's organizations. Schools organized instrumental music and singing and acting troupes, performed benefits, sponsored tea parties, and also sold tags on the streets on tag days. The Mon Keong School of Vancouver provides a well-publicized example of student effort. During the war years, Mon Keong students published over ninety essays on anti-Japanese resistance themes, their most common outlet being the KMT's New Republic newspaper, which had a special student section. They also formed singing and theatrical groups and gave benefit performances for fund-raising.

Chinese women's groups supported the war with war relief fund drives. These included teas, bazaars, and tag sales on the streets. Much of what they did was associated with white Canadian women's organizations, especially after Canada and China became wartime allies in 1941. Wartime mobilization of the efforts of every Chinese was a stimulus to the development of Chinese women's associations. In Toronto there were the Bay Street (Chinese) Women's Association and the University Avenue Chinese Women's Association. In Calgary there was a Women's Patriotic Association in existence and raising funds for resistance to Japan even before the outbreak of war in July, 1937. It continued its activities during the war with such things as the presentation of plays to raise relief funds. By the fall of 1939 a women's association in Edmonton was holding tea parties to raise relief funds. Chinese women in Vancouver organized themselves for relief work during the early fall of 1937, and in the interests of war support activity formed the Chinese Women's Patriotic Athletic Association. Athletic activity in support of patriotism was even more noticeable in Victoria where a women's lion dance team was organized and gave performances at bond sales events. New Westminster, too, had its women's association patriotic activities.

In many activities, especially after 1941, Chinese and white women worked together. A lion dance in Victoria in support of bond sales during the early years of the war was accompanied by on-street fund collection by Chinese and white women. Observing this phenomenon, the *Chinese Times* called it "the happiest day since the Chinese came to Victoria." Chinese women had definitely come out of their houses. Indeed, the appearance of Chinese women selling tags on the streets of Canada's major cities was one of the most remarkable and interesting phenomena of the war years.

TEMPORARY UNITY IN THE CHINESE COMMUNITIES

Another phenomenon of great importance at this time was the relatively high degree of unity achieved by the Chinese communities across Canada. It is fair to say that even when the Chinese organized their opposition to the 1923 Immigration Bill they did not achieve the degree of unity that was reached during World War II.

In China the onset of the war against Japan had led to the formal establishment of a United Front. The major domestic antagonists, the ruling KMT and the dissident Communists, agreed to stop fighting one another and to fight the Japanese instead. The KMT accepted the idea of opening up participation in government, at least to some degree, to Communist representatives and also those associated with politically independent groups. The United Front was a precarious thing; there was little trust among its participants. But it was considered essential for the duration of the war.

In Canada the United Front philosophy also prevailed. Rivalries from the past, such as the long-standing KMT-Freemason opposition, were to be overridden in the interest of unified support for China's war effort. This stimulus to organizational unity had long-range results in some communities but not in others. In Toronto, when the war ended, those who had led the Chinese Patriotic Federation converted this association into the Ontario Chinese Community Centre, or CCC, thereby giving Toronto what it had never had before, a community-wide CBA-type organization. The scope of this organization's authority, however, extended beyond Toronto to include all the towns and cities in Ontario where there were major Chinese communities. A similar development occurred in Winnipeg, where the local Resistance Association was converted into a Manitoba Chinese Association. Calgary, however, could not maintain or convert its wartime organization into a lasting CBA, and it was only in the 1960's, under different social conditions, that new forms of community-wide organization began to appear in that city.

After 1941 Canada and China became allies in a common struggle against Japan. In an effort to make China an equal partner and a post-war "Great Power," Canada, in common with other Western nations, negotiated in 1942 the termination of a set of 100-year-old treaties that had governed Sino-Western relations in ways the Chinese found objectionable.

Canada and China also upgraded their diplomatic relations, first to ministerial and then, by 1943, to full ambassadorial status.[29] The Canadian consulate that had existed in Nanking since 1931, under the Canadian legation in Tokyo, became an independent legation, and then an embassy, with General Victor Odlum as Canada's first ambassador to China.[30] China's consulate-general in Ottawa became an embassy, with Dr. Liu Shih-shun as China's first ambassador to Canada.[31] By the end of the war Chinese consulates had been established at Toronto and Winnipeg, and the Toronto and Vancouver consulates had been elevated to consulates-general.[32]

Canada and China also signed a general treaty in April, 1944, and a commercial agreement in September, 1946. In 1947 a Canadian loan of U.S. $60 million was made to China to be used mainly to purchase surplus war equipment. On a non-governmental level, the national Chinese War Relief Fund Association, based in Toronto, became at the end of the war an organization (Canadian Aid to China) for providing reconstruction aid to China from sympathetic white Canadians.

All of the foregoing not only enhanced KMT prestige among white Canadians; it also raised the prestige and position of KMT leaders in Canada's Chinatowns. In the major Chinese communities the various war-support associations that developed were linked to the government of China, to which nearly all China-bound aid funds of a non-personal nature were sent. In most communities war-support associations were dominated by those local Chinese most associated with the government of China. Such Chinese were likely to be the local KMT leaders. The identification of local KMT members and organizations with the Chinese government went beyond this. Criticism of the Kuomintang government in China and of KMT organizations and leaders in Canada was seen as a serious offence, threatening the required wartime unity at the least, and at the worst being considered as subversive activity.

The evidence for the strengthening of KMT influence is strongest for Toronto, where the Chinese Patriotic Federation was led continuously through the war by Chong Ying and E.C. Mark, both of them adherents of the KMT. But even in Toronto, there was no monopoly. Dr. Henry Lore, and one or two other Freemason leaders, also participated in the leadership. Even on logical grounds, it seems unlikely that the enhanced prestige and opportunities for the KMT could lead to complete KMT dominance of local organizations in Chinatowns across the country. The goals of the Chinese-Canadian communities and those of the KMT were not identical; they only were overlapping. Both wished a highly unified war-support effort. Beyond that, whatever ambitions for local KMT dominance were present, they were not shared throughout the community. The war saw the KMT move into a position of great strength in CBAs across Canada, but not necessarily one of control.

The major figures from China who visited Canada to promote the war effort reflect both partisan and United Front considerations on the part of the KMT government of China. Liu Wei-chih, Huang Wen-shan, and Wong Bock-yue were party figures whose visits to Canada were organizational in intent. For Wong it was a return to the scene of an earlier triumph, as one of the early promoters of the KMT in Canada in the World War I years. But even Wong's visit included a United Front note, since he was accompanied by the American Freemason leader, Seto Mei-tang. And Liu Wei-chih was accompanied by a veteran Freemason revolutionary, Zhao Yu (Chew Yuk).[33]

Dr. Kalfred Dip Lum, an American-educated political scientist, made over 300 speeches across North America during the war years, some of them in British Columbia. At a higher political level, T.V. Soong, Chiang Kai-shek's brother-in-law and finance minister of the government, visited Canada twice, in 1943 and 1945. His sister, Madame Chiang Kai-shek, fresh from her triumphs with the U.S. Congress in Washington, D.C., visited Ottawa and Toronto in the spring of 1943, speaking to a joint session of Parliament.

The more independent visitors were also people of note. T'ao Hsing-chih, a leader in the Mass Education movement, spent much of 1937-38 crossing the country promoting support of the war effort. Seto Mei-tang, the American Freemason leader, was an embodiment of the United Front in China in the sense that he had accepted membership in the Peoples Political Council, the major United Front body. In company with the KMT's Wong Bock-yue, he visited major Chinese communities and attended a Freemasons' national meeting. Hu Shih, the famous scholar who had accepted a wartime position as Chinese ambassador to the U.S., visited eastern Canada on at least one occasion.

Some of these speakers, Madame Chiang and Dr. Kalfred Dip Lum, for instance, addressed their exhortations as much to white Canadians as to Chinese Canadians. Indeed, the other great development of the war years was the growing sympathy of white Canadians for China and, by extension, for the Chinese in their midst. When the war began in 1937 the Canadian Chinese had on their side the CCF, which had supported the vote for the Chinese in B.C., a few interested and sympathetic church groups and leaders, and a few academics. After 1941 China was seen as an important – perhaps even a vital – ally in the Pacific War. The end of the unequal treaties and the exchange of ambassadors reflected a growing esteem for China in the eyes of Canadians.

THE PRICE OF PARTIAL ACCEPTANCE

One important factor in the evolution of more favourable white attitudes toward the Chinese in Canada was the emergence of Chinese-Canadian leaders who were unusually articulate and skilful in working with white Canadians. Two conspicuous examples of this type of leader during the 1937-47 period were E.C. Mark in Toronto and Foon Sien in Vancouver.

Ernest Chewan Mark (Mak Sik-chew) arrived in Canada in 1908 at the age of twelve. For the next few years he attended school during the day while working after school in his father's general merchandise store on Elizabeth Street.[34] He learned English at a night class sponsored by the Presbyterian Church. In 1910 he was among the founders of the Toronto Chinese YMCI, which became the largest Chinese YMCI in Canada and gave rise to the Chinese Christian Association, for many years the leading community-wide organization in Toronto's Chinatown. During the fight against the 1923 Immigration Bill, he demonstrated his ability to work with white Canadians. As English secretary of the National Club that opposed the bill, he worked with Senator William Proudfoot, leading clergymen of the Presbyterian Church, and a few sympathetic Members of Parliament. By 1925 he was Chinese passenger agent for eastern Canada for the CPR and was also devoting much time to the *Shing Wah Daily News*. Subsequently, he added other business agencies and took on more responsibility at *Shing Wah*, eventually becoming editor. He was also a leader of the Mark clan association in Toronto.

In Vancouver Foon Sien (Wong Mun-po) was, like E.C. Mark, well-educated, articulate in English, and good at working both inside and outside the Chinese community. Born in China in 1899, Foon Sien came to Canada nine years later. After a short residence in Cumberland, B.C., he moved to Vancouver. By the early 1920's he was a visible member of the Chinese community as an interpreter, a member of the Chinese-Canadian Association, and an activist in Chinese student groups. He studied at the University of British Columbia and later took a degree course from Chicago.

Although much of his formal higher education was in the area of international law, Foon Sien was a man of wide-ranging interests. In the course of his life he wrote and spoke on Chinese culture and education, immigration problems, race relations, and problems of international affairs. He was the founder of several associations, perhaps the most important being the Chinese Trade Workers' Association (1942). During the war years Foon Sien was active on the executive of the Vancouver Resistance Association. When war-support activities were to be co-ordinated with those of white Canadians he was the person most likely to be called upon. In the course of his life he was a member of several non-Chinese associations, including the Liberal Party in Vancouver's Chinatown. Both inside and outside the Chinese community Foon Sien was a negotiator. For thirty years, from the 1930's to the 1960's, he served the Vancouver CBA and the Chinese community as a negotiator on specific issues of concern. Besides these efforts on behalf of the community or groups in the community, Foon Sien also assisted individuals with immigration problems.

This kind of negotiating and defending activity was not unique to Foon Sien. Indeed, his job, as CBA external relations officer, called for it. Many other people also had done and were doing many of the same things. What was unique about Foon Sien was that he made the one issue of immigration peculiarly his own. In the 1940's and 1950's Foon Sien became famous for his annual "pilgrimages" to Ottawa in search of complete equality of immigration treatment for Chinese in Canada. His well-publicized efforts were an important step in the ultimate achievement of that goal.

Like all Chinese community leaders, Foon Sien had his critics. Among other things, some resented the way white Canadians spoke of him as the "mayor of Chinatown." Foon Sien was not that; but he was, above all, the Chinese leader most visible and best known to white Canadians. As such, he was an "external relations" officer of a kind particularly useful to the community during the years of his greatest activity.[35]

The experience of working with Chinese leaders like E.C. Mark and Foon Sien undoubtedly had a favourable effect upon white Canadians' views of Chinese Canadians. Joint fund drives furnished opportunities for experience in working together. Even before Canada and China became allies Canadian views were changing enough so that when CBA leader Charlie Ting Lim died in 1939, a Vancouver newspaper could eulogize him as "Charlie the Christian," noting his efforts in behalf of his countrymen.[36]

The Sino-Japanese War and the subsequent Pacific War furnished an opportunity for the Chinese communities in Canada to acquire enhanced status in the eyes of other Canadians. Given the opportunity to prove themselves, they did just that. While supporting the war in China, they supported the war effort in Canada. Chinese bought Canadian Victory Bonds in the total amount of $10 million. The Chinese community of Victoria was cited four times by the government for its purchases. With less than 10 per cent of the Chinese population of Canada, Victoria purchased 20 per cent of the bonds bought by Chinese.[37] Chinese did war work in shipyards and factories. Chinese farmers in B.C. exerted themselves to produce more food for Canadian troops. Chinese served as air raid wardens. And finally, over 500 Chinese born in Canada or naturalized were called into military service during World War II, as compared to some 300 in World War I. Unlike World War I, in which no Chinese served as a commissioned officer, this time some Chinese Canadians did obtain commissions, although it was not always easy for them to do so.[38] Thus, when the war ended – and even as the war was still going on – when Chinese Canadians spoke of getting their rights to equal treatment in immigration, or rights to vote, hold public office, and practise certain professions – they were not talking about gifts but about things they had paid for.

Wartime co-operation was not the only influence on white Canadian attitudes. The emergence of family life and higher living standards among Canadian-born Chinese was also a powerful force. Police in Vancouver reported less gambling there, in part, they said, because Canadian-born Chinese were less interested in that kind of activity.[39] A study of Asian standards of living in British Columbia noted a definite tendency of Canadian-born Chinese to seek living standards comparable to those of white Canadians.[40] Chinese began to move out of Chinatowns and into middle-class white neighbourhoods, although not without white resistance.[41]

Still, the war was decisive, not only because China was an ally but because it was seen as a war against the kind of injustice and inhumanity epitomized in Nazi racist doctrines. With this kind of interpretation of the war's significance, it was difficult to maintain racist policies in Canada: there was a growing feeling that the time had come to correct old injustices.

When World War II ended the Chinese communities across Canada celebrated victory by decorating Chinatowns and participating in victory parades and speech-making. The solidarity and sense of purpose of war effort activities were invigorating. White attitudes toward the Chinese were changing. Discrimination, in its overt forms at least, was becoming less common and, when it occurred, could be protested against with broader public support than before. The task of achieving full equality was not yet accomplished, but there was reason for optimism as Canada's Chinese entered a new era.

NOTES

1. Yoji Akashi, *The Nanyang Chinese National Salvation Movement, 1937-1941* (Lawrence, Kansas, 1970), pp. 126, 132-3.
2. "Inside the CBA," p. 16.
3. *Chinese Times*, 22 February 1938. Much of the information on fund-raising contained in this chapter will be found in various issues of this newspaper during the period 1937 to 1944.
4. Joseph Hope, "Wei-fao Huaqiao sanian fendou shiji," p. 8. See also Victoria *Colonist*, 12-13 August 1939; *Chinese Times*, 2, 6 December 1938.
5. Lee Tung-hai, p. 463.
6. *Chinese Times*, 7, 13, 16, 23 August, 19 October, 2, 24 November 1937.
7. *Ibid.*, 4 January, 9 June 1938.
8. *Ibid.*, 1, 8 February, 14-16, 23 June, 4 July, 5 August, 16 November 1939.
9. *Ibid.*, 10, 20, 26 February, 27 April, 10 September 1940; 21 August 1939.
10. *Ibid.*, 18 May 1942.
11. *Yungaohua Huiguan luocheng tekan*, pp. 1-2.
12. Levine, "Historical Documentation Pertaining to Overseas Chinese Organizations," pp. 97-8; *Xiandai Huaqiao renwu zhi* (Taibei, 1963), p. 219; *Shing Wah Daily News*, 23 July 1943.

13. *Chinese Times*, 2 March 1938; Levine, "Historical Documentation," p. 94; Chen Kwong Min, *Meizhou Huaqiao tongjian*, pp. 425, 427.

14. Undated [1943] flyer of Chinese War Relief Fund; Toronto *Evening Telegram*, 24 June 1943.

15. *Shing Wah Daily News*, 3 December 1946.

16. Levine, "Historical Documentation," pp. 100-17.

17. *Chinese Times*, 27 June, 5 July 1939.

18. Chen Kwong Min, *Meizhou*, p. 427.

19. Lee Tung-hai, p. 465.

20. Bill Lee, interview with Bernice Kwong, November, 1974.

21. Mrs. Gordon Yuen, interview with Bernice Kwong, November, 1974.

22. *Chinese Times*, 3 September 1937; Chen Kwong Min, *Meizhou*, p. 428; W.S. Chow, "The Chinese Community in Canada Before 1947, and Some Recent Developments," paper presented to the IXth International Congress of Anthropological and Ethnological Sciences, Chicago, 1973, pp. 16-17.

23. *Chinese Times*, 19 August 1937; 2-3 February, 2 April 1938; 8 November 1939.

24. Ban Seng Hoe, *Structural Changes of Two Chinese Communities*, pp. 91-2.

25. *Chinese Times*, 4 April 1939ff.

26. "The Chinese Community in Newfoundland," pp. 24, 75.

27. Undated [1943] flyer of Chinese War Relief Fund.

28. *Chinese Times*, 12 February 1941; on financial relations, see *ibid.*, 24 November 1939; 20 January 1940; 22 January, 7 February, 8 March 1941; 5 August 1942.

29. *Documents on Canadian External Relations*, VII (Ottawa, 1974), pp. 89ff.; Chen Kwong Min, *Meizhou*, p. 406.

30. PAC, RG 25, vol. 1687, file 80H, Keenleyside Report, 1935, gives some arguments of the mid-1930's for establishing a legation in China.

31. Chen Kwong Min, *Meizhou*, p. 406; *Shing Wah Daily News*, 23 March 1942. See also *Chinese Times*, 2 November 1941, for a biography of Dr. Liu.

32. Toronto had had a vice-consulate since at least 1912. PAC, RG 25, Annual Registers, 1912, vol. 1119, file 136. An unidentified Toronto English-language newspaper, apparently dated in 1918, refers to two Chinese consuls at Toronto. See PAC, Chief Press Censor, file 246-2.

33. *Huang Wenshan lu-Mei luncong* (Taibei, 1960), pp. 715ff.; *Chinese Times*, 18 August, 22, 29 November 1943; *Shing Wah Daily News*, 27 September, 14 October 1943; *Chinese Times*, 23-24 November 1937; 1, 7 April 1938. Chew's report of collections around the world is found in *ibid.*, 30 September, 1 October 1938.

34. Ivan Mark, "E.C. Mark, my father," unpublished ms., 1973.

35. *Quan-Jia Taishan Yi-qiao dierjie kenqin dahui tekan* (Taibei, 1975), pp. 119-20; *Huang Wenpu xiansheng aisi lu* (Vancouver, 1971), pp. 1-3.

36. Vancouver *Province*, 24 March 1939.

37. Lee Tung-hai, pp. 446-7.
38. Gordon Taylor, letter to E. Wickberg, 8 November 1973.
39. *Chinese Times*, 16 January 1939. Apparently the decline in gambling activity was temporary.
40. Carrothers, "Oriental Standards of Living," pp. 273-92, especially, pp. 285-91.
41. Mark, "E.C. Mark"; note also a few examples for Vancouver in *Wrigley's B.C. Directory* (Vancouver, 1931); *Chinese Times*, 4 February, 4 September 1941.

PART FOUR

1947-1980

FIFTEEN

Immigration: Policy and Patterns, 1947-1962

THE END OF EXCLUSION

At the end of the war, the energies of the Chinese community were focused on two main objectives: the repeal of the 1923 Chinese Immigration Act and the granting of the franchise to Chinese citizens in British Columbia. The Immigration Act, or, as the Chinese called it, the "43 Harsh Regulations," had been a source of deep humiliation to the Chinese since it came into being. Agitation for its repeal had been almost constant throughout the 1920's and 1930's. Chinese diplomats brought it up in their discussions with Canadian governments;[1] CBAs and other Chinese organizations regularly reminded Ottawa that it should be repealed; Humiliation Day was observed each year by Chinese communities across the country. During the 1920's the Eastern Canada Mission, a Protestant interdenominational organization in Toronto, regularly voted resolutions for repeal at its meetings. These were transmitted to the government with covering letters emphasizing that the 1923 law made normal family life impossible for most of the Canadian Chinese population, and created a bad impression of Canada in China, thereby hampering Canadian missionary work and trading possibilities.[2] The point about trading possibilities was re-inforced in the early 1930's by indications that China's reactions to a proposed commercial treaty with Canada were shaped and conditioned by the existence of the 1923 Immigration Law.[3]

Meanwhile, impetus for change came from another source. Beginning in early 1943 the United States moved toward abandoning its Chinese Exclusion Act, which was finally repealed in favour of a quota system in 1944. By July, 1943, Prime Minister Mackenzie King had said in the House of Commons that Canada's Chinese immigration policy was a "mistake," which needed to be corrected.[4]

Several other developments advanced the cause of repeal of the 1923 law. The upgrading of diplomatic representation to embassy level in 1943 was followed in April, 1944, by a treaty which did not deal specifically with immigration but which included general terms giving nationals of each country rights to travel and reside in the other country. It was difficult to see how the 1923 law could be sustained in the face of such an agreement. In the same year the United Nations Charter was formulated, containing statements about human rights and non-discrimination which were contradictory to some aspects of the 1923 law. The *Globe and Mail* reminded Mackenzie King of his statement in Commons and contrasted his glowing praise of China as an ally, when Madame Chiang Kai-shek visited Canada, with the realities of Canada's treatment of its own Chinese.[5] The Vancouver *Sun*, which twenty years earlier had published the racist novel, *The Writing on the Wall*, now came out in support of repealing the 1923 law.[6]

In 1946 there began a concerted effort to bring about the repeal of the 1923 law. In Vancouver the Toi-san association passed resolutions calling for its repeal and the substitution of a quota system. Foon Sien, on behalf of the association, repeatedly wrote letters to the appropriate departments of the Dominion government arguing for these changes.[7]

In Toronto the effort was the most broadly based of any in the country. As in the 1923 opposition to the proposed law, so in the agitation for its repeal, the Toronto drive was uniquely a joint white-Chinese enterprise. In 1923, leaders of the Eastern Canada Mission had joined the Chinese in their protests, and some of those leaders – for example, Reverend A.E. Armstrong and Reverend W.D. Noyes – were also leaders in the 1946 movement. Of the seventy-one names listed on the letterhead of the Committee for the Repeal of the Chinese Immigration Act, 80 per cent were not Chinese. Besides ecumenical Protestant representation in the persons of Armstrong and Noyes, there was Catholic support expressed through Father E.J. Lyons. Toronto attorney Irving Himel was a legal advisor and frequent spokesman for the group. Among the Chinese leaders were Dr. S.K. Ngai, a Toronto surgeon, Chong Ying of the KMT and *Shing Wah Daily News*, Wong Yick, editor of the Freemasons' *Hung Chung She Bo*, Professor C.C. Shih of the University of Toronto, and K. Dock Yip, one of the sons of Yip Sang of Vancouver, who, in 1945, had become the first Chinese Canadian to be called to the bar.[8]

The Committee for the Repeal of the Chinese Immigration Act was formally organized at the end of November, 1946, after a series of informal meetings. Over the next few months it sent delegations to Ottawa to speak to the Minister of External Affairs, the Minister of Mines and Resources (who had jurisdiction over immigration matters), and the Director of the Immigration Branch (under Mines and Resources). It also sent briefs to the government and wrote numerous letters to leaders of Chinese and white organizations.[9]

In its statement to the Minister of Mines and Resources, the Committee gave nine reasons for repeal:

1. The Act was in conflict with the UN charter, of which Canada was a signatory.
2. The Act was the "greatest single" cause of disturbance of the friendly relations between Canada and China.
3. The Act was a "major barrier" to the development of trade between the two countries.
4. The Act was against "all principles of humanity, morality and social welfare," by preventing normal family life for the majority of Chinese in Canada.
5. The Act was contrary to the principles of Canadian democracy.
6. Canada was now the only North American country with a special Chinese Immigration Act.
7. The Act was "counter to the recommendations of the Senate Standing Committee on Immigration and Labor in its report of August 13, 1946."
8. The CCF and the Progressive Conservatives supported its repeal.
9. Prime Minister King had already admitted in October, 1943, that it was a mistake.

By December, 1946, several newspapers were supporting repeal of the law, including the Toronto *Globe and Mail*, the Winnipeg *Free Press*, the Winnipeg *Tribune*, the Regina *Leader-Post*, and the Vancouver *News-Herald*. By February, 1947, the Toronto-based Committee for the Repeal could claim widespread support in Canadian society. The major Protestant church denominations were supporters as were both English- and French-speaking Catholic bodies; the Council of Women, several Members of Parliament, and perhaps of most importance, the Canadian Congress of Labour had thrown their support behind repeal. Subsequently, the Toronto and Winnipeg Trades and Labour Councils had added theirs.[10]

With this kind of support the real question was not repeal but what kind of arrangements would replace the old law. Although negotiations with China over a possible immigration treaty continued, the debates in Commons over repeal revealed the difficulties in arriving at the complete equality of treatment desired by the Chinese side. British Columbia's MPs made it clear that although they agreed with the rest of the country that on humane and other grounds the old law had to be repealed, they feared any new arrangement might deluge their province with dependants of the Chinese already there, all of them seen as unassimilable. Since British Columbia was still the residence of over half of the Chinese in Canada, most dependants would locate in that province. It was known that the majority of the 20,000 Chinese in B.C. were single men with dependants in China. If all were given the right to bring dependants the influx, it was said, might be enormous. In reply to this argument, the Committee for Repeal and speakers in the House of Commons pointed out that for various reasons many dependants would not come. It had been proposed that wives and children under twenty-one be the group eligible to come.

Many of the single men in Canada were at an age where their children would be too old to be eligible. Many could not afford to bring their families to Canada. In many cases the family would not wish to come and the single man already here, especially if he were old, would wish to return to China for his last years.[11]

Debate centred on which Orders-in-Council should govern Chinese immigration policy when the 1923 Act was repealed. In general, P.C. 695 covered the question of immigrants' dependants. According to its terms any immigrant who had established himself in Canada for five years might bring over members of his immediate family. This Order-in-Council did not apply to Chinese, who were covered by the 1923 Act. Two other Orders-in-Council were relevant to Asian immigration. P.C. 2115, passed in 1930, provided that Asians who were citizens could bring members of their immediate families to Canada. But it also stated that its terms were not to apply to any group whose immigration was regulated by a special act. The Chinese were the only such group. In other words, P.C. 2115 made it possible for Japanese and East Indians who were citizens of Canada to bring their families into the country, but did not do the same for the Chinese. The other relevant Order-in-Council was P.C. 1378, passed nine months after P.C. 2115. This was the Order that required Chinese and Japanese who wished to become citizens to secure the permission of their respective home governments and place advertisements in Asian vernacular newspapers in Canada before being allowed to proceed to application. In 1934 these terms were waived for Japanese.[12]

In other words, the Chinese were the only immigrant group in Canada for which there was a complete structure of special legislation and regulations limiting their opportunities to come, to be united with their families if already here, and to proceed immediately to citizenship when eligible. The only way to end this humiliation and Canada's embarrassment in the face of the UN Charter and its own professed ideals would have been to put Chinese immigration on the same basis as that of all other countries. In terms of dependant regulations, then, Chinese would come under P.C. 695 and any Chinese who had established residence in Canada would have the right to bring over members of his immediate family.

It was precisely this complete openness that B.C. still could not accept. The problem for the federal government became one of how to satisfy humanitarian, trade, and other concerns while not alienating B.C. The formula eventually decided upon was to repeal the 1923 Act and with it P.C. 1378. With the 1923 Act no longer in existence, the Chinese would automatically fall under P.C. 2115, which allowed only those Chinese who were citizens to bring their families to Canada. And since P.C. 1378 was abolished, citizenship should be easier for Chinese to obtain.

In other words, the Chinese were to get "half a loaf." There was not to be complete equality; there were still to be special regulations governing Chinese and other Asians. In the debates, M.J. Coldwell of the CCF pointed out the discrimination involved in asking only a Chinese to commit himself to Canadian citizenship as a test of his worthiness to bring relatives here, while all other immigrants had only to be residents.[13]

The 1923 Act was repealed in May, 1947, bringing to an end twenty-five years of exclusion. It was a great symbolic victory for the Chinese communities and their white supporters; but it was less than an achievement of equality. It was as far as a Canadian government – and perhaps Canadian society, too – was ready to go at the time. In his statement in the House of Commons of May 1, 1947, announcing repeal and a new policy, Prime Minister King said that immigration to Canada was a privilege and not a right, and that Canada, in common with all countries, had a right to restrict immigrant admissions. He also stated his government's willingness to make immigration treaties with individual countries.[14] Some Chinese dependants were to be let in but there was to be no general letting down of bars to Chinese immigration.

The twenty-five-year struggle to abolish the 1923 Act was over, but there remained other tasks, particularly the securing of the vote in British Columbia. The position of the Chinese was not unique: other Asians in B.C. also lacked the franchise. Discussions on this subject, therefore, involved policy and popular attitudes towards the Japanese and East Indians as well as the Chinese. During the war years the Japanese were relocated to the interior of British Columbia and to other parts of Canada and in the immediate post-war period there remained some suspicion and popular hostility towards them. The East Indians' situation was somewhat different from that of the Chinese, since the former were British subjects.[15]

In early 1945 a delegation from the Chinese-Canadian Club presented a brief to B.C. Premier Hart and his cabinet. The undemocratic nature of the denial of the franchise was noted, and Chinese-Canadian demonstrations of loyalty and responsibility through the war effort and in other ways were pointed out. It was also argued that the number of Chinese-Canadian citizens was so small that granting them the vote would not have profound political consequences for Canada.[16]

The only visible response to this petition was an amendment to the B.C. Elections Act in March, 1945, by which the franchise was awarded to all Asians who were serving or had served in World War II and any Asians other than Japanese who had served in World War I. The numbers affected were about 400 from World War II and fifty from World War I. For the moment, then, for Asians in B.C. the franchise continued to be something that had to be won by military service, not a right that went automatically with citizenship.

But that situation soon changed. The Canadian Citizenship Act, which went into effect at the beginning of 1947, defined the franchise as a part of citizenship status. Something else changed. Until 1946 the CCF had been almost alone as a political force that was committed (since 1934) to unconditional enfranchisement of Chinese citizens in B.C. Now other white groups added their political support. When a joint delegation of Chinese Canadians and East Indian Canadians appeared before the special elections act committee of the B.C. legislature in November, 1946, they had the support of the B.C. Trades and Labour Council, veterans organizations, the UN Society, civil liberties groups, churches, and business organizations.[17]

In the spring session of 1947 the B.C. legislature voted to amend the provincial elections act, thereby granting the vote to Chinese Canadians and East Indian Canadians. Since the Saskatchewan legislature had amended its elections act three years earlier to rule out an oath that had prevented Chinese from voting in that province, Chinese were now fully enfranchised in Canada and thereby entitled to all opportunities that accompanied status on the voters' list.

IMMIGRATION POLICY

The post-war world ushered in some significant changes in the character of the Chinese communities in Canada. As in so many phases of Canadian Chinese history, immigration legislation was to have a decisive effect on the possibility of community formation and continued community growth.

At war's end, the Chinese in Canada were a declining, aging population. From a high point of 46,519 in 1931, the number of Chinese had fallen to 34,627 a decade later and would decline still further to 32,528 by 1951. Until the late 1960's, Chinese communities would still be characterized by a preponderance of men. In the 1930's there had been more than thirteen men to every woman; by the middle 1940's there were only about 2,000 Chinese women of marriageable age in a total population of 23,000. In the immediate post-war period Chinese communities were still demographically imbalanced, and the "married bachelors" had been cut off from virtually all contact with their families for almost a decade.

The repeal of the 1923 Act made possible a revival of Chinese communities in Canada, at least those in the major urban centres, although the recovery was neither immediate nor dramatic. The great changes in the character and composition of the Chinese population lay twenty years in the future. The assumptions of Canadian immigration policy changed slowly and it was only in 1967 that the last vestiges of discrimination against potential Chinese immigrants were removed.

Mackenzie King's statement of May, 1947, set the tone for immigration policy through to the end of the St. Laurent administration and even through the Diefenbaker Conservative government:

The policy of the government is to foster the growth of the population of Canada by the encouragement of immigration. The government will seek by legislation, regulation and vigorous administration, to ensure that careful selection and permanent settlement of such numbers of immigrants as can be advantageously absorbed in our national economy.

. . . The essential thing is that immigrants be selected with care, and that their numbers be adjusted to the absorptive capacity of the country.

There will, I am sure, be general agreement with the view that the people of Canada do not wish, as a result of mass immigration, to make a fundamental alteration in the character of our population. Large-scale immigration from the Orient would change that fundamental composition of the Canadian population.[18]

King's statement reflects in part his own strong views. The implications for Chinese migrants were very direct: federal policy until 1962 was opposed to "large-scale immigration" from the Orient. There emerged a situation whereby Canada was anxious to encourage migration for the contribution it could give to the rapidly expanding post-war economy, yet the government was equally concerned to close the door to non-European and non-white groups which were eager to participate in that promising future. King saw the need for an enlarged Canadian population, but it was more than merely a question of size. For him the key issues were the immigrants' contribution to the economic development of Canada and the capacities of both the economy and the society to absorb immigration. Economic and social integrative aspects were occasionally put aside for humanitarian principles, as in the case of immigrants from Hungary after the events of October, 1956. But humanitarian principle hardly seemed to work for the Chinese population of Canada, and, for twenty years after repeal of the 1923 Act, leaders of the Chinese communities in Canada, sometimes in concert with allies from the non-Chinese community, sought to induce successive immigration ministers to inject more humanity into regulations that were discriminatory in their operation.

The notable feature of Canadian immigration policy has been its flexibility. Like other similar legislation before it, the 1952 Immigration Act, under which all immigration laws were administered, was couched in vague terms. It confirmed and extended the previous practice of leaving current policy to be determined by cabinet through Orders-in-Council, which, unless specifically revoked, could prevail over law.[19]

One of the first actions by Chinese Canadians in the aftermath of the 1947 repeal was directed toward one such Order-in-Council, P.C. 2115, which had restricted Asian family immigration to a citizen's wife and unmarried children under eighteen years of age. The repeal of the 1923 Act allowed wives and dependant children to enter Canada, but there were categories of close relations who did not fall within these categories. For many Chinese Canadians, who had been unable to establish families in Canada but who had, nonetheless, married in China and periodically visited their wives and children since 1923, repeal of the 1923 Act seemed a mockery. If the pre-1923 immigrants had adult children, aged parents, not to mention siblings, they were excluded from Canada. Such rules did not apply to European groups.

For Chinese Canadians this was intolerable, especially in the years after the formation of the Peoples' Republic of China in 1949, when their wives and children were living in a social situation dominated by new collectivist principles that compromised the system of remittances so critical to the economy of many families in the Sze-yap and Chung-san regions. Indeed, from the time contacts were re-established in early 1947, the conditions of life in China were chaotic for the dependants of Chinese Canadians. After 1949 many of the family members were part of the exodus to Hong Kong and Macau. Moreover, given the historic associations between KMT organization in the centres of overseas migration and the Overseas Chinese communities themselves, Canadian Chinese anxieties about dependant families in China were often well-founded.

Whatever the specifics, Chinese Canadians saw their relatives and friends in difficulties from 1947 on. They also saw that many ethnic categories of European origins were subjects of humanitarian gestures on the part of the Canadian authorities. It was clear that emigrants from eastern Europe and the German Democratic Republic were welcome as immigrants to Canada. Chinese immigrants, even with close family ties to Canadian Chinese, were systematically excluded.

The "Committee for the Repeal of the Chinese Immigration Act" was not wound up after May, 1947. Some of the leading members of the Committee, along with A.R. Mosher, President of the Canadian Congress of Labour, appeared as witnesses before the Standing Committee of Immigration and Labour of the Senate of Canada,[20] in March, 1948. Their major grievance was the continued operation of P.C. 2115. The committee brief argued that such discrimination against the Chinese continued:

> To what other conclusion can one come when the law says on the one hand you can bring your wife and children into Canada provided you are of European, South American or United States parentage, so long as you are a *resident* of the country (Order-in-Council 695). And, on the other hand, you must be a Canadian *citizen* before you can bring your wife and children into the country if you are of the Chinese or Asiatic race (Order-in-Council 2115).
>
> If this is not discrimination against people on account of their race then the word discrimination has no meaning.

The brief argued for the repeal of the regulation on the grounds that discrimination on racial grounds should be avoided in immigration law. It went to pains to point out that it was requesting only a very modest change:

> We are not asking you to open wide the gates for Chinese immigration. We are only asking you to allow the wives and children of Chinese residents of Canada to come here, giving them the same privileges as we do Europeans and South Americans.

In arguing that repeal of P.C. 2115 was humane and modest, the brief went on to point out that it would not result in substantial immigration of Chinese:

> When you consider that from 1886 to 1924, inclusive, the total number of Chinese immigrants that came to Canada was 82,369, and there are barely 34,000 people of Chinese origin left in Canada at the present time, we do not see how anyone can seriously object in the circumstances to the admission of such a number of wives and children into the country or seriously argue that it would create problems of absorption.

The Senate Standing Committee was impressed with the arguments of the delegation. In the questioning that followed the presentation of the brief, members of the Committee appeared shocked at the restrictive nature of P.C. 2115 and the effects it had had on, especially, the possibilities of family unity. Dr. S.K. Ngai was the final witness called. He presented "the Chinese position" and stated:

> The fact is that there has been a wall or barrier between the racial groups, not only internationally, but also in Canada itself. I am glad to see that the big barrier between the racial groups in the form of racial discrimination, has already collapsed, because of the repeal of the Chinese Immigration Act last year. There still remains a small wall which we have been walking around many times, and we hope that Senator Wilson and her committee here will sound the trumpet and the walls of Jericho will fall.

Senator Wilson sounded the trumpet, but the walls remained virtually intact. By mid-summer of 1948 the Chinese communities of Canada saw that their struggles to achieve a degree of equality with respect to immigration legislation were far from over. Again the organizational leadership came from Toronto, perhaps because of its proximity to Ottawa and the skills that had been acquired in two years of struggle against the 1923 Act. A small success was achieved in late 1950, when regulations with respect to the age of admissible dependant children were changed. Children of Canadian citizens of Chinese origin up to the age of twenty-one (from age eighteen) were permitted to enter Canada. This provision was interpreted somewhat liberally so that unmarried children up to twenty-five years of age could be admitted.[21]

But the basic operation of P.C. 2115 was unchanged, and it was not to be until 1956 that the Order-in-Council was finally abandoned.[22] In part, the pressure of annual visits to Ottawa by Vancouver CBA leader Foon Sien contributed to its demise. There is little doubt that Canadian demands for employment determined in substantial measure the kinds of immigrants that were welcome, but economic arguments interacted with national sentiments to produce a policy outcome that was remarkably similar to those in Australia and the U.S.[23] The Chinese communities had managed to remove some of the most crushing disabilities with respect to immigration by the mid-1950's, but in common with other non-European groups they were still at a considerable disadvantage.

There was no policy change of significance during the Conservative government of John Diefenbaker from 1957 to 1962. This was surprising, given the fierce criticism Conservatives had levelled at Liberal immigration policy while they were in opposition and the increasing dissatisfaction with the 1952 Act. In 1962, toward the end of its period in office, the Conservative government did change a key regulation, which had the effect of removing emphasis on country of origin as a major criterion of the selection of immigrants. This was very significant for the Canadian Chinese population, although the details were left to a Liberal government to administer.

For all the lack of decisiveness in formulating a new policy, Conservative administration of the Immigration Department produced one of the most dramatic and traumatic episodes in post-war Chinese-Canadian history. In 1959 the government began to grapple with the question of illegal Chinese immigration.

ILLEGAL CHINESE IMMIGRATION

It is clear that Canadian immigration law had worked to the disadvantage of Chinese residents and of potential Chinese immigrants. Even with the repeal of the Exclusion Act in 1947, disadvantages were substantial. The trauma of political events in China, and the subsequent migration of large numbers of close relatives of Chinese residents of Canada to Hong Kong, where living conditions were often far from attractive, created a substantial number of Chinese who wished to join their relatives in Canada. The operation of immigration legislation prevented them from doing so. Given such disabilities, it is little wonder that there occurred efforts to by-pass the regulations and to enter Canada illegally.

Illegal movement of Chinese immigrants to Canada had probably occurred since the first discriminatory regulation against Chinese was issued in the nineteenth century.[24] Why it assumed the political proportions that it did during the Diefenbaker government is not easy to explain, although the Deputy Minister of that period seems to have been utterly preoccupied with the problem of Chinese illegal immigration. In the middle 1950's, U.S. immigration authorities in Hong Kong had evidence of organized efforts to evade U.S. immigration law. The determination of a number of people to move permanently to North America regardless of the law had allowed the creation of an illegal immigration "industry." It was the task of this industry to manufacture Chinese

213

families, or, perhaps more commonly, fictitious membership in existing Chinese families who had some claim to entry to the U.S. Thus, in Hong Kong, file identities were manufactured which allowed ineligible categories of Chinese to enter the U.S., and it was reported that American "citizenship" could be purchased for several thousand U.S. dollars.

Canada's Immigration Office in Hong Kong, which had been one of the earliest immigration establishments abroad, had become increasingly aware that a degree of misrepresentation existed. The U.S. investigation raised several questions in the minds of Conservative policy-makers in Ottawa. In the spring of 1959, Mrs. Fairclough, Minister of Immigration, asked the Director of the Inspection Services of the Department of Citizenship and Immigration to visit the Hong Kong office and make an investigation. On his return to Canada, he reported to the Minister and to the RCMP. There followed an investigation into illegal Chinese immigration by the RCMP that lasted almost three years.

During the investigation, some members of the Immigration Service were found to be involved in questionable activities and were dismissed. In the late summer of 1959, the Hong Kong police raided several establishments in Hong Kong, arrested several dozen people, and seized vast quantities of letters and documents. It would appear that a vast illegal immigration ring was operating in Hong Kong, which was avoiding the immigration laws of Australia, New Zealand, certain Central and South American countries, and the U.S.A. in addition to Canada. The movement between Hong Kong and Canada seemed to be particularly well-organized. It was the task of the RCMP to investigate this operation in the succeeding months.

At half-past eight in the morning of Sunday, May 24, 1960, the RCMP – assisted by constables from the Hong Kong police force – simultaneously searched the major and minor Chinese communities in Canada. These included Trois-Rivières, Quebec City, Ottawa, Peterborough, Sarnia, Windsor, Toronto, London, Kingston, Winnipeg, Regina, Edmonton, Calgary, Prince George, Vancouver, and Victoria. It was one of the biggest searches in Canada's history.[25] The Chinese communities of Canada were astonished by the extent of the investigation. Some saw it as the government's response to demands to liberalize immigration legislation.[26] Whatever the reason, the offices of major Chinese organizations throughout Canada were raided, as well as many of the business premises and private residences of the leaders of the various Chinese communities. Documents were seized. The communities were in a state of shock.

Such a massive operation naturally received enormous coverage in the Canadian press. On June 9, Mr. Pickersgill, former Minister of Immigration under St. Laurent, raised the issue in the House of Commons. Commissioner Harvison of the RCMP had reported that "11,000 Chinese of the 23,000 that have come to Canada since 1946 have entered the country illegally."[27] Such a statement was political dynamite. Mr. Pickersgill, in a statement in the House, said:

> . . . having regard to the exaggeration in this whole matter and an indictment of a whole section of the Canadian Chinese Community, which has a record of obeying the law that most of us might envy, it seems to me of utmost importance that this matter be cleared up without delay.[28]

The investigation focused on how illegal migration was organized, particularly in terms of the profits that were being made through the manufacture of false documents. The English-language press ran banner headlines, such as "RCMP Squads Crack Huge Chinese Immigration Racket." It was reported that the total graft over ten years amounted to $44 million, that admission price was set at $4,000, and that "a very large part of the Canadian-Chinese community must have been involved in the scheme."[29]

Foon Sien, who had been occupied with questions of the essential unfairness of immigration law as applied to Chinese in Canada since his election as co-chairman of the CBA in Vancouver in 1948, was staggered by the enormity of the events of May 24. His initial response was to caution silence. The "National CBA," with its headquarters in Vancouver, sent a letter to Mrs. Fairclough asking for clarification of the objectives of the RCMP raids. At the end of the month Foon Sien was in Ottawa asking questions and making contact with the opposition MPs. There seems little doubt that Foon Sien had had a hand in providing information that had prompted Mr. Pickersgill's questions.

In her reply to the CBA letter, Mrs. Fairclough stated:

> I should like to report . . . that the government has no intention whatsoever to prosecute or treat unfairly any of the individuals who find themselves in this position. I feel sure that many of the Chinese themselves are most anxious to regularize their status in Canada and to relieve themselves once and for all from the feeling of insecurity which they must feel, knowing, as they do, that they have entered Canada through illegal means and are constantly subject to the dangers of exposure. . . . It is not the intention in connection with the current investigation to prosecute or deport from the country any Chinese presently in Canada who have not themselves engaged in assisting other Chinese, apart from their relatives, to enter Canada illegally.[30]

Mrs. Fairclough's statement outlined the beginnings of a program whereby illegal Chinese immigrants could regularize their status without fear of prosecution or, worse, deportation. Amnesty was one method of dealing with the short-term effects. A long-term improvement could be effected only with an overhaul of the regulations, which came, in fact, before the fall of Mr. Diefenbaker's government, in 1962.

The amnesty was to apply to all Chinese who had entered Canada illegally before July 1, 1960. It ushered in an important administrative procedure of the Ministry, the Chinese Adjustment Statement Program, modelled on the American Department of Immigration "Truthful Statement Program for Chinese," which had been introduced in 1956.

Under the Canadian program, all illegal Chinese immigrants who came forward would have their cases reviewed by the Minister of Citizenship and Immigration. Provided they had not been systematically engaged in illegal immigration and were considered to be of good moral character, they would be allowed to remain in Canada.

The Chinese residents were somewhat relieved that the government was treating with leniency immigration infractions so long as they were family-related, but there was nevertheless a good deal of uneasiness. The RCMP, with their colleagues from the Hong Kong police force, were continuing their investigations, and there was considerable tension in Chinese communities across the country.

A month after the RCMP investigations were publicly announced, a large delegation of representatives from various Chinese communities across the country came to Ottawa to express their unease.[31] The members met with Mr. Fulton, Minister of Justice, and Mrs. Fairclough. They also had a well-publicized, two-hour meeting with Prime Minister Diefenbaker. Foon Sien drew the Prime Minister's attention to systematic violations of the proposed Canadian Bill of Rights during the preliminary RCMP investigations:

> I have received reports that the police in some places freely arrest and detain Chinese under suspicion. After several hours of interrogation they were released, but at the time of their detention they could not see the lawyer retained by the CBA. The situation resembles a country under martial law. If the government does not restrict such actions, the basic rights and freedoms of the people are endangered.[32]

Most regrettable was the action of the RCMP in Prince Rupert, where the total Chinese population of about 200 were ordered to fill in questionnaires.

In November of 1962, Mr. Bell, who had replaced Mrs. Fairclough as Minister, announced the end of the RCMP investigations. The Hong Kong policemen were to return home, and there were to be simpler procedures for regularizing illegal status. It was also revealed that Chinese applicants for citizenship had been subject to substantial delays in processing their applications. Mr. Bell suggested that, in future, applications for citizenship would be processed more speedily. In the words of one Chinese newspaper, "The 907 days of fear were brought to a halt."[33]

As a result of the investigations themselves the Crown prosecuted twenty-eight people, twenty-four of whom were Chinese. Of the non-Chinese, two were acquitted, one fined, and the other drew a prison sentence. Of the Chinese, five were never brought to trial, two were acquitted, and in two cases probation was given. The rest were fined or imprisoned, or both. In no case was the sentence greater than six months, although fines up to $5,000 were levied.

The Chinese Adjustment Statement Program was continued into the 1970's. When it was abandoned in October, 1973, over 12,000 Chinese had had their status adjusted. In its last years only a hundred or so cases per year were dealt with. With its demise, a phase in the history of immigration policy that had special reference to Chinese came to an end. An older generation of leaders, who had fought against the discriminatory aspects of that policy, was beginning to disappear from the scene. Battles over immigration policy were far from over, but the standard was to be carried by a different kind of leader, the benefactors of the changing immigration legislation of 1962 and 1967.

GENERAL PATTERN OF IMMIGRATION

The repeal of the 1923 Act made it possible for Chinese to come to Canada, although for the 1947-49 period a mere 788 did so. Beginning from 1950 the numbers of Chinese immigrants increased, averaging over 2,000 per annum up to 1959, the year before the massive RCMP raids. Between 1947 and 1962, over 24,000 Chinese came to Canada. The largest concentration of Chinese in Canada remained in British Columbia, followed by Ontario, Quebec, and Alberta. Vancouver still had the largest Chinese community with other significant Chinatowns in Victoria, Toronto, Montreal, Winnipeg, Edmonton, and Calgary. But after 1947, although British Columbia continued to attract migrants, it did so less readily (in percentage terms) than, in particular, Ontario, or even Quebec and Alberta (see Appendix, Table 6).

The effects of the 1947 repeal were also reflected in the sex ratio of the Chinese population. The initial argument for repeal of the 1923 Act was that it did not allow for the establishment of families among the Chinese population. Although by 1961 the sex ratio was still imbalanced, with a total population of 36,075 males to 22,122 females, compared to its prewar composition the improvement was substantial.

This period marks the end of one phase in the distribution of Chinese in Canada. Although Chinese communities had always flourished more in the larger urban centres, such as Victoria, Vancouver, or Toronto, the rural hinterland supported some scattered Chinese population from the earliest stages. In the aftermath of exclusion, the smaller communities were not renewed. Some, such as Barkerville and Quesnel Forks, ceased to exist, while others, such as Cumberland and Ashcroft, continued with only a handful of residents. This disintegration was especially marked in British Columbia.[34]

The Chinese populations in the outlying regions had developed in the aftermath of the railroad period. Some Chinese had remained as truck farmers, restaurateurs, and laundrymen. The 1923 Act prevented the renewal of these populations, and the Depression of the 1930's obliged many to seek help in the larger urban centres of Vancouver and Victoria, or, in some instances, to return to China. In the period after 1947 the economic basis of Chinese life in the interior was seriously compromised by technological change. Truck farmers could not compete with the corporate growers of California and Idaho – the Chinese market gardeners of Vancouver Island and the potato farmers in the Ashcroft region became figures of history along with their countrymen in the hand laundry business. Only the restaurants remained viable. Paradoxically, perhaps, the restaurants brought women and children to interior locations, where they had never been. But the communities which had once been thriving and bustling were ghosts of their former selves.

A similar consolidation of the Chinese population occurred to a degree also on the Prairies, affecting particularly the smaller Alberta cities and towns, such as Lethbridge and Medicine Hat.[35] In general, throughout Canada the concentration of the Chinese population into fewer, larger urban centres continued through the 1950's, although the economies of the different provinces affected the rate at which the process occurred.

There seems to have been a general movement of the Canadian Chinese population away from the coast and toward the industrial and financial centres of Toronto and Montreal. The growth in Quebec's Chinese population during the 1950's – from 1,904 to 4,794 – is especially marked. The bulk of this population was concentrated in Montreal. Many of the immigrants were doubtless the wives and children of pre-1923 immigrants. It is interesting that the increase in numbers in Montreal coincides with a decline in importance of its Chinatown as a consequence of urban renewal. In Montreal, Toronto, and Calgary urban renewal was disruptive of the traditional communities. Only in Vancouver was the process checked. It was only in the post-1967 period that, partly as a consequence of new types of immigrants, the destruction of the traditional centres of Chinese population was vigorously resisted.

NOTES

1. House of Commons, *Debates*, 11 February 1947, vol. I, p. 319.
2. PAC, RG 76, file 827821, part 11, Eastern Canada Mission to Minister of Immigration and Colonization, 5 September 1927; *ibid.*, Eastern Canada Mission to King, 28 February 1930.
3. PAC, RG 25, vol. 1687, file 80H, Keenleyside Report, 1935; *ibid.*, vol. 1539, file 178, Eastern Canada Mission Proposal, 1930; Marler to External Affairs, 29 July 1930; Chinese Nationalist League of Canada to Minister of Immigration and Colonization, 1 August 1930; Wah On Exporters Association, Hong Kong, to Canadian Trade Mission to China [1930]; Canton Municipal Government to Canadian Trade Mission [1930].

4. House of Commons, *Debates*, 12 July 1943, vol. V, pp. 4682-3.

5. Toronto *Globe and Mail*, 30 March 1944.

6. Vancouver *Sun*, 26 June 1943.

7. For examples, see *Lethbridge Herald*, 6 December 1946; PAC, RG 76, file 23635, part 7, Foon Sien to King, 29 August 1945; *Chinese Times*, 20 May 1942.

8. Chen Kwong Min, *Meizhou Huaqiao tongjian*, pp. 414-15; Lee Tung-hai, p. 359; Toronto *Globe and Mail*, 30 November 1946, in PAC, RG 76, file 827821. Concerning K. Dock Yip as first to be called to the bar, see Vancouver *Province*, 20 September 1945.

9. Chen Kwong Min, *Meizhou*, pp. 414-15. Chen's date of 1936, rather than 1946, is clearly inaccurate.

10. PAC, RG 76, file 827821, Committee for the Repeal to King, 7 February 1947; House of Commons, *Debates*, 11 February 1947, vol. I, pp. 317, 337ff.; Toronto *Globe and Mail*, 30 November 1946.

11. House of Commons, *Debates*, 11 February 1947, vol. I, 307-45; 2 May 1947, vol. III, pp. 2696-2718, 2726-41; 5 May 1947, vol. III, pp. 2749-95.

12. *Ibid.*, 5 May 1947, vol. III, pp. 2776-9; 11 February 1947, vol. I, p. 325.

13. *Ibid.*, 5 May 1947, vol. III, pp. 2789-90.

14. *Ibid.*, 1 May 1947, vol. III, pp. 2644-7.

15. Sir Robert Holland, "Indian Immigration into Canada: the question of franchise," *The Asiatic Review*, 39 (January, 1943), pp. 168-70.

16. Lee Tung-hai, pp. 56-7.

17. *Ibid.*, p. 61.

18. House of Commons, *Debates*, 1947, vol. III, pp. 2644-6.

19. See the comments on the 1952 Immigration Act in Freda Hawkins, *Canada and Immigration: Public Policy and Public Concern* (Montreal, 1972), pp. 102-5.

20. Apart from Mr. Mosher, the witnesses appearing for the Committee were: Mr. Irving Himel, legal counsel from Toronto; Dr. A.E. Armstrong, representing the United Church and the Canadian Council of Churches (co-chairman of the committee); Rev. Father Boal, representing the Catholic Church in Toronto (co-chairman); and Dr. S.K. Ngai of Toronto (co-chairman). Also present were Mr. Dock Yip of Toronto, Mr. S. Yuen of Ottawa, and Mr. Elroy Robinson of the Canadian Congress of Labour. Mr. Himel described the Committee as "composed of Canadians from all avenues of life. The majority of its members are non-Chinese. Divisions of the Committee exist in Ottawa, Toronto, London, Kingston, Montreal, Halifax, Winnipeg, Calgary, Victoria and Vancouver." Canada Parliament Senate Standing Committee on Immigration and Labour, *Proceedings*, no. 4, Wednesday, March 10th, 1948, pp. 95-103.

21. This policy was applied beginning June 28, 1951. The Minister of Immigration, Mr. Harris, made the following statement in the House of Commons: "Having in mind the present situation in China and the known desire of parents to have their children with them, we have come to the

conclusion that we will give consideration to those cases of unmarried children up to the age of 25, to see if circumstances warrant their admission." House of Commons, *Debates*, p. 4836.

22.   SOR/56-180. We would like to thank Mr. Allen Soroka for legal detective work.

23.   Freda Hawkins' comment is instructive: "it is important to remember where Asia was in 1947. . . . [I]n the minds of Canadian Liberal government in 1947, Asia meant almost everything in the Eastern Hemisphere outside Europe. . . . Thus by excluding Asians and, by association and extension, Africans also (except South Africans) Canada was prepared to accept only one kind of immigrant from the Eastern Hemisphere – the European Immigrant." Hawkins, *Canada and Immigration*, p. 95.

24.   In the context of similar discriminatory regulations in the U.S. after 1882, documents that would allow re-entry into the U.S. and permanent residence status changed hands in the Chinese homeland for substantial sums. The U.S. immigration service was plagued with illegal Chinese immigration until the laws were liberalized in 1965. As noted previously, substantial numbers of Chinese crossed illegally from Canada to the United States after 1891.

25.   Only the declaration of the War Measures Act after the FLQ crisis in 1970 has produced an operation of comparable size.

26.   *Qiao Sheng Ribao* ("The Chinese Voice"), Vancouver, 30 November 1962.

27.   *Globe and Mail*, 25 May 1960.

28.   House of Commons, *Debates*, 1960, p. 4717.

29.   *Montreal Star*, 24 May 1960.

30.   House of Commons, *Debates*, 1960, pp. 4723-4.

31.   There were representatives from the following cities: Ottawa (2), Toronto (5), Winnipeg (1), Montreal (3), Quebec City (1), Halifax (1), Sudbury (1), Sarnia (1), Kingston (1), Windsor (2), and Vancouver (2). Foon Sien led the delegation to see Mr. Diefenbaker; Jack Sim from Ottawa and George Chow from Toronto acted as spokesmen for the delegation in their dealings with the press.

32.   *Qiao Sheng Ribao*, 12 December 1962. Jack Sim was stronger at the press conference which followed: "the Hong Kong policemen are too belligerent. They use intimidation and Gestapo methods contrary to the principles of Canadian Justice." *Montreal Star*, 24 June 1960.

33.   *Qiao Sheng Ribao*, 26 November 1962.

34.   See W.E. Willmott, "Some Aspects of Chinese Communities in British Columbia Towns," *B.C. Studies*, 1 (Winter, 1968-69), pp. 27-36.

35.   Ban Seng Hoe, *Structural Changes of Two Chinese Communities*, pp. 93-6.

SIXTEEN

Social Organization, 1947-1962

The immediate political target for Chinese organizations in Canada in 1947 had been the repeal of the 1923 Act. Related to it were demands for elementary civil rights, such as the right to the franchise at all levels of government. These were fundamental to the opportunities for the small but active and vocal groups of second-generation Chinese Canadians, many of whom were veterans and who wished to participate fully in the economy and society of a Canada that they believed was different from the Canada of their fathers' and uncles' generations. In general, these young men were not part of the established structure of influence, but they represented a new wave and a new set of possibilities. As Chinese became citizens and, by virtue of educational achievements, became professionals, the possibility of new community forms was hinted at. The lawyers, accountants, pharmacists, doctors, and dentists, although few in number until the 1960's, formed a category of Chinese who fitted uneasily into the traditional structure. Their influence, as a consequence, was at first muted, but after the mid-sixties these younger Chinese Canadians found the domination of older, traditional leaders and the structures that they operated increasingly anachronistic.

COMMUNITY ORGANIZATION

Toronto

In no community were the effects of the war experience more readily demonstrated than in Toronto. The wartime Chinese Patriotic Federation (CPF) had been enormously successful in raising money for the Chinese war effort, at least that war effort conducted by the Nationalists from Chungking. During the war years, the Federation had given primary community power to the KMT. In November, 1945, at a meeting held in the associational offices of the Lung Kong Kung-so, the Chinese Community Centre was founded. As noted above, no association, despite claimants, had ever been able to speak with unquestioned authority on behalf of the Toronto community in the 1920's and 1930's. In the immediate post-war years, however, and for two decades thereafter, the CCC (*Zhongguo Huiguan*) was able to operate as the proto-typical, community-wide association because it utilized the talents and the connections of the CPF. For all intents and purposes, the CCC was the CPF in a post-war form.

The wartime links were used to immediate effect in the agitation over repeal of the 1923 Act. The proximity of Toronto to Ottawa allowed Toronto and the CCC to take the lead nationally in the immediate post-war period and up to the early 1950's as agitation against discriminatory immigration legislation continued.

Toronto had an additional characteristic that was useful through the 1950's and 1960's, namely the support of non-Chinese organizations and individuals at various political functions. Again, this stems in good measure from the activities of the war years. After the war, such activities as the "Canadian Aid to China Committee" were continued, and in 1947 the committee, whose members were predominantly non-Chinese, sent $2.5 million to Chungking.

As the political situation in China grew more complex, and as it became increasingly difficult to trace monies handed over to the beleaguered KMT government, the activities of the committee ceased, and in late 1948 the affairs of the association were wound up. But it was through activities like these that the CCC leaders, largely supporters of the KMT government, maintained contacts with non-Chinese community leaders and politicians – at municipal, provincial, and federal levels in Canada.

Vancouver

The situation in Vancouver was very different from that in Toronto. The wartime fund-raising activities were organized as a coalition in which traditional competitors' claims to community leadership were balanced in the long-established CBA. There is little doubt that the war allowed the KMT to flourish, but not at the expense of the Freemasons, who were much stronger in Vancouver than they were in Toronto.

In the post-war period, as Chinese Canadians became active in the Canadian political process, initially in matters of immigration, the organizational support differed between Toronto and Vancouver. In Toronto the committee to fight for repeal of the 1923 Act was given its initial financial aid by the KMT. In Vancouver, the organizational support was from the CBA on the one hand, operating as a community-wide body, and on the other by a set of specialized organizations that had grown up during the war years or were formed in the immediate post-war period under the leadership of Foon Sien. In the fifties and sixties the Vancouver CBA resumed its attempts (not always successful) to speak for all Chinese in Canada. However, even the Chinese in Vancouver did not unanimously recognize the right of the CBA to speak on their behalf. The

CBA held a privileged position in the Vancouver community for a number of reasons, not the least of which were its historical claims to community leadership.

Beneath the external facade of unity in the Vancouver community simmered factionalism. The nature of conflict was familiar. It referred, as before, to the politics of China. The Freemasons had withdrawn their support from Chiang Kai-shek in 1946 and had advocated a coalition government in China. This decision shattered the wartime "united front" in the Vancouver community, although the facade of unity was preserved by the classical device of compromise. In 1948, the constitution of the executive committee of the CBA was amended to provide three co-chairmen of the body. One came from the KMT, one from the Freemasons; the balance of power was held by either the Chinese Workers Association or the Toi-san Association, the leading figure in both of these being Foon Sien.

The fragility of the arrangement was, at times, quite obvious. Nonetheless, the structure of representatives from the locality associations continued from 1918 until 1962, when an effort was made to replace it with a council of representatives from all the (traditional) associations then active. This amounted to recognition that representation on the basis of the locality association, however appropriate in the 1940's and 1950's, was no longer an accurate reflection of the true loci of power within the community, for by 1962 the community had changed substantially.

Despite the efforts at change in the early 1960's, the CBA continued to reinforce a traditional conception of the community. One reflection of this tendency was its failure to invite the dynamic (and non-traditional) Elks, Lions, and the Chinese Veterans Association to sit on the revamped CBA board. In consequence, the rising young professionals made little impact on traditional leadership positions. The younger leaders of the immediate post-war period were becoming increasingly dissatisfied with the KMT domination of the CBA and the hard-line, Cold-War attitudes that were expressed in the CBA's continued loyalty to the Nationalist government in Taiwan and its claim to be the legitimate government of China. Nevertheless, non-Chinese continued to recognize the CBA as *the* community spokesman, while most Chinese recognized its factional quality.

Other Communities

Significant growth in the size of the Chinese population occurred from the mid-fifties in both Alberta and Quebec, where the contrasts with the complexities of Vancouver and Toronto were quite marked.

The major Chinese communities of Alberta[1] – those of Calgary and Edmonton – are contrasting examples, although both were quite "traditional" until the latter half of the sixties. Calgary, rather like pre-war Toronto, had no umbrella CBA-type organization, whereas Edmonton, although somewhat smaller and also less differentiated, did have such an overarching association. In 1947 there were nine clan and locality associations in Calgary, a long-established church, and the Kuomintang. The Freemasons were not re-established there until 1954, and an umbrella association appeared only in 1969, when the tiny community was threatened by urban renewal and the traditional structure of leadership challenged by a group of articulate younger men.

In Calgary, the KMT branch organization had dominated the Chinese community since 1913. As in Toronto, the wartime collections reinforced the branch's powers and the Freemasons were almost completely eclipsed and became quite inactive for ten years or more. This is not to suggest that the KMT was in some ways equivalent to the CBA. If any organization had claims to "umbrella" status, it was the Chinese United Church, the oldest Chinese organization in Calgary.

Edmonton, by contrast, had had a CBA since 1932. It claimed to represent Chinese in Edmonton, northern Alberta, the Yukon, and the Northwest Territories. In the fifties and sixties its major work, like that of the CBA in Vancouver, to which it had clear links, was concerned with immigration regulations and related matters. The Edmonton CBA was a coalition of community interests, governed by a large executive body representing the various traditional interests in Edmonton, and it was headed by three chairmen representing the three major surname associations in the community: Mah, Wong, and Gee. The major problem also faced by the Edmonton CBA was that its structure was becoming inappropriate to changed circumstances, a fact recognized by its leaders.

Montreal, being somewhat smaller than the dominant communities of Toronto and Vancouver, had a simpler associational structure. Like Calgary and Toronto, the churches had had a significant impact in the Montreal community. Thus, although there was a CBA in Montreal, which had been an important element in mediating conflicts between the Freemasons and the KMT, its influence was diluted by the active church organizations. The Montreal community was unique in Canada in one respect: its members had to choose between an anglophone or francophone orientation. In a context increasingly dominated by francophones at both municipal and provincial levels, the political decisions were complex.

The community faced difficulties in the post-war years, and, although some of the leaders of the thirties and forties continued to be active in Chinese community politics, the dynamism of the twenties and thirties, as expressed through the activities of the YMCI, seemed lacking. The Montreal community grew in numbers in the fifties and the sixties, but community sentiment seemed to decline. But as a traditional Chinese-Canadian community, Montreal did not enjoy an overall direction. Unlike the other major Chinese communities in Canada, the Montreal community seemed in decline by the mid-1960's.[2]

Chinese communities in Quebec and the Maritimes had regarded Montreal as their major supply centre. Most of the communities in

Quebec, such as in Quebec City, Sherbrooke, Trois-Rivières, and in the mining establishments, were small and had only a minimum of organization. The towns of the Maritimes were similarly poor in organizations, and even in a relatively large centre like Halifax the 1923 Act had taken its toll. With the decline of Montreal as an organizational centre, those communities to the east also declined.

Saskatoon, Regina, and Winnipeg, although suffering like the communities of the Maritimes, came through the Depression with some semblance of organizational coherence. In each community there was a CBA; in each the CBA was dominated by the KMT, although the Freemasons held their own in Saskatoon.[3] But these communities were in decline in 1947. They had never been large, and although the war effort allowed them to maintain some semblance of organized community life, the traditional structure was ossified into an inflexible form of community politics and made the transition to the post-1962 period a difficult one indeed.

ASSOCIATIONAL FORMS

One of the major effects of the war effort was to generate pressures for traditional-style, community-wide associations in Toronto and to revive the prestige of CBAs in other communities, due to linkages with the wider society. Since immigration continued to be somewhat restricted and the new arrivals did not attempt to establish new-style associations, the associations and leaders of the early 1960's still had their roots firmly in the pre-1947 period.

The details of the associational character of various Chinese communities in this period can be seen in the Appendix. Generally speaking, there were few Chinese organizations east of Montreal. In Quebec City there was only a "cultural society." In the smaller communities of Ontario (Sudbury, London, Kingston, or Windsor, for instance) there were usually one or two small associations – often a CBA and KMT organization and sometimes a Freemason lodge, perhaps with one or two social clubs. On the Prairies a similar pattern repeated itself. In British Columbia, where the Freemasons were much stronger, smaller communities (Port Alberni, Nanaimo, Vernon) boasted lodges and sometimes substantial halls; but in many of the smaller communities they were paper organizations with a declining membership. The real estate purchases of an earlier generation allowed them to survive, but, as the Nanaimo fire of 1959 demonstrated, survival could be precarious indeed.

Political/Fraternal Associations

The Freemasons, KMT, and Constitutionalists (XZD) were the traditional fraternal associations. The first two flourished after 1947, but the XZD barely survived and only in Montreal did it have separate existence.[4] Meanwhile, newer-style fraternal organizations appeared – the Chinese

225

branches of the Elks, Lions, and Kiwanis organizations. There were Chinese veterans' organizations, which traced their solidarity to shared military service in the Second World War. Their members were the small, yet vocal, representatives of the second generation that was established before 1923. Their membership overlapped with those of the Elks and Lions. All were, unlike their traditionist counterparts, oriented to Canada and had no referent whatsoever to Chinese domestic politics. Their formation was part of an effort of the second generation – which saw itself as Canadians of Chinese origin – to gain acceptance in the general society. They campaigned for the franchise. They also formed associations that had no links with the established Chinese past in Canada. They were what have been termed "modernist" associations.[5]

The Freemasons

For the Freemasons the post-war years were marked by efforts to maintain and strengthen the organization in areas where it was weak and also to adopt some new orientations. In western Canada, where their property holdings helped maintain their strength, the Freemasons were able to construct new buildings for their branches in Calgary and in the B.C. towns of Vernon and Port Alberni. In Edmonton a Freemasons branch was re-established in 1954, but as before, the Freemasons found it difficult to maintain a strong presence in Winnipeg, in Ontario, and in places further east. Moreover, like other organizations, they suffered from the decline of Chinese populations in small towns, which in turn affected the viability of branch organizations. By contrast, the Vancouver headquarters and branch did well, although the Tai Kung School did not survive into the 1970's and the character of the Freemason ownership of the *Chinese Times* was altered.

The Freemasons could not but be influenced by political developments in China. Internationally, the political arm of the Freemasons had changed its name from Zhigongdang (Chee Kung Tang) to Minzhidang (Muncheetong). In 1946 the two major forces in China, the Kuomintang and the Communists, were on the verge of all-out civil war. In a congress in Shanghai late in that year, the Minzhidang urged an end to the hostilities that were already taking place, a position that was reaffirmed at the Havana Conference of the North American Minzhidang in September, 1947.[6] These actions placed the worldwide Minzhidang, and the Freemasons in Canada, in a neutral, mediating position in the politics of China. In Canada this was a difficult position to maintain for very long. In the Cold War politics of the early 1950's it was not easy for the Freemasons to be critical of KMT activities in Canada and yet avoid being labelled a leftist organization.

By this time, however, new opportunities were opening up in Canada. As the founding of the People's Republic precluded the maintenance of earlier organizational relationships with the homeland, so the possibility of more direct involvement in Canadian society presented itself. As the

1950's progressed, the Freemasons turned toward the Canadian scene and the changing problems of the Chinese in Canada.

The pressures of China's politics, however, were still a feature of community life in the 1950's. For the Freemasons, these centred on the newspaper *Hung Chung She Bo*, published by the Toronto branch. The allegedly "leftist" politics of the paper led to an investigation by the Montreal branch and a revamping of the paper's board of directors.[7] Problems of the paper's political position continued throughout the 1950's; in 1959 it was finally closed down as a consequence of falling revenue and a reluctance on the part of the national body to keep financing it.

The Kuomintang

The KMT was, without doubt, the most influential Chinese organization in Canada in 1947, both within the Chinese communities and, more importantly in the short run, with non-Chinese political authorities. Its wartime leadership had enabled the KMT to achieve pre-eminence in the various CBAs across the country. Many Chinese communities in the immediate post-war period were thus "represented" by an organization – a CBA or CCC – which had legitimacy in the eyes of Canadian governmental organs, but which represented KMT interests while it also attempted to speak for its community. Given its pre-eminence, the KMT was able to define its own interests as the community's interests in the post-war period. In the larger communities of Vancouver and Toronto there was some dilution of influence, but it was not marked until the 1960's, when the new immigrant composition of the Chinese ethnic community began to challenge the KMT position.

In the 1950's and 1960's, the KMT organizations had the full backing of the Chinese Nationalist diplomatic missions in Canada. The KMT-led government of the Republic of China in Taiwan continued to assert its right to "guide" local Chinese organizations in Canada and to use the CBAs as its agents in communicating with local Chinese communities. The Overseas Chinese Affairs Commission appointed a commissioner for Canada, who was normally chosen from within the ranks of senior officials of the national-level KMT organization in Canada.

An important strength of the KMT until the late 1960's was that it had been the ruling party of China until 1949, and its representatives were officially recognized in Canada as those from China until 1970. The Cold War, and Canada's involvement in the Korean War, allowed the KMT to push its particular ideological position. In 1951 the national headquarters of the KMT in Canada began to organize for "national salvation" and to plan for a movement to give community support to Nationalists in Taiwan which was to be organized through the CBAs and the consulates. In early 1952 there was an organized effort to begin an "anti-Communist crusade" in Taiwan, with reports that each Chinese organization had expectations to collect ten dollars per month from each member.[8] A high official of the Overseas Chinese Affairs Commission came to Vancouver in March, and an "Overseas Chinese Anti-Communist National Salvation Covenant Movement" was launched. During March and April, associations throughout Canada signed the agreement, and a Canada-wide "National Salvation Association" was inaugurated, with headquarters at the Chinese Public School in Vancouver.

Many Canadian Chinese, including some who were otherwise apolitical, supported these campaigns. There were many families whose relatives in China had lost their lands, or even their lives, during the Communist "liberation" of 1949 and the subsequent land reform in Guangdong. For them, Communism and a Communist China were bound to be anathema. Others, through their own personal philosophy and experience in Canada, were anti-Communist and feared the possible effects of a Communist China on Chinese-Canadian life and fortunes.

The year 1954 was the post-war zenith of KMT strength in Canada. Although its national headquarters were in Vancouver, the largest branch was in Toronto (500 members); Montreal ranked second, and Calgary was third with between 400 and 450 members. Vancouver had a membership of about 300. But the KMT seemed incapable of responding to change. To be sure, it established youth sections in Calgary, Winnipeg, Toronto, and Vancouver in the early fifties. It also encouraged Chinese Canadians to take advantage of subsidized education in Taiwan. But its efforts seemed increasingly irrelevant to the greater issues of Chinese involvement in Canadian society. Chinese-Canadian educational goals were set on *Canadian* universities, and the ideological lessons in the KMT-dominated language schools produced very few activists for the KMT cause.

Still, the KMT had had a long history of strength in Chinese communities in Canada, and it retained its control over most CBAs throughout the 1960's. It was this ability to retain control over associations that had enormous traditional influence and recognition from the non-Chinese political authorities that allowed the KMT to retain its significance in Chinese communities across Canada even as it became more and more anachronistic.

Elks, Lions, and Veterans

The Freemasons and the KMT were organizations that owed their origins to homeland politics. The Chinese Elks, Lions, and Veterans organizations, however, had their counterparts in the larger Canadian society. Indeed, such organizations formed part of a structure of nationally and internationally organized bodies. None of these organizations had any connection with the homeland, nor is there any evidence of their existence before 1947. The importance of such organizations lay not so much in the numbers that joined them, but in the composition of their membership. They provided an alternative to the traditional organizational structure of the Chinese community, especially for the small sec-

228

ond generation in the 1940's. They allowed an integrated existence rather than a retreat to the segregated existences of their childhood or the experiences of their fathers and uncles. The organizational impetus came from Vancouver – hardly surprising given the numbers of the second generation located there immediately after the war – where Chinese Elks, Lions, and Veterans organizations all were established. Further Lions clubs were established in Victoria, Toronto, and Montreal, and Veterans organizations in Toronto and Montreal.

Such organizations did not fit easily into the structure of the Chinese community. The more tradition-minded Chinese rejected them as "Canadian-controlled" and affording them little prestige. Yet, by the early 1960's, leaders in the Vancouver community could argue that such organizations could be "more daring than real [sic] Chinese organizations"[9] precisely because they were not tied to the traditional structure of the Chinese community and bound by precedent.

The Lions Club was made up of professionals in the 1950's and 1960's; the Elks had a white-collar membership; and the Veterans a working-class and small-shopkeeper membership. The Elks of Vancouver in the early 1960's have been described in the following terms:

> Not since a very early period in the history of the [Vancouver] community, when some occupational specialization according to native place was evident, has there been any indication of a particular class orientation within certain associations . . . [I]t is a reflection of the fact that the class structure of the Chinese Community has become considerably more complex since the early period of the community's history, when only two classes were operative: merchant and labourer.[10]

Indeed, the Elks, Lions, and Veterans organizations pointed to an organizational future for the Chinese communities of Canada, in which the distinctively Chinese values of a previous period were of less significance than the more general principles characteristic of the society as a whole.

The Lions and Elks were involved in welfare activities within their communities, but they were normally not concerned with the political affairs of the Chinese community, and their presence was barely noted by the Chinese media. The Veterans organizations were somewhat different. They were formed almost immediately after demobilization, in part as a vehicle for members and their families to socialize in club premises. From early 1947, the Veterans organization in Vancouver was deeply involved in the quest for the municipal franchise. Veterans had enjoyed the right to vote at the federal level since their service days and in 1947 had received the franchise at the provincial level. Success at the municipal level was not achieved until 1949, after a substantial lobbying campaign in which the CBA, the newly formed Canadian-Chinese Citizens Association, and the Veterans argued their case before the Vancouver City Council.

After the outbreak of the Korean War a "Chinese Community Canadian Troop Comfort Fund" was organized in Vancouver with a significant number of associations, including the CBA, involved. Its spearhead was, however, the Veterans organizations. Similar bodies were founded in Victoria, Calgary, Toronto, and Montreal. In the Vancouver community during the summer of 1951 $2,500 was raised, and collections also took place in Toronto and Montreal. In November, the Victoria Veterans raised $700 in just three days.

The Clan and Locality Associations

In the immediate post-war period, in common with other "traditionist" groups, clan and locality associations enjoyed a brief flowering. By the 1960's, however, they had become less central to Chinese communities in Canada, although a handful did remain powerful adjuncts to the main centres of influence.

In 1947 the issues confronting the clan and locality associations stemmed from a quarter century of exclusion and the effects of war and invasion in China, which had paralysed contacts with the homeland. Efforts to re-establish contacts with the homeland after 1947 were important for the affairs of the clan and locality associations, and for the next four years they were very busy. Contacts with the diplomatic representatives of the Chinese government were frequent in 1947 and 1948, for the regulations with respect both to remittances and possible visits were more restrictive than formerly and often unclear in their application.

Remitting funds to China presented some difficulties which had not been satisfactorily explained by the Bank of China. The famous *shui-haak*[11] had not operated out of Canada since the mid-1930's. Hence, the banking institutions were entrusted with the critical task of remitting funds. Regulations from China suggested a restriction of U.S. $100 on remitted funds.[12] How strictly this was to be applied was of great concern to individuals within the Chinese communities of Canada, whose kinsmen had suffered dreadfully in the wartime period and who wished, after at least six years of enormous difficulties in sending money, to ensure a livelihood for their wives and children in the homeland. The associations themselves had raised funds for what can be broadly termed "community welfare" in the homeland in 1947 and 1948[13] and opposed any obstacles to remitting funds to China.

In the aftermath of the Japanese occupation of southern China there was a good deal of social disorder. The collapse of the economic system, particularly the hyper-inflation, was extremely stressful. In such circumstances, "bandits" flourished, including political "bandits" and anti-KMT forces. Anti-bandit activity was a way of raising cash, particularly of valuable foreign currency, to finance the expenses of local government. Equally, local government officials could divert funds to their own uses. In early 1947 the associations in the Chinese communities of Canada were informed by Chinese central government representatives that no organization in China was allowed to raise funds in Canada without the express permission of the Guangdong branch of the Overseas Chinese Affairs Commission. As a consequence, requests for funds were increasingly channelled through the clan and, especially, the locality associations in Hong Kong. The need for funds in the homeland thus led to a flowering of activities. As Chinese residents began to return to the homeland from early 1947, the various associations once again began to collect exit fees (*chukoubiao*).

Many of the funds were earmarked for educational purposes in addition to defence. In early 1948, the Yin-ping association in Canada sent HK $32,000 for educational purposes in the county, and later in the year similar funds were sent to Toi-san and Sun-wui by the appropriate organizations. As late as September, 1949, the Mah Society in Canada received a request from the residents of Pak-sa to set up a second Mah family school.

Political events in China in late 1949, when Guangdong was incorporated into the People's Republic of China, were to change the nature of Chinese-Canadian involvement with the homeland and disrupt the activities of the clan and locality associations, and thus hasten their decline. In December, 1949, the banking authorities in Hong Kong announced that remittances would no longer be forwarded to China.[14] It was not until March, 1950, that the new government's Overseas Chinese Affairs Commission announced new procedures. Along with new rules relating to the registration of Overseas Chinese lands, and the land reform which was getting underway in Guangdong, a new direction was charted for Canadian Chinese oriented to the homeland.

Cut off from the homeland, the long-run consequence for the district and clan associations would be, with few exceptions, a decline in their vitality. That was not immediate, however, and for a short period there was an effort to substitute Hong Kong for the homeland. In early 1954, for example, after the disastrous Christmas Day fire in Shek-kip-mei, a densely crowded Kowloon squatter area in Hong Kong, the locality organizations in Canada were involved in their biggest post-1949 fund-raising drive, eventually contributing $26,000 to relief work in Kowloon. It was, perhaps, the last massive fund-raising drive by the clan and locality associations.

By the 1960's the clan and locality associations had, in general, reached a period of decline. They became important social clubs for their members, and were able to provide welfare funds from real-estate investments. The major clan associations held valuable buildings in commercially attractive locations. With the loss of "exit fees" after 1949, the most important source of income was from rentals, which allowed the associations to subsidize living accommodations for a few older members living alone. The clan associations and, to a lesser extent, the district associations became the protectors of a version of Chinese culture that, as the sixties progressed, became increasingly remote from the experiences of the second generation or, indeed, of the new immigrants from Hong Kong and other parts of the Overseas Chinese world.

With the exception of the Shon Yee Association, which had organizational links to the "modernist" trends in the Freemasons, the locality associations barely survived the severing of the China links. The clan associations retained their vitality somewhat longer, and in the complex equation of local politics within the ethnic communities, some of the larger clan associations continued to exercise substantial influence in the 1960's. However, the earlier conditions that had given rise to a community structure in which clanship and locality were important principles of social organization had changed enormously by the middle 1960's.

Commercial and Trade Associations

In many Overseas Chinese settings, commercial and trade associations are fundamental to the operation of the community. In Canada, their role was only small. It is by no means certain that the trade associations established before 1937 survived in large numbers after 1947, and, with only two exceptions, they were largely defunct by the mid-1960's. The Chinese Chamber of Commerce of Vancouver, although in operation for many years, seems to have had little impact after 1947, and Victoria's Chamber of Commerce seemed largely inoperative by the early 1950's. Until the great wave of immigration after 1967, the character of Chinese business enterprise was not fundamentally different from what it had been in the 1920's. The businessmen saw the non-Chinese service clubs (e.g., Lions) as a more appropriate vehicle for their interests.

Associations based on specialized interests were more successful. For example, associations of restaurateurs existed throughout the period in Montreal and Vancouver. An exception was the Overseas Chinese Hotel Association, which ceased operation in early 1948, a casualty, no doubt, of the lack of single male immigrants after 1923 and the settlement in *fangkou* (boarding houses) of those that lived in Vancouver.

In the 1960's, associations to protect the interests of Chinese entrepreneurs in the food business were established in Edmonton and Vancouver. The Edmonton association, called "The Chinese Businessmen's Association," was set up by the owners of small grocery stores "to increase their knowledge of the food industry and to facilitate communication between Chinese store operators and the white suppliers."[15] The initial impetus was not maintained, although it did continue to operate into the 1970's. An association of almost identical form was established in Vancouver in 1969.

Earlier associations of Chinese farmers in the Vancouver area apparently had disappeared in the 1940's or 1950's. In 1962 the B.C. Lower Mainland Farmers Cooperative Association was founded. The Chinese farmers, who grew mostly vegetables and berries, shared one important characteristic: the bulk of them were from Chung-san. This locality tie and their involvement in the one locality organization that appears to have adapted to change, the Shon Yee Association, appeared to be important elements of solidarity. The initial organizing was not easy. The forties and fifties saw the decline of interior farming communities as California vegetables invaded the market. Ashcroft, Armstrong, and Vernon, once thriving vegetable centres, declined as the farmers without families grew old and retired. Even where family help was available, times were hard.

> . . . I could see how the farmer had been kicked around by everyone. After the war, lots of immigrants came in, wives and children, and the farmers want their sons to take over the business, but the son not want to take over because living not good, working conditions not good, long hours . . . so we need an association.

A full-time manager was hired with authority to confront the vegetable wholesalers, threatening them with boycott unless guaranteed higher prices were instituted. The wholesalers accepted the growers' association, and by the mid-1960's the association was well-established and gave to the sixty or seventy Chinese farmers surrounding Vancouver a degree of security that had been impossible before.

If business organizations were few in the 1947-62 period, associations of workers were even fewer. The centre of organized workers' activities during the period was, again, Vancouver. The B.C Ferries Chinese Society, whose members were mostly cooks and kitchen personnel on the ferries, was formed in the late 1950's. It was organized to ensure cheap and convenient accommodation for members on shift work who were obliged to be absent from their homes. The association was, therefore, organized in Vancouver, Victoria, and Nanaimo: the ferry terminals. It was not involved in economic issues – that was the responsibility of a formally organized trade union – but it extended its activities beyond lodgings to leisure-time pursuits, particularly the development of an active table tennis club.

Two organizations in Vancouver went by the name "Workers Association." The Chinese Trade Workers Association had been formed in 1942 to raise issues about the tax status of married Chinese with wives in China who were unable to claim tax deductions for their wives. It was associated with the leadership of Foon Sien and for many years maintained its office in the CBA building.

A very different organization was the Chinese Workers Protective Association, which had a longer history and was one of the few Chinese organizations that was identifiably left-wing. This organization had cooperated with the KMT in the wartime fund-raising, but by early 1948 it was critical of the Nationalist conduct of the civil war and of Canada's role in it. With the support of sympathetic members of the University of British Columbia, it initiated a public debate on the propriety of

233

Canada's involvement in the Chinese civil war. Public reaction built up throughout 1948, and in December the Department of National Defence announced it would stop supplying the Nationalist forces. The association celebrated the inauguration of the People's Republic of China in October, 1949, and flew the flag of the People's Republic on January 1, 1950, while all other associations flew the KMT flag.[16]

The 1950's were difficult years for the Chinese Workers Protective Association. The intensification of the Cold War, Canada's involvement in the Korean conflict, and other disagreements over the international situation were sources of conflict. In April, 1958, the association celebrated the return of a group of local Chinese who had made an extensive visit to China. This was its last public event. It could not survive the ideological conflict that stemmed from the Sino-Soviet split and was wound up in early 1960.

Leisure/Athletic Associations

The 1947-62 period was one in which traditional forms of leisure and athletic associations persisted. One important leisure activity of the Chinese population in Canada at an earlier period was gambling. Popular Chinese culture had an array of gambling games – cards, dice, dominoes, and fantan. The existence of gambling clubs was an enormous source of tension between segments of the various Chinese communities and municipal authorities. This was especially the case in Vancouver and Toronto in the late forties and early fifties. It was reported that there were at least thirty-seven gambling clubs in Vancouver in 1947[17] and the press, both Western-language and Chinese, was replete with accounts of police raids, attempts to buy off policemen, fines for gambling, and the like.

Although there were gambling raids in Toronto, most of the activity was in Vancouver. The year 1950 began with a hundred arrests for playing fantan in the Chinese community of Vancouver. Fantan was held to be illegal in B.C., and three clubs were closed down at the end of the year because they allowed the game to be played. This became an issue throughout 1951, when the courts held that the mere fact that fantan was being played was not sufficient cause to close down Chinese clubs.[18] At this point, a *modus vivendi* was apparently established, for although there was the occasional report of gambling arrests after that, the issue never again reached the epidemic proportions of the earlier period.[19]

Sporting activities were also part of the structure of Chinese communities in Canada in the period after 1947. Some had a long history; others developed as a consequence of the newer needs of the larger second generation maturing in the late 1950's. Some of the traditional forms of Chinese recreation, in both village and urban centre, were the "martial arts" (Kung-fu in its various forms). Martial arts techniques were a part of community life, and the Freemasons were one of the most important organizations actively to preserve the tradition through the Dart Coon

Club. Several clan associations in the major centres possessed lion-dance troupes, and they also provided elementary training in martial arts.

In Vancouver, the most active athletic association of the traditional character was the Hon Hsing Athletic Club, associated with the Wong Clan Associations but drawing its membership from throughout the Vancouver community. As the generation born in the immediate post-war period came to their teens, the needs of the Chinese communities changed, and efforts were made to organize recreational activities that were Canadian, rather than Chinese, in content. The Freemasons in both Toronto and Vancouver established athletic clubs in the early 1960's which provided young people opportunities to play table tennis, chess, and basketball.

The prototypical athletic association of the new type was the Hai Fung Association in Vancouver, established in 1956. Though its membership was not large, its impact was substantial. It organized the first annual Chinatown table tennis tournament in 1958, which continues to attract players from western Canada and the United States. It also sponsored Chinese chess tournaments and volleyball, and it was involved in the organization of the basketball league.

The Hai Fung Association also sponsored traditional music and dance performances, cultural skills that were preserved in the face of Canadian-ization. These skills were part of the traditional community structure, but they seemed threatened after the war. In early 1947, for example, the Young Chinese Musical Club of Vancouver, which had been very active in the wartime fund-raising activities, closed down, and its small surplus funds were donated to St. Joseph's Hospital. Musical societies drew a small number of participants throughout the 1950's and early 1960's. Chinese opera was actively preserved by the Vancouver Jin Wah Sing, which worked closely with its American counterparts on the West Coast. During this period, musical and operatic activities were less grand than in an earlier period.

Following the repeal of the 1923 Act, young people and their needs became an important aspect of Canada's Chinese communities because of the influx of children. By the late 1950's the KMT had sponsored youth sections in several centres, and there were youth associations sympathetic to the People's Republic of China in Vancouver, Toronto, and Mont-real. The most active was the Chinese Youth Association in Vancouver, which began to publish a weekly Chinese newspaper, the *Da Zhong Bao* (The Masses), and sponsored films on developments in Mainland China. It also organized instruction in traditional instruments and formed a singing group, whose music was the music of the New China. At about the same time, organizations with similar aims and activities were founded, the East Wind Club in Montreal and the Chinese Youth Association in Toronto. On the Prairies and in Victoria, similar organi-zations were born, but their biggest growth occurred after 1970, when Canada recognized the People's Republic of China.

235

Religious Associations

In marked contrast to other Overseas Chinese settlements, Chinese religious organization was never prominent among migrants to Canada. Only the first major settlement, Victoria, continued to support a separate Chinese temple in 1947. Within the associations with a Chinese focus, the worship of deities or ancestors continued.

Christian churches, however, made a substantial impact among Chinese in Canada, although the extent of Christianity varied from community to community. In the small community of Moose Jaw, for instance, the Chinese United Church had been led by Chinese ministers since the early part of the century and was crucial in maintaining community survival in the face of disintegrative forces. The early 1960's saw the birth of a church auxiliary, which provided social facilities for Chinese women in Moose Jaw. It also ran a Sunday school, held picnics, and, with the help of the local Lions, provided English classes from 1948-49. The involvement of the Moose Jaw church in community welfare projects, particularly in providing services for new immigrants, was understandable in a small community with a minimum of ethnic organizations. The church was the only organization operating in the Chinese community until 1960, when a Chinese Athletic Association was established to cater to the needs of the growing numbers of Chinese youth.

In a major community with an array of ethnic associations, the Chinese-language churches had considerably less centrality. The Chinese United Church was active in both Calgary and Edmonton. In Edmonton its success was only modest in the 1940's and 1950's, although in 1953 a new church was built. Its congregation grew only slightly between 1953 and 1962, and its Young People's Club, started in 1954, was never active. The church also ran a school throughout the period, which provided the only Chinese-language instruction available in Edmonton. In Calgary, activities of the church were rather more extensive, and in 1954 it moved from its old quarters to a new $250,000 church. It was also well-integrated into the system of influences in the Chinese community, and "many pioneer Chinese families" were members of the congregation.

Perhaps in no community were the Christian churches more active than in Montreal, which is the only community in Canada in which Chinese Catholics are well-represented. A Chinese Catholic Mission has existed in Montreal since 1922, although it was only in 1957 that the first Chinese priest was appointed to it. The Catholic Mission had taught both French and English to Chinese children since 1916, and in 1956 it opened a language school for adults, known as the Chinese School. Although this school was active through the 1960's, the forces of urban renewal dispersed Chinese families with school-aged children throughout the city, and the viability of the school was thus threatened. It closed in 1970.

The large numbers of Chinese who moved into the Montreal region during the 1950's and 1960's were assisted in the process of adaptation by the Mission. It gave assistance to the aged and to new migrants in making contact with various government services. It also organized a Boy Scout troop, a youth club, and a folk dance club. The greatest contribution that the Catholic Mission made to the Chinese community as a whole was in its support of the Chinese hospital. The hospital had ceased to be community self-supporting by 1946, when it first received assistance from the Montreal welfare department, although several sisters attached to the Mission continued to nurse there, aiding two part-time physicians. In 1960 a baby clinic was added to the services of the hospital. In 1962 the hospital building was condemned, and its very survival was questioned, but its problems generated a response from the, by now, largely dispersed Chinese population of Montreal, which argued for its retention. "Community spirit" had fallen since the war years, but the hospital issue indicated that the community could still be mobilized over particular issues.

A second major Christian influence in the Montreal community was the Montreal Chinese Presbyterian Church. We have seen how the Presbyterian Mission had begun in the 1880's with a returned missionary from South China and Mr. Chan Nam-sing. In 1940, the son of Chan Nam-sing, Paul Chan, who was born in Montreal but who had spent the bulk of his life in China, returned to take charge of the church. In 1950, a new church building was dedicated, and it soon became the focus for the community centre which had been established in 1949. This church's congregation grew substantially during the 1950's, and like the Catholic Mission it ran an array of social services, including Chinese classes for young people and English classes for new immigrants. It also continued to sponsor its long-established Boy Scout troop and, in 1962, began to teach *Taijiquan (T'ai-chi ch'uan)*.[20]

In both Toronto and Vancouver the churches continued to develop during the 1950's and, like the churches of Alberta and Montreal, became conscious of the social needs of new immigrants. In particular, the churches became increasingly involved in providing English classes for newcomers.

The Chinese Anglican Church in Vancouver began to offer English classes in September, 1947, and others soon followed suit. The churches also moved into social issues and in doing so anticipated developments in the post-1962 period. After 1962 there would be a substantial growth in church activities and in the number of churches of fundamentalist variety. This trend was apparent by the late 1950's, but it became more significant after the great waves of immigration in the late 1960's.

LEADERSHIP, 1947-62

The principal form of social organization in Overseas Chinese communities, in their traditional form at least, is the voluntary association. The network of associations that are formed determines the pattern of influence and a structure of power.[21] In most of the Chinese communities of Canada, the Freemasons formed one locus of power in the network of associations and were opposed by the KMT as another. In many of the communities the nominal spokesman for the community, the CBA, was dominated by the KMT through a set of "traditionist" clan and locality associations, although the federative character of the CBA gave nominal membership to most if not all voices within the ethnic community.

In Vancouver in the 1950's and 1960's the Freemasons and the KMT were both represented on the executive committee of the CBA. During the chairmanship of Foon Sien (1948-60), the CBA attempted to maintain a balance by adopting the organizational compromise of three co-chairmen, one from each of the two major factions, and a "neutralist," Foon Sien. For the CBA to lean to one side or the other would have weakened its claims to be community spokesman and mediator within the community. As long as the network was composed of associations that "represented" the ethnic community, the arrangement was politically viable.

Social Characteristics of Leadership

In the Chinese communities of Canada of the nineteenth century, merchant status and wealth were the primary characteristics of leadership; by 1947 the characteristics had become more varied, for leadership could operate in the context of a far more complex network of voluntary associations.[22] Leadership in the 1947-62 period was dominated by males. If women participated, it was almost invariably in a subordinate fashion or in spheres specifically reserved for women.

The typical leader was middle-aged. A significant number had seen wartime service and, especially in the case of those who were university graduates in the immediate post-war years, had been involved in action to establish civil rights. Some had created "firsts" by joining previously inaccessible professional bodies. By the early 1950's there appeared a split in opinion and loyalty between young and old.

The traditional associational core groups (CBA, KMT, clan and locality associations) were dominated by the China-born while the Canadian-born (*tusheng*; Cantonese *tou-sang*) dominated newer bodies, for example, the Lions and such ethnic media as *The New Citizen* and *Chinatown News*, which were bilingual and oriented toward Canada rather than China. Members of the post-1947, China-born group were found in both types of association and provided energetic new leadership for some of the traditional associations.

With few exceptions, professional qualifications were not available for Chinese Canadians until after 1947. Then they were allowed to exercise the franchise and to enter a broad range of professions, and as a consequence a previously merchant-dominated leadership structure was challenged by a younger group with professional qualifications. Merchant status continued into the post-1947 period as an important characteristic simply because such men had the social networks and influence to move easily into leadership positions. Managerial personnel also became significant at this time, as some Chinese became bank managers and restaurant managers.

As the 1950's progressed, being bilingual became increasingly important. A Chinese leader could not hope to attain a position of eminence without fluent Chinese, but it became increasingly difficult to operate without fluency in English. Here the young lawyers, doctors, and dentists were at a distinct advantage. Thus, the first Chinese member to be elected to the Canadian Parliament, Douglas Jung, was a lawyer.

At any stage in the history of the Chinese communities in Canada, politics have been complex. No one community was like another. In some, particularly the smaller ones, the domination of community-wide organizations was extensive and a particular persuasion was dominant. By the early 1950's the young Canadian-born group was emerging, standing somewhat aloof from traditional principles of social alignment. Furthermore, the founding of the People's Republic in late 1949 somewhat stilled the debate on events in China. Consequently, the politics of China had less impact on Chinese-Canadian communities, and political alignments within the communities could be on other bases.

Political opinions among Chinese Canadians were now tempered by the Cold War atmosphere and the fact that Canadian forces were fighting Chinese soldiers in Korea. It was unusual for any Chinese groups to take a position sympathetic to developments in China and, of course, a number of people had suffered losses in the Guangdong land reform during 1950-52 and were therefore antagonistic. Once the Korean conflict had ceased to involve Canadians, however, the anti-Communist organizations formed in the early 1950's did not prosper, and by the end of the decade organizations (and leaders) that were openly sympathetic to the People's Republic of China became an established part of the community.

In a previous era, Chinese organizations oriented to the wider Canadian society seemed inappropriate, but in the late 1940's they were taken seriously. The Chinese Trade Workers Association of Vancouver had, of course, been founded in 1942 with that orientation. Later in the 1940's *The New Citizen*, at least at the outset,[23] adopted what might be termed an "assimilationist" position, and one of its major tasks was to present the Chinese-Canadian contributions to the *Canadian* way of life. The young second-generation leaders, although they might participate in their clan and locality associations, took care to dissociate themselves from China-oriented politics. One second-generation leader said:

> I don't want anything to do with [Chinese politics]; I don't know which side to take. I'm here in Canada but I'm also Chinese in origin, so what do I do? The Canadian government recognizes one, the English government the other, who is right? The only opposition to the Kuomintang are the Communists, and they are nothing in

Canada. . . . Personally I don't know. Why, even in travel – I would like to go to the [Far] East and see my place of origin, but where exactly should I go?

And another leader said: "Chinese politics are not any good in Canada – they can't help Chinese Canadians!"

Among China-born leaders, traditional attitudes prevailed. Although supporters of the KMT had the upper hand, traditional opposition to the KMT and a feeling of dissatisfaction with the Nationalist government during the civil-war period were sufficiently strong in Canada that conflict constantly threatened the apparent solidarity of the Chinese community. Meanwhile, Canadian politics became attractive. Although Douglas Jung entered federal politics as a Progressive Conservative, Chinese support tended to go to the party which offered the most advantageous stand on immigration policy. Harold Winch, long-time CCF/NDP member for Vancouver East, which encompassed the great bulk of Vancouver's Chinese population, was well-known as a proponent of more liberalized immigration legislation and one who went to great pains to investigate alleged irregularities by immigration officers in the treatment of Chinese immigrants and their families. The Progressive Conservatives were held responsible for the massive RCMP raids on the Chinese communities in 1959, which seriously alienated Chinese support. A Chinese branch of the Liberal Party was formed in Vancouver shortly before Mr. Pearson's success at the polls in 1962, when Douglas Jung was defeated. Over a decade was to elapse before another Chinese MP was returned to Ottawa.

Types of Leader

Many white Canadians believed the Chinese communities had a coherent and homogeneous leadership, which is one reason why the CBAs continued to receive support and attention from governments at all three levels long after they had ceased to represent the ethnic communities. There is no sense, however, in which political leadership in Canadian-Chinese communities was homogeneous in the 1947-62 period. Until 1962 there were some China-born leaders whose power base was the older associations and who operated almost totally in a Chinese environment, but they were fewer in number than before and they were becoming somewhat anachronistic. They were more comfortable speaking Chinese, had primarily Chinese friends and business contacts, and belonged primarily to associations in the CBA/KMT network. Their behaviour was likely to be traditionist and China-oriented. Such men could assume leadership roles, but only as internal leaders. Their lack of fluency in English, and perhaps their unfamiliarity with the general culture of Canada, made it difficult for them to interact with the larger society.

A second type of leader mediated between Chinese and non-Chinese contexts. Such leaders were either China-born or local-born, rarely lived in the older Chinese district, but still preferred to live in some Chinese district. While maintaining a strong belief in ethnic endogamy, they had both Chinese and non-Chinese friends, and their business and professional associates and clientele included both Chinese and non-Chinese. This type of leader was bilingual in Chinese and English. Such men belonged to the Veterans organizations, Lions, Elks, and, where Christian religion was significant, to activist church organizations. They did not see the traditional organizations as dated and used them as sources of political advancement within their communities. They saw themselves as mediators familiar with the internal characteristics of the ethnic community, yet comfortable with the dominant culture while attempting to represent the Chinese communities to the outside world.[24]

Toward the end of the 1950's and in the early 1960's there emerged a type of leader who became increasingly common – in Toronto and Montreal, they predominated – in the post-1962 period. Such leaders lived in non-Chinese neighbourhoods (in Montreal, in English-speaking neighbourhoods), were wealthy, spoke English at home, and interacted socially with non-Chinese on a frequent and continuing basis. They were oriented to the Chinese community either for sentimental reasons or because they or their families had derived their wealth from ethnic sources. They accepted positions within Chinese organizations on an honorary basis but avoided active participation within the community. Their major associational involvement was, in fact, in Canadian society as a whole, and not in its Chinese segment.

NOTES

1. The major sources of information on Alberta communities are: Ban Seng Hoe, *Structural Changes of Two Chinese Communities*; Dawson, "Chinese Urban Communities in Southern Alberta, 1885-1910"; Dawson, "The Chinese Experience in Frontier Calgary"; G. Baureiss "The Chinese Community of Calgary," *Canadian Ethnic Studies*, III, 1 (1971), pp. 43-56; and P.L. Voisey, "The Chinese Communities in Alberta: An Historical Perspective," *Canadian Ethnic Studies*, II (1970), pp. 15-29.

2. Fanny C. Davies, "A Survey of the Chinese Community in Montreal," unpublished ms., 1974.

3. F.Q. Quo, "Chinese Immigrants in the Prairies," preliminary report submitted to the Ministry of the Secretary of State, November, 1977; *Winnipeg Chinese*, pp. 16ff.

4. Indeed, as late as the middle 1970's it had an address and telephone number. We do not know whether or not it held elections.

5. The distinction between "modernist" and "traditionist" associations is made in Willmott, *The Chinese in Cambodia*, pp. 84-5.

6. In 1949 the Zhigongdang (despite the adoption of the name Minzhidang, the older name still had a great deal of currency) was a "minor" party

241

and attended the People's Political Consultative Conference. It was still operating in China in the late 1970's, although its advice was often ignored. See S. Fitzgerald, *China and the Overseas Chinese* (Cambridge, 1972), pp. 21, 32-3.

7. *Chinese Times*, 5 February 1949.

8. *Vancouver Sun*, 4 February 1953.

9. Straaton, "The Political System of the Vancouver Chinese Community: Associations and Leadership in the Early 1960's," p. 75.

10. *Ibid.*, p. 76.

11. *Shui-haak* (literally, "water guest") travelled as couriers between Overseas Chinese settlements and the points of migration.

12. See, for example, *Chinese Times*, 4 January, 26 February 1947.

13. The classic statement on these kinds of activities is Chen Ta, *Emigrant Communities in South China* (London, 1939). See also J.L. Watson, *Emigration and the Chinese Lineage* (Berkeley, 1976); Woon Yuen-fong, "Social Organization of South China 1911-1949: the Case of the Kwaan Lineage of Hoi-ping" (Ph.D. thesis, University of British Columbia, 1975). Woon's informants resided in Victoria, B.C.

14. *Chinese Times*, 3 December 1949.

15. Hoe, *Structural Changes of Two Chinese Communities*, p. 206.

16. *Chinese Times*, 5 January 1950.

17. *Ibid.*, 20 March 1947.

18. Vancouver *Province*, 1 March 1951; *Chinese Times*, 29 June 1951.

19. *Chinese Times*, 10 February 1956; 22 December 1958.

20. Rev. Paul Chan, "A Short History of the Chinese Presbyterian Church and Community Centre in Montreal," in *Mancheng Zhonghua* (Montreal, 1961), pp. 6-8; see also D.H. Rayner, "Montreal's Changing Chinatown," *Presbyterian Record* (January, 1970).

21. The most coherent accounts of the structure of power and influence have been provided for Southeast Asian Chinese communities. See, e.g., Skinner, *Leadership and Power*.

22. The data are from Vancouver and are derived from B.H. Erickson, "Prestige, Power and the Chinese" (M.A. thesis, University of British Columbia, 1966). Further analysis has been pursued by Straaton, "Political System of the Vancouver Chinese Community"; B. Lal, "Chinese Benevolent Association of Vancouver, 1889-1960: An Analytical History," unpublished paper, University of British Columbia, 1975. See Straaton, pp. 110-12, for comments on the nature of data.

23. *The New Citizen* was published in Vancouver for the first three years of its existence (1949-51). It regularly profiled Chinese Canadians who had excelled in Canadian society, e.g., Normie Kwong, the professional football player. After *The New Citizen* moved its editorial office to Toronto from Vancouver in 1951, it became much more political in its content, stressing an anti-Communist line.

24. This type is not peculiar to Canada. In Bangkok, such leaders were described as "from the periphery," since their ethnic orientation and

loyalty was mixed. M.S. Weiss reports a similar phenomenon in Sacramento, California. See Weiss, *Valley City: A Chinese Community in America* (Cambridge, Mass., 1974), pp. 209-31.

SEVENTEEN

A New Kind of Chinese

The new regulations that emerged in 1962 removed the emphasis on country of origin as a major criterion for the admission of immigrants to Canada. The desired characteristics of migrants were set out in general terms, and the ability of the migrant to establish himself was stressed.[1] The regulations emphasized the economic contribution that the immigrant could make.

These regulations worked to the advantage of Chinese migrants. For the first time since 1884 Chinese migrants would enter Canada without the burden of an immigration system systematically weighted against them. The record of the Conservative government on immigration policy was constrained by both political pressures and a lack of money,[2] but in developing largely non-discriminatory immigration regulations it registered a decisive advance. The short period that Mr. Bell was Minister was important, for he began certain changes that were carried on through the Pearson government and which resulted in a thorough revamping of the administrative structures and finally, in 1967, in a new set of immigration regulations.

Even in the 1962 regulations there were, however, remnants of racial discrimination which applied to the Chinese populations. All immigrants could sponsor relatives, but a distinction was made between immigrants from Asia or Africa and all others in terms of sponsoring all but the closest of relatives. The Diefenbaker government had intended to remove all discrimination based on race, colour, and creed, but it seems that some feared that regulations without such a discriminatory clause would allow an influx of immigrants from non-European sources. It was further assumed that such immigration would contain large numbers of unskilled people. However, in evolving an immigration policy that stressed the economic contribution a migrant could make, such an open policy was, at the last minute, thought to be intolerable.[3]

In 1967 a series of changes in immigration regulations and their administration was introduced, free of the discriminatory elements that had characterized the 1962 regulations. They gave less discretion to individual immigration offices and spelled out precisely, via the "point system," the criteria that were to be used in assessing potential immigrants.[4] Chinese were now on the same basis as all other immigrants.

The possibilities for a distinctively new kind of Chinese migrant had been opened in 1962. The 1967 changes allowed its full realization with the abolition of the restrictive rules regarding sponsorship. Immigrants with close kinship ties to Chinese Canadians were virtually the only Chinese migrants who came to Canada before 1962. After 1962, and increasingly after 1967, not only did Chinese migrate to Canada in large numbers, but there were also larger numbers of Chinese immigrants who came as unsponsored migrants, entering Canada on the basis of the skills they possessed.

The typical Chinese migrant before 1923 was rural-born, poorly educated, and without a knowledge of English. In the twenty years following repeal of the Exclusion Act, these characteristics did not change substantially; but after 1967 urban, well-educated, English-speaking Chinese came, especially from Hong Kong but also from such centres as Manila, Singapore, Johannesburg, and Lima. Their contribution to Chinese-Canadian communities has been very different from that of their compatriots of an earlier generation. In those communities long years of decline came to an end. Migration helped stimulate renewed community sentiments in the Chinese population of Canada.

IMMIGRATION AND SETTLEMENT: 1962-1975

Direct migration from China to Canada had ceased in 1949, not to be restored until 1974. The most important point of origin for Chinese migration became Hong Kong, although a few Chinese came to Canada from a variety of Overseas Chinese communities in Southeast Asia (e.g., Malaysia, Singapore, and the Philippines), southern Africa, Latin America (especially Peru), and the Caribbean.

By the middle 1960's the Chinese émigrés in Hong Kong with either family in Canada or the promise of a job there were altogether different from the migrants of a previous generation. Many had been resident in Hong Kong for a decade or more. Many had acquired English-language education in the colony. They were used to an urban environment, in contrast to their kinsmen and fellow countrymen of an earlier generation, who were country folk with peasant skills. Their general sophistication allowed for relatively easy entrance into Canada and pointed to a potential for adaptation that their predecessors could rarely have hoped to possess.

The year 1967 is important not merely for the changes in immigration regulations in Canada. In the summer of 1967 the Great Proletarian Cultural Revolution spilled across the border from Guangdong Province into Hong Kong. From May until the autumn, Hong Kong experienced bombs, strikes, demonstrations, and martial law, and for a brief period it seemed that the colony might revert to China long before the New Territories' lease was due to expire. Chinese and British residents of Hong Kong were not prepared for the eventuality of the end of Hong Kong's colonial status.[5] Thus, as immigration legislation considerably eased access to Canada, internal pressures in Hong Kong generated additional motivation to emigrate.

The abolition of restrictions also coincided with changes in conditions facing Chinese communities in other parts of the world. In Southeast Asia, although Chinese had traditionally held a dominant economic position, such dominance came under increasing pressure in the 1960's and 1970's. Political conditions in the Malay Peninsula were such that Singapore – a predominantly Chinese settlement – felt obliged to withdraw from a nation dominated by Malays to form a new city-state in 1963. Matters for the Chinese population in Malaysia grew increasingly complex with the "Bumiputra-policy," which favored the Malay at the expense of the Chinese citizens of Malaysia. In 1969 there was ugly communal rioting in Kuala Lumpur and other parts of West Malaysia, which left several hundred Chinese dead.

Pressure against Chinese in the Philippines also intensified with the declaration of martial law in 1972. Internal pressures in other parts of the world – notably South Africa, Peru, and the Caribbean area – were important in causing Chinese from a variety of locations to look to migration as a long-term solution to their difficulties. Canada became increasingly attractive throughout the 1960's and into the 1970's.

The Chinese population in Canada in the 1970's was substantially different from its counterpart a mere decade earlier. This difference can be traced in large measure to the gradual lessening of disabilities of Chinese immigrants, which allowed a population structure to emerge that was less peculiar. For example, by 1970 the sex ratio had become much more balanced. In the Maritimes, where the Chinese population had grown but slowly, the proportion of males and females still was unbalanced. The preponderance of females in Ontario as a whole (although not in Toronto itself) and in Saskatchewan was probably a reflection of the large numbers of foreign students at schools, colleges, and universities in the two provinces.

The post-1967 immigration continued the trends of the 1950's and early 1960's so that the Chinese population of Canada was even more concentrated in the urban centres. Ontario and Quebec seemed especially attractive. In effect, the major Chinese communities continued to be in Vancouver, Toronto, and Montreal, but Toronto gained an increasing share of the new migrants. By the middle 1970's, the largest community was in Toronto, and there were more Chinese in Ontario than in any other province. Growth was also marked in Quebec, where the Chinese population grew six-fold in the period after 1951, somewhat faster than the Chinese population in Ontario.

Some of the smaller urban Chinese settlements grew only modestly during the period. The nineteenth-century centre of Chinese immigration into Canada, Victoria, became only a pale replica of its former dynamism, and although it reflected the overall changes in immigration patterns, the impact seemed slight. Its nineteenth-century past was manifested in a "bachelor society" in the old centre of Chinese settlement. Its twentieth-century present was marked by the immigrants and second- and third-generation Chinese Canadians who lived in the suburbs, taking on the distinct occupational characteristics of the urban middle class, using the old "Chinatown" only as a marketing centre.

The secondary Ontario Chinese communities, such as in Kingston, Hamilton, and London, went through a process not unlike that of Victoria. The smaller communities, which had experienced a sense of liveliness in the 1920's and had borne with stoicism the difficulties of the 1930's and 1940's, did not participate in the revival of the larger communities like Toronto and Vancouver. They did not die as the communities of interior British Columbia had died, but there was no dramatic change.

Despite their increased concentration in Canada's major cities, Chinese remained scattered throughout all the provinces. In northern Ontario, for example, small clusterings (i.e., up to fifty persons) are to be found in Kenora, Sioux Lookout, Cochrane, Elliot Lake, and Espanola. The mining towns of Timmins and Sudbury and the Lake Superior cities of Thunder Bay and Sault Ste. Marie have Chinese populations in excess of 250.[6]

By the mid-1960's the sojourner Chinese was becoming a social type of the past. This was in part a consequence of changes in immigration regulations, which allowed Chinese in a large variety of settings throughout the world to migrate to Canada. Coming as they did from communities scattered around the globe, the post-1967 immigrants brought a variety of skills, sophistication, and savoir faire which reflected diverse cultural traditions. That variety was most marked in the larger urban centres, especially Toronto, where a process of accommodation and adaptation was necessary, not merely to Canadian society in general, but also to existing Canadian-Chinese communities.

The largest group of Chinese residents in Canada remained the China-born, but the China experience was filtered through Hong Kong or some Overseas Chinese community. The links with the homeland, although present, were different from those that an earlier generation of Chinese residents had enjoyed. Now Chinese Canadians could enjoy a more committed relationship to Canada than was ever possible before. The isolation that characterized the survivors of the pre-war period was not an option the new migrants were willing to accept, nor was the ambivalence toward things Chinese *and* Canadian, which was often a part of the personality of the small second generation that grew up in the period of exclusion and came to maturity in the immediate post-war period. Chinese in Canada in the post-1967 period were no longer homogeneous. Social class, point of migration, and date of migration all served to distinguish groups within the ethnic population. But the fundamental distinction inevitably related to immigration history, and the division between pre- and post-sixties migrants became the critical one.

The centrality of Chinese politics (specifically the conflict between Communists and Nationalists) was somewhat muted by the political events of the 1950's and 1960's. Sympathy for the achievements and goals of the People's Republic was publicly expressed over a broad area only after Canada's recognition in 1970 and Communist China's entry into the United Nations in 1971. The presence in Ottawa of an embassy from the People's Republic of China, Prime Minister Trudeau's visit to China in 1971, and the consequent establishment of a consulate in Vancouver in 1973 gave legitimacy to positive sentiments about New China's achievements since 1949. As the 1970's progressed it became more common for Canadians to go to China, and Chinese Canadians were able to visit their ancestral areas, many for the first time since childhood. Changing attitudes toward China had significant consequences for the structure of the community and gave rise to alternatives to traditional sources of authority within the inventory of community associations.

At a more general level, however, an older, apolitical version of the Chinese roots of Canada's Chinese population was a significant element in the character and sentiments of the population. The bulk of migrants still traced their origins, not merely to China, but to that small fragment of South China that had provided migrants to Canada and North America since the 1850's. The shared cultural experience is a basis for cooperation when other attributes are distinct, and it largely explains why traditional community organizations can persist or even flourish in an historical period marked by such sharp contrasts with other periods of Chinese-Canadian history.[7]

If continuity is an underlying theme, the dominant characteristic of development after 1967 is the extent of change, and the nature of the contrast with earlier periods. The greater part of Chinese-Canadian history had seen a preponderance of males in the population and strangely lopsided communities as a consequence. By 1971 there was only a slight preponderance of males, although history gave a peculiarity to certain age categories. The large numbers of younger men possibly reflect the attractiveness of Canadian higher education to those who are not migrants. The relatively larger number of women between fifty and seventy reflects the late marriage of pre-1923 immigrants and perhaps also the role of grandmothers in the process of adaptation.

The educational level of Canada's Chinese population by the early 1970's appeared substantial. In the country as a whole, over 20 per cent of household heads had some university education, although a somewhat larger proportion (32 per cent) had less than a grade-eight education.

This reflects, in part, a distinction between two kinds of immigrants. That part of the population that had entered as "sponsored" kinsmen of those already resident in Canada were less likely to be competent in English, and probably had fewer educational qualifications than immigrants who had entered Canada without sponsors and on the basis of their own skills, which were indexed by educational achievements.

By the early 1970's Chinese in Canada were engaged in a broad range of occupations in a variety of contexts. The great majority of gainfully employed Chinese were wage-earners; less than 10 per cent were employed on their own account.[8] Certain occupations traditionally associated with a Chinese population, whether in Canada or in other parts of the world, were apparent. Almost two-fifths were to be found in sales and personal services. In terms of an industrial classification, almost 60 per cent of the Chinese labour force were involved in either trade or service industries, but a not insignificant number – almost a fifth – were engaged in occupations that are clearly "white collar." Only a relatively small proportion were engaged in either manufacturing or primary industry, such as farming, fishing, mining, or the timber industry. Chinese market gardeners have continued to play a significant role in the Vancouver and Victoria regions – the great bulk of Chinese involved in agricultural pursuits in Canada are located in British Columbia – but their overall role in this sector has been in decline for some decades.

In smaller centres there is some concentration in the service occupations, especially restaurants, grocery stores, and, increasingly, hotels and other tourist-related activities. This reflects the status of the Chinese population as an immigrant population. Immigrants whose mother tongue is neither English nor French, coming from distinctive cultural backgrounds, may move into particular economic niches that allow the immigrant to adapt to the new culture either by doing unpleasant work requiring little skills (as working on the railroad) or by working unpleasantly long hours. Chinese in Vancouver and Victoria, and to a lesser degree in other Canadian cities, dominate the "corner" grocery stores. Hard work, long hours, diligence, and the use of established Chinese wholesaling networks help the Chinese immigrants to secure an economic foothold if they can bring together sufficient capital to initiate such an operation.

For a large part of the population, the recency of immigration and the consequent problems of adaptation give rise to a situation where the population, although coping, is not a wealthy one. The Chinese in the early 1970's were less prosperous than most ethnic groups, with only 20 per cent earning more than $11,000 in 1971. (See Table 16 in Appendix.) As the disabilities of the migration process ease, it is likely that inequality with respect to income will diminish.

In the 1970's the Chinese Canadians remain primarily an immigrant population. But to see the population only as a set of immigrants is to ignore the reality of the older, if numerically smaller, group of descendants of the pre-1923 immigrants. The Chinese population of Canada is characterized by dualities, the roots of which lie in changing immigration regulations. Thus, the population is divided between those who came to Canada before 1923 and those who came after the great changes in regulations in the 1960's. The Chinese immigrants of an earlier period developed communities and community organizations which the newer migrants have had to take into account. The newer Chinese residents have thus tended to add onto existing structures and sometimes to revive moribund ones, and, while there have been needs and problems specific to new migrants, the skills of those long resident or those adults who are "local born" have to enter the formula of adaptation.

It is not easy to pinpoint precisely why Canada became such an important area for Chinese migration in the 1960's. Certainly the places that provided immigrants were becoming increasingly unattractive at that time. The two factors that predominated in the "pull" to Canada were the presence of kinsmen and the possibility of social or economic conditions that migrants can adapt to. In Vancouver in the middle 1970's Chinese informants gave family ties as the single most important factor which impelled migration. Economic conditions were seen as attractive, however, as was the general aura of peace and tranquility that migrants believed characterized Canada. Also of significance was the nature of the educational system. In Hong Kong and, to a lesser degree, also in Singapore and Malaysia, the educational system was extremely competitive, and the strain on pupils and parents alike was substantial. The less pressured, more open system in Canada was a not insignificant element in the decision to migrate. Reasons to migrate vary with education and age. The young tend to come with less attention paid to kinship considerations. For those with higher educational levels, the economic and social climate tend to figure more prominently.

In general, the process of adaptation did not seem unduly traumatic. Difficulties could be expected to arise in the contexts of employment, education, housing, food, and language. Language sometimes posed a problem, although in 1971 77.2 per cent of the Chinese population was able to speak English, 0.4 per cent French, and 3.2 per cent both official languages; 19.2 per cent was able to speak neither.

In the larger urban centres of Canada, which were the primary points of settlement for new Chinese migrants, housing was at a premium. Population growth in Vancouver and Toronto, and, to a lesser extent, Calgary, Edmonton, and Montreal, was substantial, especially in the early 1970's, when Chinese migration to Canada was increasing. Although the migrants initially lived with relatives or in rented accommodation, the purchase of a house was a priority. Once the time had passed when restrictive covenants limited the areas where the Chinese could live, by the 1970's Chinese were scattered throughout the metropolitan areas of both Vancouver and Toronto, although certain parts of both cities remained popular. In Toronto, after urban renewal of the 1960's demolished the old Chinatown, a new Chinese residential area grew up alongside a re-established Chinatown.

Given the high levels of educational achievement of Chinese immigrants to Canada after 1967, and the significance of Canada's educational system in the decision to migrate, it is not surprising that difficulties with education did not rank high. Younger children coped easily with the system, and parental encouragement saw the entry of large numbers of "visa students" from Hong Kong, Singapore, and Malaysia, the vast majority of whom were Chinese. Chinese students were concentrated in certain disciplines, especially in applied science, medicine, and dentistry, but as the 1970's progressed, commerce, law, and the arts were attractive alternatives. As Chinese communities grew in complexity, the demand for Chinese professionals also grew. Only in the late 1940's had the maturing second generation successfully argued for the Chinese right to be represented by ethnic Chinese in such professions as law, pharmacy, and accountancy. A quarter century later the universities produced an array of Chinese professionals, whose ranks were swelled by highly qualified immigrants. Unlike their kinsmen of a generation earlier they were not hemmed in by discriminatory professional rules. While the ethnic community became an important point of reference in their professional commitments, they were not limited by it.

The generally high level of educational achievement is one reason for the relative ease with which Chinese in Canada coped with a steadily worsening labour market in the 1970's. One reason for the attractiveness of Toronto for Chinese migrants in the 1970's was the economic opportunities throughout the southern Ontario region.

One problem was that skills and training acquired abroad were not always readily transferable to the Canadian context. Civil engineers with training at a Chinese university and job experience in Hong Kong or some other part of Asia found it difficult to practise their profession in Canada without some effort to obtain local qualifications. Initial jobs often were in contexts not wholly appropriate to their training or expertise, and those jobs were often located within an ethnic context – for example, restaurant manager. Indeed, the immediate consequence of migration was to suffer a loss in occupational prestige. Certain Chinese cultural norms seemed to prevail in seeking jobs. Many immigrants relied upon introductions by friends or relations to find jobs. Relatives were particularly significant in introducing informants to jobs within the ethnic community.[9] Ties within the ethnic community, or kinship networks, were thus important in assisting Chinese migrants in the 1970's to adapt to the difficulties posed by the Canadian occupational system.

In an atmosphere of growing tolerance, Chinese Canadians were able to participate in Canadian social and economic life to a degree denied to an earlier generation. As a consequence, Chinese residents of Canada in the period after the middle 1960's were able to cope effectively with the complexities of Canadian society.

NOTES

1. The regulations were phrased as follows:
   Landing in Canada is limited to persons who comply with all the requirements respecting landing in Canada . . . and who are within one of the following classes:
   (a) a person who by reason of his education, training, skills or other special qualifications, is likely to establish himself successfully in Canada and who
      (i) has sufficient means to maintain himself in Canada until he has so established himself.
      (ii) has come to Canada, under arrangements made or approved by the Director, for placement in employment.
      (iii) has come to Canada . . . for establishment in a business, trade or profession, or in agriculture.
   See House of Commons, *Debates*, 26 October 1967, pp. 3505-7, 3531-4; 25 March 1968, pp. 8013-19.
2. Hawkins, *Canada and Immigration*, pp. 136-7.
3. *Ibid.*, pp. 129-31.
4. House of Commons, *Debates*, 26 October 1967, pp. 3505-7, 3531-4; 25 March 1968, pp. 8029-32.
5. See J. Cooper, *Colony in Conflict* (Hong Kong, 1970); Committee of Hong Kong-Kowloon Chinese Compatriots of All Circles for the Struggle Against Persecution by the British Authorities in Hong Kong, *The May Upheaval in Hong Kong* (Hong Kong, 1967).
6. Chang Lee, "Chinese in Northern Ontario," paper presented at the annual meeting of the Canadian Society for Asian Studies, Guelph, Ontario, May, 1978.
7. Indeed, an intriguing feature of a visit to Toi-san that one of the authors made in 1976 was the discovery that the county town is reminiscent of a Canadian "Chinatown." The architectural links between Canada and China are clear. In one household, in a village that was visited, the author noted a photograph of one of the grandchildren of the household head – in the graduation robes of Simon Fraser University!
8. For Canada, sources of income, according to the 1971 census, were as follows:

Source	%
Wages	37.5
Pensions	5.1
Government	1.2
Bonds and Investment	3.0
Self-employed	4.2

None	16.1
Not applicable	31.6

9. Certain universalistic norms prevailed: 70.2 per cent believed that "good job performance" was the crucial element in promotion; in the work context only 19.4 per cent deemed "personal contact with employers" significant.

EIGHTEEN

The Chinese Ethnic
Community in the 1970's

Chinese communities in Canada in the 1970's were less well-defined spatially than at an earlier time. In Vancouver, Chinatown thrived. In Toronto it was built anew, in a new location. In such places as Montreal, Calgary, Winnipeg, and Victoria, Chinatown declined. But in all settings the ethnic *community* was in resurgence. That community, even in Vancouver and Toronto, was no longer bounded by a particular spatial definition. The context in which the Chinese communities of Canada operated was vastly changed from that of the darker days of exclusion, or even of the police raids of the late fifties, but the resurgence had a distinctly traditional ring to it. Not the least among the traditional aspects of this resurgence was the continued role of voluntary associations. Even in the very different environment of the 1970's, they continued to be the cement that made the concept of a Chinese community a viable one.

As the 1970's progressed, Chinatowns, whether in their newly resurgent form or even as a shell of former substance, became a cultural focus for the increasingly dispersed and increasingly complex communities. As the community grew more varied in level of educational achievement, occupation, generation, place of origin, or whatever, the assertion of Chinese ethnic identity took on particular significance. From the early 1970's the Canadian government officially encouraged the expression of distinctive ethnic identity in the overall context of multiculturalism. Those political considerations appeared to coincide with the growth of sentiments within the varied Chinese communities to generate an ethnic identity and to demonstrate the Chinese contribution to Canadian social life in a manner that had scarcely seemed possible for an earlier generation.

While the Chinese communities as a whole were flourishing, some groups within the communities faced particular problems. One such group was the remnant of the "bachelor" community from the pre-1923 days. They were the elderly "sojourners" of the pre-exclusion period whose numbers were declining by the 1970's. Many were married, with families in China, but the links with their families were tenuous. They were the *Kam-shan a-paak* ("uncles from America") who had never returned to China. They lived in association headquarters or in co-operative housing – the so-called *fangkou*, which had been a common form of housing in the "bachelor community" days.[1] Most of these "single" old men were to be found in Vancouver, reflecting British Columbia's historical predominance as a centre of Chinese population. Such men were to be found, however, in other Chinese communities both large and small. They were largely dependent on government pensions and – isolated from kin contacts – were an important social welfare issue within the various communities.

There was also a substantial number of older Chinese women in Canada by the 1970's. Unlike the older men, they were in contact with kin networks and, indeed, many came as sponsored migrants and assisted in child-minding to allow both young parents to work. This pattern reflects traditional Chinese family structure as well as the adaptive strategy of a migrant population.[2] Many of these older women were isolated from Canadian society and, indeed, even from the Chinese communities.

The problems of the aged, although of general significance in Canadian society as a whole, had never been an issue within the Chinese communities of Canada. From the mid-1960's, and into the 1970's, however, care for the aged and the provision of facilities to meet the needs of the aged were important community issues. The issue was met, in part, by official actions. It is clear that in centres of Chinese concentration local governments assumed some responsibility for the social welfare of the aged Chinese without the resources, financial or otherwise, to provide for themselves. In Montreal by 1967, the city government had assumed a major responsibility for the Chinese hospital and the care of its twenty or so elderly, long-term care patients. This is not to suggest that the Chinese community of Montreal was not involved in the rebuilding of the new facilities. In 1967 the various organizations within the community overcame their differences and agreed on guidelines to raise money for the Chinese hospital. Almost three-quarters of a million dollars were raised. In subsequent years, however, care became increasingly a governmental responsibility. In other major centres housing provision for the elderly was an important issue. In some cases a mixture of government, traditional associations, and church initiatives improved the quality of housing for older members of Chinese communities. In one notable instance in Toronto, a home for aged Chinese was provided through the efforts of the Mon Sheong Foundation, an organization of Chinese-Canadian professional people.

Extant community organizations, including the Chinese churches, were important and predictable sources of help. Individual initiative, when backed by government assistance, was another source. In Vancouver, for example, an association for older people, which enjoyed huge success, was founded in 1971 by a particularly dynamic octogenarian, a graduate of Cornell University of the class of 1913, and manager of the Bank of China in Guangdong province until the early 1950's. He retired to Vancouver, was dismayed at the lack of facilities for older members of the community, and organized a response to those issues. By 1974 the association had 491 members; by 1977, 810. It was funded with several grants from the federal level and had established an organizational base at the Strathcona Community Centre, which, adjacent to Chinatown, served an area of the city that was predominantly Chinese. The bulk of the members were women over seventy years of age, and were from the Sze-yap. The general objectives of the association were to promote the welfare of older Chinese residents and to develop a program of meaningful activities for them.

In the post-1967 period Chinese professionals grew in number. They brought to Chinese communities an activist orientation and they formulated plans to resolve community problems, working frequently through the organizations they formed, such as the Montreal Society of Chinese Engineers, the Mon Sheong Foundation in Toronto, and the S.U.C.C.E.S.S. organization in Vancouver. As they did so, a different kind of "politics" began to emerge. In the 1950's Chinese rights as Canadian citizens were asserted and much of the argument was based on abstract notions of "social justice." The 1970's saw a substantial ethnic consciousness as a valid basis to argue for programs and facilities or for the removal of inequities.

From the late 1960's there were two versions of politics in Canadian Chinese communities. One was firmly rooted in the older community organizations and was dominated by older men whose consciousness was marked by discriminatory rules and regulations and who saw accommodation, not confrontation, as the most effective strategy. A second version was dominated by younger, professionally oriented members of the communities, who were willing to use the system and, if necessary, challenge it.

Inevitably, therefore, Chinese community politics were marked by tension and sometimes by conflict. In the context of Chinese communities this was by no means unknown. The conflicts of the 1970's, however, were often between generations and between orientations as to the role appropriate for Chinese ethnic communities in the contemporary period.

Among the major problems facing Chinese communities in the 1970's two are particularly relevant to this discussion. One was the need to integrate numerous Chinese immigrants from a wide variety of backgrounds into Canadian society. The other was to utilize the considerable talents within Chinese communities to develop a sense of ethnic identity more appropriate than the one which had prevailed during the long years of hostility and discrimination. The distinctive needs of Chinese communities after 1967 thus generated new types of organizations and new forms of politics. But even the most innovative and radical among these were operating from a base that had, in part at least, the sanctity of tradition. The past was not forgotten, and traditional responses to modern problems were not infrequent. Toronto and Vancouver were the largest Chinese communities and the most dynamic. In both, the proliferation of new groups and organizations was substantial.

> Chinese youth clubs, Chinese political associations, Chinese university student associations, Chinese *kung-fu* clubs, Chinese community service groups, Chinese workers associations, Chinese professional organizations, cultural organizations, independence organizations; the list, though not endless, is staggering.[3]

In Toronto, given the narrowness of the organizational base on the eve of the post-1967 changes in immigration legislation, the overall impact was more dramatic than in Vancouver. But in both, and in the lesser communities of Alberta, there was a similarity of development. Popular participation in community organizations was high.

In Vancouver, the 1970's saw the formation of two new locality associations that served the needs of Chinese from the Philippines. One, founded in 1972, catered almost exclusively to Philippine Chinese who trace their origins, like the bulk of the Vancouver Chinese population, to the Sze-yap region. Members gathered together on weekends to play games, read newspapers from the Philippines, and maintain a sense of togetherness. One important task that the association set itself was to assist newcomers in finding work. A second Philippine Chinese association (the Fukien Association) was founded in the mid-1970's recruiting members from Hokkien-speaking Chinese, who constitute the bulk of the Chinese in the Philippines. Its members celebrated major Chinese festivals, held dinner parties, dances, fashion shows, and bingo sessions. It was clearly associated with a Mandarin-speaking Christian church in contrast to the other Philippine Chinese association, which apparently had no significant religious underpinning.

In the context of the times, such traditional responses to the problem of adaptation were not typical. But they do indicate the potential of traditional organizational forms, even in the vastly changed 1970's. The significance of a Christian church for the Fukien Association in Vancouver draws attention to another mode of adaptation in the 1970's. In a Vancouver survey almost a quarter of the sample population belonged to a Christian church. In Vancouver, Toronto, and, to a lesser degree, Edmonton, Chinese-language churches were scattered throughout the metropolitan areas, although close to Chinese population concentrations. While long-established churches held their own, the greatest growth occurred in expressive, fundamentalist forms of worship. Data from Vancouver suggest that those born, and especially those raised, outside China were likely to be frequent churchgoers. Indeed, churches appealed to both the young and the elderly. Student Christian Fellowship groups were well-organized in the colleges and universities throughout Canada. Those with a high level of educational achievement and a prestigious occupation were more likely to be members of church groups than the less well-educated.

A related issue is the degree of traditional religious ritual that is maintained over time. Traditional Chinese religious observance had never been important in the affairs of Chinese in North America. There were the occasional temples, but cult movements of the kind that flourish throughout Southeast Asia were absent. Ritual observances most likely to survive the difficult journey from China were mortuary rituals and those relating to the worship of ancestors. The fictive kinship character of many traditional associations was reflected in their continued worship of founding ancestors or tutelary deities. Thus, in association buildings from Victoria to Halifax, a form of traditional worship survived. In Chinese commercial establishments throughout Canada, earth-god shrines, or shrines to Guan Gong, the god of wealth and patron deity of businessmen, were frequent. Among Chinese households, observance of traditional domestic rituals was only modest.

Certain festivals of a general nature, which expressed Chinese cultural identity rather than kinship obligations, were widely observed. Not least of these was Lunar New Year. In the weeks preceding New Year celebration, Chinatowns were thronged with shoppers, their stores with an array of festival foods. The atmosphere was festive and celebratory. The celebration was a cultural one, that of being Chinese. Other festivals, such as Mid-Autumn Festival or Dragon Boat Festival, were observed less grandly, being marked by feasting. Non-traditional, and essentially political, celebrations such as China's National Day, October 1st (or October 10th for KMT adherents), were also part of Chinese-Canadian identity, at least for a segmented portion of the community. Such celebrations were caught up in a different context and were perceived separately.

LEADERSHIP IN THE 1970's

Leadership in the Chinese communities of Canada has always manifested itself through networks of associations. Neither the younger professionals of the earlier second generation nor the newer Chinese residents who came to Canada from 1967 could accept the form of political leadership which prevailed up to the early 1960's. Glimmerings of dissent, which were expressed in political terms with the formation of the East Wind Club in Montreal or the Chinese Youth Association in Vancouver, indicated an underlying dissatisfaction with the character of the community. The two newspapers published by younger persons on the political left contained news about China, but also much political news about their own communities in Canada. The two are the *Da Zhong Bao* of

Vancouver and the *Duolunduo Shang Bao* ("Chinatown Commercial News") of Toronto.

The older merchant group that had survived for so long, and had a considerable fund of legitimacy within the Canadian political system as a whole, began to engage the young dissidents in the late 1960's. A major issue that brought forth new and younger leaders was urban renewal. From late in 1965, the municipal authorities in several major Canadian cities put forward plans for the redevelopment of inner urban areas that had suffered neglect over the past decades. In Vancouver, Edmonton, Calgary, Winnipeg, Toronto, and Montreal, such plans encompassed existing Chinatowns, which were thus threatened with demolition. In 1965-66, urban renewal in Toronto centred on the City Hall complex, destroying the Chinatown area that had served the growing Chinese community. Similarly, in Montreal the dispersed Chinese population could provide little organized support to maintain the small Montreal Chinatown. In both Toronto and Montreal, then, the traditional Chinese leadership appeared incapable of meeting the challenge posed by the municipal authorities backed by federal commitments to improve Canada's urban core.

In Vancouver, plans had been developing for more than ten years to raze Strathcona, the decaying residential area adjacent to Chinatown in which many Chinese and some other ethnic groups lived. In 1968, the City Council announced a project which would have bulldozed the remaining old houses and replaced them with apartment buildings. While the older merchant elite tried to affect city planning through their traditional connections with politicians, younger Chinese, many of them professionals, relied upon support from the Chinese community itself – and they got it. They organized the Strathcona Property Owners and Tenants Association (SPOTA), which aimed "to ensure that the people who live in this area will be fully informed and that their interest and their community will be protected."[4]

SPOTA achieved so much popular support that the government invited it to participate in a committee to investigate the area and propose plans for it. It was the first time in Canada that a citizens' committee had joined with three levels of government in such an endeavour. Two years of investigation produced a report recommending grant-loans to encourage local residents to upgrade their own houses while the government improved streets and amenities. Over 200 private houses were refurbished, many of them far beyond the level of subsidies provided by the Strathcona Rehabilitation Project itself.

In Alberta, the Chinese communities in Edmonton and Calgary, although somewhat dispersed, generated responses to proposals for renewal and were able to resist the general plans with some success. Calgary, in particular, set the tone for the 1970's. Municipal plans that would have demolished the existing Chinatown gave rise to a distinctive form of association, the Sien Lok Society, its name garnered from the Chinese proverb, "the greatest happiness lies in being charitable" (*Wei-shan zui-le* or, in Cantonese, *Wai-sien tsei-lok*). Formally registered as a society in November, 1968, Sien Lok was composed of Canadian-born businessmen and professionals, later to be joined by "a group of realtors and professionals who were born in China but were educated in Canada."[5] In April, 1969, the Society sponsored a National Conference on Urban Renewal as it affected Chinatowns. The conference examined the forces that threatened the very existence of Chinatowns in North American urban centres. Its concerted and energetic stand was a landmark in Chinese community action.

The Sien Lok Society represented the position that Chinatowns, although sometimes dilapidated and often neglected, were worthy of preservation. Increasingly, the argument was made that Chinatowns were not colourful reminders of a distant and exotic civilization but central to the definition of Chinese-Canadian identity. Chinatowns in the major centres of Chinese populations became increasingly the loci of Chinese cultural identity.

There were, indeed, conflicting processes. On the one hand, Chinese populations, even in the major centres of Vancouver, Toronto, and Montreal, were becoming greatly dispersed. At the same time, China-towns developed a centrality which, although different from that of an earlier generation, was nonetheless intense. "Chinatown" was no longer the only locus of organizational, residential, and cultural expression. The ghetto character of Chinese communities crumbled in the post-1947 period. But Chinatown as a cultural focus expanded. It became a living and revitalized centre. Chinese not only from Chinatown but from all over the metropolitan area would congregate there on the weekend to shop at Chinese specialty stores and sample the enormous variety of salty and sweet snacks – the justly famous *dim-sum*.

The historic decline of Canada's Chinese communities was arrested by the influx of new Chinese immigrants after the changes in immigration regulations in 1962 and 1967. The needs of the new population, and the demands of the maturing second generation, argued for a rebuilding of Canada's Chinatowns at precisely the same moment that civic authorities, often in concert with their provincial and federal counterparts, were pressing for "urban renewal," an important consequence of which would have been to eliminate Chinatowns. The prospect of the destruction of Calgary's Chinatown brought into being the Sien Lok Society.

The Calgary case is significant, not so much in what it achieved, as in what it pointed to. A form of leadership had prevailed within Canada's Chinese communities with relatively little change – even in the post-Second World War period – for over a half-century. Older leaders were not prepared to abandon their positions readily or speedily. There were, nonetheless, a set of pressures that arose, initially, about the issues of urban renewal which began to raise serious questions about the character of political leadership within Canadian Chinese communities and which argued for the emergence of new kinds of leaders who could cope more effectively with the differing sets of problems that now faced Chinese communities.

One result was a substantial weakening of KMT pre-eminence in politics in the major centres of Chinese settlement in Canada. By the middle 1970's the links between the politics of China and the politics of Chinese communities in Canada were all but broken, even though a politically conscious and sophisticated immigrant population, with a voracious appetite for newspapers, was highly conscious of homeland politics. But the role of Chinese politics in forming political factions in Chinese-Canadian communities, and the involvement of Chinese-Canadian political leaders in the political life of China which had prevailed up to the early post-war period, had become irrelevant by the late 1960's. Newer leaders sought an active involvement in Canadian cultural and political life. Older leaders, long used to particular ways of doing things, frequently could not respond positively to such actions. As one consequence, older political conflicts appeared to surface in contexts that seemed inappropriate.

The character of leadership in the Toronto community in the 1970's demonstrates with particular clarity the changing nature of community politics. Prior to the post-war immigration Toronto's Chinatown was a tiny concentration of grocery stores, a few shops catering to tourists, a collection of association headquarters, Christian churches, barber shops, and restaurants. In its new form by 1975 the Chinatown was in a new location as a thriving commercial section with a wide variety of stores and restaurants and a "new" residential segment. The transformation, even when compared to its appearance in 1970, was astounding.

The physical changes in Chinatown reflected the transformation in the social character of the community as a whole. The range in the occupational profile of the Toronto community is substantial, and its members are no longer confined to a restricted set of occupational choices. Toronto's Chinese community is large, complex, and stratified. There have developed, especially since the mid-1960's, new groups and new possibilities for leadership.

There seems little doubt that, as the size of the Toronto Chinese community has grown, so has the size of the Chinese "sub-economy."[6] The nature of that economy has changed. The garment industry is now perhaps of greater significance than restaurants or tourist-oriented stores. But certain of its characteristics remain. Immigrant Chinese whose facility in English and educational level is low are trapped in the sub-economy and become victims of the very process that has led to the renaissance of the Toronto Chinatown. In a previous generation, the traditional associations had met the needs of immigrants who were caught in the Chinese sub-economy, but after the Second World War the traditional associational structure in Toronto was in decline. It remained as a source of prestige and a medium of advancement for political leaders, but it failed to recruit new members on a large scale and seemed incapable of responding to the needs of the large numbers of immigrants in the post-1962 period. Chinese immigrants were obliged to look elsewhere to resolve certain of their difficulties.

One further complication that gave rise to an important shift in the possibilities for leadership in the Toronto community was Canada's diplomatic recognition of the People's Republic of China in 1970. The Chinese Community Centre of Ontario, like the Chinese Benevolent Associations in Vancouver and Montreal, had formed an important pillar of KMT strength in Toronto. Canada's shift in diplomatic recognition from the KMT government in Taiwan to the People's Republic of China in Peking was a political defeat for the CCC. In the aftermath of the diplomatic recognition, two of the larger family associations publicly questioned CCC legitimacy and declared their disassociation from the Taiwan-oriented politics of the CCC. Emergent political groups within the Toronto community – especially those with few ties to an earlier form of political behaviour – were encouraged by the fracturing of the older system of political solidarity to put forward alternatives to a form of community politics that seemed outmoded. This is not to suggest that the power base of the CCC crumbled immediately or that its spokesmen ceased to gain recognition from without. The CCC appeared strong. But as the community grew in size and its needs became more complex, a younger, highly sophisticated, and decidedly immigrant set of community activists was able to organize about distinctively *new* community issues which the older leadership group was slow to recognize.

As substantial numbers of Chinese immigrants, with distinctive social needs, became involved in the growing Chinese sub-economy, other Chinese immigrants of different characteristics (young, sophisticated, well-educated, in professional occupational categories) were involved in building community associations of a new kind. The complex nature of urban Canada in the 1970's and the possibilities for participation in Canadian culture in general presented a set of problems which an earlier generation of Chinese in Canada had never faced. The younger, better educated, and, above all, bilingual and bicultural immigrants adopted a service ideology which was expressed through organizations designed to assist less well-educated, unilingual, sometimes older Chinese residents to cope with the demands of the urban Canadian environment. The newer organizations thus dealt with child care, youth activities, activities for the elderly, employment, English-language classes, legal aid, income-tax preparation, and citizenship. Such activities were sometimes carried on through the older associations, or churches, but often through organizations which were able to seek funding from a variety of government agencies committed to "multiculturalism." Young Chinese professionals thus developed roles as mediators between government on the one hand

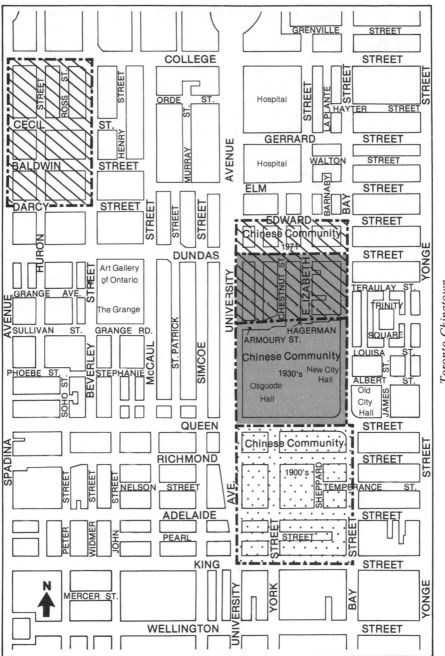

Toronto Chinatown

263

and large numbers of immigrant Chinese coping with the demands of new social expectations on the other.

The traditional role of mediator in the Toronto community had been reserved for the CCC. Inevitably the two would find themselves in conflict, more so, since the young professionals, unimpressed by the tradition that the CCC represented, questioned the right of the CCC to speak on behalf of the changed community. The nascent conflicts burst into the open as various community groups became involved in the process of planning the neighbourhood that in the 1970's was to be Toronto's new Chinatown.

From 1969 the City Planning Department in Metropolitan Toronto attempted to decentralize its operations and to involve a broader spread of citizen participation in its activities through the development of neighbourhood planning offices. The neighbourhood designated "Southeast Spadina" is predominantly Chinese and it is locally known as Chinatown. Planners attached to the local planning office established a steering committee as a vehicle for gathering opinion from a combination of residents and property owners. The committee had no precise constitution, no decision-making power, and no strict membership. Membership on the committee was defined as those who were present when it was in session. Its meetings were advertised through a variety of local media and during the first four years of its existence it developed a core membership largely composed of social service leaders. Local businessmen and the larger property owners showed little public interest in the committee's deliberations, and their involvement with the work of the committee was sporadic. A consensus developed in the committee, which argued for local stability and the maintenance of the residential character of the neighbourhood with commercial developments primarily linked to neighbourhood needs.

In 1973 the local planning office drafted a tentative development plan, which reflected the views of the steering committee. The draft plan argued for rezoning to prevent the displacement of family homes by high-rise developments. The plan also proposed limitations to the commercial development in the area and saw retention of its industrial sector – the garment industry in the southwest corner of the area – as an important economic base for neighbourhood residents.

Meanwhile, during the period of the plan's gestation, migration into the area of Chinese residents newly arrived in Canada continued at a substantial pace. These and earlier additions had made the Chinatown area so large and complex in its population that by 1975 there were strong possibilities for conflict over the future of the neighbourhood. A Chinese investment company, dominated by new entrepreneurial interests, outlined a costly development project for the centre of the neighbourhood's commercial area, which was diametrically opposed to the planning principle enunciated by the steering committee. The project was summarily rejected. The investment group, through its legal advisers, discovered that the planning office plan was only a guide for action and did not have official status. As a strategy for the right to develop its project, the investment group attacked the conception of the plan and the process through which "community opinion" had been gathered. In doing so it raised questions about ethnic political organization and set the scene for political conflict within the community about highly local issues.

The investment group was denied planning permission to launch its project in 1975. Within two years it had organized within the ethnic community and had forged a coalition between itself and other similar entrepreneurial groups and the older set of "traditional" leaders whose organizational focus was the CCC. The coalition – which named itself the Toronto Chinatown Community Planning Association – was extremely effective. It appeared before the City of Toronto Planning Board and pointed out that its membership was composed of twenty-five community organizations representing 10,000 citizens of Chinese ethnic origin. It argued that the steering committee was unrepresentative, that it had no organized base of support, and that there were no formal mechanisms for collecting opinions from within the committee. The Planning Board agreed with the coalition. It directed the steering committee to reconstitute its membership in order to demonstrate that it was a representative body and also to elect a permanent chairman and adopt parliamentary procedures in carrying out its work. The coalition succeeded in reopening the planning process for the neighbourhood and in effectively blocking the neighbourhood conception which had been developed in the early 1970's.

The success of the coalition in successfully challenging the work of the social service leaders in developing a neighbourhood plan pitted one segment of the community against another and resulted in a degree of intra-community hostility unmatched since the teens and twenties. Up to this period, relations between traditional leaders and the new entrepreneurial group had been insignificant. In a strategy to create a local environment conducive to their own economic benefit, the entrepreneurs had to demonstrate their political legitimacy, an attribute that had not hitherto been seen as important. Meanwhile, the traditional leaders saw their own claims to leadership dominance within the community gradually reduced and questioned, barely surviving the derecognition of Taiwan in 1970. The needs of the entrepreneurial group for political legitimacy dovetailed neatly into the traditional leaders' desire to reassert their claims to legitimacy.

The situation in the Toronto community in the late 1970's was both volatile and unresolved. The social service groups were obliged to demonstrate how they represented their constituency. One immediate requirement of the Planning Board's demand that the steering committee alter its composition was the choice of a chairman who could, in sum, mediate between the two broad factions. A steering committee meeting drew 500 people, the majority of whom did not live in the area. Indeed, it was reported that chartered buses brought participants from throughout southern Ontario, perhaps from as far afield as New York City! A candidate agreeable to the entrepreneurial group won handily.

The non-Chinese governmental structure was often unable to judge with precision the character of internal community politics. Its job was even more difficult, given the care with which the different positions were put and the genteel and polite manner in which official contacts were maintained. The Planning Board directed the neighbourhood planning team to develop plans that might be agreeable to both sides. That task, in the short term, seemed an impossible one. Its successful outcome would depend upon the character of politics within the ethnic community in the future.

The Toronto pattern of events was repeated with substantial similarity in the major centres during the 1970's. In Calgary the Sien Lok Society's efforts were called into question by a coalition of traditional groups calling itself the United Calgary Chinese Association.[7] In Vancouver the issues of leadership turned, ultimately, on the question of control of the Chinese Benevolent Association. A coalition of interests not unlike those of the Sien Lok Society in Calgary, or the social service group in Toronto, formed the Chinese Cultural Centre in 1972. Efforts to attract government funds were checked by non-Chinese assumptions that the CBA was the major community organization and the realization that the Chinese community in Vancouver was, in some unclear way, divided. Community dissatisfaction with the CBA leadership had been clear since the early 1970's.[8] It reached a peak in the summer of 1977 when the thorny question of KMT domination of the CBA was publicly aired. It was linked to other contentious issues in the community, such as funding for the cultural centre and urban renewal. Conflict was perhaps less divisive in Vancouver than in Toronto, although it was certainly as bitter. It was resolved, to some degree at least, with the legal challenge to the authority of the CBA. After some manoeuvring, a judicially ordered election resulted, in the fall of 1978, in a sweep of CBA directorships by the Chinese Cultural Centre group. One phase of history of the Vancouver Chinese community, in which the KMT had been politically dominant, came to a formal end.[9]

The Vancouver community had for so long been the premier Chinese community in Canada. By the late 1970's it had perhaps surrendered its position as the largest Chinese community in Canada. But in restructuring its political character so that the small and vocal second generation, in concert with the articulate and politically acute professionals, had a major voice, it now began a new phase in Chinese-Canadian history.

NOTES

1. Knowledge about the organization of *fangkou* is scanty. Recruitment to

the household was not unlike recruitment to a family or district association. Expenses of maintaining the house were shared, although individuals cooked separately.

2. The nature of Chinese-Canadian families is discussed in G.E. Johnson, "Chinese Family and Community in Canada: Tradition and Change," in J.L. Elliot, *Two Nations, Many Cultures* (Scarborough, 1978), pp. 353-71. See also Hoe, *Structural Changes of Two Chinese Communities*, pp. 263-83.

3. Richard H. Thompson, "Ethnicity versus Class: An Analysis of Conflict in a North American Chinese Community," *Ethnicity*, VI, 4 (December, 1979), pp. 306-26.

4. Donald Gutstein, *Vancouver Ltd.* (Toronto, 1975), p. 159.

5. Hoe, *Structural Changes*, p. 165. Hoe deals with the case of Edmonton on pp. 119-22. Sien Lok Society of Calgary, *National Conference on Urban Renewal and its Effects on Chinatown* (Calgary, 1969), p. i.

6. On "sub-economy," see I.H. Light and C.C. Wong, "Protest or Work: Dilemmas of the Tourist Industry in American Chinatowns," *American Journal of Sociology*, 80 (1975), pp. 1342-65; I. Light, *Ethnic Enterprise in America* (Berkeley, 1972), pp. 170-92.

7. Hoe, *Structural Changes*, pp. 130-4.

8. See, e.g., John Kirkwood, "Chinese Dragon Stirs as East Comes West," Vancouver *Province*, 30 January 1971. Chester Grant, "The Struggle for Power in Chinatown," Vancouver *Sun*, 21 February 1971.

9. The conflict occurred over a long period. See Vancouver *Sun*, 13, 14, 15 August, 8 December 1977. Also Vancouver *Province*, 8 December 1977. Also see the pamphlet by the Committee of Concerned Chinese Canadians, *Return the CBA to the Chinese Community*; "CCC, CBA and Chinese Community," *Chinese Cultural Centre Reports*, 2, 6 (September, 1977); Vancouver *Sun* and Vancouver *Province* for 30 October 1978.

NINETEEN

Conclusion

From the nineteenth century to 1947 Canada's Chinese lived in two worlds, never fully part of either. Tied in some ways to China, they were also involved in Canada. Physically removed from China, they could not participate in China's affairs. Limited in their opportunities in Canada, they could only marginally participate in Canadian affairs.

After 1947, as Canada opened up to them and as old dreams about China began to die, there was less confusion in orientation and their interest in China, while still substantial, became more a matter of generalized sympathies than of personal objectives. Yet, in another way, Chinese communities in Canada enjoyed fresh infusions of Chinese culture as a result of Canadian immigration policy. Through sponsorship and nomination of immigrants a constant stream of Chinese, predominantly from Hong Kong, replenished Chinese-Canadian communities with the urban Hong Kong version of Chinese culture. Most significant of all, the spectacular immigration of Chinese from all over the world between 1967 and the middle 1970's not only enhanced the Hong Kong influence but created a new cosmopolitanism in Chinese-Canadian communities. The long-term effects on Chinese-Canadian history of this post-1967 influx of educated, propertied Chinese can scarcely be estimated. It is abundantly clear, however, that Canada's Chinese population is still an immigrant population and yet one different in size and character from that of the Chinese population as recently as the mid-1960's.

The post-1967 change in character of the Chinese communities illustrates very well the profound effect Canadian immigration policy has long had in shaping those communities. The head tax of $500 and the exclusion law of 1923 not only limited the size but helped maintain the mostly male character of the Chinese population. That, in turn, shaped the social, cultural, and organizational life of Chinatowns, and helped perpetuate an interest in China and its politics. The immigration policy of the 1950's made Chinese family life in Canada fully possible, and the policies of the late 1960's greatly accelerated the development of wealth and professional skills within the Chinese communities.

Another major force shaping Chinese life in Canada was the reaction of white Canadians to the Chinese presence – which, of course, was closely related to immigration policy, since immigration policy normally responded to what were believed to be public sentiments. Whether or not Canada's treatment of its Chinese was worse or better than treatment of any other ethnic minority, it is significant that two unique forms of discrimination were applied in the Chinese case: only the Chinese had to pay a head tax and only the Chinese were excluded from Canada by an Act of Parliament.

Two contrasting reasons have been given for white attitudes. One view stresses economic forces; large businesses in Canada often found Chinese labour useful, at least up to 1923, while the low wages accepted by the Chinese stimulated opposition to them by white workers. Anti-Chinese sentiment, in this formulation, is the result of economic competition. The other argument cites white stereotypic expressions about the Chinese in order to demonstrate that a broad spectrum of whites – not just those whose jobs were at stake – had negative physical and cultural images of the Chinese.

There is abundant evidence for either interpretation. Anti-Chinese sentiment was usually strongest when economic conditions were critical, and especially when job competition was severe. We have seen that, especially in British Columbia, as the Chinese moved from one occupation to another, white opposition was aroused. There is, however, no denying the racism of white children's rhymes or that of the repeated literary descriptions from the nineteenth and early twentieth century of Chinese "chattering" when speaking, or being "bewildered" in every situation – the sort of things not regularly said of white persons. Friendships might exist across such racial barriers, but they were likely to be tinged with paternal affection on the part of the whites. They rarely could be intimate relationships between equals.

From the late nineteenth century to the late 1940's racial stereotypes about the Chinese provided apologies for anti-Chinese discrimination. It was said that the Chinese were unassimilable (and hence should be kept at arm's length), that they did not understand democracy (and so should not enjoy the franchise), that they were a threat to the moral well-being and physical health of the white Canadian public, and that they did not spend their earnings in Canada, sending them all to China instead.

White attitudes also were influenced by Chinese reactions to discrimination. Particularly in the decade 1900-1910 the Chinese were unfavourably compared in this respect with the newly arrived Japanese. The Japanese were seen as aggressive in the face of mistreatment; they commanded respect, even as (so Westerners thought) a Westerner would. Hence they were more likely to get it. The Chinese, by contrast, often seemed passive, accepting, anxious to avoid trouble or offence.

269

This perceived difference in "national character" was really a reflection of a difference in national power. At the time this invidious (to the Chinese) comparison was made, Japan was in a period of national euphoria. Its modernization program, after three decades, seemed hugely successful; its armies had defeated not only its Asian neighbour, China, but a white European power, Russia. The Japanese in Canada knew that they had an alert, aggressive government behind their interests. The Chinese in Canada knew that they had behind them only a government identified with weakness and confusion. Thus, the interest of Canada's Chinese in the existence of a strong China, and the pride they would later feel in the respect that China has finally commanded in recent decades, are partly the result of practical self-interest.

But whatever the degree of pride in a strong, respected China, the practical need for that has disappeared. As equal opportunity for the Chinese in Canada becomes increasingly possible and as Canadian issues and concerns increasingly pre-empt time and interest, there will be less and less time for China's affairs and China's politics, and the meaning of "China" in the consciousness of Chinese Canadians will undergo changes we can hardly predict.

A third influence that shaped Chinese-Canadian life was the interaction of Chinese culture with the living conditions of Chinese in Canada. For most of their history, Chinese-Canadian communities were "bachelor" communities. Their members were under an incredible strain. In an alien and sometimes hostile land they were separated from their families, required to work long hours and save for remittances by feats of self-denial in degrading living conditions. Under these strains, many sought release in ways brought from China – gambling and opium use. Opium addiction, ironically, was not an old Chinese custom, but a new one, stimulated by Western merchants on the China coast.

As Chinese-Canadian family life developed, it reflected both its Chinese heritage and the Canadian environment. In Chinese-Canadian families, family solidarity, individual discipline, and the leading role of elders and males all were expressions of Chinese culture; but a large proportion of families were Christians, reflecting the Canadian environment.

In the period before 1947 the large number of organizations reflected the social needs of a partly isolated "bachelor" phase. In the period since, the much more numerous and more varied organizations that have appeared reflect the great diversity now present in Chinese-Canadian communities. Despite all this extensive organizational apparatus, however, the Chinese "organizational genius" has never produced in Canada a single body that could unite all Chinese Canadians across the country. Even within individual communities, such unity has been rare and precarious. Despite frequent white supposition of master networks and controls, Chinese-Canadian society has proved to be extraordinarily fragmented and difficult to unite. The possibility of organizational unity in the future may well depend upon how Chinese Canadians see Chinese culture in relation to Canadian opportunities.

Glossary

NAMES OF ORGANIZATIONS

Local/Standard Usage	Characters	Pinyin	Identification
Aiguo Xuetang (see Oi-kwok Hock-tong)	愛國學堂		
Au Tai Mee Club	No Characters Available		
Bao Wong Wui	保皇會	Bao Huang Hui	Empire Reform Association
B.C.Lower Mainland Cooperative Association	卑詩首埠宗鬼業合作社	Beishisheng Pingyuan Nongye Hezuoshe	
Canada Evening Post (see Jianada Zhongguo Chenbao	加拿大中國晨報		
Chan Wing Chun	陳穎川堂	Chen Yingchuan Tang	Clan Association. Surname: Chan (Chen,Chin)
Cheng Wing Yeong Tong	鄭榮陽堂	Zheng Rongyang Tang	Clan Association. Surname Zheng: (Cheng, Jung)
Chee Duck Tong	至德堂	Zhide Tang	Clan Association. Surnames: Ng,Chou,Chow,Choy,Cho,Yung
Chee Kung Tong (see Chinese Freemasons)	致公堂	Zhigong Tang	
Chew Luen Society	昭倫公所	Zhaolun Gongsuo	Clan Association. Surnames: Tam,Hui,Tse.Yuan (Tan,Xu.Xie. Yuen:Tom.Hoy,Der.)
Chi-chi She	寰揖社	Jiji She	Revolutionary Society Founded In Victoria Before The 1911 Revolution.

Chin Wing Chun Tong (see Chan Wing Chun)	陳頴川|堂		
Chinatown Lions	筆埠獅予会	Huafu Shizi Hui	
Chinese Benevolent Association	中筆会舘	Zhonghua Huiguan	Vancouver CBA.
Chinese-Canadian Club	同源会	Tong Yuan Hui	
Chinese-Canadian Veterans	筆喬退伍軍人会	Huayi Tuiwu Junren Hui	
Chinese Chamber Of Commerce	中筆商業会	Zhonghua Shangye Hui	
Chinese Community Centre Of Ontario	安省中筆总会舘	Ansheng Zhonghua Zhonghuiguan	
Chinese Consolidated Benevolent Association	中筆公舘	Zhonghua Huiguan	The Victoria CBA
Chinese Elks	筆人鹿頭会	Huaren Lutouhui	
Chinese Freemasons	致公堂	Zhigongtang	
Chinese Nationalist League (see Kuomintang - KMT)	國民党	Guomindang	
Chinese New Year Festival Committee	慶祝新年筆通小組	Qingzhu Xinnian Choubei Xiaozu	
Chinese Patriotic Federation	加拿大安省筆喬抗日救國会	Jianada Ansheng Huaqiao Kangri Qiuguo Hui	
Chinese Public School	筆喬公立學校	Huaqiao Gongli Xuexiao	
Chinese Times	大筆公報	Dahan Gongbao	Vancouver-published Newspaper. It Began Publication In The Early Years Of The Twentieth Century And In 1914 Became The Official Organ Of The Chinese Freemasons.
Chinese Trade Workers	中國職工会	Zhongguo Zhigong Hui	

GLOSSARY

NAMES OF ORGANIZATIONS

Local/Standard Usage	Characters	Pinyin	Identification
Chinese Varsity Club	中國大學生會	Zhongguo Daxuesheng Hui	Chinese Student Club.UBC For Local-born Canadian-Chinese.
Chinese Vegetable Peddlers Association	菜業公會	Caiye Gonghui	Commercial Association Victoria B.C.
Chinese Voice Daily	僑聲日報	Qiaosheng Ribao	Vancouver Newspaper.
Chinese Welfare Society	華人福利會	Huaren Fulihui	Toronto Association Formed In Early 1960's. Opponent Of Ontario CCC And Publisher Of Duolunduo Shangbao.
Chinese Workers Protective Association	中華工人保障會	Zhonghua Gongren Baozhang Hui	Left-wing Vancouver Association.
Chinese Youth Association	青年聯誼會	Qingnian Lianyi Hui	Left-wing Youth Association. Vancouver. Publisher Of Da Zhong Bao.
Ching Won Musical Society	清韻音樂社	Qingyun Yinyue She	
Chong Hoo Tong	昌後堂	Chang Hou Tang	
Chong Wah School	中華學校	Zhonghua Xuexiao	Nineteenth Century Locality Association. Victoria. Locality: Poon-yue.
Chow Loon Kung-so (see Chew Luen Society)	昭倫公所		

Chun Wah Commercial Association	振華貿易團	Zhenhua Maoyi Tuan	Vancouver Business Association. Early Twentieth Century.
Chung San Fook Sun Tong (Also See Heung-san Fook Sun Tong)	中山福善堂	Zhongshan Fushan Tang	Locality Association: Chung-san (Heung-san)
Chung Shan Lung Jen Association	中山隆鎮/同鄉會	Zhongshan Longzhen Tongxianghui	Locality Association. Chung-san (Heung-san). Longchen Xiang.
Chung Shan University Alumni Association	中山大學同學會	Zhongshan Daxue Tongxuehui	
Chung Tim Fong	仲添芳	Zhong Tian Fang	Clan Association Surname: Chow (Zhou).
Chung Wah Youth League	中華青年團	Zhonghua Qingnian Tuan	Youth Branch Of KMT, Winnipeg.
Commission For Overseas Chinese Affairs	僑務委員會	Qiaowu Weiyuanhui	
Da Zhong Bao	大眾報	Da Zhong Bao	Left-wing Vancouver Newspaper.
Dai Luk Bo (Mainland Times)	大陸報	Da Lu Bao	Early Vancouver Newspaper.
Dang Sing Dang	戥誠黨	Zan Sheng Zan	Chinese Mining Company Of The 1870's. Possibly Colloquially Known As "Dancing Dan".
Dart Coon	洪門達權社	Hungmen Daquan She	Organization In The Freemasons Group.
Dat Yan School	達人學校	Daren Xuexiao	Vancouver School
Doe Kai	渡溪公所	Du Xi Gongsuo	
Duolunduo Shang Bao (Chinatown Commercial News)	多倫多商報	Duolunduo Shangbao	Toronto Newspaper

GLOSSARY

NAMES OF ORGANIZATIONS

Local/Standard Usage	Characters	Pinyin	Identification
East Wind Club	東風会	Dongfeng Hui	Left-wing Youth Association, Montreal.
Empire Reform Association	保皇会	Bao Huang Hui	"XZD"
Five Districts Association Of Hong Kong	五邑同鄉会	Wuyi Tongxianghui	The Association Represented The Four Districts Of The Sze-Yap Plus Hok-san (An Adjacent County).
Fook Sin Tong (see Chung-san Fook Sun Tong)	福善堂	Fushan Tang	
Freemasons, Chinese (see Chinese Freemasons)	洪門民治党		
Fukien Association	福建華僑鄉会	Fujian Tongxianghui	Locality Association For Hokkien-speaking Chinese From The Philippines.
Fong Loon Tong	鳳鳴堂	Fenglun Tang	Clan Association. Surnames: Seto,See,Tse (Situ,Xue,Xie). Known As Fong Lun Society In Toronto.
Gee How Oak Tin	至孝篤親公所	Zhixiaodu Qinkongsuo	Clan Association. Surnames: Chan,Wu,Yuan (Chen,Hu,Yuan). Known As Gee How Tong In Montreal.

Gee Poy Guo Tong	朱沛国堂	Zhu Peiguo Tang	Clan Association. Surnames: Chen,Gee (Zhu).
Gim Lee Yuen	金利源罐记	Jin Li Yuan Xing Ji	Early Vancouver Business Firm.
Gongyi Gongsuo	公一公所	Gongyi Gongsuo	Early Vancouver Business Association.
Hai Fung Association	海峰会	Haifeng Hui	Recreation Club. Vancouver.
Heng Tong Kung-so	横塘公所	Hengtang Gungsuo	Locality Association. Toronto.
Heungsan Fooksin Tong	香山福善堂	Xiangshan Fushan Tang	Locality Association: Heung-san (Chung-san).
Ho Lu Kong Tong	何卢江堂	Ho Lu Jiang Tang	Clan Association. Surname: Ho.
Hoi-ping Kwong Fook Tong	開平广福堂	Kaiping Guangfu Tang	
Hoi Yin Kung-so	海宴公所	Haiyan Gongsuo	Locality Association. Toi-san Xian.
Hon Hsing Athletic Club	汉升体育会	Hansheng Tiyuhui	Vancouver Athletic Club For The Surname Wong.
Hong Hang Society	No Characters Available		
Hop Kee	合记	He Ji	Early Victoria Business Firm.
Hoy Ping District Association	開平会館	Kaiping Huiguan	Locality Association,Hoi-ping.
Hoy Sun Ning Yung	台山寧陽會館	Taishan Ningyang Huiguan	Locality Association,Toi-san.
Hsin Min-kuo Pao	新民國報	Xin Minguo Bao	New Republic Daily. Published In Vancouver And Victoria By The Kuomintang.
Huaqiao Xuexiao	華僑學校	Huaqiao Xuexiao	Victoria School.
Huaxing Shiye Gongsi	華興實業公司	Huaxing Shiye Gongsi	Nineteenth Century Chinese Company. Nanaimo B.C.

GLOSSARY

NAMES OF ORGANIZATIONS

Local/Standard Usage	Characters	Pinyin	Identification
Huaying Ribao	華英日報	Huaying Ribao	Christian Newspaper. Vancouver About 1906
Hum Kwong Yee Tong	譚光裕堂	Tan Guangyu Tang	Clan Association. Surname: Tan,Tom,Hum.
Hung Chung Pao	洪鐘時報	Hong Zhong Bao	Toronto Freemasons Newspaper. Ceased Publication. 1950's.
Hung Men Hui	洪門會	Hong Men Hui	Anti-dynastic Secret Society. South China. Forbear Of Freemasons.
Hung Shun Tong	洪順堂	Hong Shun Tang	South China Forbear Of Freemasons.
Ing Suey Sun Tong (Also Ng Hoy Sun Tong)	伍胥山堂	Wu Xushan Tang	Clan Association. Vancouver. Surname:Eng (Wu).
Jen Guan Alumni Association	真光同學會	Zhenguang Tongxuehui	
Jianada Zhongguo Chenbao	加拿大中國晨報	Jianada Zhongguo Chenbao	"Left" Kuomintang Newspaper, 1920's.
Jin Hung Sing Operatic Association	振洪聲音樂社	Zhen Hung Sheng Yinyue She	
Jin Wah Sing Musical Association	振華聲音樂社	Zhen Hua Sheng Yinyue She	

Jung Wing Young Association (see Cheng Wing Yeong Tong)	新會穎川堂		
Ko Yeung Reading Room	高陽書報社	Gaoyang Shubaoshe	Clan Association. Surnames: Hui.Hoy (Xu).
Kong Chow District Association	岡州會館	Gangzhou Huiguan	Locality Association. Sun-wui
Kuan Sing Fong (see Quon Sing Fong)	群勝房		
Kuangchow University Alumni Association	廣州大學校友	Guangzhou Daxue Xiaoyouhui	
Kuomintang	國民党	Guomindang	Chinese Nationalist Party (KMT).
Kwong An Lung Company	廣安隆公司	Guang An Long Gongsi	Nineteenth Century Chinese Company. Victoria.
Kwong Chi School	廣智學校	Guangzhi Xuexiao	Victoria School Run By Yin-ping Association.
Kwong Do School	弘道學校	Hongdao Xuexiao	Toronto School Run By Freemasons.
Kwong Fook Tong	廣福堂	Guangfu Tang	Locality Association.Hoi-ping.
Kwong Hoi United Association	廣海同鄉會	Guanghai Tongxianghui	Locality Association. Toi-san
Kwong Lee	廣利	Guang Li	Nineteenth Century Chinese Company. British Columbia.
Lam Sai Ho Tong	林西河堂	Lin Xihe Tang	Clan Association. Surname: Lam (Lin.Lim.Lum)
Lee Clan Association	李氏公所	Lishi Gongsuo	Clan Association Surname: Lee (Li)

279

GLOSSARY

Local/Standard Usage	Characters	NAMES OF ORGANIZATIONS Pinyin	Identification
Lee Gee Wing Tong	No Characters Available		
Lee Kwong Kai Society	李廣溪堂	Li Gongxi Tang	Clan Association. Surname: Li From Hoi-ping.
Lee Long Sai Tong	李隴西堂	Li Longxi Tang	Clan Association. Surname: Lee (Li) From Long-sai Xiang. Hoi-ping.
Lee Tun Tsung Tong	李敦宗堂	Li Dunzong Tang	Clan Association. Surname: Lee (Li).
Leong Chung How Tong	梁忠孝堂	Liang Zhongxiao Tang	Clan Association. Surname: Leong.Leung (Liang).
Lew Mow Way Tong	廖武威堂	Liao Wuwei Tang	Clan Association. Surname: Lew (Liao)
Lian Chang Company	聯昌公司	Lian Chang Gongsi	Early Chinese Business Concern, Victoria.
Lien-ching Society	聯警社	Lian Jing She	Theatrical Group.
Lim Kow-mock Kung-so	林九牧公所	Lin Jiumu Gongsuo	Clan Association. Surname: Lim,Lam,Lum (Lin).
Lim Sai Ho Tong (see Lam Sai Ho Tong)	林西河堂		
Look Ming Reading Room	鹿鳴別墅	Luming Bieshu	Clan Association. Surnames:Wong (Wang And Huang) From Toi-san.
Lor Yu Chang Tong	羅豫章堂	Luo Yuzhang Tang	Clan Association. Surname Lo,Lor (Luo)

Lung Kong Kung Suo　　　　　Longgang Gongsuo　　　Clan Association. Surnames:
龐涵公所　　　　　　　　　　　　　　　　　　　　　Lew,Kwan,Chang,Chew
　　　　　　　　　　　　　　　　　　　　　　　　Lau,Kuan,Cheung,Chao
　　　　　　　　　　　　　　　　　　　　　　　　(Liu,Guan,Zhang,Zhao)

Le Qun School　　　　　　　Lequn Yishu　　　　　　Early Victoria School.
樂群義塾

Mah Gim Gee Tong　　　　　Ma Jin Zi Tang　　　　Clan Association. Surname: Ma.
馬金姿堂

Mah Society　　　　　　　　Mashi Gongsuo　　　　　Clan Association. Surname: Ma
馬氏公所

Man Wah School　　　　　　Wenhua Xuexiao　　　　Vancouver School.
文華學校

Mark Si Hing Tong　　　　Mai Shi Xing Tang　　Clan Association.
麥始興堂　　　　　　　　　　　　　　　　　　　　Surname: Mark (Mai).

Min Sing Reading Room　　Minxing Yuebao She　　Clan Association.
民星閱報社　　　　　　　　　　　　　　　　　　　Surnames:Wong (Wang And
　　　　　　　　　　　　　　　　　　　　　　　　Huang From Hoiping)

Minzhidang　　　　　　　　Minzhidang
(see Chinese Freemasons)
民治党

Mon Keong School　　　　　Wenjiang Xuexiao　　　Chinese School Run By
文疆學校　　　　　　　　　　　　　　　　　　　Wong Kung Har Tong.
　　　　　　　　　　　　　　　　　　　　　　　　Vancouver.

Mon Sheong Foundation　　Meng Chang Ciyou Hui　Toronto Welfare Association.
孟嘗慈幼会　　　　　　　　　　　　　　　　　　Mostly Professional In
　　　　　　　　　　　　　　　　　　　　　　　　Membership. Founded 1960's.

Nam-hoi District Association　Nanhai Huiguan　Locality Association:
南海会館　　　　　　　　　　　　　　　　　　　Nam-hoi.

Nam-ping Bitsuey　　　　　Nanping Bieshu　　　　Locality Association: Hoi-ping.
南平别墅

Nam Young Tong　　　　　　Nanyang Zhongtang　　Clan Association. Surnames:
南陽總堂　　　　　　　　　　　　　　　　　　　Yip,Dong,Jang,Sam,(Yeh,
　　　　　　　　　　　　　　　　　　　　　　　　Ding,Zheng,Cen).

GLOSSARY

NAMES OF ORGANIZATIONS

Local/Standard Usage	Characters	Pinyin	Identification
Ng Hoy San Tong	俉齊山堂	Wu Xushan Tang	
Ning Yung Yu Hing Tong (see Hoy Sun Ning Yeung)	寧陽餘慶堂	Ning Yang Yu Qing Tang	
North American Alumni Of Poy Ching	培正同學会	Peizheng Tongxuehui	Poy Ching (Pui Ching) Is A Prestigeous Hong Kong Middle School
Oi-Kwok Hok-tong	愛國學堂	Aiguo Xuetang	School Operated By Empire Reform Association (XZD).
On Hing	安興	An Xing	Chinese Company. Victoria.1870's.
Ottawa United Chinese Association	加拿大渥京中華聯誼会	Jianada Kejing Zhonghua Lienyi Hui	
Oylin Society	愛蓮公所	Ailian Gongsuo	Clan Association. Surnames: Eng.Ng.Chew.Chao (Wu.Zhou).
Qiaosheng Ribao	僑聲日報	Qiaosheng Ribao	Vancouver Newspaper
Quon Lung Sai Tong	羣龍儞西堂	Qun Lungxi Tang	Clan Association.surname: Kwan.Quon,Kuan,(Guan) From Long-sai Xiang. Hoi-ping.
Quan Sing Fong	羣勝坊	Guan Sheng Fang	Clan Association. Surnames: Chan,Kwan,Quon. (Chen,Guan).
Quong Lee	廣利	Guang Li	Nineteenth Century Chinese Mining Company.B.C.

Sam Gee	森記	Sen Ji	Chinese Company. Victoria,1870's
Sam Kee	三記	San Ji	Late Nineteenth Century Chinese Company, Vancouver.
Sam Duck Tong	三德堂	Sande Tang	Clan Association. Surnames Chow,Choy,Eng,Ng,Yeung,Young (Zhou,Cai,Wu,Yang).
Sam Yap District Association	三邑同鄉會	San Yi Torgxianghui	Locality Association For The Three Adjacent Counties Of Nam-hoi,Poon-yue And Sun-dak.
San Min Chu I Youth Corps	三民主義青年團	Sanminzhuyi Qingniantuan	San-min Chu-I Ch'ing-nien-t'uan.
Shao-nien Chung-kuo Chen-pao	少年中國晨報	Shaonian Zhongguo Chenbao	San Francisco Chinese Newspaper. Kuomintang.
Shar Duey Mutual Society	沙堆陳安會	Shadui Qiao An Hui	Locality Association, Sun-wui.
Shing Kiu Opera Company	醒僑劇場社	Xing Qiao Xishe	
Ship Toy Yen Association (She-chu Yuen Theatre Society)	涉趣園劇易社	Shequyuan Xishe	Theatrical And Recreational Association.
Shing Wah Daily News (Shing Wah Yat Bo)	醒華日報	Xing Hua Ribao	Toronto Newspaper (KMT).
Shoon Duck Association	順德堂	Shunde Tang	Locality Association: Sun-tak
Shon Yee Benevolent Association (Tit-shing Shon-yee)	鐵城崇義會	Tiecheng Chongyi Hui	Locality Association: Chung-san.
Sien Lok Society	善樂社	Shanle She	Chinese Civic Association, Calgary
Sing Dan	勝蛋	Sheng Zan	Nineteenth Century Chinese Mining Company

283

GLOSSARY

NAMES OF ORGANIZATIONS

Local/Standard Usage	Characters	Pinyin	Identification
S.P.O.T.A.	土達孔身業主协进咨协会	Shitakongna Yezhu Yu Juke Xiehui	Strathcona Property Owners And Tenants Association.
S.U.C.C.E.S.S.	中僑互助会	Zhongqiao Huzhu Hui	Vancouver Social Welfare Association Founded Early 1970's
Sue Yuen Tong	緆源統堂	Suyuan Zhongtang	Clan Association. Surnames:Lew,Louie,Fong,Kwong (Lu,Liu,Fang,Kuang)
Sun Ning Yu Hing Tong	新寧餘慶堂	Xinning Yuqing Tang	Nineteenth Century Locality Association,Victoria Locality:Toi-san.
Sun Mun-kwok Po (see Hsin Min-kuo Pao)	新民國報	Xin Minguo Bao	
Sun-wui Fook Ching Tong	新会福慶堂	Xinhui Fuqing Tang	Locality Association: Sun-wui.
Tai Cheung	泰昌	Tai Chang	Nineteenth Century Chinese Company,Victoria.
Tai-hon Kung-po	大漢公報	Dahan Gongbao	The Chinese Times.
Tai Kung Charity School	大应義塾	Dagong Yixue	Chinese School Run By Vancouver Freemasons.
Tai Soong	泰崇	Tai Sun	Nineteenth Century Chinese Company,Victoria
Tai Yoon	泰源	Tai Yuan	Nineteenth Century Chinese Company,Victoria

Tam Kung Temple	譚公廟	Tan Gong Miao	Victoria Temple Dedicated To Popular South China Deity.
Tit-sing Shon Yee (see Shon Yee Association)	鐵城崇義會		
Tong-yuen Wui	同源會	Tongyuan Hui	"Chinese-Canadian Club".
Tung Shan Reading Room	東山書報社	Dongshan Shubaoshe	
United Chinese Association (see Ottawa United Chinese Association)	加拿大柯華中崋聯誼會		
Villa Kung Shang	No Characters Available		
Wah Ying Yat Po	華英日報	Huaying Ribao	Early Vancouver Newspaper.
Wing Cheung	永昌	Yung Chang	Nineteenth Century Chinese Company, Victoria
Wong Kung Har Tong	黄江夏堂	Huang Jiangxia Tang	Clan Association. Surnames: Wong (Wang And Huang)
Wong Wun San	黄雲山公所	Wong Yunshan Gongsuo	Clan Association. Surnames: Wong (Wong And Huang)
(Minzhu) Xianzhengdang (XZD)	憲政黨	Xianzhengdang	Constitutional Party. Successor To Empire Reform Association.
Yan Chung San Tsung Tong	顏中山総堂	Yan Zhongshan Zongtang	Clan Association. Surname: Yan.
Yan Wo Sang	源和盛	Yuan He Sheng	Nineteenth Century Chinese Company, Victoria

285

GLOSSARY

NAMES OF ORGANIZATIONS

Local/Standard Usage	Characters	Pinyin	Identification
Yat Sun Po	日新報	Rixinbao	Early Vancouver Newspaper. Published By The Empire Reform Association.
Yan Wo Tong	人和堂	Ren He Tang	Hakka Association, Victoria About 1872.
Yee Fung Toy Tong	余風采堂	Yu Fengcai Tang	Clan Association. Surname:Yee (Yu)
Yee Loo Reading Room	怡盧書報社	Yilu Shubaoshe	
Yeuk Tsai School	育才學校	Yucai Xuexiao	Vancouver School
Yeuk Yan School	育人學校	Yuren Xuexiao	Vancouver School
Yeuk Ying School	育英學校	Yuying Xuexiao	Vancouver School
Yin Ping District Association (Yin-ping Tong Fook Tong)	恩平同福堂	Enping Tong Fu Tang	Locality Association, Yin-ping.
Yit Shaw Reading Room	粵秀書報社	Yuexiu Shubaoshe	
Yue San Association (Also Chong Hoo Tong)	禺山公所	Yushan Gongsuo	Locality Association. Poon-yue.
Yuet Sing Cantonese Music Club	粵聲音樂社	Yue Sheng Yinyue She	
Zhaoyi Gongsuo	昭一公所	Zhaoyi Gongsuo	Early Vancouver Commercial Association.

Zhigongdang 致公党
(see Chinese Freemasons)

Zhonghua Gongtang 中华工堂 Chinese Labour Union.

Zhonghua Ren'ai 中华仁爱周济会馆 Victoria Chinese Consolidated
Zhouji Huiguan Benevolent Association (CCBA).

CHINESE COMMUNITIES IN CANADA

Local/Standard Usage	Characters	Pinyin	Meaning
Baihua	白話	Baihua	Vernacular speech.
Bitsuey	別墅	Bieshu	Lit: "Villa". One term for association building.
Caibo	財帛	Caibo	God of Wealth.
Chongyang	重陽	Chongyang	Autumn grave worship.
Chukoupiao	出口栗	Chukoupiao	Exit fee.
Dim Sum	點心	Dianxin	Snacks and pastries eaten in teahouses.
Fangkou	房口	Fangkou	Collective households. Often based on locality or surname ties.
Fantan	番攤	Fantan	A gambling game. Bettors predict the number of buttons that will remain when groups of four are removed from a randomly selected pile.
Heung	鄉	Xiang	"Village alliance". Political unit below the xian.
Hokchiu	福州	Fuzhou	The Chinese language spoken in northern Fujian.
Hokkien	福建	Fujian	The Chinese language spoken in southern Fujian.
Huaqiao Fangong Qiuguo Gongyue Yundong	華僑反共救國公約運動		Movement to sign the "Overseas Chinese Anti-communist National Salvation Covenant".
I-fao	二埠	Erfu	Lit: "Second Port". New Westminster B.C.
Jiefang	街坊	Jiefang	"Neighbourhood".
Kam-shaan A-paak	金山亞伯	Jinshan Abo	"Uncles from the Golden Mountain" (i.e North America). Returned Overseas Chinese.
Kuan-ti	關帝	Guandi	"God of Fraternity and Wealth".
Qingming	清明	Qingming	Spring grave worship.
Sze-yap	四邑	Siyi	The four adjacent counties of Tai-shan, Hoi-ping, En-ping and Sun-wui, located in the western part of the Canton delta. Along with Chung-shan, the point of origin of most Canadian Chinese.
Tianhou	天后	Tianhou	"Goddess of the Sea". Important south China deity. Patron Goddess of Taiwan, where she is known as Matsu.
Tusheng	土生	Tusheng	"Local born". Term applied to second generation Chinese born before 1962.
Weishan Zuile	為善最樂	Weishan Zuile	"The greatest happiness lies in being charitable". The Chinese saying from which the Sien Lok Association of Calgary took its name.

288

GLOSSARY

Local/Standard Usage	Characters	Pinyin	Meaning
Xian	縣	Xian	"County". Lowest level of Chinese Imperial government. A critical locus for the identity of Chinese abroad.
Xiansheng	先生	Xiansheng	"Teacher", "Gentleman".
Yap-kong	入礦	Rukuang	Lit: "to enter the mines". Used by older immigrants in British Columbia to mean to go to the interior of the province.

289

NAMES OF PLACES AND INDIVIDUALS

Local/Standard Usage	Characters	Meyer-Wempe	Pinyin	Wade-Giles
Ah Kay	阿 熾	Ah K'ei	A Qi	A Ch'i
Ah Hing	阿 興	Ah Hing	A Xing	A Hsing
Ah Sou	阿 秀富	Ah Sau	A Shou	A Shou
Au Foo (see Charlie Foo)	區			
Cai Tingkai	蔡廷鍇	Tsui Ting-haai	Cai Tingkai	Ts'ai T'ing-k'ai
Chan Doe Gee (see Sam Kee)	陳道之	Chan To-chi	Chen Daozhi	Ch'en Tao-chih
Chan Nam·Sing	陳南星	Ch'an Naam-shing	Chen Nanxing	Ch'en Nan-hsing
Paul Chan	陳保羅	Ch'an Po-lo	Chen Baolo	Ch'en Pao-lo
Chan Sing-kai	陳陞階	Ch'an Shing-tsai	Chen Shengji	Ch'en Sheng-chi
Chan Sue-yan	陳樹人	Ch'an Shue-yan	Chen Shuren	Ch'en Shu-jen
Chan Yu	陳耀	Ch'an Iu	Chen Yao	Ch'en Yao
Chan Yu Tan	陳耀壇	Ch'an Iu-t'aan	Chen Yaotan	Ch'en Yao-t'an
Carsun Chang	張君勱	Cheung Kwan-mai	Zhang Junmai	Chang Chun-mai
Ch'en Ch'ing-yun	陳慶雲	Ch'an Hing-wan	Chen Qingyun	Ch'en Ch'ing-yun
Ch'en Chiung-ming	陳炯明	Ch'an Kwing-ming	Chen Jiongming	Ch'en Chiung-ming
Chen Lanbin	陳蘭彬	Ch'an Laan-pan	Chen Lanbin	Ch'en Lan-pin
Chen Wenxi	陳文錫	Ch'an Man-sek	Chen Wenxi	Ch'en Wen-hsi
Cheng Tien-fong	程天放	Ch'ing Tin-fong	Cheng Tianfang	Ch'eng T'ien-fang
Chew Yuk	趙昱	Ch'iu Yuk	Zhao Yu	Chao Yu
Chiang Kai-shek	蔣介石	Tseung Kaai-shek	Jiang Jieshi	Chiang Chieh-shih
Chin Fa-shen	岑發琛	Sham Fat-shaan	Cen Fashen	Ts'en Fa-shen
Chong Tsoo	張滔	Cheung Tso	Zhang Tao	Chang T'ao
Chong Ying	張子田	Cheung Tsz-tin	Zhang Zitian	Chang Tze-t'ien
George Chow	No Characters Available			
Chu Chi-ngok	徐子樂	Ts'ui Tsz-ngok	Xu Zilo	Hsu Tze-lo
Chu Hsi	趙喜	Chiu Hei	Zhao Xi	Chao Hsi
Chu P'ing-shen	趙屏珊	Chiu P'ing-shaan	Zhao Pingshan	Chao P'ing-shan
Philip Chu	No Characters Available			
Chung Gim	蔣金	Tseung Kam	Jiang Jin	Chiang Chin
Chung Shan	中山	Chung Shaan	Zhongshan	Chung-shan
Chung Yeh	蔣銳	Tseung Yiu	Jiang Rui	Chiang Jui
Cumyow (Alexander, Won)	溫金有	Wan Kam-yau	Wen Jinyou	Wen Chin-yu
Feng Chin-ch'un	馮錦淳	Fung Kam-shun	Feng Jinchun	Feng Chin-ch'un
Feng Tzu-yu	馮自由	Fung Tsz-yau	Feng Ziyou	Feng Tzu-yu
Fong Dickman	馮德文	Fung Dak-man	Feng Dewen	Feng Te-wen
Charlie Foo	區富	Au Foo	Ou Fu	Ou Fu
Foon Sien	黄文甫	Wong Man-p'o	Huang Wenpu	Huang Wen-p'u
Fujian	福建	Fuk-kin	Fujian	Fu-chien

290

GLOSSARY

Local/Standard Usage	Characters	Meyer-Wempe	Pinyin	Wade-Giles
Guangdong	廣 東	Kwongtung	Guangdong	Kuangtung (Kwangtung)
Guangxi	廣 西	Kwongsai	Guangxi	Kuanghsi (Kwangsi)
Edward Gung	龔 邦 耀	Kung Pong-iu	Gung Bangyao	Kung Pang-yao
Guo Song-tao	郭 嵩 燾	Kwok Sung-t'oh	Guo Songtao	Kuo Sung-t'ao
Heung-san	香 山	Heung-shaan	Xiangshan	Hsiang-shan
Ho Lem	何 林	Ho Lam	He Lin	Ho Lin
Hoi-ping	開 平	Hoi-p'ing	Kaiping	K'ai-p'ing
Hok-san	鶴 山	Hok-shaan	Heshan	Ho-shan (Hao-shan)
Joseph Hope	劉 先 祖	Lau Kwang-tso	Liu Guangzu	Liu Kuang-tsu
Hsia Chung-min	夏 中 民	Ha Chung-man	Xia Zhongmin	Hsia Chung-min
Hsu Chuan-li	徐 全 礼	Hui Ts'uen-lai	Xu Quanli	Hsu Ch'uan-li
Hu Han-min	胡 漢 民	Wu Hon-man	Hu Hanmin	Hu Han-min
Hu Shih	胡 適	Wu Shek	Hu Shi	Hu Shih
Huang Chi-lu	黃 季 陸	Wong Kwai-luk	Huang Jilu	Huang Chi-lu
Huang Cunxian	黃 遵 憲	Wong Tsun-hin	Huang Cunxian	Huang Tsun-hsien
Huang Hua Kang	黃 花 崗	Wong Fa Kong	Huanghuagang	Huang Hua Kang
Huang Hsing	黃 興	Wong Hing	Huang Xing	Huang Hsing
Huang Wen-shan	黃 文 山	Wong Man-shaan	Huang Wenshan	Huang Wen-shan
Huang Xiquan (Huang Sic-chen)	黃 錫 銓	Wong Sek-tsuen	Huang Xiquan	Huang Hsi-ch'uan
Hum Quan	譚 均	T'aam Kwan	Tan Jun	T'an Chun
Ing S.Hoan	吳 簇	Ng Hung	Wu Xiong	Wu Hsiung
Douglas Jung	鄭 天 華	Ching T'in-wa	Zheng Tianhua	Cheng T'ien-hua
Kang Youwei	康 有 為	Hong Yau-wai	Kang Youwei	K'ang Yu-wei
Kiang Kang-hu	江 亢 虎	Kong Hong-foo	Jiang Kanghu	Chiang K'ang-hu
Kong Moon	江 門	Kong Moon	Jiang Men	Chiang Men
Kwan Mow Lung	關 茂 龍	Kwaan Mau-lung	Guan Maolong	Kuan Mao-lung
Y N Kwan	關 耀 南	Kwaan Yu-naan	Guan Yaonan	Kuan Yao-nan
Normie Kwong	林 佐 民	Lam Tsoh-man	Lin Zuomin	Lin Tso-min
Lau Kwong-joo (see Joseph Hope)	劉 先 祖			
Art Lee	李 僑 棟	Lei K'iu-tong	Li Qiaodong	Li Ch'iao-tung
Lee Chee (see Li You-chin)	李 池 (李 佑 芹)			
Lee Chong	李 祥	Lei Ts'eung	Li Xiang	Li Hsiang
Frank Lee (Lee To-chan)	李 道 軫	Lei To-chan	Li Daozhen	Li Tao-chen
Lee Hong-yuey		No Characters Available		

291

NAMES OF PLACES AND INDIVIDUALS

Local/Standard Usage	Characters	Meyer-Wempe	Pinyin	Wade-Giles
Lee Mong Kow	李夢九	Lei Mung-kau	Li Mengjiu	Li Meng-chiu
Raymond C Lee	李耀明	Lei Iu-ming	Li Yaoming	Li Yao-ming
Lee Sai-fan	李世璠	Lei Shai-fan	Li Shifan	Li Shih-fan
Lee Yuk-chin	李育泉	Lei Yuk-ts'uen	Li Yuquan	Li Yu-ch'uan
David C Lew (Lew Hong-chung	廖鴻翔	Liu Hong-ts'eung	Liao Hongxiang	Liao Hung-hsiang
Li Congren	李宗仁	Lei Sung-yan	Li Congren	Li Tsung-jen
Li Hongzhang	李鴻章	Lei Hung-cheung	Li Hongzhang	Li Hung-chang
Li Tian-pei	李天沛	Lei T'in-p'ooi	Li Tianpei	Li T'ien-p'ei
Li Yi-te	李奕德	Lei Yik-tak	Li Yide	Li I-te
Li Ying-san	李奕三	Lei Ying-saam	Li Yingsan	Li Ying-san
Li You-chin	李佑芹	Lei Oo-k'an	Li Youchin	Li Yu-ch'in
Li Yu	李堯	Lei Oo	Li Yao	Li Yao
Liang Qichao	粱啟超	Leung K'ai-ch'iu	Liang Qichao	Liang Ch'i-ch'ao
Lim Bang	林礼斌	Lam Lai-pan	Lin Libin	Lin Li-pin
Lim, Charlie Ting (Charles L.F.Ting)	林煥庭	Lam Oon-t'ing	Lin Huanting	Lin Huan-t'ing
Lim Duck Shew	林德紹	Lam Dak-shiu	Lin Deshao	Lin Te-shao
Lim Hon-yuen	林翰元	Lam Hon-uen	Lin Hanyuan	Lin Han-yuan
James Y Lim (Jim Lim)	林举振	Lam Kui-chan	Lin Juzhen	Lin Chu-chen
Lin Li-fong	林立晃	Lam Laap-wong	Lin Lihuang	Lin Li-huang
Lin Sen	林森	Lam Sham	Lin Sen	Lin Sen
(Dr) Liu Shih-shun	劉師舜	Lau Sz-shun	Liu Shishun	Liu Shih-shun
Liu Wei-chih	劉維熾	Lau Wai-ch'i	Liu Weizhi	Liu Wei-chih
Liu Rukun	劉儒楚	Lau Ue-kwan	Liu Rukun	Liu Ju-k'un
Loo Gee Wing	盧梓榮	Lo Tsz-wing	Luo Ziyong	Lo Tzu-yung
(Dr) Henry Lore	羅景燿	Lo King-iu	Luo Jingyao	Lo Ching-yao
Louie Ming-ha	雷鳴夏	Lui Ming-ha	Lei Mingxia	Lei Ming-hsia
Low Chew-yuen	羅超然	Lo Ch'iu-in	Luo Chaoran	Lo Ch'ao-jan
Lum Jo-yin	林佐然	Lam Tsoh-in	Lin Zuoran	Lin Tso-jan
(Dr) Kalfred Dip Lum	林晋	Lam Dip	Lin Die	Lin Tieh
Luo Fenglu	羅豐祿	Lo Fung-luk	Luo Fenglu	Lo Feng-lu
Ma Chao-I	馬超俊	Ma Ch'iu-yik	Ma Chaoyi	Ma Ch'ao-I
Ma Hsin-ming	馬心銘	Ma Saam-ming	Ma Xinming	Ma Hsin-ming
Mah Seung	馬湘	Ma Seung	Ma Xiang	Ma Hsiang
Ma T K Wou	馬窺湖	Ma King-oo	Ma Jinghu	Ma Ching-hu
E C Mark (Mark Sik-chew)	麥錫舟	Mak Sek-chau	Mai Xizhou	Mai Hsi-chou
George P Mark (Mak Po-lo)	麥保羅	Mak Po-lo	Mai Baolo	Mai Pao-lo
Mark Moon	麥文	Mak Man	Mai Wen	Mai Wen
T C Mark	麥度舟	Mak Tso-chau	Mai Zaozhou	Mai Tsao-chou

GLOSSARY

Local/Standard Usage	Characters	Meyer-Wempe	Pinyin	Wade-Giles
Mei Xian	梅縣	Mooi Uen	Mei Xian	Mei Hsien
Mui-kok Heung	梅角鄉	Mooi-kok Heung	Meijiao Xiang	Mei-chiao Hsiang
Nam Hoi	南海	Naam Hoi	Nanhai	Nan-hai
Ng Mon-hing	伍文慶	Ng Man-hing	Wen Wuqing	Wu Wen-ch'ing
(Dr) S K Ngai	艾世光	Ngaai Sai-kwong	Ai Shiguang	Ai Shih-kuang
Ou-yang Keng	歐陽慶	Au-yeung Kang	Ouyang Geng	Ou-yang Keng
Pang Song	彭崇	Paang Shung	Peng Chong	P'eng Ch'ung
Pun-yue	番禺	P'oon-yue	Panyu	P'an-yu
Sam Kee (see Chan Doe-geé)	三記(陳道之)			
Sam-yap	三邑	Saam-yap	Sanyi	San-I
Sun-ning	新寧	San-ning	Xinning	Hsin-ning
San-wui	新會	San-ooi	Xinhui	Hsin-hui
Seto Mei-tang	司徒美堂	Sz-t'o Mei-t'ong	Situ Meitang	Ssu-t'u Mei-t'ang
Seto Ying-shek (Seto More)	司徒羹石 (司徒旄)	Sz-t'o Ying-shek Sz-t'u Mo	Situ Yingshi Situ Mao	Ssu-t'u Ying-shih Ssu-t'u Mao
(Prof) C C Shih	史景成	Sz King-shing	Shi Jingcheng	Shih Ching-ch'eng
Sun-dak	順德	Shun-tak	Shunde	Shun-te
Sim Fa-shen (see Chin Fa-shen)	岑發琛			
Jack Sim	No Characters Available			
T V Soong	宋子文	Sung Sz-man	Sung Ziwen	Sung Tzu-wen
Sun Yat-sen	孫中山 (孫逸仙)	Sun Chung-shaan (Sun Yat-sin)	Sun Zhongshan	Sun Chung-shan
Swatow	汕頭	Shaan-t'au	Shantou	Shan-t'ou
Sze-yap	四邑	Sz-yap	Siyi	Ssu-I
Taai-leung Heung	大良鄉	Taai-leung Heung	Daliang Xiang	Ta-liang Hsiang
Tang Hua-lung	湯化龍	T'ong Fa-lung	Tang Hualong	T'ang Hua-lung
T'ao Hsing-chih	陶行知	T'o Hang-chi	Tao Xingzhi	T'ao Hsing-chih
Toi-san	台山	T'oi-shaan	Taishan	T'ai-shan
Tom Yee	譚義	Taam I	Tan Yi	T'an I
Tong Fat	董發	Tung Faat	Dong Fa	Tung Fa
Tong Kee	董基	Tung Kei	Dong Ji	Tung Chi
Tsang Shek-chun	曾石泉	Tsang Shek-ts'uen	Zeng Shiquan	Tseng Shih-ch'uan
Tsang Shing	增城	Tsang Sheng	Zeng Cheng	Tseng Ch'eng
Tseng Chi-tse	曾紀澤	Tsang Kei-chaak	Zeng Jize	Tseng Chi-tse
(Dr) Chilien Tsur	周啓濂	Chau K'ai-lim	Zhou Qilian	Chou Ch'i-lien
Tung Koon	東莞	Tung-koon	Dongguan	Tung-kuan

NAMES OF PLACES AND INDIVIDUALS

Local/Standard Usage	Characters	Meyer-Wempe	Pinyin	Wade-Giles
Wang Ching-wei	汪精衛	Wang Tsing-wai	Wang Jingwei	Wang Ching-wei
Wong Bock-yue	黃伯耀	Wong Paak-iu	Huang Baiyao	Huang Pai-yao
Fairman Wong	黃發文	Wong Faat-man	Huang Fawen	Huang Fa-wen
Wong Man-po (see Foon Sien)	黃文甫			
Wong Sam-duck	黃三德	Wong Saam-tak	Huang Sande	Huang San-te
Wong Sam-gwai	黃深貴	Wong Shaam-kwai	Huang Shengui	Huang Shen-kuei
Wong Suey Chao	黃瑞朝	Wong Sui-ch'iu	Huang Ruichao	Huang Jui-ch'ao
Wong Suey Sang	黃瑞生	Wong Sui-saang	Huang Ruisheng	Huang Jui-sheng
Wong Tin Louis	黃天侶	Wong Tin-lui	Huang Tianlu	Huang T'ien-lu
Wong Yan-hao (see Wong Suey Chao)	黃彥豪	Wong In-ho	Huang Yanhao	Huang Yen-hao
Wong Yau-mui	黃友梅	Wong Yau-mooi	Huang Youmei	Huang Yu-mei
Wong Yick	王益	Wong Yik	Wang Yi	Wang I
Ma T.K. Wou (see Ma)	馬鏡湖			
Wu Shang-ying	吳尚鷹	Ng Sheung-ying	Wu Shangying	Wu Shang-ying
Wu Pei-fu	吳佩孚	Ng P'ooi-fu	Wu Peifu	Wu P'ei-fu
Wuzhou	梧州	Ng-chau	Wuzhou	Wu-chou
Xue Fucheng	薛福成	Tse Fuk-shing	Xue Fucheng	Hsueh Fu-ch'eng
Yang Shuwen	楊書雯	Yeung Shue-man	Yang Shuwen	Yang Shu-wen
Yin-ping	恩平	Yan-ping	Enping	En-p'ing
K Dock Yip	葉求鐸	Ip K'au-tok	Ye Qiuduo	Yeh Ch'iu-to
Yip Kew Mow	葉求茂	Ip K'au-mau	Ye Qiumao	Yeh Ch'iu-mao
Yip Sang (Ip Chun-tin)	葉生/葉春田	Ip Saang (Ip Ch'un-tin)	Ye Sheng (Ye Chuntian)	Yeh Sheng (Yeh Ch'un-t'ien)
Yip Wai-pak	葉惠伯	Ip Waai-paak	Ye Huibo	Yeh Hui-po
Susan Yipsang	葉金陵	Ip Kam-ling	Ye Jinling	Yeh Chin-ling
Paul Yu Pin (Bishop)	于斌	Ue Paan	Yu Bin	Yu Pin
Yuan Shih-k'ai	袁世凱	Uen Sai-hoi	Yuan Shikai	Yuan Shih-k'ai
Gordon Yuen	阮賡唐	Uen Kang-t'ong	Yuan Gengtang	Yuan Keng-t'ang
S Yuen		No Characters Available		
Zeng Jize	曾紀澤	Tsang Kei-chaak	Zeng Jize	Tseng Chi-tse
Zhang Yinhuan	張蔭桓	Tseung Yam-oon	Zhang Yinhuan	Chang Yin-huan
Zheng Caoru	鄭藻如	Ching Tso-iu	Zheng Caoru	Cheng Tsao-ju
Zhao Yu (see Chew Yuk)	趙昱			

Appendix: Tables

TABLE 1

Chinese Immigration and Population Estimates, 1880-1901

Year	Entries	Exits	Net Immigration	Est. Total Population
1880				3,500[a]
1881	2,939			4,383[b]
1882	8,083			12,000
1883	3,223			15,000
1884	2,762[c]			17,000
1885	1,200[d]			13,000
1886	212	829	−617	11,400
1887	124	734	−610	10,800
1888	290	868	−578	10,100
1889	892	1,322	−430	9,600
1890	1,166	1,671	−505	9,100
1891	2,125	1,617	508	9,129[b]
1892	3,282	2,168	1,114	9,110
1893	2,258	1,277	891	9,800
1894	2,109	666	1,443	10,400
1895	1,462	473	989	11,000
1896	1,786	696	1,089	11,500
1897	2,471	768	1,703	12,200
1898	2,192	802	1,390	12,600
1899	4,402	859	3,543	13,500
1900	4,257	1,102	3,155	15,000
1901	2,544	1,204	1,340	17,321[e]

a. Estimate from Public Archives of B.C. CC 30.14.
b. *Census of Canada*, 1881, I, p. 300; 1891, IV, p. 391.
c. Does not include November-December, 1884.
d. Estimate from Morton, *In the Sea of Sterile Mountains*, pp. 131, 135.
e. *Census of Canada*, 1911, II, p. 367. The adjusted figure of 1911 for 1901 is used because it puts the Chinese on the same "origin" basis as the censuses of 1911 and after.

Sources: *Census of Canada*, 1881, I, p. 300; 1891, IV, p. 391; Sedgwick, "The Context of Economic Change and Continuity in an Urban Overseas Chinese Community," p. 204; Lee Tung-hai, pp. 414-17; Morton, *In the Sea of Sterile Mountains*, pp. 131, 135; *1885 Royal Commission*, p. 398; Cheng Tien-fang, *Oriental Immigration in Canada*, p. 272.

TABLE 2

Chinese Immigration to Canada, 1947-61			
Year	Total Number of Immigrants to Canada	Chinese Immigrants	Chinese as Percentage of Total Immigration
1947	64,127	21	0.03
1948	125,414	33	0.03
1949	95,217	734	0.77
1950	73,912	1,746	2.36
1951	194,391	2,708	1.39
1952	164,498	2,328	1.42
1953	168,868	1,936	1.15
1954	154,227	1,636	1.06
1955	109,946	2,535	2.31
1956	164,857	2,093	1.27
1957	282,167	1,662	0.59
1958	124,851	2,615	2.09
1959	106,928	2,516	2.35
1960	104,111	861	0.83
1961	71,689	894	1.25

Source: Dominion Immigration Statistics, 1947-61.

TABLE 3

	Total Number of Immigrants to Canada	Chinese Immigrants*	Chinese as Percentage of Total Immigration
1962	74,586	876	1.2
1963	93,151	1,571	1.7
1964	112,606	3,210	2.8
1965	146,758	5,234	3.6
1966	194,743	5,178	2.7
1967	222,876	6,409	2.9
1968	183,974	8,382	4.6
1969	161,531	8,272	5.1
1970	147,713	5,377	3.6
1971	121,900	5,807	4.8
1972	122,006	7,181	5.9
1973	184,200	16,094	8.7
1974	218,465	14,465	6.6
1975	187,881	13,166	7.0
1976	149,429	12,736	8.5

Immigration to Canada and Chinese Immigration, 1962-1976

* During 1962-66, statistics were kept with respect to "ethnic origin." From 1967, the relevant tables record "country of former residence" and "country of citizenship." Between 1967-70 the category China/Chinese (country of former residence) is linked with citizens of China, Britain and Colonies, Portugal, Other Asia, etc. Migrants of Chinese ethnic origin who did not migrate from a place on the China mainland (i.e., Hong Kong or Macao) or Taiwan and did not hold Chinese citizenship would not appear under the category China/Chinese. Thus, Overseas Chinese who held citizenship in their country of residence do not appear in the total.

Totals after 1967, therefore, somewhat underestimate the number of ethnic Chinese "arrivals." It is not easy to judge how significant this may be, but in 1966 Chinese from the West Indies numbered 233, from "Other Asia," 285, from India, 86, and from the U.S., 69 (i.e., about 20 per cent). As immigration of Chinese increased into the 1970's, underestimation of ethnic Chinese was in excess of 1,000 arrivals per annum. From 1971 the categories "Hong Kong" and "Taiwan" appeared under "country of former residence." There will be some non-Chinese in the Hong Kong totals, but the bulk are ethnic Chinese. Of pre-1967 arrivals, one-sixth were from places other than China, Hong Kong, Macao, and Taiwan, and this proportion is likely to have grown with the removal of restrictions on non-relatives.

Source: Canada Immigration Division, Department of Manpower and Immigration, Immigration Statistics, 1962-76.

TABLE 4

Counties of Origin for Some Chinese in Canada, 1884		
County	*Per cent*	*Number*
The Four Counties (Sze-yap)	*63.6*	
Toi-san (Sun-ning)	22.9	1,158
Hoi-ping	18.8	949
Sun-wui	12.2	615
Yin-ping	9.7	491
The Three Counties (Sam-yap)	*18.3*	
Poon-yue	15.8	798
Sun-dak	1.5	78
Nam-hoi	1.0	51
Other Counties	*18.2*	
Hok-san	6.0	302
Tsang-shing	3.9	195
Chung-san (Heung-san)	2.2	111
Po-on	1.6	81
Fa-uen	1.2	62
Yeung-kong	1.0	51
Tung-koon	1.3	64
Other*	1.0	50
TOTAL		5,056

* Including Saam-shui, Sze-wui, Tsung-fa, Ng-wa, Hing-ning, Wai-yeung, Ko-ming, Lok-cheung, Mui-uen, Ching-uen, Sun-hing, Yeung-chun, and unspecified.

Source: David C.Y. Lai, "Home County and Clan Origins of Overseas Chinese in Canada in the Early 1880s," *B.C. Studies*, 27 (1975), p. 6.

TABLE 5

Geographical Distribution of Chinese Population by Provinces, 1901-1941

Year	Province	Chinese Population	Total Province Population	% of Population Chinese	B.C. Chinese as % of total Chinese
1901	B.C.	14,885	178,657	8.30%	86%
	Alberta	235	73,022	.32%	
	Saskatchewan	41	91,279	.04%	
	Manitoba	206	255,211	.08%	
	Ontario	732	2,182,947	.03%	
	Quebec	1,037	1,648,898	.06%	
	N.B.	59	331,120	.02%	
	N.S.	106	459,574	.02%	
	P.E.I.	4	103,259	.004%	
1911	B.C.	19,568	392,480	5.99%	70%
	Alberta	1,787	374,663	.48%	
	Saskatchewan	957	492,432	.19%	
	Manitoba	885	455,614	.19%	
	Ontario	2,766	2,003,232	.11%	
	Quebec	1,578	2,005,776	.08%	
	N.B.	93	351,889	.03%	
	N.S.	134	492,338	.03%	
	P.E.I.	6	93,728	.01%	

1921				60%
B.C.	23,533	524,582	4.49%	
Alberta	3,581	588,454	.61%	
Saskatchewan	2,667	757,510	.35%	
Manitoba	1,331	610,118	.22%	
Ontario	5,625	2,933,662	.19%	
Quebec	2,335	2,361,199	.10%	
Maritimes	514	1,000,328	.05%	
1931				**60%**
B.C.	27,139	694,263	3.91%	
Alberta	3,875	731,605	.53%	
Saskatchewan	3,501	921,785	.38%	
Manitoba	1,732	700,139	.25%	
Ontario	6,919	3,431,683	.20%	
Quebec	2,750	2,874,255	.10%	
Maritimes	602	1,009,103	.06%	
1941				**60%**
B.C.	18,619	817,861	2.28%	
Alberta	3,122	796,169	.39%	
Saskatchewan	2,545	895,992	.28%	
Manitoba	1,248	729,744	.17%	
Ontario	6,143	3,787,655	.16%	
Quebec	2,378	3,331,882	.07%	
Maritimes	569	1,130,410	.06%	

Source: *Census of Canada*, 1911, II, pp. 340-1, 368-9; 1921, I, pp. 354-5; 1931, II, pp. 294-7; 1941, IV, pp. 4-18.

TABLE 6

Provincial Distribution of the Chinese Population in Canada, 1941-1971

Province	1941	%	1951	%	1961	%	1971	%
Newfoundland	—	—	186	(0.6)	445	(0.8)	610	(0.5)
P.E.I.	45	(0.1)	35	(0.1)	43	(0.1)	25	—
Nova Scotia	372	(1.1)	516	(1.6)	637	(1.1)	935	(0.8)
New Brunswick	152	(0.4)	146	(0.4)	274	(0.5)	575	(0.5)
Quebec	2,378	(6.9)	1,904	(5.8)	4,794	(8.2)	11,905	(10.0)
Ontario	6,143	(17.7)	6,997	(21.5)	15,155	(26.0)	39,325	(33.1)
Manitoba	1,248	(3.6)	1,175	(3.6)	1,936	(3.3)	3,430	(2.9)
Saskatchewan	2,545	(7.3)	2,144	(6.6)	3,660	(6.3)	4,605	(3.9)
Alberta	3,122	(9.0)	3,451	(10.6)	6,937	(11.9)	12,905	(10.9)
British Columbia	18,619	(53.8)	15,933	(49.0)	24,277	(41.6)	44,315	(37.3)
Territories	3	—	41	(0.1)	134	(0.2)	200	(0.1)
Total	34,627		32,528		58,197		118,815	

Source: *Census of Canada*, 1941, 1951, 1961, 1971.

TABLE 7

Chinese Population of Some Major Cities, 1911-1941

Year	City	Chinese Population	Total Population	Chinese Population as % of total
1911	Vancouver	3,559	100,401	3.54%
	Victoria	3,458	31,660	10.92%
	Calgary	485	43,704	1.11%
	Edmonton	130	24,900	.52%
	Winnipeg	585	136,035	.43%
	Hamilton	162	81,969	.20%
	Toronto	1,099	376,538	.29%
	Ottawa	168	87,062	.19%
	Montreal	1,197	470,480	.25%
	(all others under 100, except Cumberland, B.C.)			
1921	Vancouver	6,484	117,217	5.53%
	Victoria	3,441	38,727	8.89%
	Calgary	688	63,305	1.09%
	Edmonton	518	58,821	.88%
	Winnipeg	814	179,087	.45%
	Toronto	2,134	521,893	.41%
	Montreal	1,735	681,506	.28%
1931	Vancouver	13,011	246,593	5.28%
	Victoria	3,702	39,082	9.47%
	Calgary	1,054	83,761	1.26%
	Edmonton	467	99,197	.59%
	Winnipeg	1,033	218,785	.47%
	Toronto	2,635	613,207	.42%
	Ottawa	305	126,872	.24%
	Montreal	1,982	818,577	.24%
	Halifax	129	59,275	.22%
1941	Vancouver	7,174	275,353	2.61%
	Victoria	3,037	44,068	6.89%
	Calgary	799	88,904	.90%
	Edmonton	384	93,817	.41%
	Winnipeg	719	221,960	.32%
	Toronto	2,326	667,457	.35%
	Ottawa	272	154,951	.18%
	Montreal	1,708	903,007	.19%
	Halifax	127	70,488	.18%

Source: *Census of Canada*, 1911, II, pp. 372-3; 1921, I, p. 542; 1931, IV, pp. 900-18; 1941, IV, pp. 456ff.

303

TABLE 8

Naturalization by Provinces and as
Proportion of the Chinese Population of Each Province

Year	Province	Chinese Population	Naturalized	% of Total
1901	British Columbia	14,201	375	2.6%
	N.W.T.	252	25	10.0%
	Manitoba	167	42	25.1%
	Ontario	629	129	20.5%
	Quebec	982	61	6.2%
	Marit./Unorg. Terr.	144	36	25.0%
1921	British Columbia	23,533	573	2.7%
	Alberta	3,581	268	7.4%
	Saskatchewan	2,667	147	5.6%
	Manitoba	1,331	76	5.9%
	Ontario	5,625	503	9.3%
	Quebec	2,335	147	6.7%
1931	British Columbia	24,009	713	3.0%
	Alberta	3,535	310	8.8%
	Saskatchewan	3,335	195	5.8%
	Manitoba	1,598	149	9.3%
	Ontario	6,524	1,107	17.0%
	Quebec	2,506	307	14.8%
1941	British Columbia	14,667	480	3.3%
	Alberta	2,604	259	9.9%
	Saskatchewan	2,235	146	6.5%
	Manitoba	1,042	80	7.7%
	Ontario	5,010	775	15.5%
	Quebec	1,953	248	12.7%
	New Brunswick	110	25	22.7%
	Nova Scotia	273	33	12.1%
	P.E.I.	27	9	33.3%

Source: *Census of Canada,* 1901, I, p. 448; 1921, II, pp. 426ff; 1931, IV, pp. 592ff; 1941, IV, pp. 170ff. Note that the 1931 and 1941 Chinese populations for each province given here are less than the totals in Table 5. Because of differences in census cross-classification these tables are only roughly comparable to each other.

TABLE 9

Christian Chinese in Major Urban Areas by per cent of Total Chinese in these Cities, 1931 and 1941

Year	City	Chinese Population	Christians	% Christians
1931	Vancouver	13,011	565	4.3%
	Victoria	3,702	418	11.3%
	Calgary	1,054	300	28.5%
	Edmonton	467	144	30.8%
	Winnipeg	1,033	258	25.0%
	Toronto	2,635	1,183	44.9%
	Ottawa	305	181	59.3%
	Montreal	1,982	565	28.5%
	Halifax	129	99	76.7%
1941	Vancouver	7,174	1,424	19.8%
	Victoria	3,037	510	16.8%
	Calgary	799	259	32.4%
	Edmonton	384	135	35.2%
	Winnipeg	719	169	23.5%
	Toronto	2,326	885	38.0%
	Ottawa	272	196	72.1%
	Montreal	1,703	570	33.5%
	Halifax	127	84	66.1%

Source: *Census of Canada*, 1931, IV, pp. 900ff; 1941, IV, pp. 138ff.

TABLE 10

Male/Female Populations and Sex Ratios of Specific Communities

Year	Community	Males	Females	Male/Female ratio
1921	Vancouver	5,790	585	10/1
	Victoria	2,938	503	6/1
	Cumberland, B.C.	802	52	16/1
	Vernon, B.C.	136	31	4.5/1
	Nanaimo, B.C.	379	54	7/1
	New Westminster, B.C.	702	45	17/1
	Calgary	649	39	16/1
	Edmonton	501	17	30/1
	Saskatoon	220	8	27/1
	Regina	246	4	60/1
	Moose Jaw	177	11	16/1
	Winnipeg	790	24	33/1
	London	210	18	12/1
	Kingston	96	0	
	Hamilton	347	27	13/1
	Toronto	2,019	115	17/1
	Ottawa	273	9	30/1
	Montreal	1,628	107	15/1
	St. John	83	0	
	Halifax	138	2	60/1
1931	Vancouver	11,952	1,059	11/1
	Victoria	3,192	510	6/1
	New Westminster	561	38	15/1
	Calgary	969	85	12/1
	Edmonton	440	27	17/1
	Toronto	2,482	153	15/1
	Ottawa	274	31	9/1
	Montreal	1,811	171	11/1

TABLE 10—*Continued*

Year	Community	Males	Females	Male/Female ratio
1941	Vancouver	5,973	1,201	5/1
	Victoria	2,549	488	5/1
	Calgary	694	105	7/1
	Edmonton	358	26	14/1
	Winnipeg	679	40	17/1
	Toronto	2,073	253	8/1
	Ottawa	231	41	6/1
	Montreal	1,510	198	7/1
	Halifax	106	21	5/1

Source: *Census of Canada*, 1921, I, p. 542; 1931, II, pp. 494ff; 1941, IV, pp. 456ff.

TABLE 11

Males/Females in the Chinese Population of Canada by Province, 1971

	Male	Female
Maritimes	64.7	35.3
Quebec	53.5	46.5
Ontario	48.6	51.4
Manitoba	59.4	40.6
Saskatchewan	48.0	52.0
Alberta	62.2	37.8
British Columbia	51.1	48.9
		N = 1241

Source: *Census of Canada*, 1971.

TABLE 12

Reported Size and Composition of Chinese Communities in British Columbia, 1879-80

Date of Report	District	Total Chinese	Women	Total in Business	Miners	Cooks and Servants	Labourers	Vegetable Gardeners	Wood-cutters	Laundry	Barbers	Others[e]	Criminal Convictions 1879
12.2.80	Victoria	2,370	70	322	1,100[a]	400	0	100	95	100	20	163	68
1.12.79	Nanaimo	437	2	15	23	18	347	0	0	13	9	10	8
27.2.80	New Westminster	250-300	?10	0[b]	0	0[b]	0[b]	0[b]	0[b]	0[b]	0	0	6
27.11.79	Yale	45	4	9	26	6	6	0	0	0	0	0	1
2.12.76	Kamloops[c]	35	2	2	19	3	7	0	0	1	0	1	0[b]
22.10.79	Forks Quesnelle	385	10	12	305	7	5	5	0	3	0	38	0
22.11.79	Richfield	491	25	26	428	0	0	8	0	4	0	0	2
10.11.79	Kootenay	81	1	3	70	0	0	4	0	0	0	3	0
11.12.79	Cassiar[d]	600	5	30	300	0	0	0	0	6	0	260	0

a. This figure is given as "miners and fishermen."
b. Present, but no number given.
c. Figures for Kamloops from a name provided in lieu of numbers.
d. Figures for Cassiar all approximate.
e. "Others" include the following: Victoria: 60 tailors, 21 cigar-makers, 52 shoemakers, 7 transport workers, 3 doctors, 20 pedlars; Nanaimo: 7 butchers, 3 pedlars; Kamloops: 1 tailor; Forks Quesnelle: 3 butchers, 5 carpenters and blacksmiths, 30 no occupation; Kootenay: not given; Cassiar: "Unable to find anything to do . . . had to finally leave the district in a state of destitution."

Source: Public Archives of British Columbia, CC. 30.14. C44.

TABLE 13

Occupations of Chinese in British Columbia, 1884			
Employers and professionals		180	2%
Merchants and restaurateurs	132		
Doctors	40		
Teachers	8		
Tradesmen and self-employed workers		992	9%
Barbers	53		
Carpenters	28		
Pedlars (vegetable, fish, and sundries)	67		
Tinsmiths	2		
Sailors	3		
Laundrymen	158		
Vegetable gardeners	114		
Bricklayers	25		
Charcoal burners	34		
Printers	3		
Butchers	13		
Woodcutters and bark-strippers	422		
Prostitutes	70		
Miners and farmers in the interior		1,585	15%
Workers in Chinese establishments		563	5%
Store employees	302		
Shoemakers	130		
Brickmakers	60		
Cigarmakers	28		
Clothing operators	36		
Matchmakers	7		
Workers for non-Chinese enterprise		5,932	57%
Railway construction	2,900		
Coal mines	791		
Canneries	709		
Farm labour	720		
Ditchdiggers	156		
Sawmill hands	267		
Servants and cooks	279		
Unspecified labourers	110		
Newly arrived workers		602	6%
Families		617	6%
Married women	55		
Children	55		
Boys between 12 and 17	507		
		10,471	100%

TABLE 14

Chinese Occupations, by Province, with percentage of Laundry and Restaurant Businesses

Year	Province	Laundry	Restaurant	Retail	Labour	Agriculture	Profess. and Manag.	% Laundry	% Restaurant
1921	B.C.	680							
	Alberta	516	1,316	101	226	361	1	15%	40%
	Saskatchewan	548	1,368	42		184	5	20%	50%
	Manitoba	464	461	42	81		5	35%	35%
	Ontario	2,300	1,875	218	483	64	9	40%	33%
	Quebec	1,359					6	50%	
1931	B.C.	752	3,744	1,310	8,231	4,196	21	3%	16%
	Alberta	566	1,922	204	97	291		17%	60%
	Saskatchewan	572	2,087	104		67		18%	70%
	Manitoba	475	778	59		30		30%	50%
	Ontario	2,508	2,722	95	122	105	4	40%	45%
	Quebec	1,272	718	81	33	13	3	54%	30%
	Maritimes	206	263	4				40%	52%
1941	B.C.	474	2,639	845	2,857	3,220		3%	20%
	Alberta	270	1,348	254	93	489	5	10%	50%
	Saskatchewan	217	1,398	206		238	1	9%	60%
	Manitoba	235	552	50		87		20%	50%
	Ontario	1,584	2,491	483	233	261	31	24%	33%
	Quebec	971	751	391	106	31	16	30%	20%
	Maritimes	132	232	225		13	13	13%	22%

Source: *Census of Canada*, 1921, IV, pp. 656ff; 1931, VII, pp. 430ff; 1941, VII, pp. 322ff. The 1921 census does not separate Chinese from other Asians. Since few Asians other than Chinese were found outside B.C., "Asia" has been used for provinces other than B.C. and no data are entered for B.C. The 1941 materials include other Asians for all provinces except B.C. but provide separate listings for each group in the case of B.C. Hence, "Asiatic" is used for other provinces and "Chinese" for B.C.

TABLE 15

Chinese Population of Canada, Montreal, and Toronto: Occupational Profile, 1971

	% Canada	% Montreal	% Toronto
Manager	1.1	9.3	2.2
Science/engineering	7.1	9.3	9.7
Medicine	5.3	—	4.4
Religion	0.4	—	0.7
Teaching	2.6	2.3	5.2
Social science	0.7	—	0.7
Artistic, recreational	0.5	—	1.5
Clerical	12.1	11.6	21.6
Sales	9.7	2.3	7.5
Services	27.9	32.5	22.4
Farming	2.2	—	0.7
Primary production	0.2	—	—
Processing	3.1	2.3	0.7
Fabricating	7.3	9.3	9.7
Construction	0.7	2.3	0.7
Transport	0.7	—	1.5
Other	4.8	2.3	3.0
Not Stated	13.1	16.3	7.5

Source: *Census of Canada*, 1971.

TABLE 16

**Chinese Population of Canada, Montreal, and Toronto:
Income, 1971**

Income	% Canada	% Montreal/Toronto
Less than $2,000	4.5	4.8
$2,000-$3,499	7.8	6.9
$3,500-$4,999	9.8	11.4
$5,000-$7,999	20.4	19.1
$8,000-$10,999	16.3	16.2
$11,000-$13,999	10.3	10.0
$14,000-$19,999	7.0	6.7
$20,000-$24,000	2.7	1.4
Over $25,000	2.1	2.0
Loss/None/Not applicable	18.8	20.3
	N = 1241	N = 369

Source: *Census of Canada*, 1971.

TABLE 17

Kuomintang Branches in Canada, 1913-14

British Columbia

Victoria	New Westminster
Vancouver	Revelstoke
Arrowhead	Rossland
Ashcroft	Trail
Barkerville	*Alberta*
Cache Creek	Calgary
Chemainus	Canmore
Clayoquot	Macleod
Clinton	Medicine Hat
Cranbrook	Edmonton
Duncan	*Manitoba*
Enderby	Brandon
Extension	*Ontario*
Fernie	Hamilton
Ft. Steele	London
Golden	Ottawa
Grand Forks	Toronto
Greenwood	*Quebec*
Kamloops	Montreal
Ladner	Quebec City
Ladysmith	*Newfoundland*
Lulu Island	St. John's
Mission	*Nova Scotia*
Nelson	Halifax

Sources: "Chinese Business Directory," 1913; Ban Seng Hoe, *Structural Changes of Two Chinese Communities in Alberta, Canada,* pp. 136, 188.

TABLE 18

Cheekungtong Branches, 1919

British Columbia		Alberta
Victoria	Rossland	Calgary
Vancouver	Nelson	Medicine Hat
Ladner	Vernon	Blairmore
Port Hammond	Kamloops	Lethbridge
New Westminster	Chemainus	Bow Island
Chilliwack	Duncan	*Saskatchewan*
Nanaimo	Kaslo	Saskatoon
Cumberland	Kelowna	*Manitoba*
Sidney	Princeton	Winnipeg
Salmon Arm	Fernie	*Ontario*
Agassiz	Quesnel	Windsor
Alberni	Grand Forks	London
Prince George	Keremeos	St. Catharines
Prince Rupert	Bevan	Hamilton
Barkerville	Cranbrook	Toronto
Revelstoke	Cobble Hill	*Quebec*
Trail	Armstrong	Montreal
		Quebec City

Source: List of Branches represented and unrepresented at First National Convention of CKT, Victoria, December, 1919. A slightly different list may be compiled from the program of the North American constitutional conference of 1919. The changes are: addition of Merritt, B.C.; deletion of Chemainus, Duncan, Kaslo, and Armstrong, B.C., addition of Regina, Saskatchewan, and Chatham, Welland, and Ottawa, Ontario. The result is 49 branches, rather than 48.

TABLE 19

Clan Associations in Vancouver, Toronto, and Calgary in 1923

Vancouver	Surnames	Toronto	Surnames	Calgary
Wong Kung Har Tong	Wong	Same		Same
Wong Kung Har Tong Hq.	Wong			
Wong Wun San	Wong			
Wong Wun San Hq.	Wong			
Lu Ming Bitsuey	Wong from Toi-san			
Lee Long Sai Tong	Lee	Same		
Lee Tun Tsung Tong	Lee			
Lee Kong Kai Tong	Lee from Hoi-ping			
Lim Sai Ho Tong	Lim (Lam, Lum)	Same		
Chin Wing Chun Tong	Chin (Chan)	Same		
Cheng Wing Yeong Tong	Cheng (Jung)			
Mah Gim Gee Tong	Mah			Same
Mah Gim Gee Hq.	Mah			
Ng Hoy San Tong	Ng	Ng Hoy San Fong	Ng	
Oylin Kung-so	Chow, Ng	Oylin Fong	Chow	
Chee Duck Tong	Chow Ng, Cho, Choy, Yung			Same
Yee Fung Toy Tong	Yee			Same
Leung Tong How Tong	Leung			Same
Lew Mo Wai Tong	Lew			
Lor Yu Chang Tong	Lor			
Kuan Lung Sai Tong	Kuan			
Lung Kong Kung-so	Lau, Kuan, Cheung, Chao	Same		

TABLE 19—*Continued*

Vancouver	Surnames	Toronto	Surnames	Calgary
Fong Loon Tong	Seto, See	Same		
Nam Yeung Tong	Sam (Sim), Yip, Teng	Nam Yeung Fong	Sam (Sim), Yip, Teng	
Sue Yuen Tong	Louie, Fong, Kwong			Same
Chow Loon Kung-so	Tom, Hoy, Der, Ts'e, Yuen			
		Mark Si Hing Tong	Mark	

Note: Fortunately the associational data are the most complete for these three cities, which represent different kinds of community: Vancouver, with a population of about 6,000, contained 60 per cent of Canada's Chinese; Toronto, the second-largest community, was the biggest in eastern Canada; and Calgary, with a population of 650, represented a small prairie community. This and the following table taken together give the reader a fairly clear picture of the associational life in these centres during the 1920's. See Edgar Wickberg, "Some Problems in Chinese Organizational Development in Canada, 1923-1937," *Canadian Ethnic Studies*, XI, no. 1 (1979), pp. 88-98.

Sources: Willmott, "Chinese Clan Associations," p. 35; *Chinese Times*, 1914-1923; *Dulangdu Qingnian Hui, Jianlou baogao* (Donor list of 1924); Hoe, *Structural Changes of Two Chinese Communities*, pp. 128ff. Note that the existence of the Chee Duck Tong in Calgary is indicated by *Chinese Times*, 1920, and not by Hoe.

TABLE 20

Other Associations in Vancouver, Toronto, and Calgary in 1923

Vancouver	*Toronto*	*Calgary*
Community-wide		
CBA	CBA; YMCI (Chinese Christian Assn. or Chinese Assn.); Resist the Bill (of 1923) Hq. Assn.	
Fraternal-political		
CKT (Freemasons)	CKT (Freemasons)	CKT (Freemasons)
Dart Coon		Dart Coon
KMT	KMT	KMT
HCT	HCT	HCT
District		
Yu Hing Tong (Toi-san)	Same	
Hoi Ngai Kung-so (Toi-san)	Same	
Kwong Hoi United Assn. (Toi-san)		
Hoi-ping Kwong Fook Tong (Hoi-ping)		
Low Kong (Hoi-ping)		
Yue San Chong Hoo Tong (Poon-yue)		
Tit Sing Shon Yee Wui (Heung-san)		Same
Heung-san Fook Sun Tong (1 or 2 surnames, Heung-san)		
Sun-wui Fook Ching Tong (Sun-wui)		
Shar Duey Mutual Society (Sun-wui)		
Yin-ping Tong Fook Tong (Yin-ping)		
Yin-ping Hq. (Yin-ping Tong Fook Tsung Tong)		
Trade Associations		
Chamber of Commerce	Chinese Business Assn. (Merchants Club)	
Chun Wah Commercial Assn.		

TABLE 20—*Continued*

Vancouver	Toronto	Calgary
Trade Associations (Continued)		
Vegetable Retailers Assn.		
Shingle Mill Workers Assn.		
Zhonghua Gongtang (Chinese Labour Assn.)		
Youth Organizations		
Tong-yuen Wui (Chinese Canadian Club)	YMCI/CCA	
Chung Wah Youth League (and Boy Scout Troop)	Methodist YMCA	
Schools		
Oi-kwok School (XZD)	Overseas Chinese School (YMCI– Presbyterian)	Chinese Public School
Chinese Public School (KMT)		
Churches		
Presbyterian	Same	
United	Same	Same (YMCA)
Anglican		
Christ Church of China (Indep. and ecumenical)		
Newspapers		
Tai Hon Kung Bo (Chinese Times; CKT)		
Sun Mun-kwok Bo (New Republic; KMT; in Victoria)	Shing Wah Yat Bo (Shing Wah Daily News; Daily by 1922; KMT)	
Theatrical and Sports		
Freemasons Athletic Club	Shijie Zhongxi She	
Various theatre groups		
Reading Rooms		
Several		

Sources: Same as for previous table. Note the inclusion of the Victoria newspaper among Vancouver associations. In politics and in organizational leadership there was a considerable overlapping of the Vancouver and Victoria communities. In this case, the Vancouver newspaper represented the Freemasons in western Canada, the Victoria paper the KMT in the same region.

TABLE 21

Associations in Vancouver, Toronto, and Calgary established between 1923 and mid-1937

Vancouver	Toronto	Calgary
Community-wide		
Resist-Japan and Save-the-country Assn.	Same	(Edmonton CBA)*
Political-fraternal		
Freemasons Hq.		
	Dart Coon	
District Associations		
Toi-san Ning Yung Wui-kuan (reorganized form of Toi-san Yu Hing Tong) Hoi-ping Hq. Yue San Tsung Sun Kuk (Yue San Hq.) Kong Chow Wui-Kuan Hq. (Sun-wui) Nam Ping Bitsuey (Yin-ping)	Kong Chow Wui-Kuan	
	Heng Tong Kung-so	
Clan Associations		
Man Sing Reading Room (Wong from Hoi-ping)	Wong Man Sing Kung-so Wong Wun San Wui-kuan	Wong Wun San Kung-so
Lee-si Kung-so Lee-si Kung-so Hq. Lim Sai Ho Tong Hq.	Same	Same
	Lim Sai Ho Tong	Same
Lim Kow Mock Kung-so Chin Wing Chun Tong Hq. Cheng Wing Yeong Tong Hq.		
		Mah Gim Gee Tong
Oylin Kung-so Hq. Chung Tim Fong (Chow) Sam Duck Reading Room (Ng, Choy, Cho, Yung) Lor Yu Chang Tong Hq. Kuan Lung Sai Tong Hq.	Chee Duck Tong	

319

TABLE 21—*Continued*

Vancouver	*Toronto*	*Calgary*
Clan Associations (Continued)		
Kuan Sing Fong (Kuan, Chan)	Kuan Lung Sai Tong	
Lung Kong		
Kung-so Hq.		
		Lung Kong Kung-so
Fong Loon Tong Hq.		
Sue Yuen Tong Hq.		
Ko Yeung Reading Room (Hoy)		
Ho Lu Kong Tong (Ho)		
Yan Chung San Tsung Tong (Yan Hq.)		
Gee See Kwok Tong (Gee)		
Trade Associations		
Chinese Workers Protective Assn.		
	Western-style Restaurant Owners assn.	
Chinese Actors Benevolent Assn.		
Overseas Chinese Farmers Assn.		
Overseas Chinese Produce Merchants Assn.		
Chinese Produce Wholesalers Assn.		
Federation of Overseas Chinese Agric. Producers and Merchants		
Vancouver Mainland Growers Coop. Assn.		
Women's Organizations		
Chinese Women's Assn.	Toronto Chinese Women's Assn.	Calgary Women's Assn.
Youth Organizations		
University of British Columbia Chinese Student Assn.		
Vancouver Chinese Schools Students Fed.		
Schools		
Mon Keong (Wong Assn.)		
Tai Kong (Freemasons)		

320

TABLE 21—*Continued*

Toronto	Calgary	Vancouver
Schools (Continued)		
Kwong Chi (Yin-ping Assn.)		
Yeuk Ying		
Yeuk Tsai		
Yeuk Yan		
Man Wah		
Chong Wah		
Oy Loon		
Ming Loon		
Dat Yan		
Overseas Chinese Educ. Assn. Canada Branch	Kwong Do (Freemasons-XZD)	
Newspapers		
Canada Evening Post (*Jianada Zhongguo Chenbao*— "left" KMT: 1920's only)		
	Hung Chung (She) Bo (Freemasons)	
Theatrical and Sports		
Ching Won Musical Soc.	Lien Kiu theatre group	Lien Ching society
Jin Wah Sing Opera Co.	She Chu yuen theatre society	San Lien theatre group
Sing Kiu Opera Co.		
Chinese Student's Athletic Club	Jin Hung Sing opera co. (Freemasons)	Chinese Public School Theatre Group
Chinese Tennis Club		
Reading Rooms and Speech Clubs		
Several		

* Claimed to represent all Chinese in Alberta when founded in 1932. Hoe, *Structural Changes of Two Chinese Communities*, p. 88.

Note: There is, necessarily, some imprecision about this list. Many organizations were formed after 1923 and lapsed before 1937. A case in point is the Western-style Restaurant (Chinese) Kitchen Workers Union, which existed throughout the 1920's in Vancouver and closed about 1931. We have excluded all such organizations except the newspaper *Canada Evening Post*. In the case of the Vancouver schools, it is not likely that all of them existed in 1937, but, with the exception of the first three listed, which are known to have existed, it is not clear which of the others was still in operation at that time. Headquarters organizations in Vancouver have been listed separately because the associations themselves usually do so. If they were not so listed here, the Vancouver list would have been shorter by a dozen names.

Sources: *Yu Shan Zonggongsuo jinian ce; Kaiping Zonghuiguan tekan; Lin Xi Ho ba zhounian zhuankan; Shing Wah Daily News*, July, 1940, July, 1941; *Chinese Times*, 1923-1937, and 1960's to 1970's, especially 24 May 1924, 26 May 1926, 7 June 1942; Hoe, *Structural Changes*, pp. 128-221; PABC, Attorney General's Correspondence Inward, 1925-1937, file 236-2: "Chinese Societies," (unsigned) Report on Chinese Associations Operating in British Columbia, 1935; Levine, "Historical Documentation Pertaining to Overseas Chinese Organizations," p. 90; *Qiao Sheng Ribao (The Chinese Voice*, Vancouver), 1970's; *The New Republic* (Vancouver), 1970's; information furnished by associations to Harry Con.

TABLE 22

Unofficial List of KMT Branches, 1937

British Columbia	*Saskatchewan*
Vancouver	Saskatoon
New Westminster	Regina
Victoria	Battleford
Kelowna	*Manitoba*
Trail	Winnipeg
Nanaimo	*Ontario*
Quesnel	Toronto
Port Alberni	Hamilton
Prince George	Ottawa
Prince Rupert	Kingston
Cranbrook	Brantford
Duncan	Sudbury
Kamloops	Windsor
Alberta	Niagara Falls
Edmonton	Fort William
Calgary	Welland
Medicine Hat	*Quebec*
Blairmore	Montreal
Lethbridge	Quebec City
	New Brunswick
	Saint John
	Canada Headquarters: Vancouver

Source: *Chinese Times*, 15 June 1937. This list represents the branches present at the funeral of a KMT leader in June, 1937.

TABLE 23

Freemason Branches in the 1920's

First District

HEADQUARTERS: VICTORIA, B.C.
  Sidney
  Chemainus
  Duncan
  Ladysmith
  Cumberland
  Courtney
  Cobble Hill
  Alberni
  Nanaimo
    (all in B.C.)

Second District

HEADQUARTERS: VANCOUVER
  New Westminster
  Agassiz
  Chilliwack
  Port Hammond
  Haney
  Ladner
  Prince Rupert
  Prince George
    (all in B.C.)

Third District

HEADQUARTERS: KAMLOOPS, B.C.

  Armstrong
  Vernon
  Revelstoke
  Rutland
  Salmon Arm
  Penticton
  Kelowna
  Enderby
  Chase
  Merritt
  Ashcroft
  Keremeos
  Princeton
    (all in B.C.)

Fourth District

HEADQUARTERS: NELSON, B.C.

  Cranbrook
  Trail
  Rossland
  Hell's Bar
  Grand Forks
  Kaslo
  Fernie
  Kimberley
  Creston
    (all in B.C.)
  Blairmore
  Bellevue
  Coleman
    (all in Alberta)

Fifth District

HEADQUARTERS: CALGARY

  Hanna
  Medicine Hat
  Lethbridge
  Fort Macleod
    (all in Alberta)
  Saskatoon, Saskatchewan
  Regina, Saskatchewan

  Winnipeg, Manitoba

Sixth District

HEADQUARTERS: TORONTO

  London
  Hamilton
  St. Catharines
  Sault Ste. Marie
  Ottawa
  Niagara Falls
  Welland
    (all in Ontario)

Seventh District

HEADQUARTERS: MONTREAL
  Quebec City
  Halifax

Source: Second Freemasons National Convention Programme, Lethbridge, 1924. There were changes thereafter. By 1926 Vernon had replaced Kamloops as the Third District headquarters. (*Chinese Times*, 6 April 1926). In 1932 the Sixth and Seventh Districts were merged with Toronto as the headquarters.

TABLE 24

Associational Structure in Montreal, ca. 1960

Community

Chinese Benevolent Association

Montreal Chinese Hospital

Fraternal/Political

Constitutionalist Party (Empire Reform Association)

Freemasons

Kuomintang

East Wind Club

Clan

Chau Lum Society

Gee How Tong

Yee Fong Toy Tong

Lee Family Association

Sam Dark Tong

Wong Won Sun Society

Wong Kong Har Tong

Commercial

Montreal Chinese Restaurant Association

Leisure/Athletic

Dart Coon Association

Musical

Yuet Sing Cantonese Music Club

Religious

Chinese Catholic Mission

Chinese Presbyterian Church

Chinese YMCI

Sources: *Chinese Times*; Fanny C. Davies "A Survey of the Chinese Community in Montreal," manuscript, 1974; *Montreal Chinese Directory*, 1962.

TABLE 25

Chinese Associations in Toronto, ca. 1960

Community

Chinese Community Centre (of Ontario) (CCC)
Chinese Canadian Association

Political/Fraternal

Freemasons
Kuomintang

Clan/Locality

Chin Wing Chun Tong
Chin Association
Chau Lun Kung-Sol
Fong Lun Society
Lee's Family Association
Lee Yu Society
Lim Gow Mock Benevolent Association
Lem Sai Ho Tong
Low Kong Society
Lung Kong Kung-Shaw
Lung Kong Tin Yee Association
Villa Kung Shang
Wang's Family Centre
Wong Wun Shun Society
Yee's Family Association
Kwong Hoi Association
New Kwong Hoi Association

Schools

Chinese School

Leisure/Athletic

Dart Coon
Hon Sing Athletic Club

Musical/Dramatic

Cantonese Music Society
Chinese United Dramatic Club
Ship Toy Yen Association

Other Leisure

8 "social clubs"
Free Chinese Youth Centre
Chinese Welfare Association

Church

Chinese Anglican Church
Chinese Presbyterian Church/Chinese YMCI
Chinese United Church
Chinese Catholic Church
Chinese Evangelical Baptist Church
Chinese Gospel Church

Newspaper

Shing Wah Daily News

Sources: *Chinese Times*; Levine, "Historical Documentation Pertaining to Overseas Chinese Organizations"; *Metropolitan Toronto Chinese Directory*, 1961-63.

325

TABLE 26

Chinese Associations in Winnipeg, ca. 1960

Community

Chinese Benevolent Association

Political/Fraternal

Freemasons
Kuomintang*

Clan

Gee How Oak Tin Association
Lee Family Association
Mah Society
Wong Wun Sun

School

Chinese Public School

Leisure

Chinese Dramatic Society
Chinese Students of University of Manitoba
6 "social clubs"

Church

Chinese United Church of Winnipeg

* Note that the Chinese Youth Association and the Chinese Canadian Citizens Association of Manitoba were also organized by the KMT but did not appear to have separate organizational status.

Source: F.Q. Quo, "Chinese Immigrants in the Prairies."

TABLE 27

Chinese Associations in Calgary, ca. 1960

Community

    Chinese Cemetery Committee

Political/Fraternal

    Chinese Freemasons

    Kuomintang

Clan/Locality

    Wong's Affinity Association (Wong Wun Shan)

    Sue Yuen Tong

    Mah Society

    Yee Fong Toy Tong

    Leung Tung Hao Tong

    Lung Kong King-So

    Lam Sai Ho Tong

    Lee's Association

    Ho Yee Society

    Shon Yee Association

    Chung Shan Association

Schools

    Chinese Public School

Leisure

    Chinese Dramatic Club

    3 "social clubs"

Churches

    Chinese United Church of Calgary

    Chinese Pentecostal Church

Sources: Hoe, *Structural Changes of Two Chinese Communities; Chinese Times.*

TABLE 28

Chinese Associations in Edmonton, ca. 1960

Community

Chinese Benevolent Association

Political

Freemasons

Kuomintang

Clan Associations

Mah Society

Wong Kong Har Tong

Gee Poy Kuo Tong

Commercial

Chinese Businessmen's Association

Schools

Chinese United Church School

Leisure

Chinese Dramatic Club

5 "social clubs"

Church

Chinese United Church

Alumni/Students Association

Chinese Students Association (University of Alberta)

Sources: Hoe, *Structural Changes of Two Chinese Communities; Edmonton and Northern Alberta Chinese Directory.*

TABLE 29

Chinese Associations in Vancouver, ca. 1960

Community

    Chinese Benevolent Association

Political/Fraternal

    Chinese Freemasons
    Chinatown Lions
    Chinese-Canadian Veterans
    Chinese Elks
    Kuomintang

Clan

    Chau Luen Society
    Chan Wing Chun
    Fong Loon Tong
    Gee How Oak Tin Association
    Cheng Wing Yeung Association
    Ng Suey Sun Tong
    Ko Reading Room
    Lim Yeung Sai Ho Tong
    Lee Clan Association
    Leong Chung How Tong
    Lew Mu Way Society
    Lore Yee Jang Tong
    Lung Kong Tien Yee
    Lee Kwong Kai Society
    Look Ming Reading Room
    Ming Sun Reading Room
    Mah Society
    Nam Yeung Tong
    Oylin Society
    Quon Lung Sai Tong
    Sue Yuen Tong
    Tung Shan Reading Room
    Wong Kong Har Tong
    Wong Wun San Yee Fung Toy Tong
    Yee Hing Reading Room
    Yee Loo Reading Room
    Yit Shaw Reading Room

TABLE 29—*Continued*

Locality

Sam Yap District Association
Nam Hoi District Association
Yue San Association
Shoon Duck Association
Five Districts Association of Hong Kong
Toi-san Ning Yung
Hoi-ping Association
Yin-ping Association
Kong Chow District Association
Shon Yee Benevolent Society
Chung Shan Lung Jen Society

Commercial

B.C. Lower Mainland Cooperative Association
Chinese Chamber of Commerce
Chinese Trade Workers Association

Chinese Language Schools·

St. Xavier School (Catholic Centre)
Chinese Public School
Tai Kung Charity School (Freemasons)
Mon Keong Chinese School

Leisure/Athletic

All Chinese Basketball League
Chinese Bowling Club
Chinese Golf Club
Masonic Athletic Club
Hai Fung Association
Hon Hsing Athletic Club
Tai-Chi Chuan Exercise Club

Others

Chung Wah Cubs and Scouts
Chinese Varsity Club
Chung Wah Youth League
Overseas Chinese Students Association
Y.W.C.A.–Pender Street
Chinese Youth Association

TABLE 29—*Continued*

Others (Continued)

        Ngai Lum Musical Society

        Jin Wah Sing Musical Society

        Ching Won Musical Society

Charity

        Charlie Kent Golden Anniversary Charity Foundation

        Community Chest

        Red Feather/Red Cross

        Free China Relief Association

Alumni

        North American Alumni of Poy Ching

        Chung Shan University Alumni Association

        Jen Guan Alumni Association

        Kuangchow University Alumni

Other

        Chinese-Canadian Citizens Association

Chinese Religious Groups

        Chinese Anglican Church

        Chinese Catholic Centre

        Christ Church of China

        Chinese Lutherans

        Chinese Pentecostals

        Chinese Presbyterians

        Chinese United Church

Newspapers

        Chinatown News

        Chinese Times

        Chinese Voice Daily

        Da Zhong Bao

        New Republic Daily

Sources: *Chinese Times*; K. Straaton, "The Political System of the Vancouver Chinese Community: Associations and Leadership in the Early 1960's"; *Vancouver Chinese Directory*.

TABLE 30

Chinese Associations in Victoria, ca. 1960

Community

Chinese Consolidated Benevolent Association
Chinese Hospital

Political/Fraternal

Chinese Freemasons
Kuomintang

Clan

Chew Lun Kung-so
Chow Oy-lin Association
Lee Family Association
Lim Sai Ho Tong
Lung Kong Tien Yee Association
Mah Society
Sue Yuen Tong
Wong Kung Har Tong
Yee Fung Toy Tong
Yee Hing Tong

Locality

Chung-shan Hook-sin Tong
Doe Kai
Hoy Ping Association
Hoy Sun Association
Kong Chow Association
Three District Associations
Tit-shing Shan Yee
Yan-ping Association
Yue-shan Association

Schools

Chinese Catholic Mission School
Chinese Public School
Yue-shan Chinese School

Commercial

Chinese Chamber of Commerce
Chinese Dry Cleaners Association
Chinese Vegetable Pedlars Association

Leisure/Athletic

Chinese Students Athletic Club
Dart Coon Club
5 "social clubs"

Religious

Chinese Catholic Mission
Chinese Presbyterian Church
Chinese Y.M.C.A.
Chinese Christian Community Centre
Tam Kung Temple

Source: *Victoria and Vancouver Island Chinese Directory.*

FIGURE 1. The Network of Chinese Associations in Vancouver, Early 1960's

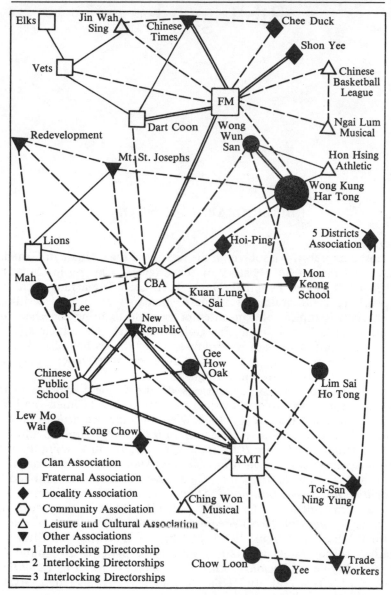

Figure 1 shows how the structure of interlocking membership gives rise to the three factions identified with the KMT, Freemason, and "neutralist" positions. The KMT had memberships interlocked with the "traditionist" clan, locality, and music associations; the Freemasons were linked with organizations not oriented toward China such as the Chinese Veterans, Elks, and the increasingly Canadian-oriented Shon Yee Association. The model for this analysis is found in G.W. Skinner, *Leadership and Power in the Chinese Community of Thailand* (Ithaca, N.Y., 1957).

Source: K. Straaton, "The Political System of the Vancouver Chinese Community," p. 100.

Bibliography

BIBLIOGRAPHICAL NOTE

General Sources
The most comprehensive source on the history of the Chinese in Canada is *Jianada Huaqiao Shi* [History of the Overseas Chinese in Canada] (Taibei, 1967) by Lee Tung-hai (David T.H. Lee). The arrangement of this work reflects traditional Chinese standards of history writing. Organization is topical and no attempt is made to bring together the various subjects into a single, integrated narrative. Nevertheless, this book is the result of years of careful research by the leading historian of Chinese-Canadian society and serves as an excellent reference work. As such, it deserves translation into English.

The social and political dimensions of the Chinese experience in Canada have been ably treated by such scholars as David Chuen-yan Lai, Ban Seng Hoe, and Peter S. Li. Lai's works include two articles on the Victoria Chinese Benevolent Association in *B.C. Studies*, nos. 15 and 18; two demographic studies (in *B.C. Studies*, no. 27, and in V. Ujimoto and G. Hirabayashi (eds.), *Visible Minorities and Multiculturalism* [Toronto, 1980]); and a study of Victoria's Chinatown in C.N. Forward (ed.), *Residential and Neighbourhood Studies in Victoria* (University of Victoria Department of Geography, 1973). Hoe's major work is *Structural Changes of Two Chinese Communities in Alberta, Canada* (National Museum of Man, 1976). Li's historical writings on Chinese-Canadian social status and family and work patterns are found in *Canadian Review of Sociology and Anthropology* (vol. 16), *Canadian Ethnic Studies* (vol. 12), and Ujimoto and Hirabayashi (eds.), *Asian Canadians: Regional Perspectives*.

Those able to read Chinese should move quickly beyond these works to the single most important source for our book, the *Chinese Times* (Tai Hon Kung Bo). An almost complete file of this daily newspaper from 1914 to the present is available in the University of British Columbia

Library. The earlier issues maintain especially good coverage of news of Chinese communities outside of B.C. as well as those within. Editorial viewpoints are those of the Chinese Freemasons. Our book is the first to make major use of this extremely valuable research source. For the history of Chinese organizations we have used anniversary souvenir publications, as well as the *Chinese Times* and interviews.

White reactions to the Chinese are best approached through Peter Ward's *White Canada Forever* (Montreal, 1978) and several articles by Patricia Roy, including two in *B.C. Studies*, nos. 18 and 31, and "The Oriental Menace in British Columbia," in S.M. Trofimenkoff (ed.), *The Twenties in Western Canada* (National Museum of Man, 1972). For late nineteenth-century white perceptions, we made the most use of James Morton's *In the Sea of Sterile Mountains* (Vancouver, 1973) and R.E. Wynne's "Reaction to the Chinese in the Pacific Northwest and British Columbia, 1850-1910" (Ph.D. dissertation, University of Washington, 1964). Morton's is a popular but generally reliable narrative. It seems to be based largely on the English-language press, but there are no references or bibliography that would allow one to check. Wynne's dissertation draws heavily upon B.C. legislation to provide a convenient and documented account of the development of anti-Chinese sentiment in British Columbia. Tien-fang Cheng's *Oriental Immigration in Canada* (Shanghai, 1931) remains useful and is also of historical interest, since the author was both a Chinese student in Canada and a political activist in the Toronto Chinese community.

Among the archives, the most useful for this book were the Public Archives of Canada; the United Church of Canada Archives at Victoria University of the University of Toronto; and the Vancouver City Archives. The basic files in the PAC are those in the Immigration Section (Record Group 76). Files 23635, 729921, and 827821 provide basic coverage from the last years of the nineteenth century to the 1950's. At the United Church Archives, the files of the Presbyterian Church in Canada, Mission to the Chinese in Canada, boxes 3 and 6 (B.C. and Montreal, 1880's-1920's) were most useful. The basic documents at the Vancouver City Archives are the City Council Minute Books and the series of City Clerk's Incoming Correspondence.

Issues

Two controversial research issues within the Chinese-Canadian communities are the origins of the Cheekungtong (Freemasons) and the founding date of the Vancouver Chinese Benevolent Association. The first is a question of when the first Freemason unit was founded and what relationship the various Hongmen-type units bore to each other in late nineteenth-century British Columbia. Some of the details are discussed in Stanford Lyman, W.E. Willmott, and Berching Ho, "Rules of a Chinese Secret Society in British Columbia," *Bulletin of the School of Oriental and African Studies, London University*, XXVII, 3 (1964), and in Lee Tung-hai's book. The second question may be pursued in Lee's book.

335

A third controversy, recently introduced in Canada but of long standing in the United States, is whether Chinese immigrants were sojourners who did not plan to remain here and avoided involvement in North American affairs, or whether they wished settlement and involvement but were rejected on racist grounds. The question is raised in Anthony B. Chan, "The Myth of the Chinese Sojourner in Canada," in Ujimoto and Hirabayashi (eds.), *Visible Minorities and Multiculturalism*.

"Overseas Chinese" Comparisons

Whether or not seen as sojourners, Chinese Canadians and their history are also a part of the history of Chinese overseas migration and hence are included in the comparative literature. Indeed, reference to the general literature on overseas Chinese is one of the best ways to illuminate otherwise unclear aspects of Chinese-Canadian history. The best known generalizers on overseas Chinese history and society are the late Maurice Freedman, G. William Skinner, and Wang Gungwu. Freedman's most general statements are found in G. William Skinner (ed.), *The Study of Chinese Society: Essays by Maurice Freedman* (Stanford, Calif., 1979). See also the obituary bibliography compiled by Skinner in *American Anthropologist*, 78 (1976). Of Skinner's own work, the two books on Thailand are broader in their implications than their titles suggest. *Chinese Society in Thailand: An Analytical History* (Ithaca, 1957) provides an historiographic model; *Leadership and Power in the Chinese Community of Thailand* (Ithaca, 1957) supplies a model of leadership analysis for overseas Chinese communities. Skinner's "Change and Persistence in Chinese Culture Overseas: A Comparison of Thailand and Java," *Journal of the South Seas Society*, 16 (1960), is an early statement of factors bearing on ethnicity and assimilation in relation to overseas Chinese. Of Wang Gungwu's many writings, the most directly applicable here is "Chinese Politics in Malaya," *China Quarterly*, 43 (July-September, 1970), which suggests a broadly useful way to look at the political orientations of overseas Chinese.

Yen Ching-hwang's works are among the best for studying the early political links between the overseas Chinese and China. *The Overseas Chinese and the 1911 Revolution* (London, 1976), although focused on Malaya, contains much that is comparable to Canada. "Ch'ing's Sale of Honours and the Chinese Leadership in Singapore and Malaya (1877-1912)," *Journal of Southeast Asian Studies*, I (September, 1970), deals with a special aspect of the relationship. For relations since 1949, the indispensable work is Stephen FitzGerald, *China and the Overseas Chinese* (Cambridge, 1972). On the special subject of remittances, see, for the early twentieth century, Charles Frederick Remer, *Foreign Investment in China* (New York, 1922), and for the post-1949 era, Wu Chunhsi, *Dollars, Dependants and Dogma: Overseas Chinese Remittances to Communist China* (Stanford, Calif., 1967).

Overseas Chinese social organization takes its models from social organization in China but has its own dynamics. The latter are broadly explored in Lawrence Crissman, "The Segmentary Structure of Urban Overseas Chinese Communities," *Man*, New Series, II (June, 1967). Single-country case studies may be found in Donald E. Willmott, *The Chinese of Semarang: A Changing Minority Community in Indonesia* (Ithaca, 1960); William E. Willmott, *The Chinese in Cambodia* (Vancouver, 1967) and *The Political Structure of the Chinese Community in Cambodia* (London, 1970); and Edgar Wickberg, *The Chinese in Philippine Life, 1850-1898* (New Haven, 1965).

South China "Home" Territory

To understand fully the Chinese in Canada, one must know something of the Guangdong province environment from which they came, with which they maintained contact, and to which many eventually returned. The economic environment, social forms, and leadership standards, and the effects of emigration in relation to these Guangdong communities have all received some study. Rural economic conditions are most directly approached through Chen Han-seng's *Landlord and Peasant in China* (New York, 1936), the fruit of surveys by the most experienced Chinese rural investigator, a man strongly committed to change in rural China. The Chinese lineage is of fundamental significance in this region, and the classic works are two by Maurice Freedman: *Lineage Organization in Southeastern China* (London, 1958) and *Chinese Lineage and Society: Fukien and Kwang-tung* (London, 1966). The lineage in its Guangdong setting and in relation to its migrant members in Canada is discussed in Yuen-fong Woon, "Social Organization of South China, 1911-1949: The Case of the Kwaan Lineage of Hoi-ping" (Ph.D. dissertation, University of British Columbia, 1975). Lineage, leadership, varying organizational forms, and many other topics are treated by James W. Hayes in his *The Hong Kong Region, 1850-1911* (Hamden, Conn., 1977) and in several articles, particularly in the *Journal of the Hong Branch. Royal Asiatic Society*. Although Chen Ta's *Emigrant Communities in South China* (New York, 1940) deals with Fukien, his findings about the effect of overseas migration and remittances upon communities with members abroad are generally applicable to such "home" communities in Guangdong. The background chapter in Ezra Vogel's *Canton Under Communism* (Cambridge, Mass., 1968) furnishes a useful summary of political and social conditions in Guangdong province before 1949. G. William Skinner's "Marketing and Social Structure in Rural China," *Journal of Asian Studies*, XXIV (November, 1964), is applicable to Guangdong.

U.S. Comparisons

Inevitably, there are similarities in the adaptation of Chinese to the two North American environments, and, hence, comparable developments in social forms and individual life patterns. American immigration policies, although somewhat different from those in Canada, did have an effect on Canadian policies from time to time. The whole question of organiza-

337

CHINESE COMMUNITIES IN CANADA

tional and other relations between American Chinese and Canadian Chinese awaits study. The most recent general history of the Chinese in the United States is Jack Chen, *The Chinese of America* (San Francisco, 1980). An excellent summary by the leading authority is H.M. Lai, "Chinese," in Stephan Thernstrom (ed.), *Harvard Encyclopedia of American Ethnic Groups* (Cambridge, Mass., 1980), pp. 217-34. An earlier work, Gunther Barth's *Bitter Strength: A History of the Chinese in the United States, 1850-1870* (Cambridge, Mass., 1964), was a focal point of controversy in the American version of the sojourner-racist rejection controversy. Stanford Lyman's *Chinese Americans* (New York, 1974) is the work of an American sociologist with experience in the study of the Chinese in Canada. One of the best community studies is that of M.S. Weiss: *Valley City: A Chinese Community in America* (Cambridge, Mass., 1974). The classic oral history is Victor and Brett Nee, *Longtime Californ'* (Boston, 1974). Two generalized versions of individual life patterns are the sociological classics by Paul C.P. Siu: "The Isolation of the Chinese Laundryman," in E. Burgess and D.J. Bogue (eds.), *Contributions to Urban Sociology* (Chicago, 1964), and "The Sojourner," *American Journal of Sociology*, LVIII, 1 (1952).

Both Canadian Chinese and Canadian governments were aware of the treatment of the Chinese in the United States. Changes in American policies affected Canada's policies. An important example is that of Canadian awareness that the United States was repealing its exclusion of the Chinese in 1943. Information on this point is found in PAC, RG 76, file 826734, part 2.

SELECTED BIBLIOGRAPHY

I. Unpublished Documents
   Personal
   Governmental and Institutional

II. Published Government Documents

III. Unpublished Manuscripts

IV. Books and Articles in English

V. Newspapers and Magazines in English

VI. Books, Articles, and Unpublished Materials
   in Chinese and Japanese

VII. Newspapers and Magazines in Chinese
   and Japanese

I UNPUBLISHED DOCUMENTS

Personal

Cumyow, Alexander W. Personal Papers, ca. 1900-1935. Special Collections Division, UBC Library. In English.

Foon Sien (Wong Mun-po). Personal Papers and Newspaper Clippings, 1930's-1950's. Special Collections Division, UBC Library. In English.

Lin Shih-yuan, Chinese Consul, Vancouver. Letterbook, 1914. Original in Public Archives of Canada. Copies in Glenbow Foundation, Calgary, and in Special Collections Division, UBC Library.

Mark, E.C. Scrapbooks of newspaper clippings concerning Canadian Chinese support for the war against Japan, 1937-1945.

Governmental and Institutional

Public Archives of Canada

RG 6. Secretary of State. E 1 Chief Press Censor for Canada; vol. 37, file 168, 168A; vol. 86, file 246-1, 246-2.

RG 7. Governor-general. G 21; vol. 239, file 348A.

RG 18. RCMP. G 1.

RG 25. External Affairs. Annual Registers, 1912, 1922; vol. 1119, file 136; vol. 1133, file 477; vol. 1135, file 1045; vol. 1142, file 308; vol. 1162, file 878; vol. 1472, file 515; vol. 1524, file 867; vol. 1539, file 178; vol. 1599, file 333; vol. 1687, file 80 H; vol. 1803, file 729; vol. 1867, file 263; G 1, file 379.

RG 76. Immigration. file 826734; file 831196; China, Consulate, Vancouver, Letterbook, 1914-1915; Loring Christie Papers, Subject files, file 76.

RCMP Archives

HQ files 1921-HQ-189E-2; 1922-HQ-189, Q-1; 1923-HQ-189E-1; 1929-HQ-189-3-3-1 (files on enforcement of narcotic drug laws).

Public Archives of Alberta

Premier's Office files, Acc. 69.289/1207 (1936-37).

Public Archives of British Columbia

CC 30.14.C44, 247/79, 363/79, 55/80; Department of Attorney-general, microfilm, roll 1; Attorney-general's files, register of depositions; Attorney-general's files, Lew Letterbooks, 1907-09; Attorney-general's correspondence, inward, 1925-37: file 236-2; Notebooks of the Hon. Mr. Justice Crease, vol. 18.

Public Archives of Newfoundland

File on the Wo Fen Game murder case.

Vancouver City Archives

Knowlton Papers, vol. 1: "History of the Cariboo Road" by Walter Moberly; McLean letter to City Clerk, 15 November 1900; H.J. Cambie letter to J.M.R. Fairbairn, 4 September 1923; W.H. Gallagher, Docket, n.d.; Annual Report of the Vancouver Board of Trade, 1889; Gambling Investigation, 1928 (typescript, 11 vols.); Council Minutes, 1889; "Incoming Correspondence," vol. 17, 1885; License Board Report Book, 1886-1889 and 1903-1909.

United Church of Canada Archives, Toronto
Board of Foreign Missions, general correspondence. Box 1, file 19; "A Religious and Missionary Survey of the Chinese," typescript, 1919 (probably by S.S. Osterhout).

II PUBLISHED GOVERNMENT DOCUMENTS

Canada. Department of Trade and Commerce. *Trade of Canada* (year ended December 31, 1940). Ottawa: Dept. of Trade and Commerce and Dominion Bureau of Statistics, 1941.

Canada. Parliament. House of Commons. *Commons Debates*, 1903-1968.

Canada. Parliament. House of Commons. *Commons Journals*, 1879.

Canada. Parliament. Senate. Standing Committee on Labour and Immigration. *Proceedings*, March 10, 1948, and April 15, 1953.

Census of Canada, 1870/1-1971.

A Collection of Public General Statutes of the Colony of Vancouver Island - Passed in the Years 1859, 1860, 1861, 1862, and 1863. Victoria: Evening Express, 1864.

Consolidated Statutes of British Columbia. Victoria: R. Wolfenden, Government Printer, 1877.

Correspondence, Reports of the Ministers of Justice, and Orders in Council Upon the Subject of Dominion and Provincial Legislation, 1867-1895. Ottawa: Government Printing Bureau, 1896.

Documents on Canadian External Relations. Vol. VII, 1939-1941. Ottawa: Department of External Affairs, 1974.

_____. Vol. VIII, 1939-1941. Ottawa: Department of External Affairs, 1976.

Journals of the Legislative Assembly of the Province of British Columbia, 1880. Victoria: Richard Wolfenden, Government Printer, 1880.

Laws of British Columbia. Victoria: Government Printing Office, 1871.

Northwest Census, 1885. Ottawa, 1886.

"Report of the Chief Controller of Chinese Immigration, 1919," in *Annual Report of the Department of Immigration and Colonisation.* Ottawa: King's Printer, 1919.

_____, 1920.

_____, 1922-23.

Report of Losses Sustained by the Chinese Population of Vancouver, B.C., 1907. (Royal Commission: W.L. Mackenzie King.) Ottawa: Government Printing Bureau, 1908.

Report of Mr. Justice Murphy, Royal Commission Appointed to Investigate alleged Chinese Frauds and Opium Smuggling on the Pacific Coast, 1910-11. Ottawa: Government Printing Bureau, 1913.

Report of the Royal Commission Appointed to Inquire into the Methods by which Oriental Labourers have been Induced to Come to Canada. Ottawa: Government Printing Bureau, 1908.

Report of the Royal Commission on Chinese Immigration. Ottawa: Printed by Order of the Commission, 1885.

Report of the Royal Commission on Oriental Immigration. Ottawa: Printed by S.E. Dawson, 1902.

Revised Statutes of Saskatchewan, 1909. Regina: J.A. Reid, Government Printer, 1911.

Statistics Canada. *Canada 1976.* Ottawa, 1975.

Statutes of Canada, 1885. Ottawa: Queen's Printer, 1885, Chapter 71, 1885: Chinese Immigration Act.

Statutes of the Province of British Columbia, 1878. Victoria: Richard Wolfenden, Government Printer, 1878.

Statutes of the Province of British Columbia, 1896. Victoria: Richard Wolfenden, Government Printer, 1896.

———, 1921. 2 vols. Victoria: William H. Cullin, King's Printer, 1921.

Statutes of the Province of Saskatchewan, 1944. 2 vols. Regina: Thos. H. McConica, King's Printer, 1944. Vol. I.

Statutory Orders and Regulations, 1950, 1956. Ottawa: Queen's Printer, 1950, 1956.

III UNPUBLISHED MANUSCRIPTS

Bassett, R. "Enforcement of the Opium and Narcotic Drug Act, 1920-1940," manuscript, RCMP Headquarters, 1972.

Chow, W.S. "The Chinese Community in Canada Before 1947, and Some Recent Developments," paper presented to the IXth International Congress of Anthropological and Ethnological Sciences, Chicago, 1973.

Davies, Fanny C. "A Survey of the Chinese Community in Montreal," manuscript, 1974.

Dawson, J. Brian. "Chinese Urban Communities in Southern Alberta, 1885-1910," Master's thesis, Department of History, University of Calgary, 1976.

Erickson, B.H. "Prestige, Power and the Chinese," Master's thesis, Department of Anthropology and Sociology, University of British Columbia, 1966.

Johnson, Arthur J. "The Canadian Pacific Railway and British Columbia, 1871-1886," Master's thesis, Department of History,

University of British Columbia, 1936.

Laforet, Andrea. "Folk History in a Small Canadian Community," Ph.D. dissertation, University of British Columbia, 1974.

Lal, Brij. "The Chinese Benevolent Association of Vancouver, 1889-1960: An Analytical History," manuscript, 1975.

Lawrence, Gary Kenneth. "The Windsor Chinese Community," manuscript copy used. Published in Chinese Students Association, *University of Windsor Magazine* (December, 1976).

Lee, Chang. "Chinese in Northern Ontario," paper presented at the annual meeting of the Canadian Society for Asian Studies, Guelph, Ontario, May, 1978.

Levine, Paul. "Historical Documentation Pertaining to Overseas Chinese Organizations," Master's thesis, Department of Asian Studies, University of Toronto, 1975.

Loggy, Gillian. "The Chinese Immigrant in British Columbia: A Survey of the Years 1858-1923," manuscript, 1972.

Mark, Ivan. "E.C. Mark, my father," manuscript for private circulation, 1973.

"Memoirs of Anna Ma," manuscript, ca. 1973.

Memorial University of Newfoundland, Chinese Student Society, comp. "Chinese Community in Newfoundland," manuscript, St. John's, 1977(?).

"Project Integrate: An Ethnic Study of the Chinese Community of Moose Jaw," Report of a Summer O.F.Y. Project, Moose Jaw, 1973.

Quo, F.Q. "Chinese Immigrants in the Prairies," Preliminary Report Submitted to the Ministry of the Secretary of State, November, 1977.

Sedgwick, Charles P. "The Context of Economic Change and Continuity in an Urban Overseas Chinese Community," Master's thesis, Department of Sociology, University of Victoria, 1973.

Snowden, Mary Ann. "Chinese Settlement in British Columbia. A Process of Segregation and Integration," paper, Cariboo College, Kamloops, B.C., 1973.

Straaton, K. "The Political System of the Vancouver Chinese Community: Associations and Leadership in the Early 1960's," Master's thesis, Department of Anthropology and Sociology, University of British Columbia, 1974.

Taylor, Gordon R. "An Investigation of Chinese Schools in Canada," Master's thesis, McGill University, 1933.

Thompson, Ric. "Class as Context: An Analysis of Conflict in a North American Chinese Community," manuscript, Department of Anthropology, University of Michigan, 1977.

Woon, Yuen-fong. "Social Organization of South China, 1911-1949: The Case of the Kwaan Lineage of Hoi-ping," Ph.D. dissertation,

University of British Columbia, 1975.

Wynne, Robert Edward. "Reaction to the Chinese in the Pacific Northwest and British Columbia, 1850-1910," Ph.D. dissertation, University of Washington, 1964.

IV BOOKS AND ARTICLES IN ENGLISH

Adachi, Ken. *The Enemy That Never Was: A History of Japanese Canadians.* Toronto: McClelland and Stewart, 1976.

Akashi, Yoji. *The Nanyang Chinese National Salvation Movement, 1937-41.* Lawrence, Kansas: Center for East Asian Studies, University of Kansas, 1970.

Angus, H.F. "The Legal Status in British Columbia of Residents of Oriental Race and their Descendants," in *The Legal Status of Aliens in Pacific Countries*, ed. Norman Mackenzie. London: Oxford University Press, 1937. Pp. 77-88.

Armentrout-Ma, Eve. "A Chinese Association in North America: The Pao-Huang Hui from 1899 to 1904," *Ch'ing-shih wen-t'i,* IV (November, 1978), 91-111.

Balf, Mary. *Kamloops: A History of the District up to 1914.* Kamloops, B.C.: Kamloops Museum, 1969.

Baureiss, Gunther. "The Chinese Community of Calgary," *Canadian Ethnic Studies*, III (June, 1971), 43-56.

Berton, Pierre. *The Last Spike.* Toronto: McClelland and Stewart, 1971.

Biography of Yip Sang. Hong Kong: privately published, 1973(?). In English and in Chinese. See *Yeh Ch'un-tien Chuanji.*

Boorman, Howard L., ed. *Biographical Dictionary of Republican China.* New York: Columbia University Press, 1967-71. Vols. I, II.

British Columbia Directory for 1884-85. Victoria: R.T. Williams, 1885.

Cappon, P. "The Green Paper: Immigration as a Tool of Profit," in *Modernization and the Canadian State*, ed. D. Glenday *et al.* Toronto: Macmillan of Canada, 1978. Pp. 372-7.

Carrothers, W.A. "Oriental Standards of Living," in *The Japanese Canadians*, by Charles H. Young and Helen R.Y. Reid, ed. H.A. Innis. Toronto: University of Toronto Press, 1938. Pp. 199-292.

Chan, Anthony B. "The Myth of the Chinese Sojourner in Canada," in *Proceedings of the Asian Canadian Symposium II*, University of Guelph, ed. Gordon Hirabayashi and K. Victor Ujimoto. Ottawa: Multiculturalism Directorate, 1978. Pp. 106-10.

Chan, Rev. Paul. "A Short History of the Chinese Presbyterian Church and Community Centre in Montreal," in *Mancheng*

Zhonghua Jidujiao Qingnian Hui Jinxi Jinian Tekan. Montreal: privately published, 1961. In English and in Chinese.

Cheng, Tien-fang. *Oriental Immigration in Canada.* Shanghai: Commercial Press, 1931.

Clark, Cecil. *Tales of the British Columbia Provincial Police.* Sidney, B.C.: Gray's Pub., 1971.

Committee of Concerned Chinese Canadians. "CCC, CBA and Chinese Community," *Chinese Cultural Centre Reports*, II (September, 1977).

_____. *Return the CBA to the Chinese Community.* Vancouver: privately published, 1977(?).

Davis, Morris, and Joseph F. Krauter. *The Other Canadians.* Toronto: Methuen, 1971.

Dawson, J. Brian. "The Chinese Experience in Frontier Calgary," in *Frontier Calgary: Town, City and Region 1875-1914*, ed. A. Rasporich and H. Klassen. Calgary: University of Calgary; McClelland and Stewart West, 1975. Pp. 124-40.

FitzGerald, Stephen. *China and the Overseas Chinese.* Cambridge: Cambridge University Press, 1972.

Glynn-Ward, H. (Hilda Glynn Howard). *The Writing on the Wall. With an Introduction by Patricia E. Roy.* Toronto: University of Toronto Press, 1974.

Grant, Chester. "The Struggle for Power in Chinatown," Vancouver *Sun*, 21 February 1971.

Gutstein, Donald. *Vancouver Ltd.* Toronto: James Lorimer & Co., 1975.

Hawkins, Freda. *Canada and Immigration: Public Policy and Public Concern.* Montreal: McGill-Queen's University Press, 1972.

_____. "Canada's Green Paper on Immigration Policy," *International Migration Review*, IX (1975), 237-49.

Henderson's British Columbia Directory, 1906. Vancouver: L.G. Henderson, 1906.

Henderson's British Columbia Directory, 1908. Vancouver: L.G. Henderson, 1908.

Henderson's British Columbia Gazetteer and Directory, 1889. Victoria: L.G. Henderson, 1889.

Henderson's British Columbia Gazetteer and Directory, 1900-1901. Victoria: L.G. Henderson, 1901.

Henderson's Vancouver City Directory, 1914. Vancouver: L.G. Henderson, 1914.

Hoe, Ban Seng. *Structural Changes of Two Chinese Communities in Alberta, Canada.* National Museum of Man Mercury Series, Canadian Centre for Folk Culture Studies Paper Number 19. Ottawa: National Museum of Man, 1976.

Holland, Sir Robert. "Indian Immigration into Canada: The Question of Franchise," *The Asiatic Review*, XXXIX (January, 1943), 167-172.

Howay, F.W. *British Columbia From the Earliest Times to the Present.*

Vancouver: S.J. Clarke, 1914. Vol. II.

Howay, F.W., W.N. Sage, and H.F. Angus. *British Columbia and the United States. The North Pacific Slope from Fur Trade to Aviation*. Toronto: Ryerson Press, 1942.

Johnson, G.E. "Chinese Family and Community in Canada: Tradition and Change," in *Two Nations, Many Cultures*, ed. J.L. Elliot. Scarborough, Ont.: Prentice-Hall of Canada, 1978. Pp. 353-71.

Johnson, Richard Byron. *Very Far West Indeed*. London: Sampson Low, Marston, Low and Searle, 1872.

Kirkwood, John. "Chinese Dragon Stirs as East Comes West," Vancouver *Province*, 30 January 1971.

Lai, David Chuen-yan. "Chinese Attempts to Discourage Emigration to Canada: Some Findings from the Chinese Archives in Victoria," *B.C. Studies*, 18 (Summer, 1973), 33-49.

_____. "The Chinese Consolidated Benevolent Association in Victoria: Its Origins and Functions," *B.C. Studies*, 15 (Autumn, 1972), 53-67.

_____. "Home Country and Clan Origins of Overseas Chinese in Canada in the Early 1880s," *B.C. Studies*, 27 (Autumn, 1975), 3-29.

_____. "Socio-economic Structures and Viability of Chinatown," in *Residential and Neighbourhood Studies in Victoria*, ed. C.N. Forward. Western Geographical Series, No. V. Victoria: University of Victoria, Department of Geography, 1973. Pp. 101-29.

Lai, Vivien. "The New Chinese Immigrants in Toronto," in *Minority Canadians: Two Immigrant Groups*, ed. J.L. Elliot. Scarborough, Ont.: Prentice-Hall of Canada, 1971. Pp. 120-40.

Lao Bo. "Hostages in Canada: Toronto's Chinese (1880-1947)," *The Asianadian*, I (Summer, 1978), 12.

Lee, Carol F. "The Road to Enfranchisement: Chinese and Japanese in British Columbia," *B.C. Studies*, 30 (Summer, 1976), 44-76.

Light, I. *Ethnic Enterprise in America*. Berkeley: University of California Press, 1972.

Light, I., and C.C. Wong. "Protest or Work: Dilemmas of the Tourist Industry in American Chinatowns," *American Journal of Sociology*. LXXX (May, 1975), 1342-65.

Lyman, S. "Contrasts in the Community Organization of Chinese and Japanese in North America," *Canadian Review of Anthropology and Sociology*, V, 2 (1968), 51-67.

Lyman, S., W.E. Willmott, and Berching Ho. "Rules of a Chinese Secret Society in British Columbia," *Bulletin of the School of Oriental and African Studies*, XVII, 3 (1964), 530-9.

Macfie, Matthew. *Vancouver Island and British Columbia*. London: Longman, Green, Longman, Roberts, and Green, 1865.

MacInnis, Grace. *J.S. Woodsworth, a Man to Remember.* Toronto: Macmillan of Canada, 1953.

McClung, Nellie. *The Stream Runs Fast.* Toronto: Thos. Allen and Sons, 1965, reprint.

Millien, C., E. Woo, and R. Yeh. *Winnipeg Chinese.* Ottawa: Department of the Secretary of State, 1971.

Morley, Alan. *Vancouver: From Milltown to Metropolis.* Vancouver: Mitchell Press, 1961.

Morton, James. *In the Sea of Sterile Mountains. The Chinese in British Columbia.* Vancouver: J.J. Douglas, 1973.

Nee, Victor G., and Brett DeBary Nee. *Longtime Californ'.* Boston: Houghton Mifflin, 1974.

Ormsby, Margaret A. *British Columbia: A History.* Vancouver: Macmillan of Canada, 1958.

Osterhout, S.S. *Orientals in Canada.* Toronto: United Church of Canada, 1929.

Palmer, Howard. "Anti-Oriental Sentiment in Alberta, 1880-1920," *Canadian Ethnic Studies*, II, 2 (1970), 31-57.

Paterson, T.W. "Cumberland's Ghosts," Victoria *Daily Colonist,* 17 September 1967.

Paupst, K. "A Note on Anti-Chinese Sentiment in Toronto," *Canadian Ethnic Studies*, IX, 1 (1977), 54-9.

Phillips, Paul. *No Power Greater: A Century of Labour in B.C.* Vancouver: B.C. Federation of Labour, 1967.

Programme of Freemasons San Francisco Constitutional Conference, 1923. In Chinese.

Programme of Second National Freemasons Conference, Lethbridge. In Chinese.

Ramsey, Bruce. *Barkerville.* Vancouver: Mitchell Press, 1961.

_____. *Ghost Towns of British Columbia.* Vancouver: Mitchell Press, 1971.

Rayner, D.H. "Montreal's Changing Chinatown," *Presbyterian Record* (January, 1970).

Roy, Patricia. "Educating the East: British Columbia and the Oriental Question in the Inter-War Years," *B.C. Studies*, 18 (Summer, 1973), 50-69.

_____. "The Oriental Menace in British Columbia," in *The Twenties in Western Canada*, ed. S.M. Trofimenkoff. Ottawa: National Museum of Man, 1972. Pp. 243-58.

_____. "The Preservation of the Peace in Vancouver: The Aftermath of the Anti-Chinese Riot of 1887," *B.C. Studies*, 31 (Autumn, 1976), 44-59.

Roza, Gustavo da. *A Feasibility Study for the Redevelopment of Chinatown in Winnipeg.* Winnipeg: Winnipeg Chinese Development Corporation, 1974.

Sampat-Mehta, R. *International Barriers. Aliens, Immigration and Citizenship in Canada.* Ottawa: Canadian Research Bureau, 1973.

Sien Lok Society of Calgary. *National Conference on Urban Renewal*

347

and its Effects on Chinatown. Calgary: privately published, 1969.

Skinner, G.W. *Leadership and Power in the Chinese Community of Thailand.* Ithaca, N.Y.: Cornell University Press, 1957.

Sudain, James. *Alex Dunsmuir's Dilemma.* Victoria: Sunnylane Publishing Company, 1964.

Sugimoto, Howard S. "The Vancouver Riots of 1907: A Canadian Episode," in *East Across the Pacific,* ed. Hilary Conroy and T. Scott Miyakawa. Honolulu: University of Hawaii Press, 1972. Pp. 92-126.

Thompson, Richard H. "Ethnicity versus Class: An Analysis of Conflict in a North American Chinese Community," *Ethnicity,* VI, 4 (December, 1979), 306-26.

Tou, Father Thomas. "A Brief History of the Chinese Mission and its School," in *Mandike Zhonghua Tianzhutang chengli wushi zhounian jinian tekan, 1922-1972.* Montreal: privately published, 1972. In English and in Chinese.

"A Town's Ghosts Wait for the End," *Canadian Magazine,* 6 January 1966.

Trasov, G.E. "History of the Opium and Narcotic Drug Legislation in Canada," *Criminal Law Quarterly,* IV (January, 1962), 274-82.

Trimble, William J. *The Mining Advances into the Inland Empire. A Comparative Study of the Beginnings of the Mining Industry in Idaho and Montana, Eastern Washington and Oregon, and the Southern Interior of British Columbia; and of the Institutions and Laws Based upon That Industry.* Bulletin of the University of Wisconsin, Number 638, History Series, vol. 3, no. 2. Madison, Wis.: University of Wisconsin, 1914. Pp. 137-392.

Voisey, Paul. "Two Chinese Communities in Alberta: An Historical Perspective," *Canadian Ethnic Studies,* II, 2 (1970), 15-29.

Ward, W. Peter. "The Oriental Immigrant and Canada's Protestant Clergy, 1858-1925," *B.C. Studies,* 22 (Summer, 1974), 40-55.

——. *White Canada Forever.* Montreal: McGill-Queen's University Press, 1978.

Wickberg, Edgar. "Chinese and Canadian Influences on Chinese Politics in Vancouver, 1900-1947," *B.C. Studies,* 45 (Spring, 1980), 37-55.

——. "Chinese Associations in Canada, 1923-1947," in *Visible Minorities and Multiculturalism: Asians in Canada,* ed. Victor Ujimoto and Gordon Hirabayashi. Toronto: Butterworths, 1980. Pp. 23-31.

——. "Chinese Organizations and the Canadian Political Process: Two Case Studies," in *Ethnicity, Power and Politics in Canada,* ed. J. Dahlie and T. Fernando. Toronto: Methuen, 1981. Pp. 172-76.

Willmott, W.E. "Approaches to the Study of the Chinese in British Columbia," *B.C. Studies,* 4 (Spring, 1970), 38-52.

_____. "Chinese Clan Associations in Vancouver," *Man*, LXIV (1964), 33-7.

_____. *The Chinese in Cambodia*. Vancouver: University of British Columbia Publications Centre, 1967.

_____. "Some Aspects of Chinese Communities in British Columbia Towns," *B.C. Studies*, 1 (Winter, 1968-9), 27-36.

_____. *The Political Structure of the Chinese Community in Cambodia*. London: Athlone Press, 1970.

Wong, Dukesang. "The Golden Mountains of Dukesang Wong," in *We are Their Children. Ethnic Portraits of British Columbia*. Vancouver: Commcept Publishing, 1977. Pp. 31-40.

Woodsworth, Charles James. *Canada and the Orient*. Toronto: Macmillan of Canada, 1941.

Wrigley's B.C. Directory. Vancouver: Sun Directories, 1931.

V NEWSPAPERS AND MAGAZINES IN ENGLISH

B.C. Workers News, February, 1935.

Calgary Herald, September, 1907; April, 1954.

The Citizen (Ottawa), December, 1946-January, 1947.

The Colonist (Victoria, B.C.). Also *The British Colonist* and *The Daily Colonist*, 1860-1947.

Evening Telegram (Toronto), March, 1942; April, 1943; June, 1943.

The Globe and Mail. Also Toronto *Globe.*, September, 1907; March, 1944; November, 1946; May, 1960.

Halifax Mail, January, 1947.

Manitoba Free Press, 1922.

The Montreal Star, March, 1922; May, 1960

The New Citizen (Vancouver and Toronto), 1949-1952.

New Westminster Herald, 1879.

The Province (Vancouver), 1896-1978.

The Sun (Vancouver), 1914-1978.

Vancouver News, 1886-1887.

Vancouver News-Advertiser, 1891.

Vancouver World, 1922-1923.

Victoria Times, 1906-1947.

Winnipeg Tribune, December, 1946.

The Worker, March, 1927.

VI BOOKS, ARTICLES, AND UNPUBLISHED MATERIALS IN CHINESE AND JAPANESE

Amano, Motonosuke 天野元之助 , Shina nōgyō keizai ron 支那農業經濟論 (The agricultural economy of China). 2 vols. Tokyo, 1940-1942.

"Benxiao jianshi" 本校簡史 (A short history of this school), in Wenjiang Xuexiao chuangxiao wushi zhounian jinian tekan, 1925-1975. 文疆學校創校五十週年紀念特刊 (Fiftieth anniversary of Mon Keong School, Special publication). Vancouver, 1976.

"Benxiao xiaoshi" 本校校史 (A history of this school), in Jianada Weiduoli Zhonghua Huiguan chengli qishiwu, Huaqiao Xuexiao chengli liushi - zhounian jinian tekan 加拿大域多利 中華會館 成立七十五, 華僑學校成立 六十週年紀念特刊 (Seventy-fifth anniversary of the Victoria CCBA and Sixtieth anniversary of the Victoria Chinese School, Special publication). Victoria, 1960. Part III.

Chan, Rev. Paul S. 陳保羅牧師. "A short history of the Chinese Presbyterian Church and Community Centre in Montreal; Mandike Zhonghua Jidujiao Changlao Hui ji jiaoyuguan jianshi" "滿地可中華基督長老會及教育館簡史" in Luishiba zhounian jinian tekan, Mancheng Zhonghua Jidujiao Changlaohui 六十八週年紀念特刊,滿城中華基督教長老會. ("Montreal Chinese Presbyterian Church, 68th Anniversary Issue"). Mimeographed. Montreal, 1965. In Chinese and in English.

Chen, Kwong Min. 陳匡民 Meizhou Huaqiao tongjian 美洲華僑通鑑 . ("The Chinese in the Americas"). New York, 1950.

SELECTED BIBLIOGRAPHY

Chen, Yingjie 陳庭傑 . "Taishan yiqiao dierjie kenqin dahui xianyan" 台山邑僑第二屆懇親大會獻言 (Preliminary statement about the Second National Conference of Toisanese), in Quan-Jia Taishan yiqiao dierjie kenqin dahui tekan 全加台山邑僑第二屆懇親大會特刊 (Second National Conference of Toisanese, Special publication). Taibei, 1975.

Ch'eng T'ien-fang 程天放 . Ch'eng T'ien-fang zaonian huiyilu. 程天放早年回憶錄 (Ch'eng T'ien-fang's reminiscences of his youth). Taibei, 1968.

Feng, Hefa 馮和法 . Zhongguo nongcun jingji ziliao 中國農村經濟資料 (Materials on the Chinese rural economy). 2 vols. Shanghai, 1933. pp. 936-995.

Feng, Tzu-yu 馮自由 . Geming yishi 革命逸史 (Memoirs of the Revolution of 1911). Taibei, 1965.

_____. Huaqiao geming kaiguo shi 華僑革命開國史 (History of the overseas Chinese revolutionary and early republican activities). Taibei, 1953.

_____. Huaqiao geming zuzhi shihua 華僑革命組織史話 (An informal history of revolutionary organization among Overseas Chinese). Taibei, 1954.

_____. Zhonghua Minguo kaiguo qian geming shi 中華民國開國前革命史 (History of the pre-Republican Revolution) 2 vols. Taibei, 1954. Vol. II.

Guan, Qiyi 關其逸 . "Jianada Huaqiao jiaoyu shilue" 加拿大華僑教育史略 (A short history of Overseas Chinese education in Canada), in Jianada Weiduoli Zhonghua

Huiguan chengli qishiwu, Huaqiao Xuexiao chengli liushi zhounian
jinian tekan. Part IV.

Guangdong jingji nianjian 廣東経済年鑑 (Economic
yearbook of Guangdong province). Lienxian, 1941.

Guangdong nongye gaikuang diaocha baogao 廣東農業概况調查報告
(Report of a survey of agrarian
conditions in Guangdong province). Canton, 1930. Book 2, Volume 2.

Ho, Ping-ti 何炳棣 . Zhongguo huiguan shilun
中國会館史論 (An historical survey of
landsmannschaften in China). Taibei, 1966.

Hope, Joseph (Lau Kwong-joo) 劉先祖 . "Wei fao Huaqiao
sanian fendou shiji" 域阜滎僑州年奮鬥事跡
(An historical account of thirty years of struggle by the Victoria
Chinese), in Jianada Weiduoli Zhonghua Huiguan chengli qishiwu,
Huaqiao Xuexiao chengli liushi – zhounian jinian tekan. Part IV.

Huang, Jisheng 黄寄生 . "Jianada Yungaohua Taishan
Ning Yang Huiguan shilue" 加拿大雲高滎台山寧陽会館
史畧 (Short history of the
Toi-san Ning Yung Huiguan of Vancouver), in Taishan Ning
Yang Huiguan liushi zhounian jinian tekan 台山寧陽会館
六十週年紀念特刊 (Sixtieth anniversary, Toi-san Ning
Yung Huiguan, Special publication). Taibei, 1958.

Huang, Kongzhao 黄弘昭 "Yungaohua Taishan Huiguan kenqinhui
shimo jixu" 雲高滎台山会館是親会姤末記序
(Preface to Proceedings of the national convention of Toisanese)
in Quan-Ken Taiqiao shoujie kenqin dahui shimo ji 全坎台僑
首屆恳親大会姤末記 (Proceedings of the first

national convention of Toisanese) n.p., n.d. (1931).

Huang, Wen-shan 黃文山 . Huang Wen-shan lu-Mei luncong
黃文山留美論叢 (Essays from Huang Wen-shan's stay in
North America). Taibei, 1960.

Huang Wenpu xiansheng aisi lu 黃文甫先生哀思錄 (Memorial
volume of Mr. Wong Mun-po (Foon Sien). Vancouver, 1971.

Huang, Xiquan 黃錫銓 . "Xie zai Quan-Jia Taishan yiqiao
dierjie kenqin dahui zhi qian" 寫在全加台山邑僑第二屆
懇親大會之前 (Preliminary notes on the
second national convention of Toisanese), in Quan-Jia Taishan
yiqiao dierjie kenqin dahui tekan.

Huang Yunshan Zonggongsuo dierjie Quan Jia kenqin dahui daibiaotuan
xiuding zhangcheng 黃雲山總公所第二屆全加懇親
大會代表團修訂章程
(Second national convention, Wong Wun San Association, Revised
constitution). n.p., 1954.

Huaqiao jingji nianjian 華僑經濟年鑑 (Overseas Chinese
economy yearbook), ed. Huaqiao jingji nianjian bianji weiyuanhui.
Taibei, 1977.

"Inside the CBA". Quan-Jia Zhonghua Zhonghuiguan gaikuang
全加中華會館概況 comp. Lee Doe Chuen. Taibei, 1969.
李道全

"International Chinese Business Directory." Wanguo jixin bianlan
萬國寄信便覽 , ed. Huang Jin 黃金
San Francisco, 1913. In Chinese and English.

Jianada Ansheng Zhonghua Zonghuiguan niankan 加拿大安省中華會
館年刊 (Annual of the Ontario Chinese
Community Centre). Toronto, 1973.

Jianada Dulangdu Zhonghua Jidujiao Qingnian Hui jianlou baogao
加拿大都朗度中舉基督敎青年会建樓報告.

(Progress report, Toronto Chinese Young
Men's Christian Institute). Toronto, 1927.

Jianada Taishan Ningyang Zonghuiguan zhangcheng   加拿大台山寧陽
總分館章程.   (Constitution of the Toi-san
Ning Yung Association, 1932). Copy available in the Foon Sien
Papers, Special Collections Division, University of British
Columbia Library.

"Jianada tebie Dangbu"   加拿大特別党部   (Canada Special Party
Branch), in Kuo Min Yat Po (San Francisco).   國民日報
Sixth anniversary special publication. n.d. (1933?)

Jianada Yungaohua Zhonghua Huiguan juxing chongxiu luocheng kaimu
dianli tekan 加拿大雲高華中榮會館舉行重修落成
開幕典礼特刊   (Vancouver CBA building
renovation and re-opening ceremony, Special publication).
Vancouver, 1952.

Kaiping Zonghuiguan tekan 開平縂会館特刊 (Special
publication of the Hoi-ping Association). Vancouver, 1947.

Kingston KMT. Jianada Qingshitun Zhongguo Guomindang jiuzhou jingguo
dangwu 加拿大頃士頓中國國民党九週經過党务.
(Kingston KMT. Nine years of Party affairs). Kingston, 1924.

Lee, Tung-hai (David T.H. Lee) 李東海
"Cuxi tanxin gonghua sangma" 促膝談心共話桑麻   (Intimate
talks about everyday matters) in Quan-Jia Taishan yiqiao dierjie
Kenqin dahui tekan.

_____. Jianada Huaqiao shi 加拿大華僑史
(History of the Overseas Chinese in Canada). Taibei, 1967.

354

_____. "Ningyang Huiguan yuanliu kao" 寧陽會館源流考
(Origins of the Toi-san Ning Yung Association), in Quan-Jia
Taishan yiqiao dierjie kenqin dahui tekan.

_____. ("Tung-hai"). "Jianada Huaqiao de ·shaochang fenpu ho
zhiye de yanjiu" (東海) 加拿大華僑的消長分佈
和職業的研究 (Growth, distribution and
occupations of the Chinese in Canada), in Jianada Weiduoli
Zhonghua Huiguan chengli qishiwu, Huaqiao Xuexiao chengli liushi -
zhounian jinian tekan. Part IV.

Liang, Qichao 梁啓超 . Xin Dalu yuji 新大陸遊記
(Travels on the new continent). Taibei, 1967.

Liang, Rencai 梁仁彩 . Guangdong jingji dili
廣東経済地理 (Economic geography of
Guangdong province). Beijing, 1956.·

Lim, Bang 林礼弡 . "Wei-fao Zhonghua Huiguan zhi
yange ji Huaqiao Xuexiao chuangli zhi yuanqi" 域阜中華會館之
沿草及華僑學校剙立之綠起 (The history of the
Victoria CCBA and the founding of the Chinese School), in
Jianada Weiduoli Zhonghua Huiguan chengli qishiwu, Huaqiao
Xuexiao chengli liushi - zhounian jinian tekan. Part IV.

Lin, Honggong 林洪公 . Jianadaren fadong Xinhai Geming
zaocheng minguo 加拿大人發動辛亥革命造成民國
(How Canadians promoted the 1911 Revolution and the creation of
the Chinese Republic). n.p., n.d.

Lin Xi Ho Zongtong kaimu jinian kan
林西河總堂開幕紀念刊 (Opening of Lim Sai Ho headquarters,
Commemorative volume). Vancouver, 1947.

Mancheng Zhonghua Jidujiao Qingnian Hui jinxi jinian tekan

滿城中華基督教青年會金禧紀念特刊 (Chinese Young Men's Christian

　　　Institute, Montreal, Golden anniversary special publication),

　　　Montreal, 1961.

Programme of Freemasons San Francisco Constitutional Conference, 1923.

及洲 洪門第三次懇親大會代表團修訂聯絡根本章程 民國十二年

Programme of Second National Freemasons Conference, Lethbridge, 1924.

北美洲坎拿大洪門致公堂 第二次懇親會代表團重修聯絡根本
章程. 民國十三年.

Quan-Jia Taishan yiqiao dierjie kenqin dahui tekan

全加台山邑僑第二屆懇親大會 特刊 (Second national conference

　　　of Toisanese, Special publication). Taibei, 1975.

Shouding 鑄鼎 "Dui Wei-cheng Ningyang Yu Qing Tang gaizu zhi

　　　shangque" 對維城寧陽餘慶堂改組之商榷 (A discussion

　　　of the reorganization of the Victoria Ningyang Yu Qing Tang) in

　　　Quan-Ken Taiqiao shoujie kenqin dahui shimo ji. Essay Section.

Tou, Father Thomas 杜寶田神父 "A brief history of the

　　　Chinese mission and its School"; "Breve histoire de la Mission

　　　Chinoise et de son Ecole"; "Mandike Huaren Tianzhujiaotang ji

　　　Xuexiao zhi jinxi"; 滿地可華人天主教堂及學校之今昔

　　　　　　　in Mandike Zhonghua Tianzhutang

　　　chengli wushi zhounian jinian tekan, 1922-1972. (Fiftieth

　　　anniversary publication, Montreal Chinese Catholic Church)

　　　滿地可中華天主堂成立五拾週年紀念特刊.
　　　Montreal, 1972. In Chinese, English and French.

"Tung-hai". See Lee, Tung-hai. "東海 看李東海

Wong, Sam-duck 黃三德. . Hongmen geming shi

洪門革命史 (Revolutionary history of the Hongmen). n.p. 1936

356

Wu Xianzi 伍憲子 . Zhongguo Minzhuxianzhengdang dangshi 中國民主憲政黨黨史 (History of the Chinese Democratic Constitutionalist Party). San Francisco, 1952.

Xiandai Huaqiao renwu zhi 現代華僑人物誌 (Biographies of contemporary Overseas Chinese notables). Taibei, 1963.

Yeh Ch'un-t'ien xiansheng chuanji 葉春田先生傳記 (Biography of Yip Sang). Hong Kong, 1973?

Yimin Jianada bidu 移民加拿大必讀 (Essential reading for immigrants to Canada), ed. Ma Qing 馬青 . Hong Kong, 1977.

Yinian guanwu baogao (1936-1937) 一年館務報告 (Report of one year's administrative affairs, 1936-1937), Comp. Yungaohua Zhonghua Huiguan 雲高華中華會館 (Vancouver CBA) Vancouver, 1937.

Yu Shan Zonggongsuo luocheng jinian ce 禺山總公所落成紀念冊 (Volume commemorating the inauguration of the Yu Shan Association headquarters). Vancouver, 1949.

Yue Yun 岱雲 . "Yungaohua Zhonghua Huiguan chengli niandai zhi kaozheng" 雲高華中華會館成立年代之攷證 (An investigation into the founding date of the Vancouver CBA), in Jianada Weiduoli Zhonghua Huiguan qishiwu, Huaqiao Xuexiao chengli liushi - zhounian jinian tekan. Part V.

Yun-fao Jianada Huang Jiangxia Zongtang zhangcheng 雲埠加拿大黃江夏總堂章程 (Constitution of the Wong Kong Har Tong Headquarters, Vancouver). Vancouver, 1955.

Yun-fao Zhonghua Huiguan you minguo ershibanian zhengyue yiri zhi
sanshinian shieryue sanshiyiri zhengxinlu

雲埠中華會館由民國二十八年正月一日至卅年十式月
卅一日徵信錄

(Statement of business accounts of the Vancouver CBA covering
January 1, 1939 - December 31, 1941). Vancouver, 1942.

Yungaohua Lin Xi Ho Zongtang Jiumu Gongsuo bazhounian jinian dahui
zhuankan 雲高華林西河總堂九牧公所八週年紀念
大会專刊 (Special publication of the
meeting commemorating the eighth anniversary of the Vancouver
Lim Sai Ho-Kow Mock organization). Vancouver, 1941.

Zhao Chengxin, 趙承信 "Guangdong Xinhui: Cixi tudi
fenpei diaocha" 廣東新会：慈溪土地分配調查
(Research on land distribution in Szekei Village,
Sunwui county), Shehui xuejie 社会学界 (Sociology
world), V (1929). Excerpted in Feng Hefa, Zhongguo nongcun
jingji ziliao. pp. 936-995.

Zhongguo Guomindang zai haiwai. Gedi dangbu shiliao chugao huibian
中國國民党在海外吞地党部史料初稿案编
(The Guomindang overseas. Selected historical materials from
various branches). Taibei, 1961.

Zhuo Zhengfeng 卓正豐 . "Kaiping xian nongye gaikuang
diaocha baogao" 開平縣農業概況調查報告
(Report of an investigation on general agricultural
conditions in Hoi-ping county), in Guangdong nongye gaikuang
diaocha baogao shu. Guangzhou, 1930. Book 2, Volume 2, pp. 48-55.

_____. "Zhongshan xian nongye diaocha baogao"

中山縣農業調查報告 (Report of an investigation on

agriculture in Chung-san county), in Guangdong nongye gaikuang diaocha

baogao shu. Book 2, Volume 2, pp. 141-148.

VII NEWSPAPERS AND MAGAZINES IN CHINESE

The Chinese Times. Tai Hon Kong Bo (Da Han Gong Bao)

大漢公報 (Vancouver), dates used: 1914-1966.

The Chinese Voice (Qiao Sheng Ribao).

Dates used: November - December, 1962.

僑聲日報

Hsin Min-kuo Pao. Sun Mun Kwok Po (The New Republic).

Published daily in Victoria 1912-1958 and daily in Vancouver, 1958-   .

新民國報

Hung Chung She Po (Toronto), dates of publication

1926-1959.

洪鐘時報

Shing Wah Daily News. Shing Wah Yat Bo. (Toronto),

dates used: November 24, 1928; July 1941; February 1943; June-September

1943; December 1943; December 1946.

醒華日報

Index